Germ
Queer

German Feminist Queer Crime Fiction

Politics, Justice and Desire

FAYE STEWART

McFarland & Company, Inc., Publishers
Jefferson, North Carolina

LIBRARY OF CONGRESS CATALOGUING-IN-PUBLICATION DATA

Stewart, Faye, 1972–
   German Feminist Queer Crime Fiction : Politics, Justice and
Desire / Faye Stewart.
     p.   cm.
   Includes bibliographical references and index.

   ISBN 978-0-7864-7845-3 (softcover : acid free paper) ∞
   ISBN 978-1-4766-1443-4 (ebook)

   1. Detective and mystery stories, German—History and
criticism.   2. Feminist criticism—Germany.   3. Queer
theory—Germany.   I. Title.
PT747.D4S74 2014
833'.087209—dc23   2014000032

BRITISH LIBRARY CATALOGUING DATA ARE AVAILABLE

Front cover: long alley (© 2014 iStockphoto/Thinkstock)

Manufactured in the United States of America

*McFarland & Company, Inc., Publishers
  Box 611, Jefferson, North Carolina 28640
   www.mcfarlandpub.com*

To my accomplices, the avengers:
and we are on our way

Contents

Acknowledgments

Though research in the humanities is often thought of as a solitary pursuit, this monograph was seen to completion with the assistance and support of several institutions and individuals whom I would like to recognize. Thanks go first to the Department of Modern and Classical Languages and the College of Arts and Sciences at Georgia State University for summer support and a semester of research leave. I laid the groundwork for this study at Indiana University, where I received fellowships for research in Bloomington and Berlin. This project was truly a feminist endeavor and owes a great deal to the energies and collaborative spirit of colleagues and friends. I am especially obliged to editor Lisa Kuppler and novelist Christine Lehmann for illuminating conversations about their work, and to scholars Claudia Breger, Katrin Sieg, and Phyllis Betz, for their generous encouragement of my own. I would also like to thank Hester Baer, Heidi Denzel de Tirado, Sabine Gross, Corinna Kahnke, Britta Kallin, Vincent Kling, Sonja Klocke, Philip Lewis, William Nichols, Simone Pfleger, James Rolleston, and Carrie Smith-Prei for their thoughtful comments on drafts of my work. I benefited from discussions with fellow members of the Coalition of Women in German and with my colleagues and students at Georgia State; I owe a particular debt of gratitude to my department chair, Fernando Reati, for his guidance through the publication process. I also wish to thank the anonymous reviewers of the manuscript for their enthusiastic support of this project. Words cannot express how grateful I am for the constant encouragement of my partner in crime, Amy Gremillion, and my parents, Joan and Philip Stewart.

One of my favorite parts of researching this book was the adventure of finding the primary literature, much of which is unavailable in American libraries, therefore necessitating on-location explorations in Germany and Austria. Thanks in large measure to the extensive collection of crime novels and liberal loan policies at the Spinnboden Lesbian Archive and Library in Berlin, I had the opportunity to devour many more books than I could afford to purchase, and to discover new authors and texts that became central to my project. (A tip for Berlin travelers: with its overstock of donated books, Spinnboden is the ideal place to acquire inexpensive volumes of feminist fiction and theory.) I spent countless hours perusing the inventory of bookstores specializing in crime fiction and feminist, lesbian and gay literature, and the owners and staff of Hammett, Anakoluth, and Prinz Eisenherz in Berlin, and Frauenzimmer in Vienna (which closed its doors due to financial pressures in 2007), generously shared their knowledge with me and helped me locate out-of-print editions. In Hamburg, I was warmly received by the team at Argument, publishers of the feminist Ariadne series, who also provided me with wonderful reading suggestions. These exchanges with others who were passionate about my research area shaped my project in exciting and unexpected ways.

Preface: Cracking Codes

Crime may not pay, but it certainly enthralls. At the most fundamental level, this book asks why and how. Crime literature has always reflected society, social conditions, and social change. While it entertains and educates, it is also a popular forum for social critique, where writers and readers alike can explore transgressions and resistance and imagine alternative forms of order. Mystery fiction introduces its readers to the most admirable and most despicable specimens of humanity, eliciting both desire and repulsion. It juxtaposes fantasy and action, stability and chaos, and perhaps most of all, obtuseness and insight. And insight into mystery is enabled and shaped by the deciphering of codes. Queer crime merits our attention because it complicates and reconfigures the codes, forcing a reckoning with narrative traditions, reader expectations, and the cultural function of literature.

This book posits a capacious definition of queer crime that allows us to investigate the shifting ways in which the crime genre constructs meaning. The dislocations of meaning and the breaking of rules that shape the genre are nowhere more in evidence than in queer crime, which foregrounds gender, sex, and sexuality. It is extraordinarily versatile and typically proposes—like life itself—a multiplicity of solutions. Through the attempt to contextualize criminality and through the work of detecting and interpretation, mystery fiction creates a space for experimenting with identity and codereading, which come to the fore in queer crime. The investigator's success, like that of the criminal, requires a deft negotiation of social environments that is often facilitated by the use of masquerade, exaggeration, evasion, and other deceptions. The characters' efforts to escape detection or to catch villains reveal a good deal about cultural values and their potency in dictating the stakes of human interactions, from the most basic interpersonal communications to transnational politics. The interplay between characterization and larger cultural issues encourages us to understand the figures in queer crime as literary interventions into current events and contemporary debates.

German Feminist Queer Crime Fiction reads German-language mystery novels of the last three decades as allegories about twentieth- and twenty-first-century upheavals in Europe, raising questions about human behavior and justice, the horrors of extremism, the changing shape of the nation, and the possibilities of democracy. The criminals, victims, investigators, and witnesses that populate these narratives do not materialize in a void; they are products of specific historical and cultural settings and embody the collective hopes and fears of an era. From serial killer housewives and megalomaniacal evangelists to homophobes and xenophobes, bisexuals and transsexuals, the characters appearing in queer crime stories are metaphors for changing social and political relations. I analyze these developments through the lens of genre fiction, which allows me to tell the cultural history of contemporary Germany and Austria from a new perspective. My primary literature consists of German-language novels written by female authors between 1984 and 2003, and I dissect these mysteries with the help of tools provided by queer and feminist theory, cultural studies, and scholarly writing on crime and detective fiction. Though my readers may not be familiar with many of the *Krimis* [crime novels] that are at the focus of this project, I hope to make these texts come to life by interweaving close readings with discussions of social transformations in and around Germany since the 1980s.

Having been raised by American-born professors of French in a bilingual household in North Carolina, having read and been read to in both English and French as a child, and having early tried to make sense of adult conversations about narrative, metaphor, and metonymy, I grew up deciphering linguistic and cultural codes. I have memories of trying to work out the mysteries of language and culture at the age of five, when my parents spent two semesters doing research in Europe and I went to school first in the suburbs of Paris and then in the south of France. (As a child, I believed that the word *sabbatical* meant "in France.") Upon returning to the United States, I had to relearn my native language and the cultural codes that had once been familiar. My decision to study comparative literature in college and then to home in on German might be read as a continued expression of my fascination for language as well as a determination to shape my own professional and linguistic identity, separate from that of my parents. My book, then, reflects a longstanding interest in language, storytelling, and codebreaking.

Since girlhood, I have loved crime and detective novels. My childhood heroines were teen sleuths Nancy Drew and Trixie Belden, and I later came to admire the quirky Miss Marple and the adventurer Mrs. Pollifax, the academic Kate Fansler, and medical examiner Kay Scarpetta. I also enjoyed narratives featuring the likes of the Hardy Boys, Sherlock Holmes, and the rogue Tom Ripley, but owing perhaps to my upbringing in a feminist household, I especially delighted in shrewd, strong, and stubborn female sleuths who pursued the elusive and often ugly truths hidden beneath innocuous surfaces. These women taught me to question commonly accepted narratives and read between the lines. Though the pleasures of reading mystery fiction consist largely of the challenge of cracking the code and the gratification of encountering the solution at the story's close, my preference has always been for plots that pose uncomfortable questions, eschew closure in favor of open endings, and implicate their readers in the process of interpretation. I relished short stories like Edgar Allan Poe's "The Murders in the Rue Morgue" as well as novels like Agatha Christie's *The Murder of Roger Ackroyd* and Barbara Wilson's *Gaudí Afternoon*, which forced me to confront my expectations and assumptions and to consider my complicity in assigning meaning to certain details. Crime fiction exists in a variety of forms—short stories and series of novels, detective literature and psychological thrillers—and each text positions itself among intersecting discourses as it participates in, reworks, or abandons generic conventions.

I began learning German in college, and my search for summer reading material to deepen my comprehension of the language inevitably led me to the familiar crime genre. The first book I read entirely in German was Friedrich Dürrenmatt's *Der Richter und sein Henker* [*The Judge and His Hangman*], and I was hooked. If, at first, I gravitated toward mysteries because their narrative structures kept me motivated to finish the books, I soon fell in love with learning about the cultural history of German-speaking countries through classic tales of criminality and justice. Friedrich Schiller's *Der Verbrecher aus verlorener Ehre* [*The Criminal from Lost Honor*] and Bertolt Brecht's *Die Dreigroschenoper* [*The Threepenny Opera*] depicted the depths of human depravity while highlighting the significance of the social conditions under which murder and mayhem unfold. Heinrich von Kleist's *Michael Kohlhaas* and Franz Kafka's *Der Process* [*The Trial*] illuminated the extent to which violence and abuse can masquerade under the name of justice. And E. T. A. Hoffmann's *Das Fräulein von Scuderi* [*Mademoiselle de Scudéri*], Annette von Droste-Hülshoff's *Die Judenbuche* [*The Jew's Beech*], and Bernhard Schlink's *Der Vorleser* [*The Reader*] had me pondering the ways in which categories of gender, ethnicity, and class interface with portrayals of criminal transgressions, their investigation, and the reestablishment of social order.

The graduate program in Germanic Studies at Indiana University, where I completed my doctorate, had a cultural studies orientation and my teachers encouraged me to marry my interest in popular literature with my research agenda. Though crime and detective stories have become the subjects of an abundance of scholarly work in the last three decades, few critics have focused on the intersections among mystery fiction, feminist and queer theory, and

German cultural history. I set out to explain what was special about queer crime stories, positing that there was a structural relationship between solving crime and decoding sexuality. After completing the dissertation I continued to investigate this question, and I began to understand that the queer facets of feminist crime novels serve the broader purpose of mediating discontent with local, national, and global trends. The boundary-crossing desires and practices of queer characters convey ambivalence toward contemporary developments, from the fall of the Wall and European expansion to debates about gay marriage and asylum policies. This insight brought about a shift in gears several years into the project, and I ultimately decided to write this book about queer German crime fiction—and the anxieties it elicits—as a symbolic means of surrender and resistance to cultural movements.

The literary quality of queer crime novels can naturally vary just as much as the crimes themselves, but all of them set out to reveal and simultaneously to conceal essential, compelling truths about modern society. This indeed is what I believe makes them queer: they foist upon the reader the responsibility for making sense of their mysteries. The novels on which I concentrate here are among the finest, most gripping, and most complex of the genre—those whose maddening ambiguities haunt us long after the reading is over.

Introduction:
The Queer Crime Genre

A marriage of mystery fiction and queer concerns, queer crime literature celebrates the pairing of the political with the sexual and the unexpected revelations this produces. Crime fiction traffics in the investigation and interpretation of identities and the problems that arise in concealing and revealing them. The genre's preoccupation with identity provides fertile ground for queer approaches not only to characterization, but also to storytelling, reading, and analysis. Offering both entertainment and social commentary, crime fiction's narratives of transgression locate their subjects within specific historical and cultural contexts, thus affirming or interrogating existing forms of order. Queer mysteries bring this socially critical perspective together with representations of boundary-crossing genders and sexualities, inviting readers to interpret queer figures and themes as literary incursions into cultural traditions and political discourses.

What associations does the word *queer* evoke, and what can it bring to the study of crime fiction? Though vernacular usage has normalized the term as a synonym for homosexual, its range of meaning extends far beyond this crude definition. The queer mystery is a subgenre of popular literature that develops the tension among diverging understandings of *queer* as a fixed referent and as a destabilizing approach. On the one hand, the term has solidified as a general and stable signifier of gendered and sexualized acts and positionalities that do not align easily with binary gender categories and heterosexual norms. Such affiliations include not only homosexuality, but also a range of other non-normative desires, practices, and embodiments, such as asexuality and bisexuality; cross-dressing and transgenderism; intersexuality, androgyny, and genderqueerness[1]; and questioning and transitioning. On the other hand, particularly in scholarly usage, *queer* has come to refer more broadly to subversive strategies and gestures, movements against the grain that trouble or challenge commonly accepted practices: these processes are often ongoing and resist closure.[2] In both cases, the queer or queering entity can cause disruptions, and queer mysteries invite readers to interpret these disruptions as cultural and political commentaries. Crime fiction narrates investigations of the social and psychological circumstances of transgressive acts, and the solutions it offers (or withholds) speak volumes about the assumptions, perspectives, and ideologies that it implicitly endorses.

As readers, we expect crime novels to create tension by asking questions and to resolve that tension by answering them. Though a long-standing convention of the genre is that narrative closure brings with it coherent solutions to the mysteries at hand, innovative crime fiction uses this formula to manipulate reader expectations, encouraging readers to come to mistaken conclusions or to question the solutions the texts themselves provide.[3] The queer mystery offers both affirmative and subversive approaches to reader expectations and literary conventions. Playfully engaging the search for identification and closure that detective stories traditionally deploy, queer narratives present gender and sexuality as mysteries and stress the necessary processes of reading and interpreting in constructing identity and solving crime. Open endings, multiple plausible solutions, and ambiguous or absent answers to the questions raised: these building blocks of the crime genre are further emphasized in the queer subgenre, through which texts highlight misreadings alongside, and often instead of, correct or reliable interpretations. Queer crime fiction encourages conflicting or contradictory readings of both crime and sexuality and therefore requires reader interventions in order to make sense of these dual mysteries. This study argues for a nuanced understanding of what constitutes a queer text and proposes that examining the queer facets of recent crime stories opens up interpretive possibilities for understanding the multifaceted critiques the narratives elaborate.

This project approaches genre fiction from a cultural studies perspective, deploying close readings of previously unresearched texts as a framework for examining divisive issues in recent and contemporary German and European social histories. Revealing the politics at play in queer feminist crime novels, this book demonstrates that queer objects of study and queer methodologies can afford new insights into the ways in which popular texts mobilize the implications of desire and identity in elaborating their cultural critiques. This study's queer objects are detective and mystery narratives by German-speaking women from the 1980s to the 2000s, and its queer methodologies draw interdisciplinary connections among fictional texts, theoretical discourses, political practices, and the realities of queer life.[4]

Queer mysteries have played a crucial role in shaping the German feminist crime genre, contributing to its enduring popularity since the 1980s. The classic

Frauenkrimis [women's crime novels] exemplified by Pieke Biermann's *Potsdamer Ableben* [Potsdam Demise] and Ingrid Noll's *Die Häupter meiner Lieben* [*Head Count*][5] feature queer characters and themes that negotiate contemporary discourses on the politics of gender and sexuality and offer visions of political action and social change. Women writers of German crime fiction in the 1980s, 1990s, and 2000s interrogated the legacies of the feminist and gay rights movements in an era that saw rapidly evolving roles and opportunities for women and minorities. Their work bears witness to the cultural shifts that accompanied tremendous transformations in the shape and perceptions of the German state as a nation, and as a member of the expanding European Union and the global community. While a burgeoning body of scholarship asserts the significance of feminist crime fiction and its political interventions, little research exists on the queer subgenre. Through close readings of ten mysteries in their evolving social contexts, this study examines previously unexplored works by mainstream authors such as Susanne Billig and Christine Lehmann; popular feminist and lesbian writers including Gabriele Gelien, Corinna Kawaters, and Katrin Kremmler; and the lesser-known Martina-Marie Liertz. It also offers new perspectives on the work of three successful authors who have long been recognized for their contributions to feminist crime literature, Biermann, Noll, and Edith Kneifl. This investigation uses four conceptual frameworks: the study of crime and detective fiction; feminist and queer theory and politics; German and Austrian national identities and the European community; and globalization and transnational migrations.

One of the goals of this study is to bring to the attention of English-speaking readers and scholars the significant contributions made by German writers to the mystery genre.[6] This discussion of feminist German crime novels is grounded in general scholarship on crime and detective fiction and demonstrates that German texts share numerous concerns with mysteries from other national traditions, especially Anglo-American narratives. Perhaps more than any other kind of fiction, crime stories easily cross national borders—questions of order, violence, detection, and justice have universal appeal—and yet German crime novels are rarely found in English translation. One popular theory is that they do not travel well because of their geographical and cultural specificity.[7] This assessment seems all the more apt in view of the growth and popularity of the *Regionalkrimi* [regional crime novel] subgenre in recent years. But it is precisely the ethnic flavoring of German-language mysteries that makes them so compelling for many audiences: they negotiate a distinctive balance, situating themselves within a global literary genre and exploring the unique qualities of German people, places, and traditions. This textual terrain is the ideal setting in which to pose questions about how genre interfaces with language and culture, and to delve into the nuanced relationships among enduring institutions—such as the nuclear family and the nation-state—and processes specific to German and Austrian cultures of a certain era—such as the rise of autonomous feminism, the integration of the European economy, and the development of historical consciousness in post-fascist and post-socialist societies. German crime fiction, then, is the site of an intriguing and illuminating dialogue between the local and the global, the national and the transnational.

German feminist crime fiction arose out of the protest cultures and countercultures of the late 1980s and early 1990s. It is a highly politicized subgenre, created largely by intellectuals and socially engaged women who write crime fiction as a means of expressing discontent with social relations, reaching like-minded readers, and making political interventions through their work. The legacies of the rights movements of the late twentieth century are palpable in the feminist *Frauenkrimi*, which is anchored in the contexts of radical feminist politics, the gay rights movements, and autonomous and antifascist activism. Confronting social inequalities and the ways in which they intersect with evolving economic relations during and after the end of the Cold War, *Frauenkrimis* attest to the lasting influence of the New Left by investigating oppression and justice, forms of democracy, and socialist and anticapitalist discourses. At the same time, they bear witness to ideological shifts away from post–1968 movements and the mainstream rights movements, and toward queer and antiglobalization politics. The novels explore continuities among totalitarianism, democracy, and transnationalism, both by probing the relationships between bureaucracy and violence, and by keeping a critical distance from state governments and public officials. Likely due at least in part to Germany and Austria's fascist and socialist histories and in part also to the legacies of autonomous countercultures, there is a paucity of police detectives in the feminist *Frauenkrimi*, a tendency that it shares with German-language crime writing in general. Of the novels I analyze in this study, only one (Biermann's *Potsdamer Ableben*) has a police protagonist. When police officers do appear, they are more often than not incompetent, corrupt, or at best unreliable. The German tradition also includes few of the private eyes so common to the American detective genre, perhaps because such figures are, particularly from a leftist feminist point of view, too individualistic and antisocial. In fact, most of the main characters in German feminist crime fiction are amateur investigators or criminals. The amateur gumshoes featured in the novels discussed here are journalists, students, activists, and accountants who take a personal interest in crime (if they are not directly involved) and have ties to the communities in which they do their sleuthing. When *Frauenkrimis* focus on perpetrators, they are usually average women, from housewives and mothers to artists and adventurers, whose misdeeds seek to right the wrongs they suffer or witness. Portrayals of these protagonists, whether they commit or investigate crimes, tend to stress their roles as agents of justice who act when the law fails to intervene appropriately. The German feminist crime novel thus emphasizes the social and political commitment of ordinary citizens to confronting injustice and upholding democratic ideals.

Toward a Definition of a Hybrid Subgenre: The Queer Feminist *Frauenkrimi*

The term *Frauenkrimi* sounds deceivingly simple. But genre definitions are never so easy as they might seem, and with the *Frauenkrimi* as with most other literary traditions, competing definitions accentuate different trends and conventions. Literally translating as "women's crime novel," the label announces the centrality of gender in a genre commonly defined as mystery fiction written by, for, and about women. This seems straightforward enough, but as Nicola Barfoot points out in one of the few monographs to examine the German *Frauenkrimi*, such a gloss is problematic: "The slogan 'von, für und mit Frauen' is frequently quoted, a definition which is simple on the surface but in fact covers a complex of ideas about the significance of authorial gender, about content, and about audience and intention."[8] Indeed, *Frauenkrimi* is a contentious term, and numerous authors, critics, and scholars have rejected the category as discriminatory or critically unproductive.[9] Moreover, a traditional definition of the genre according to the genderedness of its subjects, readers, and writers works to marginalize or exclude a number of noteworthy texts: some mysteries, such as Pieke Biermann's Karin Lietze series and Christine Lehmann's Lisa Nerz novels, which are popular among male as well as female readers, introduce rather masculine female investigators while also featuring roughly equal numbers of key male and female characters in their crime intrigues. Still other *Frauenkrimis*, such as Maria Gronau's Lena Wertebach books, are published under pseudonyms and cannot be verified as the work of female authors.[10] In view of the challenges such texts can pose to traditional understandings of the genre, I offer a pragmatic definition of the *Frauenkrimi* as a crime story that underscores and reflects on the femaleness of its writers, subjects, and audiences, but not to the exclusion of other gender identities. This description theorizes femaleness, together with femininity, as multiple and as non-exclusive, encompassing a range of positionalities and affiliations that circulate in and around the texts. Defined in this way, the category of the *Frauenkrimi* can include novels published under female pseudonyms or by male writers; narratives featuring masculine, transgendered, and genderqueer figures; and texts consumed by diverse audiences. While maintaining the focus on femaleness that marks earlier descriptions of the genre, my broad definition seeks to recuperate the term *Frauenkrimi* from its detractors by emphasizing the critical value of its approach to identity constructions and their far-reaching implications: the ways in which the genre strategically orients our perspectives as readers, critics, and scholars to the intersections between identity and narrative, and the ways in which this affects how we read and understand texts. At the same time, such a characterization effectively queers the category by destabilizing the fixity and centrality of gender that its name implies.

In calling attention to the significance and constructedness of gender, my definition above implies that the *Frauenkrimi* brings with it a feminist perspective. But because critics disagree about the *Frauenkrimi*'s relationship to gender politics, I attach the qualifier *feminist* to the body of texts that form the focus of this study. Feminist *Frauenkrimis* turn a critical eye to sexism and inequality, opening up the binary gender system and its concordant social power structures as categories of analysis. Literary and cultural history suggests that there are connections between the explosion of feminism into popular culture in the 1980s—as a 1984 mystery novel claims, "der Feminismus wurde gesellschaftsfähig" [feminism was becoming socially acceptable][11]—and the emergence of *Frauenkrimi* as an identifiable and marketable trend at the end of the decade.[12] Perhaps due to this confluence of political and social developments, scholars such as Kirsimarja Tielinen identify the *Frauenkrimi* as inherently feminist, though the implication is not that the crime genre automatically becomes feminist simply by virtue of its writers' and characters' femininity, but rather that the term itself has come to be associated with texts that embrace and interrogate feminist politics.[13] Anja Kemmerzell asserts that there are two different kinds of *Frauenkrimis*: the mainstream type and the feminist variant; what differentiates the latter from the former is an "Akzentverlagerung" [shift in emphasis] toward women's experiences in relation to their social, legal, and psychological contexts.[14] Feminist *Frauenkrimis* also tend to represent crime differently than do their mainstream counterparts: Sabine Wilke contends that the transgressions and investigations they dramatize are typically inflected by the gender, sexuality, and social status of their perpetrators, victims, and investigators (256). The novels at the heart of my study bear witness to Wilke's claim, for even when the crimes themselves are not sexually motivated, the social milieus in which their authors locate them call attention to the political dimensions not only of gender, but also of race, class, and ethnicity. Such is the case, for example, with the murder of an attractive Afro-German man in the autonomous subcultures of Corinna Kawaters's *Zora Zobel findet die Leiche* [Zora Zobel Finds the Body], and with the theft of a tourist's passport in Katrin Kremmler's transnational crime story *Die Sirenen von Coogee Beach* [The Sirens of Coogee Beach]. Kawaters and Kremmler share with their contemporaries a literary worldview that homes in on extremism and the conditions of possibility for participatory democracy, highlighting the inclusions and exclusions that modern political forms require. As Katrin Sieg demonstrates in two studies of *Frauenkrimis* by Pieke Biermann and Doris Gercke, such texts often take feminism itself as their object of investigation, and their self-conscious assessments of political theory and action participate in the larger feminist project of critiquing reigning ideologies and trends such as socialism, capitalism, fascism, and globalization in unified Germany and the European Union.[15] Feminist crime novels are politically engaged: they examine and interrogate social order and injustice, looking through the lens of gender critique to analyze justice, citizenship, oppression, human rights, and the politics of public space. The genre maps out the limitations posed by existing forms of theory and action and proposes strategies of resistance, envisioning the world as changeable.

Queer crime fiction, like queer identity, is a conceptual paradox that requires unpacking. Notions of identity and genre crystallize around a more or less fixed set of ideas about practices and expectations, and yet these norms are subject to change. Queering them calls for a shift in emphasis to the ways in which they evolve, resist containment, signify newly and differently, and ultimately become quite messy. The meaning of *queer* that organizes this study is, as indicated above, twofold, stressing both fixity and flux. The term *queer* has been used and understood in many ways, and in recent years scholars have argued that the proliferation of its connotations and its resulting indeterminacy have rendered it theoretically useless.[16] While I do not disagree that the contingency and diffusion of *queer* effectively defuses its meaning, I contend that its versatility also attests to the concept's power to open up new and fruitful perspectives for the interpretation of cultural phenomena. In fact, my project, in which *queer* designates both a subject and an approach—a textual positionality and a readerly strategy—necessitates this very versatility. Its focus is the manifold intersections among these notions of *queer* and recent variations on the theme of the crime genre. These include the queerly gendered and sexualized characters crime stories introduce; the interpretive work these characters do in their efforts to solve crime and to read and categorize one another; the reader's own attempts to make sense of these representations; the ways in which narratives challenge the conventions of crime and detective fiction; and the forms and functions of suggestion, ambiguity, and openness in the novels. While such tropes are noteworthy in and of themselves in bringing into relief the unspoken and often invisible expectations that regularly shape our interactions with cultural texts, identifying them is just a first step in this study, which examines how genre fiction's queer figures and gestures trouble social norms and explores the implications of these disruptions. These are starting points for writing a new narrative of social history. I view queer crime's characters and themes as metaphors for cultural critique, and I interpret their indeterminacy, flexibility, and the unease they cause as potent commentaries on life and politics in contemporary Germany and Austria, and in Europe and the world beyond.

One of the meanings of the term *queer* that this study engages relates specifically to sex and sexuality. By identifying the novels I investigate as queer, I seek to address a gap between feminist scholarship on the *Frauenkrimi* and on lesbian crime writing. There is a tendency in some scholarly discussions of the *Frauenkrimi* to overlook sex, glossing over the ways in which it resonates meaningfully in crime stories. Sexuality is not peripheral but rather central to the genre, and its constructions and connotations color multiple dimensions of the narratives. Not only do the devastating and illegal dimensions of violent or non-consensual erotic acts play out in the crimes such texts narrate—like harassment, abuse, and rape—but the portrayal of women as actively desiring sexual beings rewrites the conventions of the male-dominated detective story in which women are more often objects than subjects of desire. Sieg and Wilke are among the few scholars who acknowledge the political and literary significance of depicting sexuality in the *Frauenkrimi*, from sexual violence against women to women's sexual labor and same-sex desires. By stressing romantic and erotic yearnings, the feminist *Frauenkrimi* asserts the place of sexuality in the formation of female subjecthood and the exercise of power. In contrast, feminist scholarship on lesbian crime fiction in particular has long recognized the subgenre as a hybrid form of popular fiction in which romance and eroticism play central roles, occasionally to the point of displacing the mystery plot.[17] Though queer mysteries are a related subgenre, they are not identical to lesbian crime fiction, and one of the ways in which they tend to differentiate themselves is in the treatment of desire.[18] As Phyllis Betz, Brigitte Frizzoni, and Maureen Reddy point out, the lesbian mystery is heavily invested in the affirmation of lesbian subjectivities and desires, which frequently comes to expression in stories about coming out, the pursuit of a romantic partner, and falling in love.[19] The queer mystery sets itself apart from this trend in lesbian crime fiction by rejecting the possibility of romantic love, either in favor of explicit representations of unromantic eroticism, or in the service of channeling unfulfilled desires into political action. In many queer crime novels, romance is sublimated or dismissed entirely, such as in Biermann's *Potsdamer Ableben* and Susanne Billig's *Sieben Zeichen: Dein Tod* [Seven Signs: Your Death]. If romance does play a central role in the queer crime novel, then it almost always serves as a means of introducing a new political dimension into the crime story, as in Gabriele Gelien's *Eine Lesbe macht noch keinen Sommer* [One Lesbian Does Not Make a Summer] and Christine Lehmann's *Training mit dem*

Tod [Working Out with Death]. These texts by Gelien and Lehmann also resist classification as lesbian mysteries because their female protagonists are attracted to both men and women. Like other queer crime stories, they portray gender and desire as fluid and contingent, interweaving depictions of sexuality with their larger social critiques. By extension, lesbian mysteries in which romance, reader identification, and closure receive heavy emphasis—women fall in love with women and find happy endings, while the crime investigations are neatly tied up, leaving no loose threads at the novels' conclusions—do not fall under this characterization of queer crime fiction.[20]

Feminist studies of crime fiction have been an area of intense scholarly interest in the last twenty years. In examining the sociopolitical dimensions of queer crime novels together with their depictions of sex and sexuality, my work complements the foundations laid by two scholars who have published trailblazing inquiries into Anglo-American feminist and lesbian crime literature, Sally Munt and Phyllis Betz.[21] Munt's *Murder by the Book? Feminism and the Crime Novel*, a study of feminist discourses in women's crime fiction, reveals the ideological investments underlying representations of women as perpetrators, victims, and investigators, paying special attention to forms of justice, resistance, and social change. Phyllis Betz's *Lesbian Detective Fiction: Woman as Author, Subject and Reader*—the only book-length analysis of lesbian crime fiction—stresses the personal dimensions and public consequences of identity formation within the novels and investigates the texts' encouragement of reader identification with the fictional figures. While both studies examine the ways in which the formula of genre fiction intersects with the genderedness of its subjects and consider the roles that sexuality plays in this interaction, neither addresses the problem of indeterminacy. Taking cues from Munt's political contextualization and from Betz's examination of character and reader positionalities, I explore what happens when texts do not offer coherent answers on either level. What happens when a reader, who expects to solve a riddle, cannot find a clear answer on questions of gender or sexuality? How can we make sense of nuanced or ambiguous social commentaries? What interpretations do the texts encourage or discourage? In exploring the interface between characters and readers in the queer subgenre of crime literature, my book develops arguments that pertain to the genre as a whole and contribute to larger debates in gender and sexuality studies about narrative, authorship, politics, violence, nationhood, and human rights.

The expression *queer crime* is seldom used and virtually absent in discussions of crime literature.[22] My decade-long investigation into the subgenre has uncovered only three other sources that employ this terminology, all of which use the qualifier *queer* to underline gender and sexuality, but in different ways. Editor Lisa Kuppler's 2002 collection *Queer Crime: Lesbisch-schwule Krimi-*

geschichten [Queer Crime: Lesbian and Gay Crime Stories], an anthology of
fourteen short stories by German- and English-speaking authors, announces
queer crime as a category; the prospective reader presumably knows or can
infer what queer crime *is*.[23] But no explicit definition of the category can be
found within the pages of *Queer Crime*. Kuppler's subtitle offers a clue, suggesting that it is synonymous with gay and lesbian crime fiction—and, to be
sure, some contributions to Kuppler's anthology emphasize homosexual positionalities above all others: for instance, Frank Goyke's "Happy Birthday" and
Katrin Kremmler's "Sydney Affairs" are populated almost entirely by gay or
lesbian characters. But though gay and lesbian mysteries may have a place in
the queer genre, crucial distinctions exist between these categories. A strict
definition of queer as homosexual would exclude many of the complex, messy,
and seemingly unreadable identities that drive *Queer Crime*'s intrigues, from
the transgressive lesbian and the gay man who sleep together in Manuela Kay's
"Scheißbullen" [Crap Cops] and the bisexual lover in Susanne Billig's "Dora,"
to the semen-stealing male-to-female transsexual and the pregnant drag king
in Carlo de Luxe's "Yin-Yang Gang-Bang." Populating the pages of these mysteries and others in Kuppler's collection are characters whose desires, acts, and
performances cannot be adequately captured by the label homosexual. Queer
crime, then, is not just shorthand for gay and lesbian mysteries.[24] At the online
bookstore Rainbow Sauce, which devotes a page to "Queer Mysteries and
Thrillers," the rubric emphasizes other identities—to the exclusion, however,
of gay and lesbian texts. The separation of queer mysteries and thrillers from
the categories of gay and lesbian novels suggests that queer crime constitutes
a distinct class of its own. The store's website describes *queer* as a catchall for
odds and ends that do not fit under other rubrics: "This section is basically
for books that feature bisexual and transgender characters in mystery novels
and thrillers."[25] Such a description suggests an affinity between queer crime
and boundary-crossing identities and practices that do not align exclusively
with male or female gendered embodiment or with desire for sexual objects
of one gender alone. My definition of queer crime demarks a wider terrain
than Rainbow Sauce's description implies, but it overlaps with the bookstore's
understanding of the genre as embracing realms of identification beyond gay
and lesbian. As used by Brigitte Frizzoni, the only scholar in whose work I
have encountered the expression *queer crime*, the label—which Frizzoni short-
ens to *Q-Krimi* [q-crime]—is shorthand for GLBTI crime fiction (133).[26] Not
only does Frizzoni understand *queer* more broadly than Rainbow Sauce's
description suggests, but she also applies the concept to the plot of the queer
crime story, arguing that the text theorizes about gender and sexuality through
the investigation it narrates. The queer mystery, she maintains, intertwines
queer positionalities with the development of the crime narrative, presenting

gender and sexuality "als eigentliches (Krimi-)Rätsel" [as the real (crime) riddle, 133] and unveiling identity as merely a semblance of coherence: this is precisely what differentiates it from crime fiction of a more general kind.[27] In connecting the crime genre's riddles of identity to its portrayals of gender and sexuality, Frizzoni gestures toward one of the two crucial ways in which I contend that the crime genre becomes queered. This queerness, I argue, also radiates outward and resonates in multiple other dimensions of the stories, serving as an allegorical means of commenting on social developments—for example, in Kawaters's *Zora Zobel* books, the queer narrator embodies the widening rift between autonomous and radical feminist politics, and in Billig's and Noll's books, such characters signal unease with German unification, the expansion of the EU, and concurrent shifts in Germany and beyond. In other words, queer crime challenges social norms pertaining to the binary gender system and heterosexual privilege, while also linking such critiques with wider cultural discourses.

My strategically broad definition of queer crime is more inclusive than the texts represented in this project may seem to indicate. None of the novels at the heart of this study is written by a male author, and though some do feature pivotal male figures, such as Biermann's *Potsdamer Ableben* and Lehmann's *Training mit dem Tod*, in which women and men work together to investigate crime, my focus on the politics of the *Frauenkrimi* and its relationship to feminist discourses effectively works to exclude many texts by and about men. My interest lies especially in characters who are multiply marginalized, often by their gender and their sexuality, in a literary tradition historically dominated by white, middle-class, heterosexual male writers and characters. Most of the investigators, criminals, victims, and witnesses at the center of the narratives I analyze here are female-embodied, and their genders entail some identification with femininity—though a few, such as Biermann's Karin Lietze and Lehmann's Lisa Nerz, as well as Cora in Noll's *Die Häupter meiner Lieben*, are quite androgynous. Some of these main characters are ostensibly heterosexual, such as Noll's Cora and Billig's Helen Marrow, and some identify as lesbian, such as Gelien's Gabriele, but even those with seemingly stable sexualities go through transitions or moments of indeterminacy, suggesting that they are neither strictly straight nor exclusively gay: they may be closeted or coming out, or they have affections for or intimate relations with both men and women. The many significant and complex queer crime texts that are written by men and emphasize masculinity, such as Michael Roes's *Der Coup der Berdache* [The Berdache's Coup] and Wolf Haas's *Der Knochenmann* [*The Bone Man*], as well as Carlo de Luxe's contribution to Kuppler's collection mentioned above, do not play a central role in this study. This also means that the vast genre of gay crime fiction remains unconsidered by my critique, though the strategies I offer here for interpreting queer texts could certainly be engaged in the analysis of novels introducing male-embodied figures. In an article reviewing gay German crime novels from 1980 until today, James Jones, the only scholar who has undertaken an analysis of the subgenre, provides a cultural history of representations of homosexuals and the changing face of the German nation.[28] Many of the trends and themes Jones identifies in gay mysteries—eroticism, the power of the closet, and the effects of German unification and political issues affecting queer populations—resonate with the queer *Frauenkrimis* I discuss here. As the genre of queer crime grows in a cultural context where gender categories are becoming more contingent and less relevant than ever before, we are likely to witness the development not only of more frequent intersections and overlaps among gay, lesbian, feminist and queer crime fictions, but also of new lines of queer inquiry into the production, reception, and analysis of these fascinating texts.

Queer German Crime Fiction as Cultural History

Queer German crime fiction has proliferated in the last quarter century. Emerging together with the feminist *Frauenkrimi*, it appeared during the 1980s, coinciding with the transition from the second to the third wave of feminism, the birth of queer theory, a burgeoning awareness of alternative genders and sexualities in the popular media, and a concurrent boom in feminist and queer writing in popular fictional genres. In Germany and Western Europe, these trends accompanied massive sociopolitical transformations like the collapse of the Soviet Bloc, the restructuring of the German nation, and the globalization of Western Europe that fertilized the ground for new forms of cultural expression. These wide-ranging changes brought about a paradigm shift to which popular literature bears witness: the breakdown of ruling ideologies ushered in postmodern skepticism and do-it-yourself cultures emphasizing the democratic potential of making one's own meaning. These changes produced a heightened awareness of processes of reading and the life and death stakes of misreading. The authors of queer feminist thrillers and mysteries, who include—in addition to the nine authors features in this study—Annette Berr, Thea Dorn, Christine Grän, Maria Gronau, Uta-Maria Heim, and Antje Rávic Strubel, among a great many others, invite their readers to question commonly accepted "certainties" not only by interrogating mainstream conceptions of identity and the politics in and beyond them, but also by leaving unsolved riddles for their readers to tackle on their own. Queer crime is a contemporary genre that articulates cultural critique while privileging possibilities over definitions and foregrounding questions rather than concrete answers.

This project's chronological framework provides a historical overview of German queer feminist crime writing, with each of its four units engaging in a comparative analysis of two or three texts from a particular era organized around a specific theme. Each set of texts reveals how different groups of authors have used the crime genre to work through issues of political action, the family unit, rights and recognition, and citizenship and belonging. Chapters 1 and 2 historicize and politicize the origins of the queer German mystery and investigate early feminist novels for evidence of contemporary discourses on the politics of gender and sexuality. Chapter 1 analyzes changing and relational forms of feminist theory and practice in three of the first *Frauenkrimis* of the mid–1980s, Corinna Kawaters's *Zora Zobel findet die Leiche* [Zora Zobel Finds the Body, 1984] and its sequel, *Zora Zobel zieht um* [Zora Zobel Moves In, 1986], and Pieke Biermann's *Potsdamer Ableben* [Potsdam Demise, 1987]. These politically engaged queer feminist detective novels interrogate the ongoing relevance and efficacy of the dominant model of second-wave radical feminism that had crystallized in West Germany in the previous decade. Reading the queer investigators in Kawaters's and Biermann's mysteries as extensions of the authors' activism, chapter 1 argues that Kawaters's novels narrate the emancipation of radical feminist action from autonomous concerns and interprets Biermann's text as a rejection of second-wave feminism in favor of a queer transnational alternative. The texts disclose the wide spectrum traced by the representation of identity politics in the genre. I explore how constructions of gender and sexuality influence and inform the novels' characterization and narrative perspective, social critique, and the structure and resolution of narrative conflict.

Detective stories were one form of crime fiction that feminist writers employed; another was the psychological thriller, or the perpetrator crime novel. German and Austrian psychological thrillers of the early 1990s located the sources of violence, oppression, and injustice in bourgeois marriage and the nuclear biological family, and explored the potential for feminist empowerment and action both at home and abroad. Chapter 2 complements the focus in chapter 1 on representations of queer investigators by analyzing their counterpart, queer criminals, in psychological thrillers or *Täterinnenkrimis* [female perpetrator crime novels]. Edith Kneifl's *Zwischen zwei Nächten* [Between Two Nights, 1991] and Ingrid Noll's *Die Häupter meiner Lieben* [Head Count, 1993] invite their readers to interpret domestic arrangements and queer family units as feminist commentaries on the violence of heterosexual relationships in contemporary Europe. In addition to emphasizing the subtle, everyday ways in which the institution of the family serves to perpetuate and conceal gendered violence, these novels position this process in migrations and intersections between cultures: Austria and the United States in Kneifl's text, and

Germany and Italy in Noll's. This chapter reads queer figures and same-sex intimacies in these *Täterinnenkrimis* within their historical context as negotiations of psychological, geographical, and gendered boundaries. The texts' queer transnational visions raise crucial questions about identity, ethnicity, and representation in late twentieth-century Austria, post-unification Germany, and the expanding European Union.

In the post-unification era, debates about gay and transgender rights came to the fore and made their way into romance and detective stories, which thematized relationships between identity and politics. Queer crime fiction, like the related lesbian mystery, which has been described as a hybrid genre, often includes an emphasis on the erotic; however, in queer mysteries, romance is typically fleeting at best and impossible at worst. The three texts at the focus of this chapter bring together romance, crime, and social commentary by probing the implications for feminist, gay, and transgender politics when queer female detectives develop romantic or erotic desires for masculine and male-embodied figures. Gabriele Gelien's *Eine Lesbe macht noch keinen Sommer* [One Lesbian Does Not Make a Summer, 1993], Christine Lehmann's *Training mit dem Tod* [Working Out with Death, 1998], and Martina-Marie Liertz's trilogy, *Die Geheimnisse der Frauen* [The Secrets of Women, 1999], playfully intertwine conventions of crime and romance fiction by highlighting the identity trouble caused when a queer woman falls in love with a mysterious man in the course of an investigation. The three texts offer different solutions to the riddle of the attractive man's identity—the first man is gay, the second transgendered, and the third a woman passing as a man—that can be read as metaphors about the social significance of gender and sexuality. These books intervened in debates surrounding the rights movements of the 1990s, confronting contemporary issues from sexism and homophobia to gay marriage and gender reassignment.

Since the 1990s, the queer German mystery genre has increasingly opened up to textual complexities and narrative forms that push the boundaries of genre; it has also turned outward to address political and cultural issues beyond the borders of Germany and an expanding Europe. Mysteries of the mid- to late 1990s and 2000s explore transnational migrations, postcolonialism, citizenship, and asylum politics, as well as the globalization of religion and the media, ideological imperialism, and international corruption. Chapter 4 examines these themes as they relate to the structural tropes of the closet and coming out, which are thematized in detective fiction's concealment and revelation of identities. The focus of the chapter is mysteries in which the revelation or affirmation of one identity category serves to distract readers and diegetic characters from another, closeted, identity that has direct bearing on the crime investigation. In Susanne Billig's *Sieben Zeichen: Dein Tod* [Seven Signs: Your Death, 1994], the closeting of a journalist who goes undercover to research an

Anglo-American cult invites a critique of cultural imperialism and global religion, while also functioning as a metaphor about awakening to queer desires and coming out. By contrast, Katrin Kremmler's *Die Sirenen von Coogee Beach* [The Sirens of Coogee Beach, 2003] mobilizes representations of hidden perpetrator identities in Sydney's lesbian milieus to expose the shortcomings of German and Australian asylum policies in protecting human rights. These novels offer visions of the devastating and yet vital potential of the transnational flows made possible by the opening of borders and revisions of citizenship and immigration laws at the turn of the twenty-first century.

The consideration in this book of these ten works—from the early work of Kawaters and Biermann in the 1980s to mysteries by Lehmann and Kremmler in the late 1990s and 2000s—as characteristic examples of queer crime fiction opens up new questions and possibilities for investigating the diversity of German feminist crime writing. First and foremost, it permits a fresh look at feminist crime that historicizes the emergence of queer mysteries and draws a clear link between feminist and queer crime fiction. Second, a textual analysis that refrains from assuming that characters are by default heterosexual orients itself to perceive queer traces that can reveal much about the interplay of gender and sexuality with other identity constructions such as class, age, ethnicity, race, and nation. An examination of these constructions provides access to new insights into the politics of representation and agency in narrative as well as in cultural history. And third, it seeks to identify queer dimensions extending beyond characters' identities into other parts of the narratives. The novels in question also lend queer contours to their themes, structures, approaches to the crime genre, and social commentaries. Through close readings of ten novels by nine authors, this project explores the diverse voices and political orientations that find expression in queer feminist crime fiction.

Note about Language and Citations

In order to make this study accessible to readers both with and without knowledge of German, I have supplemented citations from primary German-language texts with my own English translations in the following format: "Original auf Deutsch" [English translation]. The same format is used to provide and translate German titles, names, and terminology. Due to the differences between German and English grammar and syntax, it was necessary in some cases to alter word suffixes or word order before embedding German citations into my English writing. Such alterations are indicated by square brackets within the original German citation. An empty set of square brackets—[]—indicates that I have dropped a suffix from the cited text.

CHAPTER 1

Detecting Scattered Feminisms: Politics and Activism in West German Mysteries

> The ideal reader of the feminist crime novels of the 1980s is a woman familiar with the problematization of the western feminist project which took place in the late 1970s.... The reader of these novels would already be informed by the way feminism in the 1980s had extended its interrogation of gender into a "politically correct" embrace of diverse counter-cultural projects.
> —Sally R. Munt, *Murder by the Book?* (60)

Written by authors as famous for their political activism as for their mystery fiction, early feminist *Frauenkrimis* of the 1980s staged literary interventions into contemporary discourses, testing the limits of feminist philosophies and practices. With the emergence of literature by women that emphasized female perspectives for mass consumption, this era marked a turning point: feminism had become mainstream, marketable, even digestible, and the controversial ideas that had been circulating in the public arena since the late 1960s found their way into popular cultural forms. *Frauenkrimis* take up the critical tendencies of the *Neue Deutsche Krimi* [New German crime novel] and the *Soziokrimi* [socially critical crime novel], quintessentially German genres of the 1960s and 1970s that brought leftist intellectual viewpoints to tales of social order and transgression and tackled galvanizing issues in postwar and divided Germany. Coupling this approach with the representation and empowerment of identities marginalized in a literary tradition dominated by heterosexual white male writers and characters, *Frauenkrimis* of the eighties can be linked with other contemporary crime stories that politicized identity by introducing German readers to sleuths from minority groups and vesting them with agency.[1] Not only offering entertainment, but also holding up a critical lens to politics of representation in contemporary culture, *Frauenkrimis* use the crime genre to examine the legacies of scattered feminist movements of the late twentieth century. This political gesture is not unique to German feminist crime fiction but can also be found in Anglo-American mystery writing of the era, as scholar Sally Munt demonstrates in her authoritative study, *Murder by the Book?* This chapter builds on the foundation laid by Munt in connecting crime novels to their political contexts by examining German women's mysteries of the eighties for evidence of shifting conceptions of gender and sexuality and other social changes. In Germany and elsewhere, female sleuths with a range of sexual desires led a rapidly growing readership on investigations of criminal transgressions in politically charged cultures and countercultures where their gender and sexual identities were under constant negotiation and had far-reaching implications.

Feminism was and remains a contested term. In the early to mid–1970s, the campaign against Paragraph 218, the section of the German legal code outlawing abortion, brought together West German activists from various political camps in a shared struggle.[2] By the mid–1980s, however, the unifying cause of the previous decade had given way to diverging trends within the feminist movement.[3] On the one hand, the proliferation of women's political groups, publishing houses, bookstores, health collectives, and academic programs had resulted in the institutionalization and mainstreaming of feminism, a development that autonomists decried as antipathetic to countercultural struggles.[4] On the other hand, what had by the 1980s become the dominant model of radical feminism was just one of many forms of feminism that shaped contemporary debates. The coexistence of diverse feminist factions—such as radical, militant, socialist, materialist, autonomous, lesbian, separatist, antiracist, New Age, and various combinations thereof—encouraged discussion among activists, intellectuals, and public figures about the most effective and desirable forms of political action. Topics such as abortion, the sex industry, motherhood and child care, housework, domestic violence, women in the workforce, racism, women in political leadership, and relationships to law enforcement and the government took central stage in these discussions. No longer unified or singular, the "feminist movement" had become a constellation of complex relations among changing sociopolitical configurations. Forms of feminism informed and challenged one another; it therefore is no wonder that crime literature, a genre intimately concerned with justice and social change, bears witness to the shifting and relational posturing of different feminisms.

The mid-eighties witnessed the publication of three queer feminist novels by two female writers whose work participates in the tropes that would come to be known as defining elements of the *Frauenkrimi*. Set in the West German metropolitan areas of Bochum and Berlin, Corinna Kawaters's *Zora Zobel findet die Leiche* [Zora Zobel Finds the Body, 1984] and *Zora Zobel zieht um* [Zora Zobel Moves In, 1986] and Pieke Biermann's *Potsdamer Ableben* [Potsdam Demise, 1987] invite readers to engage in critiques of social, cultural, and political forces by following murder investigations led by queer female sleuths. Kawaters and Biermann were activists in the emancipatory struggles of the era, and became famous—or, in the case of Kawaters, infamous—for endorsing militant autonomism and prostitution. For them, crime fiction was a political tool. Their books offer political possibilities embedded within stories about law and order, murder and mayhem, sex and romance, and the individual and society. They also take the dominant model of radical feminism to task, dismissing it as stultified and shortsighted, and instead advance visions of semi-autonomous and socialist feminist theory and action.

Together with other women writers of their era, Kawaters and Biermann were instrumental in bringing the German *Frauenkrimi* to life with their queer feminist narratives. This chapter proposes a classification of their early novels as queer feminist *Frauenkrimis*, arguing that the political dimensions of Kawaters's and Biermann's fiction are intimately intertwined with the gendered and sexual identities of their detective figures. It also undertakes an analysis of the queer and feminist features of these texts, which are not limited to characterization but also include plot structure, voice, and themes, that provide clues for a decoding of their social commentaries. I work with a strategically broad understanding of the *Frauenkrimi*, building on Sabine Wilke's definition:

> Frauenkrimis sind—und das definiert sie—Kriminalgeschichten, die von Frauen geschrieben werden und um frauenrelevante Themen kreisen beziehungsweise Frauen als Hauptcharaktere vorstellen.... Die Themen dieser Frauenkrimis umfassen unter anderem Frauen als Opfer von gentechnologischen Manipulationen während der Schwangerschaft, die Männlichkeit von Wissenschaft und Geschäftswelt, die Probleme von allein erziehenden Müttern, die Frau als Opfer von alltäglicher Gewalt in der Familie, sexuellen Missbrauch von Töchtern, Frauenfreundschaften und Frauenliebschaften, die Probleme von Prostituierten und die Frau als Opfer, aber auch Täterin in sado-masochistischen Beziehungen [256].

> [*Frauenkrimis* are—and this defines them—crime stories written by women and dealing with themes relevant to women or introducing women as main characters.... The themes of these *Frauenkrimis* include, among others, women as victims of genetic engineering during pregnancy; the masculinity of science and the business world; the problems of single mothers; women as victims of everyday violence in the family; the sexual abuse of daughters; friendships and love affairs among women; the problems of prostitutes; and women as victims, but also as perpetrators, in sadomasochistic relationships.]

Wilke's account aligns the *Frauenkrimi* with feminist perspectives and implies the inclusion of queer figures: her definition locates gender constructions at the center of a genre that investigates the oppression and victimization of women as well as their empowerment and their alliances; it also makes specific mention of same-sex romantic relationships. Wilke includes the names of ten *Frauenkrimi* authors among whom Biermann appears, but not Kawaters.[5] However, in view of Wilke's description and the similarities between Biermann's novelistic debut and Kawaters's first two books, it would be appropriate to locate Kawaters among the ranks of *Frauenkrimi* authors. Like Biermann's *Potsdamer Ableben*, Kawaters's *Zora Zobel findet die Leiche* and *Zora Zobel zieht um* introduce female sleuths as main characters—and, in fact, the use of a first-person voice in Kawaters's books assigns greater significance to the female protagonist's experiences than does Biermann's rotating third-person narrative perspective. Moreover, all three texts stress themes relevant to women that Wilke either names or implies: sexual and domestic violence; the politics of women's sexual labor; friendships and political alliances among women; same-sex desire, romance, and eroticism; women in bureaucratic institutions; and gender politics in the male-dominated worlds of business and entertainment. It therefore seems reasonable both to describe Kawaters's Zora Zobel novels as *Frauenkrimis* and to qualify these works alongside Biermann's as vehicles for feminist and queer critiques. Attesting to the influence of evolving theories about gender and sexuality on the crime genre, Kawaters and Biermann spin tales of murder investigations that negotiate authority, agency, and action. The following analysis collects evidence from their mysteries: unattractive corpses, investigative processes that uncover the killers' motives, the sleuths' involvement in erotic seductions, and collaborations with and among police officers. Reading these and other traces within their sociohistorical contexts allows for an interpretation of Kawaters's and Biermann's literary experiments as invitations to examine the discourses of politics and identity that crystallize in popular culture of the eighties.

From Autonomous Rebel to Feminist Radical? Corinna Kawaters's *Zora Zobel findet die Leiche* (1984) and *Zora Zobel zieht um* (1986)

The Zora Zobel series of the mid–1980s vividly documents the protest cultures of the New Left in which author Corinna Kawaters participated, inviting readers to explore the evolving relationship between leftist alternative scenes and radical women's movements of the era. Kawaters became notorious for her affiliation with the feminist guerrilla group Rote Zora [Red Zora], which claimed responsibility for numerous politically motivated attacks on private and public institutions over a period two decades, beginning in the mid–1970s.[6] In hopes of avoiding prosecution for her involvement in militant violence, Kawaters fled Germany in 1987 and remained an international fugitive until 1995, when she returned to her homeland to face charges of terrorism.[7] This personal history contributed to the popularity of Kawaters's first two Zora Zobel novels, whose titles and eponymous heroine were inspired by Rote Zora.[8] Like her creator, protagonist and narrator Zora Zobel participated in the urban leftist scenes of the 1980s. The alleged parallels between Kawaters's life and art were deemed so striking that her fiction served as evidence in the trial against her in the late 1990s.[9] Published in Germany before Kawaters went into exile, *Zora Zobel findet die Leiche* and *Zora Zobel zieht um* highlight a number of issues that motivated the author and her contemporaries to political action: squatters' rights, opposition to Paragraph 218, and critiques of privatization and the sexual exploitation of women. *Zora Zobel findet die Leiche* (cited hereafter as *Zora1*) came out in 1984 with Zweitausendeins [Two thousand one], a Frankfurt-based press with connections to writers of the so-called *68er-Generation* [generation of 1968]. The press's reputation, along with the book's female protagonist and lively depictions of autonomist subcultures, helped Kawaters find eager readers among leftist and feminist radicals of the mid–1980s. *Zora1* was an underground hit, and within the first year appeared in four editions; eight editions had come out by 1986, when Kawaters published the sequel *Zora Zobel zieht um* (cited hereafter as *Zora2*), this time with Focus press. Both books became cult classics, praised by critics and scholars as transitional texts noteworthy for their portrayals of political activism on the cusp of the *Frauenkrimi* boom. A long-anticipated third installment in the series, *Zora Zobel auf Abwegen* [Zora Zobel Takes Detours], appeared in 2001 with Espresso but did not receive the same level of exposure or recognition as its predecessors.

Though contemporary author and critic Sabine Deitmer otherwise rejects the label *Frauenkrimi* as belittling, she draws upon Kawaters's work to provide the only definition of the term *Frauenkrimi* that she finds acceptable: a story in which all characters are female.[10] Deitmer's analysis highlights the paradigmatic second book in the Zora Zobel series, but it begs the question whether *Zora1* can also be categorized as a *Frauenkrimi*—and if so, which standards would justify such a classification.[11] The single criterion that Deitmer explicitly embraces, that all characters be female, does not apply to *Zora1*, in which men occupy numerous roles integral to the crime story: victim, perpetrator, police officers, comrades, and romantic interests. Deitmer's cursory discussion of *Zora1* instead highlights its representation of the lifestyles and social visions of contemporary autonomists.[12] Other critics, such as H.P. Karr, have also been more apt to depict Kawaters's books as predecessors rather than representatives of the *Frauenkrimi* movement.[13] In a move similar to Deitmer's,

Nicola Barfoot distances Kawaters's oeuvre from other works she identifies as feminist *Frauenkrimis*.[14] In spite of these nods from Deitmer, Karr, and Barfoot, Kawaters and her Zora Zobel series remain unmentioned in many scholarly investigations of women's crime writing in German.[15] This omission may be deliberate, given the author's involvement in leftist terrorism, though it may also have to do with other factors, such as the novels' subcultural appeal and publication with lesser-known presses.

These common gestures of exclusion notwithstanding, Kawaters's landmark Zora Zobel books do fit quite comfortably into the generic category of the feminist *Frauenkrimi*. Not only do *Zora1* and *Zora2* introduce a strong, politically active, female protagonist, but they also tell her story from a feminist viewpoint, placing constructions of gender and sexuality under the microscope while casting a critical eye on social injustices relating to race and class as well.[16] Kawaters's feminist interventions come to expression within the contexts of crime narratives that fulfill traditional criteria for classification under the rubric of detective fiction: each mystery is set in motion by a murder, and the narrative follows the investigation until its closure, relating these events from the perspective of the investigator.[17] While Zora is not a professional sleuth, her work as an amateur gumshoe begins, like that of her literary predecessors Sherlock Holmes and Miss Marple, when police investigations falter.[18] In describing Zora's crime-solving endeavors, the texts' rhetoric recalls descriptions of detective work: in *Zora1*, Zora decides "den Mordfall selbst aufzuklären" [to throw light on the murder case herself, 56] uses "detektivisch[e]" [detective-like, 81] skills in seeking out "Indizien" [clues, 80], and promises her collaborator Rita, "unsere 'Ermittlungen' geheim zu halten" [to keep our "investigations" secret, 111].[19] Additionally, both books emphasize the psychological and political dimensions of relationships and alliances among women, thus partaking in both feminist and *Frauenkrimi* conventions. Zora's friendship with sidekick Rita, who helps tie up the investigations in both books, receives substantial narrative emphasis and develops overtly queer dimensions in *Zora2*.

Together, *Zora1* and *Zora2*'s portrayals of German sociopolitical formations of the 1980s construct an allegory about socialist feminism's negotiations of Marxist values, autonomous activism, gender and sexuality, and radical lesbian feminist politics. The subtext of *Zora1* relates the narrator's disillusionment with the male-dominated leftist culture in which she is involved, even as she sympathizes with autonomists resisting urban development and capitalist entrepreneurism. Zora's investigation of the murder of a love interest exposes the autonomous scene as rife with ideological inconsistencies and sexist presumptions. By emphasizing Zora's critical distance as a participant observer of leftist subculture, *Zora1* sets the stage for the narrator's departure from this environment in *Zora2*, when she explores radical feminism and lesbian politics. Here, too, Zora maintains a critical distance from the culture in which she participates. The following analysis of Kawaters's first two books fleshes out the political transition their narrator undergoes while also showcasing the ways in which the novels' feminist and queer dimensions contribute to a reading of the series as a sociohistorical allegory.

Kawaters's heroine begins *Zora1* as an activist bound in solidarity by antifascist and anti-imperialist sentiments with the punks, hippies, and ex-convicts in her social circle. Protest politics are at the heart of the story, inflecting both the crime plot and the truncated romance Kawaters narrates. The setting is Bochum, one of several densely populated cities in the industrial West German Ruhr Valley, which, like Berlin and other large urban centers in the northern part of the Federal Republic, saw the evolution of a sizable APO [*Außerparlamentarische Opposition*, extraparliamentary opposition] movement and the proliferation of autonomous subcultures throughout the 1970s and 1980s.[20] The text offers colorful depictions of alternative counterculture, renowned for its activism as well as for its aestheticization of hedonism: many scenes highlight the clothing styles, musical tastes, preferred intoxicants, communal orientation, and political ramblings of Zora and her comrades. It is in this social environment that Zora first meets the attractive Afro-German Werner Kern, an encounter that sets off her first adventure as an amateur detective with a heterosexual seduction. She attends a neighborhood party at a squat house occupied by leftist activist friends, where a drunken flirtation with Werner culminates in a night of passion. The next day, however, Zora is furious to discover her new lover's secret identity as the owner of the occupied building in which they met. Werner, "dieses miese, kleinkapitalistische Schwein" [this awful, petit bourgeois pig, *Zora1* 5], embodies the very bourgeois values against which Zora and her comrades fight. She visits Werner to demand an explanation, but closure of their brief affair comes only in the form of his death when she finds his bloody corpse and becomes the prime suspect in the murder investigation. The police are unable to identify a culprit, though there is no shortage of suspects, as everyone in Zora's social circle has a motive for killing Werner. In their eyes, he is no innocent victim: as the offspring of an American occupation soldier and the inheritor of a building slated for demolition to make room for a new expressway, Werner personifies the worst kinds of evil—imperialism, colonialism, entrepreneurship, and urban sprawl. Driven by a desire to clear her name as well as a personal interest in the victim, Zora secretly takes on the murder investigation with the assistance of her best friend Rita. The amateur sleuths focus on Werner's greedy, fascist relatives, who are reprehensible but innocent of the crime. As she and Rita run out of credible suspects, Zora turns her attentions back to the squat house and renews a past flirtation with Kalle, an old friend recently released from prison. But this potential relationship, like Zora's one-night romance with Werner, is short-lived and ends with a shocking revelation about her suitor's past. Zora identifies the former drug dealer and activist Kalle, who knew Werner before being incarcerated, as the culprit: he killed Werner, an informant, to avenge his betrayal.

The demise or dismissal of the male object of desire is one of the ways in which *Zora1* participates in feminist crime fiction themes, and it is also crucial to the novel's development of Zora's feminist transformation. With Werner's death, *Zora1* establishes a queer trope that also structures its sequel: the men Zora desires die or—as in the case of Kalle—are unveiled as killers. The novel introduces Zora's attraction to a man, and the tension this produces momentarily drives the plot, but the stakes of desire change when Zora discovers the man's dead body. This development, which precludes the possibility of a romantic heterosexual relationship, resonates with Sally Munt's assertion that the dismissal of romance is a common gesture in socialist feminist crime fiction, which directs narrative focus away from individual fulfillment and onto issues with wider social significance (74). Werner's death sets the crime plot in motion, leaving the female protagonist to work through her feelings by solving the mystery of his murder and investigating her political surroundings. This dynamic performs a feminist reversal of the gendered conventions of crime fiction that traditionally cast men as mystery solvers and women as victims or distractions.[21] The novel's initial heterosexual flirtation gives way to a celebration of female bonding and solidarity when Zora collaborates with a close female friend who provides emotional and material support throughout the grieving process and the crime investigation. This structure, which takes on greater significance in *Zora2*, links several conventions of the feminist *Frauenkrimi*: the representation of sex and desire; a dismissal of romance in favor of solving crime; an emphasis on female same-sex alliances; and a feminist critique of sexism and patriarchal traditions.

Though romance is fleeting at best, desire and sex play pivotal roles in the narrative. The emphasis on the erotic is a trait shared by many queer and lesbian crime novels.[22] The opening sequence culminates in a graphic, three-page description of Zora and Werner's sexual encounter, replete with details about their positions and emissions. Narrated by Zora, these representations of nudity, desire, and bodily functions announce the book's sex-positive politics and claim an erotic subjecthood for its protagonist. When Zora insists that Werner wear a condom, he chides her by calling her a "Feministin" [feminist, *Zora1* 19], but complies with her terms. This scenario positions Zora's brand of feminism within contemporary discourses about femininity and women's bodies, distancing her from the cult of motherhood and instead aligning her with campaigns for access to contraception, the legalization of abortion, and celebrations of women's sexual agency, although any political tension generated by the exchange with Werner dissipates in the ensuing sexual contact. By contrast, the novel's end stresses platonic over sexual desire: though Zora is attracted to Kalle and yearns for his companionship, she is uninterested in intercourse. Their unromantic date is fraught with gendered preconceptions, and Zora wonders whether there is a heterosexual dynamic to this exchange: "Warum ist das mit den Typen bloß immer so schwierig?" [Why is it always so difficult with men? *Zora1* 140]. Zora's frustration with men comes to expression again when she finds evidence that pinpoints Kalle as Werner's sought-after murderer. *Zora1* thus concludes with an echo of the opening structure that does away with heterosexual romance. The final sentence, in which Zora tells herself, "du hast kein Glück mit den Männern!" [you have no luck with men! *Zora1* 143], foreshadows the departure from heterosexual desire and the explicit introduction of queer sexuality in *Zora2*.

Although it is not until the end of the sequel that the reader learns that Zora and Rita's relationship likely extends beyond a close friendship, their alliance in *Zora1* begins to take on queer dimensions because it replaces a heterosexual flirtation. The text also provides clues that Zora and Rita may be more than friends, but these signs are never unambiguous. "Meine Freundin" (depending on context, the phrase can translate as "my female friend" or as "my girlfriend," *Zora1* 7), the description Zora offers to introduce Rita, could indicate any relationship ranging from a strictly nonsexual friendship to an exclusive romantic liaison. The range of connotations that these two simple words evoke recall Sabine Wilke's discussion of the *Frauenkrimi*'s concerns, which include the themes of "Frauenfreundschaften und Frauenliebschaften" [friendships and love affairs among women, 256]. The phrase "meine Freundin" also appears repeatedly in *Zora2*, where its meaning remains unspecified, even though other evidence points to an intimate relationship between Zora and Rita. *Zora1*, however, provides no explicit indication of this apart from depictions of the two women as close and affectionate.[23] Double entendres like the above appear elsewhere in connection with discussions of sexuality, providing further indications of the narrator's queerness while also suggesting that her queer desires resist explicit articulation. When sparks first begin to fly with Werner, Zora recalls that it has been a long time since she has slept with a man (*Zora1* 16). On the one hand, if we assume—due to a lack of evidence to the contrary—that Zora is by default heterosexual, then the statement raises no questions. On the other hand, the explicit mention of a masculine object allows for the interpretation that Zora's sexual practices are queer, and that she has indeed had same-sex contact more recently than heterosexual intercourse. But though such passages open up same-sex desire, romance, and sexual acts as interpretive possibilities, they remain at the level of suggestion. Such queer double entendres, which are abundant in the text, link desire with politics. They implicitly challenge the assumption of a default heterosexuality for Zora and, by evoking same-sex desire as a possibility, but not as a utopian alternative to heterosexuality, they give contours to an emerging feminist sensibility.

The critique of the cult of motherhood is one of *Zora1*'s most explicit interventions into contemporary feminist discourse. Though the campaigns to increase the availability of day care and to decriminalize abortion had brought many feminist and left-wing activists together to fight for common causes between the late 1960s and the mid–1970s, other disputes began to drive wedges among feminists groups. These included, in addition to debates over unpaid housework and autonomy versus institutionalization, the divisive notion of *neue Mütterlichkeit* [new motherhood]. Some feminists, influenced by New Age philosophies, embraced motherhood as a celebration of women's difference: pregnancy and childbirth offered experiences of biological connectedness and intimacy available only to women and afforded them special insights. George Katsiaficas describes this tendency as part of an "inward turn in the movement ... that verified the feelings of some women that their femininity—including their motherly intentions (or actuality)—was not to be denied" (76). Others, like Kawaters's Zora, held unfavorable views of what they perceived as the conceit of women who heralded exceptionalist notions of femininity: "Jede einzelne von ihnen hält sich für ein solches biologisches Wunder, daß es unbedingt fortgesetzt werden muß" [Every single one of them sees herself as such a biological miracle that she must absolutely procreate, *Zora1* 77]. Zora's objections to such philosophies align her with those feminists in radical, lesbian, and antiauthoritarian camps who rejected motherhood on the grounds that it was oppressive, denoting an acquiescence to gendered social expectations dictated primarily by men. A self-interview by the militant feminist group Rote Zora published in the same year as *Zora1* espouses a stance, shared by Kawaters's feminist sleuth, that opposes the trend toward family politics and new motherhood (603). *Zora1* depicts the cult of motherhood as the unreflected acceptance of patriarchal definitions of the nation at a time when politicians began aggressive campaigns to slow the decline of the German population due to a decreasing birth rate.[24] Rather than allowing that childbearing can be aligned with leftist ideological goals, Zora condemns it as a regressive egotistical indulgence that negates political consciousness. Addressing the motherhood debate permits the text to deliver a socialist analysis of individualism, which it dismisses in favor of a post-human ecological fantasy. The alternative vision that Zora sarcastically offers—to spike the water supply with contraceptives in order to liberate the planet from its human burdens— sardonically implies a critique of biomedical technology, another hot-button issue for radical feminists of the era.

Zora1 also highlights political debates of the mid–1980s that galvanized leftist youth movements around issues such as globalization, consumer culture, and the environment, while at the same time pointing up political hypocrisy and blind spots in autonomist theories and practices. The squatters and their allies in Kawaters's novel deliberate the means and ends of their grassroots activism, planning go-ins to protest demolition and construction projects and demonstrations for the legalization of marijuana. Zora's droll narrative perspective draws particular attention to the contradictions between her autonomous friends' ideologies and lifestyles: they campaign against nuclear energy but use spray paint to make political art; decry the environmental impact of the auto industry and yet own gasoline-guzzling cars; or, like Zora and Rita, refuse to buy fruit from South Africa but relish the "geradezu perverses Vergnügen" [downright perverse pleasure] of eating McDonald's while acknowledging "das Problem des amerikanischen Kulturimperialismus" [the problem of American cultural imperialism, *Zora1* 117]. Though Zora registers her own hypocrisy in this regard, she critiques the false morality of the squatters' blind and uncompromising adherence to ideological convictions: "Daß diese linken Spießer noch nicht mal über den Gartenzaun ihrer blöden Vorurteile schauen konnten!" [That these leftist yuppies could not even see through the blinders of their own prejudices! *Zora1* 32]. Indeed, while imperialism, capitalism, and fascism, personified by Werner and his relatives, represent villainous, totalitarian monoliths for autonomous politics, Zora's insider perspective on factions of the New Left reveals their own ruthless tendencies toward absolutes and repression. Emma Rentschel, the foster parent charged with raising Werner because his white German birth mother feared her brothers' xenophobic rage over her Afro-German progeny, ostensibly cautions Zora against men who embrace political absolutes: "Sie müssen sich vor gleichgeschalteten Männern in acht nehmen" [You must beware of assimilated men, *Zora1* 68]. The term *gleichgeschaltet* [assimilated] can refer to a range of ideological forms and manifestations in which political beliefs dictate the assimilation of sociocultural practices, but often carries connotations of fascism in general and National Socialism in particular: *Gleichschaltung* was a central principle of the Nazi dictatorship under Hitler.[25] Zora interprets Emma's riddle as a warning against right-wing fascism, but concedes that its ambiguity poses a hermeneutic problem requiring further consideration: "Die Faschisten! Aber die Bullen? Die sind doch genauso gleichgeschaltet" [The fascists! Or the cops? They are just as assimilated, *Zora1* 73]. On the one hand, the narrator acknowledges more than one possible interpretation of Emma's portent, but on the other hand, she misreads it as an allusion only to conservative, state-oriented *Gleichschaltung*—though this assumption dovetails with the term's most common referent in German history. By contrast, left-wing extremism, which posed a significant threat to public life and national security in West Germany throughout the 1970s and 1980s, remains in Zora's blind spot. She thus comes to the mistaken conclusion that Werner's uncle Ludwig, who is known to associate with fascist sympathizers, is his murderer, when in fact the killer is one of her militant leftist friends. The final revelation of the murderer as a popular member of the autonomous scene functions as a powerful reminder of the devastating potential of assimilationism at both the right and the left extremes of the political spectrum.

Kawaters's first novel intervenes in contemporary discourses about political activism by dramatizing the journey of a socialist-leaning woman who is dedicated to the radical egalitarian promise of autonomous politics, but who begins to reevaluate the position of gender and desire in the leftist student scene. The investigator's inability—or refusal—to see the danger of violence lurking within her own entourage reads as a metaphor for the omnipresence of sexist attitudes and the blindness of her male comrades to gender-based oppression. Emma's cautionary allusion to *gleichgeschaltete Männer* masculinizes the threat, and Zora's experiences indicate that duplicity and double standards hide behind the solidarity and harmless façades of the men she meets in the alternative scene. Their chauvinistic attitudes toward women are reminiscent of the rift between the Left and feminists.[26] Verena Stefan, author of the groundbreaking feminist text *Häutungen* [*Shedding*, 1975], and the Rote Zora terrorists were among the many cultural figures who witnessed and documented the fracturing of leftist and feminist groups in the 1970s and 1980s and took left-wing political cultures to task for their blindness toward the sexist dynamics they propagated. Similarly, representations of autonomist men in *Zora1* reveal that, despite their lofty egalitarian ideals, their fixation on class contributed to the marginalization of women within power structures where male authority positions remain unquestioned.[27] Leftist men like Bernd, a former lover of Zora's whose bitterness toward her stems "aus alten Besitzvorstellungen" [from old notions of ownership, *Zora1* 55], represent the banality of this hypocrisy: whereas Bernd resists capitalism and the privatization of property, he expects romantic relationships to entail certain proprietary rights over women. This rhetoric resonates with members of Rote Zora's account of their top priority, resisting the exploitation of women as commodities, which they assert finds everyday expression "in den ehelichen Besitzverhältnissen" [in marital structures of ownership, Rote Zora 600]. The Rote Zora feminists allege that sexism consistently manifests itself within leftist cultures, where the distribution of labor all too often takes conventionally gendered forms: "Wir wollen keine 'linke' Arbeitsteilung nach dem Motto: die Frauen für die Frauenfragen, die Männer für allgemeine politische Themen" [We do not want a "leftist" division of labor based on the motto: women for women's issues, men for general political concerns, 599]. But it is precisely along such gendered lines that squatter politics play out in *Zora1*: male occupants and supporters preside over organizational meetings where political actions are planned, while women's contributions consist of painting signs, chastising one another, and pontificating about the benefits of marijuana. When Zora unknowingly betrays her own political convictions by sleeping with the building owner Werner and a male colleague demeans her by revealing her transgression at a squat house meeting, Zora feels disrespected by both her lover and her comrades, the latter of whom take the opportunity to condemn her for lacking moral standards. Evidence of sexism appears in symbolic form as well: when Kalle takes Zora for a ride on a motorcycle allegedly borrowed from a friend, she must perch over an icon of a large-breasted woman painted on the tank, which she fails to read as a sign of Kalle's deceit. This scenario ironically complements Zora's earlier, feminist-inflected declaration that men who do not allow women to drive their cars are to be mistrusted (*Zora1* 15); more dangerous even are those men who adorn and ride vehicles bearing erotic images of women. By exposing the pervasiveness of sexist stereotypes, symbols, and double standards, these details of Kawaters's *Frauenkrimi* illustrate the cultural context in which radical autonomous feminism crystallizes and emerges from within male-dominated leftist milieus in the mid–1980s.[28]

Sexual politics also come into relief in the representation of characters and institutions outside of autonomous subculture. *Zora1* develops a feminist perspective in conjunction with a socialist critique of capitalism, colonialism, and racism. Zora's workplace, an export firm, and her womanizing boss, who fires her in part because of her relationship to the squatters (*Zora1* 58), are positioned as antagonistic to her sociopolitical alliances. Zora experiences dismissal from her job as a liberation from corporate culture and rampant sexism. She finds the structural and interpersonal dynamics of her workplace revolting and reserves special disdain for her female colleagues in bookkeeping, who become complicit in fulfilling their supervisor's misogynistic expectations by acting "diensteifrig, modebewußt und demütig, wenn der Chef in der Nähe ist" [eager to serve, fashion conscious, and humble, when the boss is around *Zora1* 25]. Crises of masculinity often bring about the oppression of women, upon whom it falls to rebuild the male ego with performances of feminized inferiority and deficiency. *Zora1* mentions that this was also the case in postwar Germany, when many women relinquished the more active roles they had assumed during the war; the late 1940s and 1950s saw a return to conservative sexual mores and patriarchal power structures in both public and private life (75–78). Zora disparagingly likens contemporary West Germany to the rubble years, criticizing women's motives for bearing children as selfish and politically counterproductive. In the postwar era, unmarried women such as Luise Kern, Werner's birth mother, sought out affairs with American occupation soldiers in hopes of a better life. Instead of further analyzing the oppressive conditions under which women attempted to negotiate agency, Zora critiques Luise's choice to have a child as selfish and exploitative (*Zora1* 77). Zora has greater compassion for Werner, the secret offspring who lived out the consequences of his mother's choices as a dark-skinned outsider in an eccentric foster family in the overwhelmingly monocultural landscape of rural Germany. However, Werner's place as the heir of the apartment building that her friends inhabit illegally, and which he plans to demolish for financial gain, also positions him as a problematic object of sympathy, a bourgeois entrepreneur who stands to benefit from displacing leftist squatters. Though Zora's perspective is decidedly feminist, her feminist viewpoints do not materialize in a void; rather, her attitudes toward gender and oppression inform and are informed by other identity categories such as class and race.[29] *Zora1* thus positions itself as a leftist and feminist text that engages in a critical assessment of both political forms through its portrayals of heterosexual and queer characters in the contemporary German cultural landscape.

Like Verena Stefan's unnamed narrator in the second-wave feminist text *Häutungen*, Kawaters's Zora expresses skepticism about the compatibility of Marxist socialist and radical feminist protest politics.[30] Feminist tendencies in *Zora1* evince a prelapsarian preoccupation with sexual politics from within alternative counterculture. In *Zora2*, by contrast, there remains no trace of the autonomous squatter scene that is so pivotal to narrative development in its predecessor; instead, the sequel analyzes feminist theory and practice from within a woman-centered environment. In thus repositioning its narrator-investigator, *Zora2* takes up another part of Stefan's project in *Häutungen*, the exploration of the relationship between feminist autonomy and lesbian identity. Kawaters's portrayals of gendered geographies come to life in an era that witnessed the proliferation of women's and lesbian coalitions, gay rights advocacy concerns, and profeminist men's groups aiming to bring autonomism, activism, and militant methods together with a heightened focus on gendered and sexualized oppression. *Zora2* also embraces socialist perspectives, but here we witness a distinct shift in emphasis when they are combined with a focus on gender, highlighting the exploitation of women in a market economy.

As its title announces, Kawaters's second novel—*Zora Zobel zieht um* [Zora Zobel Moves In]—narrates Zora's move into a new apartment, which is accompanied by her entry into a new social circle, a neighboring *Frauen-WG* [*Frauenwohngemeinschaft*, women's shared living community]. Her geographical relocation to a feminized milieu marks an explicit confrontation with the political stakes of lesbian feminist culture. The mystery is set in a women's world, as Deitmer notes in her praise of Kawaters's version of the *Frauenkrimi* (245), and key scenes unfold in gendered spaces like the *Frauen-WG*, a bar on ladies' night, and an all-girl peepshow. With this feminized profile, *Zora2* takes up a lesbian literary trend that Paulina Palmer identifies as a "more radical option" than merely replacing some of the key male roles in the traditional detective novel with women: erasing men from the narrative altogether "focuses attention very firmly on relationships and encounters *between women*" ("Lesbian Thriller" 93, emphasis in original). Though its cast of stock mystery fiction characters—including a police officer, one murder victim, two killers, and several suspects—is almost entirely female, *Zora2* does introduce one important male figure, but his demise at the beginning of the story both rewrites the conventional casting of women as beautiful corpses and clears the way for an emphasis on same-sex relationships in a crime investigation driven by and exclusively involving women. Such gendering, Palmer maintains, "place[s] both the narrative and psychological interest of the text emphatically" in same-sex alliances ("Lesbian Thriller" 93). However, in *Zora2* the consequences of the text's feminine constellations are not limited to the narrative and psychological levels; they radiate into the political realm by bringing into relief connections and conflicts among women from a range of socioeconomic and professional backgrounds.

The only male character to appear in the novel is the first of two murder victims, Stefan Lange, who runs a bakery together with his mother, Zora's landlady Irmela Lange, on the ground floor of the apartment building they all inhabit. The queer structure of desire and narrative that takes shape in *Zora1* with the Werner storyline—heterosexual attraction, followed by the mysterious death of the alluring man, the discovery of his corpse, and the murder investigation—finds repetition in Zora's short-lived contact with Stefan.[31] They meet just once, when Zora initially views the apartment; she interprets her brief encounter with the attractive young man as "ein gutes Zeichen" [a good sign, *Zora2* 8] and immediately signs the lease.[32] However, the first night she spends in her new home ends with the discovery of Stefan's corpse in the street below. Together with the help of her female friends and neighbors in her building and in the *Frauen-WG* across the street, Zora solves Stefan's murder as well as a second murder, the mysterious death of Stefan's stripper girlfriend Ilona. In both cases, the culprits are female and the motives ostensibly defensible from a leftist feminist point of view. Stefan's death is revealed to be the accidental consequence of his assault on Anne, a taxi driver from the *Frauen-WG*, who defends herself against undesired sexual advances; during the altercation, a drunken Stefan falls and suffers a fatal injury. Ilona, however, is a victim of murder at the hand of Stefan's mother Irmela, who kills the stripper in an act of vengeance, angry that Ilona exploited both her and her son in order to bankroll her luxurious lifestyle.

A queer parallel between Zora's first two adventures in sleuthing is the visualization of the male corpse, which signals a crucial transition in the queer structure of desire. Zora is the first to find Werner's and Stefan's bodies: each discovery brings about the shift of the attractive male's status from object of desire to object of investigation. Zora's "heimliche Hoffnung" [secret hope, *Zora2* 15]—likely a romantic interest in Stefan—gives way to horror in the moment when she sets eyes on the corpse. The sight of the dead man deaestheticizes and deromanticizes him, removing him from the realm of sexual desirability. Investigative work also has the effect of uncovering skeletons in the murder victims' closets, thereby making the men even less attractive: Werner, a capitalist investor and informer, and Stefan, an abusive exploiter of women, become ever more reprehensible as the narratives unfold. In *Zora1* and *Zora2*, the death of the attractive man and the impossibility of pursuing an affair with him serve a further purpose of clearing the way for the protagonist to explore desire with someone else, but *Zora2* gives this dynamic a queer twist by bringing Zora into sexual contact with a woman.

The amateur sleuth's dialogues with feminist figures in and around the *Frauen-WG* convey an equivocal attitude toward "hard" radical feminism and interrogate the conflation of feminism with lesbianism.[33] Zora's move into the new neighborhood sets the narrative in motion and places her at the margins of a gynocentric space that is accessible to her but from which she can maintain a critical distance. The narrator registers varying degrees of attraction and aversion to the apartment's four female occupants: her closest ally is the stoner Resy, a friend whom Zora once accompanied to an abortion clinic; Zora is uncertain how to read the elusive Anne, the cab driver implicated in Stefan's death; and she is suspicious of the outspoken lesbians Hertha and Sybille, who are a couple. The lesbian lovers embody the 1970s slogan, "Feminism is the theory; lesbianism is the practice"[34]: the only inhabitants of the space whose sexual identity is clearly delineated, they are explicitly aligned with radical lesbian feminism. Perceiving this philosophy as dogmatic, Zora sympathizes with more moderate views. Hertha, whom the narrator disdainfully identifies as "die Härte" [the hard one, *Zora2* 34] in reference to her brashness and militant posturing, personifies multiple negative stereotypes. Hertha's vitriolic rhetoric locates her in constant opposition to patriarchal traditions and men in general. For instance, she maintains that her filthy living space is a form of resistance against gendered clichés regarding housework; Zora, however, takes a critical stance toward such hostile outlooks by judging the level of disorder as a "ziemlich peinliche Trotzreaktion auf das Klischee" [rather embarrassing act of defiance against the cliché, *Zora2* 36–37]. The text distances its protagonist from man-hatred, represented by the lesbians, who are pleased to learn of Stefan's death and suggest that the kind of man he represents does not deserve to live.

By contrast, the attraction to Stefan experienced by both Zora and Resy communicates more open-minded attitudes toward the male sex. Alternating disdain and desire for Hertha not only signal the narrator's ambivalence toward her misandrist and separatist politics, but also demonstrate the seductive appeal that such a clear-cut worldview can have: Zora is momentarily drawn into Hertha's political and sexual world. Although Zora's interrogation of Hertha regarding the relationship between her sexuality and her politics indicates a critical stance toward radical feminism's focus on patriarchy and gendered oppression to the exclusion of other social issues, she later provides material support for lesbian feminist activism by helping disseminate illegal flyers for a *Frauenabend* [women's meeting, *Zora2* 77]. Hertha and Zora's collaborative effort to advertise the meeting culminates in a drunken sexual interaction, implying a direct relationship between the political and the sexual. Hertha, who cajoles Zora into participating in both activities, also infects Zora with her opinions: the protagonist approaches a more militant position when she asserts that a woman getting away with murdering a man could help even the score in the battle of the sexes (*Zora2* 110). But when Zora's ambiguous friend-lover Rita points out the radicalism motivating such rhetoric—"Seit wann spielst du denn die harte Feministin?" [When did you begin to play the hard feminist? *Zora2* 110]—the narrator tacitly concedes that it is not a faithful representation of her political views but rather merely a trace of her fleeting desire for Hertha. Indeed, our detective-heroine does not buy into the one-dimensional delineation of good and bad along a gendered divide, and by choosing Rita over Hertha as her ally and potential lover,[35] Zora symbolically rejects the lesbian feminist's extremism and aligns herself with Rita's more moderate views. Zora ultimately turns away from the "radical vision that emancipation can only be accomplished by lesbian autonomy" (Moyrer 137) that we find in the work of Verena Stefan and other contemporary writers who embraced utopian lesbian separatist philosophies in the 1970s and 1980s. *Zora2*'s mediation of sexual politics instead indicates a preference for a more nuanced approach to feminism and its relationship to sexuality.

This does not mean, however, that the text abandons radical feminist causes. Kawaters addresses several contemporary issues, from Paragraph 218 and motherhood to sexual labor. Together, these concerns underline convergences of the personal and the political in the debates over the control of women's bodies. The campaign against Paragraph 218, arguably the most central and unifying cause of German feminist action in the late twentieth century, comes up in the history of Zora and Resy's friendship, which began with Resy's unwanted pregnancy. Though it is not known whether Kawaters participated in Rote Zora's originary act of bombing the *Bundesverfassungsgericht* [Federal constitutional court] in Karlsruhe in 1975 after it suspended a 1974 law decriminalizing abortions in the first trimester, the author clearly conveys her sympathy with the militant group's pro-choice stance in *Zora2*. The 1986 novel appeared after years of feminist campaigns had brought about the liberalization of laws and popular opinions on abortion. A revision of Paragraph 218 went into effect in 1976, allowing for the termination of pregnancies for specific *Indikationen* [(usually medical) reasons] in the first trimester: these included not only medical grounds, but also criminal and social circumstances, which required third-party verification. However, the *Strafgesetzbuch* [German criminal law code] still held, as it does today, that abortion was generally unlawful outside of certain sanctioned cases. Zora and Resy's experience highlights the difficulty of gaining the consent necessary to obtain a legal abortion, and the two women become mouthpieces for pro-choice arguments, entering into verbal battle with an antipathetic social worker who resists Resy's right for a "soziale Indikation" [social reason, *Zora2* 29]. The name of the office, Pro Familia,[36] suggests a pro-life posture, one that is apparently shared by the women's clinic that performs the procedure, where dozens of baby pictures greet patients entering the reception area (*Zora2* 30). Taking up a thread developed in *Zora1*, the sequel offers a tongue-in-cheek critique of the cult of motherhood in an anecdote about an acquaintance, a "Magic-Mama, Indianer-Mutter, Hexenfrau" [magic mama, Indian mother, witch-woman] who had, against the narrator's advice, had two children: "Sie ist über ihre Kinder zu einer Weisheit und Abgeklärtheit gekommen, um die ich sie immer wieder beneide" [Through her children she has acquired a wisdom and clarity that I envy time and again, *Zora2* 47]. A caricature of New Age femininity, the mother calls on her intuition to offer Zora a cryptic message of support, and disappears from the novel as quickly as she appears. "Magic Mama" drives the narrative forward by encouraging Zora to pursue the crime investigation, offering up a contrast to another model of femininity that Zora critiques, the strippers she interrogates in the following scene. By locating the novel's peepshow in spatial opposition to the women's bookstore across the street, Kawaters signals her position within what Katrin Sieg characterizes as "discourses (including feminist ones) that use prostitution as metaphor for the horror and immorality of exploitation" ("Postcolonial" 156). Revulsion, the narrator's dominating reaction to the multisensory peepshow experience, is tempered—slightly—by her sympathy for the strippers, including a single mother and a struggling student, reluctant practitioners of a dangerous, demeaning, and unpleasant profession. The sex workers collaborate to bring about improvements in their work conditions by agreeing on low performance standards of minimal physical exertion and minimal exposure of flesh during their rotations. But Kawaters's portrayal of the strippers' moderately successful cooperation is quite different from the emphatically affirmative gesture we witness in Pieke

Biermann's crime series, which invites its readers to celebrate a prostitute coalition that "models a feminist state and economy" (Sieg, "Postcolonial" 158). *Zora2* offers nothing more than a fleeting vision of feminist solidarity in the sex industry, destabilized by the new hire of beguiling and self-centered pinup Ilona, who raises the bar with her act and stops at nothing to increase her earnings. This representation implicates the market economy in gendered oppression through the assignment of monetary values to women. According to this scenario, alliances among women are at best only marginally effective in bringing about change within patriarchal structures that reward exploitative and individualistic behaviors. Kawaters's intervention into contemporary debates about sex work proposes a socialist feminist reading of the profession as negligibly lucrative vis-à-vis the high cost of alienating women from their bodies, their labor, and one another.

Kawaters's second novel espouses a socialist feminist worldview, which finds expression in the crimes and the investigations that uncover their social causes. The genre conventions of the mystery are mobilized to communicate Marxist critiques of privatization and capitalism and feminist critiques of the bourgeois family and the sex industry that resonate with Rote Zora's mission: "die Ausbeutung der Frau als Sexualobjekt und Kinderproduzentin aus dem 'Privatbereich' herauszureißen" [to rip the exploitation of women as sexual objects and producers of children out of the "private domain," Rote Zora 599]. *Zora2* presents two corpses that signify the evils of sexism and exploitation, especially Stefan. An interpretation of the lone male character as the epitome of male-embodied sexual desire might lead to the facile conclusion that the text, like other socialist feminist crime stories, "positions male sexuality as intrinsically oppressive" (Munt 61). Kawaters's narrative, however, refrains from conflating Stefan with all men; he simply serves as a vehicle for the interconnected oppressions against which socialist feminism takes aim. As a regular patron of an all-girl peepshow who finances his addiction to strippers by stealing from his mother, Stefan embodies the exploitation of women on several levels. His readiness to buy his lover Ilona out of her profession as a stripper aligns him with a chauvinistic view of women's bodies as possessions trafficked among men; Stefan is compared, like other peepshow patrons, to a pimp (*Zora2* 56). By revealing his transgressions, the murder investigations "uncover patriarchal 'motive' (of keeping the female body as private property), and expose the 'crime' of masculinity, of men's control of women's sexuality" (Munt 61). The young man's repeated transgressions against multiple women make him a paradigm of villainy, the incarnation of a misogyny that systematically flattens femininity with property, sexual objecthood, and financial opportunity. Stefan's treachery directly benefits his girlfriend Ilona, who capitalizes on her suitor's romantic interest: she is revealed to be a selfish, money hungry diva complicit in the oppression of women. Together, victims Stefan and Ilona symbolize the individualism, alienation, and banal corruption of upwardly-aspiring bourgeoisie and industries that traffic in female bodies. Their attractiveness, which Zora registers before she discovers the darker sides of their story, warns that exploitation and chauvinism can lurk beneath deceptively innocuous façades.

The narrative's socialist feminist tendency also comes to expression in sympathy for the female culprits, who are themselves victims of abuse and exploitation. Anne is remorseful over her involvement in Stefan's death, but other characters recognize his demise as the deliverance of a potential victim from an incursion on her sexual agency. The investigations uncover evidence that Stefan's death was accidental, exculpating Anne. The manslaughter victim is exposed as the true criminal, and his demise manifests itself as a justified—if unintended—outcome of abusive male behavior. The text intimates a feminist critique of marriage and motherhood in the portrayal of Stefan's physically and emotionally battered mother Irmela, whose son not only steps into his deceased father's shoes and perpetuates a cycle of alcoholism and abuse, but also condemns her to financial servitude by liquidating her hard-earned savings before she can retire.[37] A devoted mother, hard worker, and repentant murderer, Irmela is depicted in a benevolent light: in a fit of rage, she avenges herself against Ilona, the woman she holds responsible for manipulating her son's thievery and then killing him. Two simultaneous feminist conspiracies aim to protect the culprits from prosecution: Hertha and Sybille plan Anne's escape, while Zora, Rita, and an elderly neighbor help Irmela flee the country. But the story ends with both perpetrators in police custody (though Anne is only called in as a witness), and while Zora and her friends are dismayed to learn that their efforts to "save" Irmela have failed, they are relieved that they will not be charged with abetting. The ambivalence of this conclusion invites the reader to consider the stakes of feminist action and its relation to justice.

By painting a portrait of a sympathetic and yet adversarial police detective, the mystery addresses a key issue in autonomist politics: the relationship of activism to state institutions. Kommissarin Lederschuh [Commissioner Leathershoes] functions as Zora's doppelgänger—both women investigate the murders—and evidence indicates that Zora deems her a worthy opponent. Though the amateur sleuth recognizes the immense challenge of competing with "Frau Lederschuh und ihrem Apparat" [Mrs. Leathershoes and her apparatus, *Zora2* 48], she stubbornly persists and solves the cases first—and escapes prosecution for obstructing justice. One could read this as a victory for our autonomous socialist feminist heroine, but one must also concede that Zora's investigation is not entirely in line with an autonomist approach that, as the Rote Zora militants declare, "der Kontrolle und dem Zugriff des Staatsapparates entzogen ist" [is removed from the control and reach of the state apparatus, 598]. When interrogated by Lederschuh, Zora indulges the police officer's ramblings about bureaucracy and ironically describes the exchange as a "Gespräch unter Fachfrauen" [conversation between professional women, *Zora2* 72], suggesting that she sees herself on equal footing with the professional detective and conjuring up images of solidarity. Of course, the unemployed stoner Zora circulates outside of the law, and the two investigators do not work toward a shared goal: Lederschuh aims to apprehend the culprits, while Zora collaborates to cover up their identities. But the separate and yet intersecting crime-solving work undertaken by the two women "confounds the conventionally strict demarcation between the law breaker and the law enforcer" (Munt 64); it also troubles the common depiction of rebels as heroes and police officers as enemies in autonomous subcultures. By contrast with *Zora1*, where the narrator adopts an explicitly autonomist stance in opposition to law enforcement, in *Zora2* she shows compassion for the police detective, whose character takes a more nuanced, benign form.[38] The humanization of one bureaucratic representative is, however, not an all-out celebration of bureaucracy; the text also articulates skepticism regarding the state's capacity to serve justice: "Versteht eine Richterin mehr von Gerechtigkeit, weil sie weiß, wie die Paragraphen heißen?" [Does a (female) judge understand justice any better because she knows the legal code? *Zora2* 141].[39] Such cynical turns in *Zora2* subtly signal the "ablehnendes Verhältnis zur staatlicher Politik" [oppositional relationship to state politics, Rote Zora 603] advocated by Rote Zora, but stop short of adopting the more militant approach of challenging the legal apparatus in which contemporary terrorist groups engaged. It is unclear whether *Zora2* intends to offer this approach as a political possibility or a semiautonomous compromise, or whether it aims to interrogate the effectiveness of cooperation with state institutions and dismiss sympathy for officers of the law as counterproductive. The final lines of the novel seem to encourage the latter interpretation—after climbing out of a police car, Rita declares to Zora, "sowas passiert uns nicht wieder" [this will not happen to us again, *Zora2* 143]—but its message about activism and the state is ultimately left to the reader to decode.

Zora Zobel's adventures in sleuthing in the mid–1980s constitute a unique contribution to the genre of the German-language feminist *Frauenkrimi* that would become a market sensation in the ensuing years. Kawaters's 1984 and 1986 novels record a specific moment in West German protest history, when leftist and radical feminist autonomisms took diverging paths. Kawaters's detective "is represented as a 'subject,' her identity and way of life a product of the fragmented discourses and sub-cultures of the contemporary urban scene" (Palmer, "Lesbian Thriller" 94). Like the radical feminist protagonists of Claudia Wessel's 1984 crime story *Es wird Zeit*, Zora survives "die bedrohliche Reise durch die Männerwelt" [the ominous journey through the world of men, 12], but she narrates this experience through a critical perspective informed by Marxist critique. The depiction of a queer amateur investigator who changes camps from *Zora1* to *Zora2* represents an attempt to negotiate the shared stakes of socialist and feminist values. Engaging in the leftist debates of its era while also offering up gender and sexuality as categories of political analysis, Kawaters's mysteries undertake a critical inquiry into the constraints and promises of countercultural ideologies.

The Feminism That Dare Not Speak Its Name: Political (In)Action in Pieke Biermann's *Potsdamer Ableben* (1987)

Pieke Biermann is widely recognized as one of the earliest authors of the feminist *Frauenkrimi* that emerged in Germany in the 1980s and claimed a central place in the literary market in the following decade. Biermann is likely most famous for her popular series of Berlin crime novels, beginning with the late Cold War era *Potsdamer Ableben* (1987), which received considerable critical attention as one of the first three novels published in the newly-established crime series with the leftist intellectual Rotbuch press. The series continued into the unification and post-unification periods with *Violetta* (1990) and *Herzrasen* [Racing Heart, 1993], both appearing with Rotbuch, and both of which earned Biermann the prestigious *Deutschen Krimi Preis* [German Crime Prize], in 1991 and 1994. A fourth installment with the mainstream press Goldmann, *Vier, fünf, sechs* [Four, Five, Six, 1997], completed the series and placed second in the 1998 German Crime Prize competition. Biermann is also known for her activism in the women's liberation movement and more specifically as the public face of the German *Hurenbewegung* [whores' movement] of the 1980s: she campaigned for prostitutes' right to legal work and benefits, held lectures, organized public events, and helped found an advocacy group called Hydra.[40] Though Biermann allegedly stopped working as a prostitute in 1980, the year in which Hydra was established, she remained engaged in this cause throughout the following decade.[41] Her interest in working women and feminism has also produced scholarly publications, including her first two books: based on her Master's thesis, the self-published *Das Herz der Familie* [The Heart of the Family, 1977] focused on women's unpaid domestic labor; and *Wir sind Frauen wie andere auch!* [We Are Just Like Other Women! 1980] is an appeal for women's legal control over their sexuality and advocates for the legalization of prostitution. As Katrin Sieg suggests, it seems fitting to view

Biermann's crime novels as an extension of her activism (156). Biermann's intellectual pursuits, political work, and fiction writing are linked by shared concerns for the legacies of second-wave feminism, the new women's movements of the 1980s and 1990s, and their interfaces with late twentieth-century capitalist and socialist cultures before and after the fall of the Wall. Through her fiction, Biermann stages interventions into contemporary discourses about mainstream women's liberation movements and explores alternate forms of political theory and action. The representation of feminism in Biermann's novels is by no means unified: the author depicts different feminist ideologies in various characters whose interactions and struggles reveal changing attitudes toward the possibilities, limitations, and challenges feminist approaches face in the specific sociopolitical contexts of West Berlin and the Federal Republic of Germany in the final years of German division.

Biermann's scholarly and political engagements have made her popular with academics: not only are her crime novels and short stories often taught in literature courses at the graduate and undergraduate levels in Germany and abroad, but her fiction has also been the subject of several scholarly analyses. Unlike Corinna Kawaters and the other authors considered in this study of queer crime on whose writing little or no research exists, Biermann's fiction forms a node of scholarly interest, due in part to its critical success and in part to Biermann's notoriety as an activist, journalist, translator, and former prostitute. The present study, however, differs from existing work on Biermann's writing both in its sustained analysis of her first novel and in its treatment of police commissioner Karin Lietze as key to the narrative's articulation of a feminist critique.[42] In developing this interpretation, I seek to shed light on a blind spot in some scholarship on Biermann, which, in focusing on narrative style, realism, and the social space of the city, looks past the central role that forms of feminism play in her fiction.[43] My analysis of these discourses in Biermann's novelistic debut is indebted to Katrin Sieg's essay on the feminist critique of globalization in Biermann's Berlin crime series, but seeks to complicate Sieg's interpretation of the novels' political vision by exploring the crucial role Karin Lietze plays in connecting two central sets of characters: the police officers and the prostitutes. I also tackle a dimension of Biermann's work that Nicola Barfoot believes has been overlooked—a prostitute's romantic interest in Lietze (130)—as a key element of this text's negotiation of feminism.

Though *Potsdamer Ableben*'s crime plot, structure, and narrative voice play significant roles in conveying its multilayered political commentary, characterization is arguably the most crucial dimension of the novel's feminist vision. Biermann develops contrasts among forms of feminist thought and action through characters that, alone or in collaboration with others, embody different visions of and approaches to social issues. On the one hand, the lone self-described feminist figure in the novel, journalist Regine Trübner-Zaecke, who shares more than a few features with renowned German activist Alice Schwarzer, repeatedly decries the oppression of women and ongoing patriarchal domination. On the other hand, two constellations of characters that are not overtly associated with feminism, the gender- and queer-inclusive police homicide unit and the coalition of female prostitutes who work the Tiergarten district, embody feminist coalitions and professional spheres. Linking these two feminist work environments is head police commissioner Karin Lietze, who has professional and social connections to the streetwalkers. By vilifying Zaecke and celebrating the police and the prostitutes, the novel issues an unmistakable judgment about different forms of feminist theory and action, identifying those that do not call themselves *feminist* but rather work in socially beneficial ways as the most effective. Biermann's book rejects Zaecke's version of feminism as self-serving, vitriolic, and destructive, embracing instead a semi-autonomous coalitional feminist model that includes both grassroots activism and state involvement in democratic change.

Ableben begins, in the tradition of the detective novel, with a corpse. When Béatrice Bitterlich, the unpopular culture editor for a radio show, collapses onto the buffet table at a high profile media event, there is no shortage of suspects in her poisoning death. Populating the entertainment industry are numerous figures who despise Bitterlich for her unapologetically crude language, offensive commentaries, sex-positive stance, and career ladder-climbing promiscuity; the widespread animosity she engendered reveals the ugly side of the music business, where misogyny, exploitation, and violence hide beneath its glamorous sheen. Bitterlich's close friend and colleague, the dogmatically radical feminist Regine Trübner-Zaecke, is among the prime suspects, but Zaecke points the finger at Hans-Jürgen Wielack, the chauvinistic manager of a boy band who supplements his income by blackmailing prominent homosexuals in the industry. Zaecke becomes all the more suspicious because she seizes her friend's untimely death as a political and a professional opportunity: the occasion gives her cause to crusade for universalist feminism—she immediately declares Bitterlich a victim in the war of the sexes, a target of misogynist rage directed at a successful career woman—and she profits from Bitterlich's demise by securing a headlining position on the radio show commemorating the deceased's life. Though Zaecke is ultimately exculpated in her friend's fatality, she remains an antagonistic character throughout the novel and is further vilified by her involvement in other crimes, including conspiracy, vigilantism, contributing to the delinquency of minors, theft, and involuntary manslaughter. She emerges from the narrative no more positive a figure than the reprehensible Wielack, her sexist counterpart who is complicit in Bitterlich's accidental death (he intended to poison someone else, but not to kill anyone) as well as in the rape and exploitation of an underage member of a girl group he managed. Zaecke collaborates with the rape victim's older sisters to avenge Wielack's crimes by breaking into his apartment, tying him up, and documenting his forced confessions of the rape of the young singer, the inadvertent killing of Bitterlich, and the blackmail of prominent media figures. Though the novel ends with the uncovering of these crimes and the closure of the cases, neither criminal is brought to justice: Wielack dies of a heart attack after his confessions, and Zaecke absconds with his list of blackmail targets. This ending implies that the cycle of crime and corruption will merely continue with Zaecke extracting money from Wielack's celebrity extortion victims.

In featuring the dreadful Zaecke as the narrative's outspoken feminist voice, Biermann casts that which claims the label of *feminism* in distinctively unflattering hues. Readers of Biermann's mystery might find that several dimensions of Zaecke's character recall the qualities of real-life feminist icon Alice Schwarzer, a prominent activist in the German public sphere since the 1970s who remains, four decades later, one of the most widely-recognized figures associated with second-wave feminism. Both are journalists: like Schwarzer, who established the still-running women's magazine *Emma* in 1977, Zaecke is an experienced journalist who works in a "Frauendomäne" [women's domain], managing a paper called the *Wochenspiegel* [Weekly Mirror].[44] Zaecke's condemnation of the male-dominated media—and explicit condemnation of journalists Augstein and Nannen (38)—brings to mind Schwarzer's public confrontations with the editors of the weekly news magazines *Der Spiegel* [The Mirror] and *Stern* [Star] in the seventies and eighties.[45] These parallels are clearly not intended as celebratory gestures on Biermann's part: the embodiment of Schwarzer's radicalism in the unpleasant figure of Regine Trübner-Zaecke, whose name alone implies social disturbance (*trüben* means "to tarnish" or "to trouble," and the name *Zaecke* recalls both *Zecke*, "tick," and *Zicke*, "she-goat," a colloquialism for *bitch*), serves as a send-up of her politics.

Ableben's rotating narrative perspective offers the reader multiple views of Zaecke, none of which is favorable. The fictional feminist's irritating voice receives heavy emphasis, repeatedly introducing her presence as an auditory intrusion; in two scenes, Zaecke does not appear in person, but her voice, broadcast over the radio and captured in a home recording, engenders adverse listener reactions.[46] The representation of Zaecke as "die Stimme des Feminismus" [the voice of feminism, 36] projects feminism as a nuisance and resonates with a common perception of Schwarzer: even today, Carrie Smith-Prei observes, Schwarzer "remains German feminism's sole voice of authority."[47] Although Zaecke's universalist stance claims a collective female subjecthood— she frequently speaks from a plural first-person *wir* position—this ostensibly inclusive positioning masks the ideological exclusion of entire categories of women, including the prostitutes who are so crucial to Biermann's understanding of feminist coalitional action.[48] Margaret McCarthy points out that "Schwarzer's feminist politics have long been criticized for collapsing the differences among women in the name of a unified 'we.'"[49] This critique persists today, evidenced by recent allegations that Schwarzer's ubiquitous media presence drowns out other feminist voices.[50] In addition to Zaecke's rhetoric and positioning, her hot-button causes are also aligned with Schwarzer's enduring political interests in the issues of abortion, prostitution, pornography, and the subjugation of Muslim women. Schwarzer sees women as timeless victims and espouses the radical feminist view that, as Leslie Adelson notes, "patriarchy is the root and only root of all evil."[51] Similarly, Zaecke likens the oppression of women to the Holocaust and speaks in ahistorical clichés, railing against a "Patriarchat, das sich seit Tausenden von Jahren an Schwestern vergriff" [patriarchy that has been assaulting sisters for thousands of years, 93]. Ultimately, Zaecke represents a totalizing, stultified, and obsolete ideology unable to reconcile itself with a changing cultural landscape.[52] Only by manipulating the underage sisters of a rape victim into conspiring with her to carry out vigilante justice is Zaecke able to gain support for her philosophy; however, by exploiting and abandoning her accomplices, Zaecke exposes herself as a hypocritical crusader for women's solidarity, an advocate for a bankrupt utopian vision. In bringing *Ableben*'s crime plot to a close with Zaecke's disappearance before she can be brought to justice, Biermann communicates more than mere distrust in this brand of universalist feminism: the novel distances itself from such performances of political conviction and opens up a space for other forms of feminist theory and practice.[53]

Perhaps the most promising form of feminism, the novel implies, is not that which proclaims its views in the name of feminism, but rather social action that emerges from coalition-building, compromise, community-minded outlooks, and transnational solidarity. This political formation manifests itself in a group of prostitutes who work the Tiergarten district in the heart of Berlin, at the center of which is a trio consisting of the older Helga, the motorcycle-riding Kim, and Kitty, a married mother of two. *Ableben* comments on contemporary feminist discourse about sexual labor by elevating its streetwalkers above the violence, abuse, and exploitation that permeate the rest of its narrative universe. In contrast with the antiprostitution and antipornography stances we encounter in feminist texts such as Kawaters's *Zora2* that cast sex workers as victims of oppression, Biermann vests her prostitutes with agency, a voice, and even humor; they do not need to be liberated or redeemed, but rather empower themselves. The prostitutes form an autonomous working coalition that produces a number of benefits: they protect one another by keeping records on their clients; defend their source of income by averting street sweeps; found an advocacy group called *Migräne* [Migraine]; and organize a successful demonstration to raise money and awareness about the use of condoms to prevent the spread of AIDS. This coalition resembles the model of "shared feminism" that Sara Lennox describes as "an uneasy achievement that emerges in specific contexts in response to concrete needs" (495): it fulfills the professional needs of working-class prostitutes who work the same neighborhood, and it involves compromise. Biermann's streetwalkers pool resources: Kim shares the wealth by buying her colleagues breakfast after working a "Big Spender" (49); Kitty routinely invites the homeless Helga to dine and bathe in her home; and the maternal Helga helps the girls working the night shift with bookkeeping and stands in for her younger colleagues while they attend their demonstration. These mutually supportive activities advance the prostitutes' working conditions and overall quality of life; the whores thus function as the political antithesis of their foil Zaecke in "embody[ing] a pragmatic as opposed to a utopian model of sexual politics" (Sieg 159). Though Sieg rightly asserts that Biermann's vision of feminism is limited by the inclusion of only white women in the prostitutes' coalition and the remarkable absence of non–European women from its ranks (174–77), it is significant that the organization is nonetheless transnational in composition, with members of French, Italian, and Slavic origins.[54] The reach of the demonstration they organize at the novel's end also extends beyond the boundaries of the Cold War era island of West Berlin; the giant pink condom-shaped zeppelin they launch travels "in Richtung Potsdamer Niemandsland und weiter nach Osten" [in the direction of the Potsdam no-man's land and father eastward], broadcasting a sex-positive, health conscious message across the national border, which could benefit, or at least entertain, "die Mädels auf der drübenschen Seite" [the girls on the other side, 164]. The story's conclusion with this event expresses optimism about the potential for such political formations to effect change domestically as well as internationally. The inclusionary gesture toward East German women denotes transnational solidarity with practitioners of the "oldest profession in the world" and constitutes a noteworthy exception to the forms of white West German feminist theory that have been criticized for disavowing their own ethnocentric positioning.[55] The novel's title also conveys a transnational vision: *Potsdamer Ableben* is a play on words recalling the *Potsdamer Abkommen* [Potsdam Agreement] of 1945 that declared the terms for the occupation of Germany by the Allied powers. But since the book gives the last word to the prostitutes who occupy the liminal space of the Potsdamer Straße, it invites its reader to imagine a state in which whores are cultural ambassadors, sexual politics belong in the public forum, and women play a central role in deciding how to use and occupy public spaces.

An integral piece of this vision is police officer Karin Lietze, the commissioner at the head of the homicide division investigating Bitterlich's death. Though the reader can certainly find evidence in Biermann's mystery to support an interpretation of the prostitutes as its protagonists—even though they are only peripherally involved in the crime plot—my reading of the novel emphasizes Lietze as a pivotal figure. The lead investigator's queer feminist contours are critical to *Ableben*'s alternative social vision, and an evaluation of Lietze as a queer feminist emphasizes the political implications of the shifting and boundary-crossing dimensions of her gender, sexuality, and professional alliances. This analysis engages both senses of the term *queer*, calling upon its more fixed connotation as a signifier of gender performances and sexual desires that do not align themselves with a strict understanding of femininity and heterosexuality, and mobilizing the term as a destabilizing approach to commonly accepted practices and social norms.

The police detective's gender identity, which takes on queer dimensions in intermingling performances of femininity and masculinity, contributes to her ease of movement through the novel's various social spheres and equips her with the gendered cultural capital to engage in productive transactions with other occupants of these spheres. Lietze's shifting gender positionality travels along a continuum of feminine masculinity, described by Claudia Breger as including "the interplay of 'butch' and 'femme' gestures or more generally of identity markers coded as distinctively masculine with others coded as distinctively feminine."[56] This interplay of codes and roles provides a medium through which the narrative exposes the socio-symbolic implications of gender performances. Lietze's feminine masculinity facilitates circulation within both the traditionally male-dominated, white-collar sector of law enforcement and the feminized, proletarian milieu of prostitution. Movement through these professional realms brings into relief gendered market relations in which capitalist bureaucracy and the conditions of production are conventionally associated with masculinized authority and buying power, while the producers of goods and providers of services are feminized. Lietze, who has short hair, prefers men's clothing and cologne, and smokes cigarillos, performs a more butch identity at the police precinct, where she has authority over male colleague Lothar Fritz, who is in turn feminized by a history of complying with the mandates of his strong-willed wife. One of the greatest challenges Lietze faces in her job stems neither from the demands of police work nor from the negotiation of her position as a female authority figure, but rather from her incapacity to perform the typically feminized task of making coffee. Unable to operate the electric coffeemaker, Lietze is dependent on Mimi Jacob, her Jewish secretary, to enable her caffeine addiction. The investigator's professional performance of masculinity also involves using tobacco and alcohol as currency, giving her buying power in transactions with male officers, from whom she obtains goods and information in exchange. The representation of this work environment emphasizes the measures its leader takes to maintain a gender-neutral and nonhierarchical atmosphere. Lietze goes against the trend in mainstream feminist rhetoric to challenge the use of gendered terminology in the workplace by adding feminine suffixes to masculine words. She instead rejects the feminine versions in favor of the masculine-gendered base nouns, preferring the title *Kommissar* [(male) commissioner] and the slang term *Bulle* [cop; literally, bull] to their feminine counterparts.[57] Though one could argue that such rhetoric effectively masculinizes the policewoman, it also has the consequences of placing the female professional on equal linguistic footing with her male colleagues and assigning significance to status over gender: as *Erster Kriminalhauptkommissar* [first chief commissioner], Lietze outranks *Kriminalkommissar* [commissioner] Detlev Roboldt and *Kriminalhauptkommissar* [chief commissioner] Lothar Fritz. But their interactions remain largely uncolored by these hierarchical differences—Lietze even reprimands Roboldt for addressing her as *Chef* [boss], stressing instead teamwork and communication.

Beneath the tough exterior of this macho professionalism, the police commissioner also has a femme side, and it is her feminine insecurities that facilitate intimacy and exchange with her prostitute friends who circulate in an almost exclusively female milieu. With her white-collar job, Lietze has a higher social status than the streetwalkers, but she approaches them not from a position of legal authority or financial power as might another police officer or a prospective client, but rather from a position of relative weakness.[58] Only in the company of the prostitutes does Lietze verbalize her vulnerabilities, confessing self-consciousness about her appearance and romantic life. Not only does she disclose her crush on a younger man, but she also regales the whores with intimate details of her one-night stand. In return, Lietze gains emotional support as well as useful evidence. Her most vulnerable moment occurs in the presence of Kim, who subsequently provides the investigator with a piece of information crucial to solving the case. In contrast with the cigarillos and beer that serve as tender in transactions with male colleagues, emotional currency plays a central role in Lietze's exchanges with the female prostitutes.

With a younger man named Klaus Jalta as their object, Lietze's erotic desires suggest a reading of the police commissioner as heterosexual. But the subplot of the budding romance between Lietze and Jalta works both to dismiss the possibility of romantic love and to deflect sexual tension onto political action. Munt maintains that feminist crime novels of the 1980s take "the representation of sexual politics to be a key feminist agenda" (61). A comparison of *Ableben*'s opening and closing passages lays bare its agenda, which it conveys by thematizing movement from a personal to a political sexual arena: the novel begins with a private and incomplete heterosexual sex act and ends with public homosocial bonding. As if in anticipation of the failure of romance, the book opens with a coitus interruptus: the first line, "Das Klingeln kam mittendrin" [The ringing came right in the middle, 9], announces the call of duty summoning the investigator to a crime scene, requiring her to abandon the pursuit of sexual fulfillment with the attractive young man in her bed.[59] This scenario underlines Lietze's relative position of power over Jalta. Not only do her professional obligations determine the outcome of their truncated nighttime recreation, but she also uses more formal language, distancing herself by addressing him in a formal register with the pronoun *Sie*, while Jalta speaks in Berlin dialect and attempts without success to mollify Lietze's standoffishness by repeatedly using familiar *du* forms. These initial discrepancies between the lovers' linguistic habits suggest a deep-seated incompatibility that becomes increasingly obvious to Lietze as their short-lived romance unfolds.

The closing scene of the novel features a number of striking differences from the interpersonal politics and sexual geographies of the introductory passage. By contrast with the opening in which Lietze is called away from a private engagement to fulfill her duty as a public servant, the final scene has Lietze leaving work in a hurry to witness a political demonstration, the launch of the prostitutes' condom balloon. When a colleague misreads Lietze's haste as motivated by an impending romantic engagement, the text creates a parallel with the opening scenario but replaces sexual desire for a man with desire to participate in a feminist event. As she watches the zeppelin fly away, Lietze finds closure to her brief liaison with Jalta: "So müßten Affären zu Ende gehen, dachte sie, einfach davonschweben in einen strahlenden Himmel" [This is how affairs should end, she thought, simply drift away into a radiant sky, 164]. While the story begins in the intimate space of Lietze's bedroom, it concludes in the street, on the Tiergartenstraße where Helga, Kim, and Kitty work. And whereas the opening passage highlights unfulfilled desire, unsuccessful communication, and issues of identity, the final scene narrates the police officer bonding with Helga and Kim over the resounding success of their rally to advocate for prostitute rights, raise awareness about AIDS, and promote the use of condoms. The demonstration's prominence in the final scenes underlines its structural and political significance for the novel as a whole. The beginning and ending of the novel construct a narrative frame that exchanges heterosexual romance for homosocial collaboration, bringing sexuality from the private space of the boudoir into the public forum of urban geography.

This narrative structure takes on queer contours when we consider Lietze's position as a boundary-crossing object of sexual desire—and the possibility that she harbors queer desires too. Jalta is not alone in pursuing Lietze; he competes for her attention with leather-clad biker Kim, who also has a crush on the police officer and demonstrates a general sexual interest in women, though she takes male clients on the streets.[60] Because Lietze is discreet about her own emotional turmoil over Jalta, he is unaware of her reciprocated desire for him and questions her motives. Unsettled by Lietze's aloofness, Jalta expresses his anxiety in an aggressively questioning invitation to coffee: "Wem darf ich denn jetzt einen Espresso machen, dir, Katrin, oder Ihnen, Madame? Oder soll ich eine Geschlechtsumwandlung beantragen?" [For whom might I make an espresso, you Katrin, or you Madame? Or should I apply for a sex change? 72]. The seemingly irrelevant reference to a sex change conveys Jalta's unease with Lietze's performance of identity. While he may simply seek to convey his feeling of emasculation in the detective's commanding presence, his expression of self-doubt interrogates her presumed heterosexuality. Jalta insinuates that a woman might make a better partner for this female officer of the law, and perhaps he is correct. Kim also appears uncertain about how to read Lietze's sexuality, though her reaction to Lietze's disclosure of attraction to Jalta—"kannste mir mal sagen, wieso det ausgerechnet 'n Kerl sein mußte?" [can you tell me why it's got be a guy, of all people? 57]—may simply convey disappointment rather than doubt.[61] But it could also read as evidence of Lietze's queer desire, indicating that she has romantic affections for women too. Barfoot notes that critics have ignored the "hint of a possible past or future susceptibility to feminine charms on Lietze's part" (130).[62] Indeed, the queer contours of Lietze's characterization become meaningful to a reading of her as pivotal to the novel's political vision. The text's dismissal of Jalta as a potential love object involves the transfer of the detective's interest toward the whores in general, as noted above, and to Kim in particular. Lietze's rejection of Jalta has a direct positive consequence for the prostitutes: when she turns down Jalta's gift of a digital notebook, he offers it to Kim, who then passes it on to Helga for use in keeping track of *Migräne*'s files. On Lietze's only social outing with Jalta, she flirts with Kim instead of her date, and the rendezvous ends with Lietze crying in Kim's arms in the ladies' room. Kim comforts Lietze while preaching about the problems with men. Although unsuccessful in gaining Lietze's affections, Kim nonetheless comes again into physical contact with her in the final scene when she gives her a celebratory kiss on the mouth as she recounts the success of the *Migräne* demonstration (163). Having begun with Lietze's interrupted sex with Jalta, the novel ends by positioning her with Kim, thus suggesting that something may yet come of this alliance.[63]

Lietze's professional and personal connections to the prostitutes code her as a feminist figure while queering the parameters of her occupation. The detective and the whores work together by sharing information, which is beneficial to both parties. Helga, Kitty, and Kim provide Lietze with information about a suspect that furthers her crime investigation. However, this relationship goes beyond the traditional professional association of a police officer with her informants: Lietze also offers Helga, Kitty, and Kim vital assistance in planning the illegal demonstration and balloon launch, by informing them of a scheduled police celebration that will keep her colleagues occupied and therefore less likely to interfere with the unlicensed event. Lietze's participation in coordinating the event suggests that she is willing to risk compromising her career because she believes in the feminist causes of promoting safe sex and raising money for the prostitutes' coalition. The detective's alliance to the prostitutes both crosses the boundaries of legality and crosses into the personal. Typically, a policewoman's relationship to sex workers would be determined by the dictates of her job and exclude socializing. But Helga, Kitty, and especially Kim become Lietze's confidantes, functioning as her only social circle outside of her coworkers in the precinct. Aware of the taboo nature of this association, the investigator ruminates: "Die Behörde möchte ich sehen, die genug Phantasie hat, um sich vorzustellen, daß die Beziehungen eines Mordkommissars weiblichen Geschlechts zu drei Bordsteinschwalben andere sein könnten als die, die man in diesem Beruf zu V-Leuten eben hatte" [I'd like to see a government agency that has enough fantasy to imagine that a female homicide detective's relationships to three streetwalkers could be different from those that one typically has to informants in this job, 53]. In evoking fantasy and profession, the text invites its reader to envision other unconventional alliances among these women—one might imagine, for instance, the female police officer as a consumer of the whores' sexual services, or perhaps even as a former streetwalker and colleague of theirs. When Lietze accepts an invitation to join the trio for breakfast, she boards a car "mit vier normalen Leuten drin vom Bordstein" [with four normal people from the sidewalk in it, 53]; by assimilating Lietze into the category of street workers, the narrative makes a normalizing gesture toward what might otherwise be perceived as an exclusively queer relationship.[64]

    The functional forms of feminism that Biermann's *Ableben* offers are thus not limited to its representations of the streetwalkers and their autonomous network, but entail the participation of the state. Had the prostitutes organized their demonstration without a police officer's support, it would have been unlikely to succeed. Sieg alleges that Biermann's optimistic representation of law enforcement glosses over the ways in which state structures promote and conceal the very regimes of power and exploitation against which the prostitutes resist (167–68). Indeed, Biermann does not problematize her rather affirmative rendering of police officers as cooperative and politically correct. But

Biermann's insistence on positive portrayals of public institutions suggests that they are pivotal to her feminist project and that effective political interventions involve the participation of agents across the social and legal spectrum. Power and privilege make certain acts of resistance possible, and an alliance with law enforcement officers, civil servants, and other authority figures can be instrumental in achieving political goals. The text thus advances a combination of coalitional work and legal action in opposition to autonomous politics and vigilante justice.[65] Of course, such interventions would require working-class citizens to have faith in the capacity of bureaucratic representatives to work with them toward a shared vision of justice. By interrogating the political naïveté of a one-dimensional "Antibullen-Programm" [anti-cop agenda, 120], *Ableben* challenges the trend in feminist literature to mistrust officers of the law and politicians or to categorize them unilaterally as participants in the oppression of the disenfranchised. In contrast with this stereotype, Lietze's professional environment is remarkably democratic: the gender-balanced and queer-inclusive homicide division she heads[66] embodies the leftist optimism engendered by the rise of the West German Green Party in the 1980s, which was committed to the equal representation of women and men in its leadership. Lietze's position in command of her division functions as a metaphor for a female head of state, a connotation that rises to the level of dialogue when Lietze mentions a hypothetical "grüne Bundeskanzlerin" [Green female chancellor, 130]—the feminized term, which is noteworthy because of Lietze's usual rejection of *-in* suffixes, emphasizes the centrality of femaleness to this vision. But instead of thematizing the struggle to place women in positions of power, the text presents Lietze's leadership status as a fait accompli and explores the political acts that become possible with the support of a profeminist framework.[67] The novel's optimism on this count, however, is neither unbounded nor utopian: its overall vision of social order and transgressions is rather cynical, in line with noir traditions of detective fiction.

In her work on West German feminist movements, Ute Gerhard traces the transitions in trends among radical activist formations in the 1970s and 1980s, noting a shift toward autonomism in the eighties.[68] Despite their autonomous beginnings in the seventies, feminist politics had, to a certain extent, become institutionalized and mainstream by the end of the decade; this was followed by the fracturing of the movement into a differentiated set of parallel autonomous movements during the eighties. The position of gender and the notion of the patriarchy came under critical scrutiny in theories and practices that explored alternative approaches to political change. Pieke Biermann's first novel arrives at precisely this moment, witnessing the waning influence of second-wave feminist thought and the renewed proliferation of autonomous organizations. However, while *Potsdamer Ableben* does testify to the rejection of radical feminism and the rise of autonomous formations, it does not argue for autonomous feminist action alone. Instead, it both celebrates some forms of autonomous politics, such as the prostitutes' professional collaboration through *Migräne*, and foregrounds a vision of institutional reform and bureaucratic involvement in activism. Biermann's text develops a plurality of semiautonomous feminisms that work toward change from the ground up as well as from the top down and can best be described as coalitional. The collaborations we observe among and between the prostitutes and the police officers are democratic and local; they target specific needs and require communication and compromise by all parties. Though the particular aims and scope of the collaborative campaigns represented in the novel are limited to local cultural contexts and geographies, the final image of the condom balloon floating into East German territory proposes that such actions have great potential and could ultimately bring about transnational awareness and wider shifts. Biermann's novel thus delivers a differentiated set of feminist alliances and acts that promise to effect political change.

Conclusion: Reading the Detective

Frauenkrimis of the eighties brought political activism into the pages of popular texts. The crime novel, a genre traditionally associated with male-embodied reason and macho heterosexual agency, developed radical new contours through the feminization and political inflection of the detective. Feminism and its interventions took popular and digestible forms in the figures of female detectives who worked toward social justice by undertaking crime investigations, unveiling inequality and oppression, and empowering themselves and others through coalition building and mutual support. Zora Zobel, Karin Lietze, and their cohorts are more than just amusing fictions about clever, investigating women; they are metaphors for the emancipatory struggles of the era. During and through their investigations, these feminist protagonists confront the vestiges of sexism, homophobia, classism, and other structural injustices in late twentieth-century West German society. The narratives in which they appear also celebrate female sexuality and eroticism by making the investigators the subjects and objects of desire for both men and women. The amateur and professional detectives in Corinna Kawaters's and Pieke Biermann's crime novels of the mid–1980s signal the disintegration of patriarchal traditions and embody visions of change.

Not only in their depictions of investigators, but also in representations of the milieus in which these figures circulate, do crime novels offer commentaries on contemporary social problems. The themes of bureaucracy, urban countercultures, economic power, the sex industry, and romantic relationships among women figure prominently in these narratives and recall controversies that animated left-wing and feminist movements throughout the 1970s and 1980s. With their queer feminist *Frauenkrimis*, Corinna Kawaters and Pieke Biermann embed complex negotiations of feminist debates in a popular genre about social transgression and the reestablishment of order. Kawaters and Biermann do not take the idea of *feminism* for granted, but rather form their own working definitions of the concept and demonstrate that it emerges in response to specific needs and in particular contexts. Though readers and critics have argued the relative appeal and accessibility of Kawaters's and Biermann's narratives and politics, the success of their novels attests to a certain zeitgeist. These authors' literary interventions into political discourses issue a farewell to second-wave feminism, depicted as a remnant of a bygone era. With their semiautonomous, socialist-inflected perspectives, Kawaters and Biermann anticipate the discussions about globalization, racism, migration, and integration that would become central to evolving forms of feminism and wider political debates with the fall of the Iron Curtain and the expansion of the European Union.

CHAPTER 2

National Pathologies:
Psychological Thrillers
as Cultural Critiques

"Das is gar nich die richtige Mutter!" flüsterte [die Nachbarin]. "Die
Mutter vonner Ariane is vorm halben Jahr gestorben. Brustkrebs! Und
die Gernot hatte mit der zusammgelebt. Und jetz' kämpft se gegen die
Großmutter vonne Ariane ums Sorgerecht. Wird se aber nich kriegen,
die is doch lesbisch! 'n echt lesbisches Paar war das. Möcht' bloß wissen,
wie die an das Kind gekomm' sind!"

—Birgit Rabisch, "Eier im Glas" [1]

["That's not even the real mother!" whispered the neighbor. "Ariane's
mother died six months ago. Breast cancer! And that Gernot had lived
with her. And now she's fighting Ariane's grandmother for custody.
But she won't get it; she's a lesbian! A real lesbian couple, they were.
I'd just like to know how they got hold of that kid!"]

Birgit Rabisch's short story "Eier im Glas" [Eggs in a Glass, 1992] has
many of the hallmarks of conventional detective fiction: a puzzling murder, a
discerning investigator, and the revelation that the killer sought to protect a
secret and conceal other crimes. However, "Eier im Glas" also departs from
tradition in a number of ways: the police detective is a pregnant woman, the
murderer and her victim are both lesbians, and the narrative perspective conveys sympathy for the female and lesbian victims of social injustice.[2] Rabisch's
mystery reveals what is at stake when crime fiction negotiates the gendered
and sexualized dynamics of relationships, family politics, and women's health.
By casting a critical eye on femininity and desire, the author addresses contemporary sociopolitical issues such as sexism and homophobia in the workplace, reproductive rights, and post-unification shifts in the German economy.
The female and lesbian characters become vehicles of feminist commentary
and social critique, and the story ends with the triumph of female agency and

insight: the detective solves the case, an accomplishment that will likely advance her career. Closure, however, comes at a high cost to others: the murderer, a lesbian doctor who was herself a victim of blackmail, has seen the end of her illustrious career, and non-biological mother Regine Gernot will likely lose custody of the child she raised with her deceased female partner. Rabisch simultaneously empowers her pregnant female detective and aligns lesbianism with criminality and victimhood, thereby embracing some feminist ideals but rejecting others. Homosexual characters embody the very problems demanding to be solved, while solving crime and reestablishing order, by contrast, remain the undisputed domain of heterosexuals. This crime story celebrates the successes of the feminist movement while also laying bare its limitations in late twentieth-century Germany. Like other *Frauenkrimis* of its time, "Eier im Glas" diagnoses the underlying causes of crime as historically and culturally specific.

The two award-winning novels at the focus of this chapter, Edith Kneifl's *Zwischen zwei Nächten* [Between Two Nights, 1991] and Ingrid Noll's *Die Häupter meiner Lieben* [*Head Count*, 1993], share with Rabisch's story the strategy of mobilizing queer feminist characters to articulate contemporary social critiques. They differ from "Eier im Glas" in one key way, however: they eschew the figure of the detective, focusing instead on criminals and the social and psychological circumstances of their transgressions. In so doing, they follow in the footsteps of a German classic, Alfred Döblin's social portrait *Die beiden Freundinnen und ihr Giftmord* [*The Two Girlfriends and Their Murder by Poisoning*, 1924], the narrativized study of a real-life legal case about lovers Ella Klein and Margarete Nebbe, who conspired to kill Klein's abusive husband in 1922 and allegedly also planned to kill Nebbe's husband. Döblin's sympathetic depiction of the murdering twosome investigates the women's motives for killing and develops a commentary on the psychosocial effects of structural crises in the turbulent years of the Weimar Republic. *Die beiden Freundinnen* emphasizes Klein and Nebbe's humanity and casts them as victims of sexual abuse, violence, and other transgressions; in so doing, it explores questions about social class, bourgeois marriage, gender inequality, psychic health, and justice.[3] By highlighting the perpetrators and their experiences but leaving his readers to come to their own conclusions about the meaning of his text, Döblin engaged in a queer critique of his era.

While the conventional detective story begins with a crime and follows its investigation and the search for a perpetrator, another tendency in the crime genre—seen in texts by Döblin, Kneifl, and Noll, among others—inverts this formula. Instead of introducing the criminal act as the initial conflict requiring resolution through an investigation that reconstructs the history leading up to it, psychological and suspense thrillers commonly emphasize context and back stories and culminate in crime, narrating the lives of seemingly ordinary figures whose experiences provide a context for the transgressions they later commit. The act of the crime (or, in many cases, the repeated perpetration thereof) then develops as a solution to a problem rather than as the problem itself, functioning as a narrative climax or denouement. We might view Döblin's story as an early psychological thriller, a generic tradition in which Kneifl and Noll participate. Psychological thrillers typically place greater weight on the internal motivations for violence than on its external effects. Because they focus on the criminal instead of the investigator and emphasize the process of becoming a perpetrator, they do not often narrate police investigations of the crimes committed. Indeed, if one can speak of an *investigation* at the heart of this type of crime novel, then its subject is the psychosocial circumstances under which people become complicit in murder, abuse, vigilantism, and other violent transgressions.

Though the subgenre of the psychological thriller may appear to have little in common with mafia sagas like Mario Puzo's bestseller *The Godfather* (1969), they have a shared interest in the interface between crime and the family, the oldest and most basic social structure in human history. As John G. Cawelti points out in his canonical study of genre fiction, one of the legacies of Puzo's novel and the blockbuster film it inspired (Francis Ford Coppola, 1972), which "established a new fashion in the portrayal of crime," was the popularization of the term "the family" to refer to a criminal organization.[4] This domestic metaphor plays with the tension between traditional values and the threats of social change, moral decline, and upheaval: on the one hand, the family serves to protect and guide individual interests, and functions as a building block for other social structures; and, on the other hand, it endangers the safety of individuals and the security of the whole by organizing and concealing violence and corruption. Cawelti posits that *The Godfather* and other crime stories of its era convey a "dark message," the "disturbing irony that a 'family' of criminals might be more humanly interesting and morally satisfactory than a society of empty routines, irresponsibly powerful organizations, widespread corruption, and meaningless violence" (79). In feminist thrillers by Kneifl and Noll, too, the family materializes as literal and symbolic force, a nexus of power and the cause of conflict. Here, however, I propose that the family functions not, as Cawelti implies, as an alternative setting to those other forms and experiences of social order he mentions—"empty routines, irresponsibly powerful organizations, widespread corruption, and meaningless violence"—but rather as the paradigmatic source and ultimate manifestation of these social problems. Kneifl and Noll locate violence in the home, a traditionally feminized space, and pinpoint the causes of crime as bourgeois marriage, biological relationships, imbalances of control, and the confinement of women to domestic spaces and gendered roles. By harnessing the trope of the family to trouble accepted notions of female agency, friendship, and mobility, Kneifl and Noll offer socially critical fantasies of female-embodied revenge and control. In their late twentieth-century texts, these writers pick up threads that Döblin wove into his social portrait of two killers in the 1920s, but they bring these themes into a contemporary sociopolitical context, mobilizing them as commentaries on gender relations and inequality in post–Wall Germany and Austria.

The novels of Ingrid Noll, which explore the inner lives and secret desires of women who commit gruesome crimes, are among the most famous examples of psychological thrillers in German-language literature. Sometimes described as *Täter(innen)krimis* [(female) perpetrator crime novels]—as opposed to *Ermittler(innen)krimis* [(female) investigator crime novels]—such stories by Noll, Kneifl, and contemporaries like Sabine Deitmer and Elfriede Czurda, are commonly narrated from the first-person perspective of the perpetrator or from a perspective that favors the mental processes and experiences of a murderess. Two early examples of such texts, Kneifl's *Zwischen zwei Nächten* and Noll's *Die Häupter meiner Lieben*, feature homosocial and homosexual relationships between women who kill their brothers, lovers, and lovers' husbands; but unlike Döblin's real-life murderesses, these leading ladies metaphorically and literally get away with murder. In addition to emphasizing the subtle, everyday ways in which the institution of the family serves to perpetuate and conceal gendered violence, these novels stage such representations in migrations and intersections between cultures: Austria and the United States in Kneifl's text, and Germany and Italy in Noll's. This chapter reads queer figures and same-sex relationships in these two *Täterinnenkrimis* from the early 1990s within these contexts as negotiations of psychological and geographical boundaries and vehicles for sociopolitical commentary. The texts' queer transnational visions raise crucial questions about identity, representation, and national belonging in late twentieth-century Austria, post-unification Germany, and the expanding European Union.

A Queer Social Psychology of Crime:
Edith Kneifl's *Zwischen zwei Nächten* (1991)

Kneifl's debut novel *Zwischen zwei Nächten* develops a queer feminist critique of Viennese society, exploring the conditions of possibility for female agency and interrogating the relationship among narrative authority, social power positions, and gender and sexuality. Kneifl's crime story articulates a preoccupation with the political dimensions of gender and sexuality that res-

onates with the work of late twentieth-century Austrian feminist authors Ingeborg Bachmann and Elfriede Jelinek. All three writers take a critical stance
toward Austrian history and culture by spotlighting power, abuse, and violence
against a backdrop of postwar Viennese bourgeoisie that sets the stage for violent confrontations between female subjects and male-dominated institutions.
While critics and reviewers have compared Kneifl's work to that of Bachmann
and Jelinek, the latter two are not usually associated with the category of crime
fiction, though all three authors could be said to subvert the traditional gendering of literature by working with and rewriting masculine genres.[5] One of
the generic conventions they share is the slippage between victim and perpetrator positions in their portrayals of female artists who resort to violent, self-
annihilating, and criminal acts as means of survival in a sexist world. I read
Kneifl's *Zwischen zwei Nächten*, like Bachmann's and Jelinek's work, as distinctively Austrian in that it highlights the violence of a gendered social existence. Like the writing of her predecessors, Kneifl's novel couples these
gendered representations with queer characters and mysteries of identity, forcing its reader to make sense of its closure, commentary, and context.

Published in 1991, *Zwischen zwei Nächten* is one of the earliest Austrian
contributions to the German-language *Frauenkrimi*.[6] It is also one of the first
queer crime novels published in Austria, together with Elfriede Czurda's *Die
Giftmörderinnen* [The Poison Murderesses] from the same year.[7] For her debut,
Kneifl became the first Austrian and the first female author to win the prestigious Glauser Prize in 1992.[8] *Zwischen zwei Nächten* has appeared in multiple
editions and Kneifl's subsequent crime novels and numerous short stories and
essays have earned her recognition and acclaim throughout the German-
speaking world and beyond. Her writings have also made their way into the
visual media: the 1997 novel *Ende der Vorstellung* [End of the Performance]
was adapted into a film version as *Taxi für eine Leiche* [Taxi for a Corpse,
Wolfgang Murnberger, 2002] and televised by the Austrian network ORF.
However, despite these landmarks, few critics have written about Kneifl's fiction in general or *Zwischen zwei Nächten* in particular. Aside from Kirsimarja
Tielinen's study of the 1999 novel *Allein in der Nacht* [Alone in the Night],
there is only one other existing publication on Kneifl: Elena Agazzi's 2005
essay, "Psychologie und Verbrechen in Edith Kneifls Kriminalromanen" [Psy-
chology and Crime in Edith Kneifl's Crime Novels], which draws connections
among Kneifl's oeuvre, psycholanalytical structures, and the generic conventions of the psychological thriller. Agazzi's cursory remarks on *Zwischen zwei
Nächten*, however, do not connect its psychological themes to its sociocultural
critique of gender and sexuality, as I do here. In the following pages, I offer a
multifaceted interpretation of Kneifl's novel that intertwines a psychological
reading of its main characters with the story's feminist and queer dimensions.

By describing the novel as a psychological thriller, publishers and critics of *Zwischen zwei Nächten* point to the text's juxtaposition of an investigative structure with a psychological discourse.[9] Commentaries and reviews, however, fail to mention that the psychological mystery extends to the very identity of the novel's two main characters, Ann-Marie Jonas and Anna Beckmann, who take the form of alter egos. The central questions that the mystery poses, as its title suggests, regards the *between* status of the chronology and narrative of the crime, Anna's murder, which transpires between the two nights narrated and is the subject of the investigation. But an equally crucial issue is the *between* of Anna and Ann-Marie's bond: how close are they, are they simply intimate friends or are they split personalities? Their friendship develops into a romantic and sexual relationship and thus brings a queer dimension to this complex psychology. Dualities and repetitions permeate the novel's content and structure, intensifying the tension between parallel narratives and interpretations and leaving multiple questions open at the end.

Time bears structural significance in the story, which builds suspense by alternating between past and present tenses in scenes set before and after Anna's mysterious death. The account favors the third-person perspective of Ann-Marie, who, like a detective investigating a crime, has no direct access to the events that unfolded during Anna's final hours. She must piece together the witnesses' subjective and conflicting accounts to create a coherent narrative of her friend's demise. The accounts of both nights begin with Ann-Marie's return to her hometown of Vienna following a transatlantic voyage from her current residence in New York City. Most of the action takes place in Anna and her husband Alfred's Vienna home, a luxurious flat that also houses their successful architecture firm. In the first night, Ann-Marie and Anna's long-awaited reunion after years of transatlantic correspondence begins awkwardly and ends in passionate lovemaking. During this intimate encounter, Anna confesses that she intends to leave her cruel husband, sell the firm, and move to New York to start a new life with Ann-Marie. But on the very day when she plans to leave Vienna, Anna takes a fatal fall from her seventh-story balcony and is found lifeless in the courtyard below, a death the police immediately pronounce suicide. The second night begins with Anna's funeral, where Ann-Marie discusses her friend's mysterious death with other guests. The evening culminates in a dramatic confrontation: alone with Alfred in the apartment, Ann-Marie accuses him of murdering Anna, then pushes him over the balcony, so that Alfred ultimately meets his demise in the same way as did his wife.

At the level of character, two dualities are crucial to the novel's development and pose problems for its interpretation. On the one hand, the text calls upon its reader to make sense of the remarkable similarities and differences between Anna and Ann-Marie, and on the other hand, the antagonism between the two women and Alfred drives the crime story. Depending on how the reader decodes these relationships, at least two different readings of the text are possible. On the surface, it is the tale of a tragic queer romance that ends with a feminist act of vengeance. But the novel also reads as a psychological story of the return of the repressed; this account mobilizes the metaphorical dimensions of the same-sex love affair. This is precisely what makes the text so queer: the reader must decide how to interpret these relationships in order to solve its mysteries because the case is not closed at the novel's end. The following discussion fleshes out both interpretations, emphasizing their feminist and queer facets.

The overlap between the names Anna and Ann-Marie, which begin with the same syllable, can cause confusion for readers. This unexplained coincidence encourages a conflation of the two characters. The names are synthesized when Anna calls Ann-Marie *Annemarie*, suggesting a composite identity, one that is potentially as "unzertrennlich" [inseparable] as the lifelong friends.[10] The name *Annemarie* indicates both a proximity and a distancing, as only Anna uses it to address her friend, and Ann-Marie changes it when she moves away, an event that marks a caesura in their relationship.

On the surface, Anna and Ann-Marie are polar opposites: aside from their devotion to one another, the only things they have in common are that they grew up in Vienna and have a propensity for substance abuse. Otherwise, they are poles apart—physically, professionally and psychologically. Shy, conservative and wealthy, Anna is unhappily married to an abusive man and Viennese high society; by contrast, the outspoken, bohemian Ann-Marie has brightly-dyed hair and lives independently in a run-down apartment. Although both women work in art and design, their professional experiences are very different: an accomplished architect and business owner, Anna retires from practicing design because the demands of a conformist market inhibit her creativity; and Ann-Marie, who ekes out a living by working odd jobs and painting apartments, finds inspiration in industrial garbage on the streets of New York, from which she creates one-of-a-kind works of art. Anna rejects bourgeois mores silently and passively, but in so doing, does violence only to herself; and Ann-Marie's outward rejection of Viennese society culminates in the murder of Alfred, the man who personifies it.

A psychological reading of this multifaceted polarization encourages an interpretation of the two characters that emphasizes not their difference, but rather their sameness. The intense mutual attraction and emotional codependency they share raise questions about whether Anna and Ann-Marie are queer alter egos, that is, not just friends and lovers, but rather two sides of one person that cannot coexist. Ann-Marie embodies the rebellious tendencies that Anna represses in order to conform to familial and professional expectations; the decisive moment in this repression comes when Ann-Marie emigrates to America. Their subsequent love affair can be understood as a metaphoric longing for psychic unity. But the romance is short-lived due to Anna's inability to extricate herself from the web of repression in which she is caught. Anna's death thus figures as both a defeat and a victory: it represents the ultimate failure of psychic unity, but it also signals Ann-Marie's survival due to her successful breakout from the oppressive culture that swallows Anna.

Zwischen zwei Nächten reads as a feminist case study in repression, examining the violence that an impermeable, paternalistic and misogynistic, and profit-driven society does to the female subject. The characterization of Anna and Ann-Marie as alike and yet different resonates with Sigmund Freud's doppelgänger trope in "Das Unheimliche" [The Uncanny, 1919]. Freud explains that a doppelgänger embodies those dimensions of the ego that cannot come to expression or find fulfillment due to repression.[11] In Kneifl's novel, the creation of an alter ego could be triggered by Anna's bourgeois inhibitions, failed breakout from patriarchal legacies, and assimilation into a socially conservative milieu. Her alter ego, Ann-Marie, personifies Anna's rebellious desires and unfulfilled dreams, emerging as a funky, free-thinking feminist who escapes the world in which Anna remains trapped. Kneifl's text thus diagnoses the root of Anna's psychic condition as social and cultural. *Zwischen zwei Nächten* stages the tension between Anna and her heritage as a *Wiederholungszwang* [repetition compulsion]—the subconscious tendency to reenact past psychological traumas—whereby she returns to the parental home, the source of her repression, and internalizes patriarchal expectations so completely that she continues to submit to them even after the demise of her literal father. Anna's parents determine the course of her life: like them, she studies architecture, and despite early attempts to disentangle herself from their finances, demands, and dreams, she eventually follows in their footsteps. Though she initially rejects her father's job offer and strikes out on her own, Anna's struggle to establish herself as a freelance architect falls short of her luxurious daydreams, so she joins her father's firm, where she becomes obsessed with money and success. This return to the parental fold and bourgeois values erodes Anna's agency and triggers her psychological disintegration: "Gefangen im altbekannten Wohlstand, krank vor Ehrgeiz und Profilierungssucht—die Phase ihrer Selbstzerstörung begann" [Trapped in familiar prosperity, sick with ambition and an addiction to recognition—the phase of her self-destruction began, 145]. Significantly, the repression of Anna's own desires and aspirations, which are supplanted by those of her parents, occurs simultaneously with Ann-Marie's unannounced relocation to New York. Ann-Marie's departure also reads as a closeting of the potentially subversive queer desires that Anna contains in order to live a conventional, heteronormative life. While the novel's New York is no paradise either, the freedom and anonymity its social wilderness provides seem preferable to the oppressive superficiality of Vienna, described as "eine tote Stadt" [a dead city] and "eine Stadt der Toten" [a city of the dead, 102], which offers only familiar patterns of repression, self-negation, and, ultimately, death. The novel aligns Vienna with the suffocation and outright negation of female subjects who are socially deviant or marginalized in any way.

Anna inherits the family home and business, and, in the absence of her biological father, she submits to the tyranny of Alfred, whose social status, professional ambitions, and assumption of authority over Anna position him in continuity with her domineering parents. The alternative to a heterocentric bourgeois routine with an "überflüssige[n] Ehemann" [useless husband, 11] is an unluxurious but emotionally fulfilling life with—or as—her alter ego, Ann-Marie. But, like her failed separation from her parents, Anna's attempt to leave Alfred also fails: her death intervenes as a consequence of her inability to gain control of her life. Ann-Marie, in going back to Vienna, embodies the return of the repressed, but unlike Freud's doppelgänger, which originates as a means of self-preservation (258), Ann-Marie is unable to protect the ego, Anna. Nevertheless, by murdering Anna's oppressor and symbolic father, Ann-Marie does succeed in saving herself and other female subjects that could fall victim to his violence.

The narrative overtly engages in a feminist psychological discourse that underlines Anna's position as a victim and Alfred's complicity with an oppressive social order. The adulterous husband's tyranny is so complete that he is the likely cause of Anna's psychosis, which he ostensibly produces. Alfred is an architect and not a psychologist, but his bourgeois social standing brings with it cultural authority, and his diagnoses of Anna are delivered in psychological rhetoric that both prescribe and describe her condition: he alleges that his wife is frustrated, paranoid, and depressed. To the reader, however, Alfred's characterization of Anna as delusional in the days leading up to her death may seem exaggerated in comparison with the accounts provided by other characters, who admit that Anna was depressed and drinking heavily but do not consider her insane or capable of suicide. The reader, who accesses these events through Ann-Marie's perspective, never learns the unequivocal truth about Anna's psychological state or her death, and can be certain of only one thing: Ann-Marie believes Alfred to be not only an abuser, but also a cold-blooded killer. Even if Alfred did not push his wife off the balcony, it seems justified to hold him responsible for her death, as he is undoubtedly to blame for encouraging her self-negation and enabling her downfall.

A reading of Anna and Ann-Marie as alter egos allows for a further reading of Alfred, whose name also begins with the same letter, as yet another side of this complex psyche. The scenario in which Anna dies at the hand of Alfred, who is then killed by Ann-Marie, is a battle not only for psychic survival, but also for control of the narrative. Anna experiences growing psychological and physical isolation in conjunction with a loss of voice and agency. She even fears that Alfred will take away her legal autonomy: "Er drohte nicht nur einmal, mich für verrückt erklären zu lassen.... Eine Zeitlang befürchtete ich, er würde versuchen, mich entmündigen zu lassen" [He threatened more than once to have me declared insane. For a while I feared he might try to have me declared incompetent, 77]. Anna's suspicions are justified after her death, when Alfred persists in silencing her voice by denying the existence of her diaries. Ann-Marie tries to recuperate Anna's journals as a means of preserving her— and their—story, but the implication is that, rather than allowing Anna's account to live on for others to read, Alfred destroys the documents, which likely inculpate him, to ensure that only his story survives. The only first-hand record of this woman's experience of abuse and annihilation in a patriarchal society is thus effaced and replaced by a male-dominated narrative. Vested with the credibility of his gender and class, Alfred has the cultural authority to recount his version of Anna's psychic disintegration and demise, which, for lack of evidence to challenge it, becomes the commonly accepted narrative.

Such a reading encourages a comparison to Bachmann's *Malina*, in which the gendered personae of a female protagonist and an aggressive man also struggle for control of the narrator's identity. Mark Anderson's characterization of *Malina* as "detective novel of the psyche" is an apt depiction of the psychological intrigue in Kneifl's novel as well.[12] Kneifl's Anna and Bachmann's unnamed first-person narrator *ich* [I] are similar in several ways: traumatized by their fathers, they both become involved in metaphorical three-way relationships that symbolically represent the negotiation of a gendered selfhood as a war between the masculine and the feminine. Through these negotiations, Anna and *ich* lose their voices, agency, and ultimately their very identities and lives. The power struggles with the male figures of Alfred and Malina do violence to the female subjects and threaten to efface the female narratives altogether.[13] Kneifl's representation of Anna, however, not only stresses "die labile Psyche emanzipierter Frauen" [unstable psyche of emancipated women, Agazzi 101] but also confronts the social conditions that bring about psychic collapse, and though she dies, her story ends on a more optimistic note. Anna differs from Bachmann's *ich* in one key way: she has a female alter ego who survives and avenges her. These generational conflicts offer a feminist critique of authority structures and social injustices that resist the formation of strong, autonomous female subjects in late twentieth-century Vienna. The gendered subjects produced under such circumstances face self-negation, psychological disintegration, and death, or else they themselves become perpetrators and perpetuate the cycle of violence.

Kneifl's *Zwischen zwei Nächten* articulates an overt feminist critique of bourgeois Austria through its representation of architecture as a microcosm of Viennese society rife with sexism, classism, and corruption. The novel's critical stance is most palpable in its portrayal of Alfred, which underlines his villainy in multiple ways: he is a member of a society in which money is the highest value, a practitioner of a sexist and corrupt profession, and a self-absorbed chauvinist responsible for Anna's personal and professional discontent.[14] Though they are initially happy together, Alfred and Anna's marital bliss is short-lived. Their problems begin when Anna has an abortion and Alfred reacts by sending Anna to therapy: "Er hielt es für anormal, daß ich das höchste Glück einer Frau, die Mutterschaft, verweigerte" [He considered it abnormal that I rejected the greatest joy of a woman, motherhood, 78]. Because Anna refuses to play the role of subservient wife and mother, Alfred retaliates by openly displaying his affair with one of her employees, a woman described as more docile—and therefore more traditionally feminine—than his wife. Alfred stages Anna's lavish funeral as a celebration of his freedom and a business opportunity: attending hand in hand with his mistress, Alfred seeks to attract and impress important clients. In prioritizing the show of affluence over what might be deemed the more socially appropriate response, mourning at the loss of a loved one, Alfred's behavior indicates that, in this society, the superficial display of wealth has higher value than even the superficial display of emotion. Kneifl's depiction of a sympathetic Anna exposes Viennese society and in particular the institution of architecture as pathologically obsessed with success, prosperity, and appearances.

Those with less fortune and those who deviate from these norms circulate at the margins of this society, embodied not only by Ann-Marie, but also by Anna's housekeeper, Frau Maricek, and her nameless alcoholic son. The Mariceks, like Ann-Marie, are outsiders to the Austrian *Wohlstandsgesellschaft* [affluent society], and their marginality spins out along multiple axes: appearance, class, and national belonging.[15] The presumably Slavic origin of the name Maricek recalls Austria's expansionist past, in particular the multiethnic Austro-Hungarian Empire. The Mariceks are the only two characters aside from Ann-Marie who express doubts about the official story of Anna's suicide. The alignment of marginality with the reluctance to believe a commonly accepted account suggests that belonging to a community entails not only the proper socioeconomic background, but also the unquestioning acceptance of collective narratives. Kneifl approaches the legacies of fascism through this critique of contemporary Austrian society's conformist mentality, acceptance of accounts provided by those with wealth and power, and inability to tolerate difference. Although *Zwischen zwei Nächten* manifests greater concern with issues of class and gender than with race and ethnicity, its reflections on difference and violence bring to mind associations with the Third Reich. Its publication coinciding with a rapid upswing in the popularity of Austrian right-wing political groups in the late 1980s and early 1990s, Kneifl's text questions the "politische Naivität" [political naïveté, 14] of upper-class citizens like Anna, whose financial well-being and ignorance shield them from confronting social realities of the past and present. Alfred is also a player in this scenario: even the "feudale[] Sektbar" [feudal champagne bar, 92] he frequents is metaphorically saddled with the burdens of past social injustices. Uttered in the space of this bar, whose patrons are presumably arrogant and wealthy, Alfred's assertion that his wife could not have truly befriended Frau Maricek—he asks Ann-Marie, "Glaubst du im Ernst, daß Anna einer Putzfrau ihre wahren Gefühle gezeigt hätte?" [Do you seriously believe that Anna would have shown her true feelings to a cleaning lady? 92]—takes on both classist and fascist overtones. While Frau Maricek is careful not to voice her suspicions aloud, her teenage son tells Ann-Marie he suspects that Anna's death was perhaps "weder ein Unfall noch ein Selbstmord" [neither an accident nor a suicide, 42]. His mother immediately silences him for fear that he might be heard. However, shunned by the other funeral attendees, the Mariceks do not have the cultural authority to speak of their suspicions or to mention Anna's happiness at the prospect of leaving her Viennese home to start a new life. The impermeable social boundary that separates them from high society is policed by the silencing of their narrative and by a pattern of figurative and literal violence. In linking ethnic identity with cultural authority and belief in shared narratives, Kneifl's novel conjures the specter of National Socialism and suggests that continuities exist between the xenophobic political order of the Third Reich and the implicit social violence of excluding minorities from full participation in bourgeois society in the late twentieth century.

Anna, on the other hand, belongs to this *Wohlstandsgesellschaft* and chooses to remain a part of it for much of her life. But even in a seemingly powerful position as a business owner, Anna feels professionally marginalized on the basis of her gender. She indicts the world of architecture, to which she has devoted much of her life, as "durch und durch männlich" [masculine through and through, 73], aligning the profit-driven amorality of her occupation with patriarchy and misogyny. Anna voices a feminist critique of the male colonization of women's accomplishments for financial gain, professional success, and social acceptance: "Obwohl Männer massenhaft schlecht oder mittelmäßig sind, schreiben sie vor allem uns diese Attribute zu. Nicht selten nehmen sie dann Ideen oder Entwicklungen von Frauen auf und sind mit diesen sofort auf dem Markt präsent. Von den Frauen fehlt jede Spur" [Although men are largely bad or mediocre, they attribute these qualities above all to us. Not infrequently, they then adopt women's ideas or innovations, with which they immediately gain a market presence. No trace remains of the women, 74]. This passage indicts not only architecture as a misogynistic profession, but the entire society for which it is emblematic. Women's contributions are valued, but only insofar as they support the successes of men, who are the real beneficiaries of women's labor, which is trafficked on the male-dominated market. In evoking an empire that shows no trace of the women who helped build it, Anna foretells her own death and the male-dominated market presence that will survive her in the form of her firm.

Anna's death is murder by occupation: she dies in the very building that houses her company, which designs buildings. Although her demise—or Alfred's, for that matter—cannot be fully ascribed to architecture, it is significant that both characters fall to their deaths from the terrace that separates their apartment and office, spaces linked to Anna's professional alienation and social isolation. The apartment building is symbolic for an entire constellation of sociocultural and economic circumstances: it is near Mariahilfer Straße, a posh inner-city quarter associated with consumerism and high culture. Vienna is one of the few cities whose architectural treasures have survived the wars of the twentieth century largely undamaged, and it is also the internationally acclaimed home of many successful contemporary urban projects. In the context of this history, the vilification of architecture in *Zwischen zwei Nächten* takes the tone of a pointed cultural critique. The very cultural forms that lure millions of tourists a year to Austria are portrayed as responsible for the death of an individual who devotes much of her life to creating them. Architectural motifs permeate the novel, reiterating the multiple connections between gender, female sexuality, physical confinement, and patriarchal power structures.

Though the sex scene between Anna and Ann-Marie does not come until the novel's final pages, their queer relationship is the subject of the entire narrative. They share everything, even men; this dimension of their relationship hints at a queer triangulation of desire (for a more nuanced discussion of this structure, see the next section on Noll's *Die Häupter meiner Lieben*). Thirty years later, both women are conscious of an explicit desire for one another that they do not express directly. The text suggests that Anna's bourgeois inhibitions also affect her expression of love for Ann-Marie: "Da Anna unfähig war, ihre Zuneigung anders zu zeigen" [Because Anna was incapable of showing her affection in any other way, 12], she tries to redirect her desire by giving Ann-Marie financial support. Over the years, Ann-Marie becomes increasingly aware that her friend has "nicht nur rein freundschaftliche Gefühle" [not only purely friendly feelings, 16]. Despite hints that Anna and Ann-Marie have been deeply and madly in love with each other for their entire lives, to label them *lesbians* would not be faithful to the text. Prior to sleeping together, both women have affairs primarily, if not exclusively, with male lovers. Anna is depicted as less promiscuous than Ann-Marie—she dated men before Alfred but married him a virgin—and the only instance of desire for another woman is trivialized as a typical girlhood crush on a gym teacher. Ann-Marie, on the other hand, has had many lovers, but these are typically casual affairs, like her occasional nighttime visits with Jeff, an African-American neighbor, and they become less frequent over time, signaling a waning interest in men (122–23). Ann-Marie appears to become increasingly attracted to women, such as Mira, a younger friend to whom she feels drawn because she resembles Anna. Mira's openness to Ann-Marie also denotes the potential queerness of this friendship: "Mira war für jeden Unsinn zu haben" [Mira was up for any kind of mischief, 123]. Based on this evidence and the lack of any indication that Anna or Ann-Marie identifies as strictly straight or gay, a description of their desires and acts as *queer* would therefore seem most appropriate.

The word *lesbian* does appear in the novel but not until the very end, just as the brief narrative of the women's singular sexual encounter begins, but the lovers themselves never use the term; in fact, they avoid defining their relationship aloud. Rather, the expression appears only in the contexts of imagined misreadings or exaggerated performances of their relationship. Ann-Marie envisions how the media might construe it if Alfred were to kill her: "Im Geiste sieht sie schon die Schlagzeile der kleinformatigen Zeitung von morgen abend: 'Lesbe folgt heißgeliebter Freundin in den Freitod'" [She could already visualize the headlines of tomorrow evening's small-format newspaper: "Lesbian follows beloved girlfriend in suicide," 163].[16] Here, in an imagined misinterpretation of a hypothetical death as a sensationalized scandal, the identifier *Lesbe* seems hyperbolic and, the context would seem to imply, inaccurate. Alfred appears to be alone in suspecting his wife's romantic involvement with Ann-Marie, but his performance of the jealous husband doesn't fool her; Ann-Marie knows he only plays the role to unnerve and manipulate her. Ann-Marie and Anna's brief adult affair unfolds entirely behind closed doors, though Ann-Marie remembers that, when they were young, she and Anna sometimes enjoyed pretending to be a lesbian couple in public but never in private (164). The pleasure the girls derive from this show suggests that they are channeling—and downplaying—their latent queer desires into a public performance as a means of bypassing an intimate exchange. The attempt to limit the performance of queer desire to social settings is, however, not entirely successful. It is revealed that there was also intimate contact, even though Ann-Marie cannot remember it.[17] The encounter, an ostensibly isolated occasion during their college years when Ann-Marie and Anna shared an apartment in Vienna, explicitly goes beyond a friendly cuddle: "Ihre Küsse waren verlangend und ihre Umarmungen nicht mehr ganz unschuldig. Schließlich schliefen sie ein, fest umschlungen wie zwei Kinder, die sich fürchten" [Their kisses were desirous and their embraces no longer entirely innocent. Eventually they fell asleep in a tight embrace like two frightened children, 165]. While the description of the embrace suggests a mutual desire for greater intimacy, the allusion to the innocence of fearful children holding each other for comfort moderates its sexual implications. Aside from the overt representation of same-sex intimacy, the later adult sexual encounter between the two women has further queer dimensions. An apparent role reversal positions the usually shy and introverted Anna in an active role, initiating caresses that lead to closer contact. Suspecting that Anna is dazed and unaware of her actions, Ann-Marie "wagte nicht, sich zu rühren" [didn't dare move, 163]—it is almost as if she were playing dead. Though elsewhere she is outspoken and assertive, here a physically unresponsive Ann-Marie, who is apparently motivated by a fear of disrupting the mood, passively consents to these intimate acts. The text does not depict the lovemaking directly, but rather implies it through elision. Reminiscent of a cross-cutting film montage, the narrative is structured contrapuntally, oscillating at irregular intervals between short passages from the two titular nights. The scenes relaying Anna and Ann-Marie's queer reunion jump from a tender caress, to kissing, disrobing and declarations of love, and finally to cigarette smoking. Each scene is interrupted by a snapshot from the later night in which Ann-Marie confronts Alfred. Even if the cigarette at the end of the sequence is a symbolic postcoital cliché, the reader can be no more certain about what happens between Anna and Ann-Marie than about how Anna dies. This destabilizing strategy presents the reader with incomplete information, both actively and passively queering the narrative.

Unlike the traditional detective novel, *Zwischen zwei Nächten* does not offer narrative closure by providing an unequivocal solution to the mystery of Anna's death. To be sure, the question of how and why Anna died is, from Ann-Marie's point of view, a closed case. Even though Alfred claims innocence and Ann-Marie realizes that she will never know exactly what happened on Anna's last night alive, Ann-Marie is certain of Alfred's guilt. Because the unembodied third-person narrator largely favors Ann-Marie's perspective, which is not only partial, but also unstable, Kneifl's reader has no recourse to any objective story about Anna's death.[18] The implication of the novel's resolution is clear: whether Anna committed suicide or met her demise at the hand of another is hardly significant. Even if the reader wishes to see Ann-Marie as a heroine, it is not necessary to accept that Alfred murdered Anna, for, as Agazzi asserts, "Auch wenn sich Anna umgebracht hätte, wäre die Wut Ann-Maries genauso groß gewesen" [Even if Anna had committed suicide, Ann-Marie's rage would have been just as intense, 105]. In addition to affirming that she aligns herself with Ann-Marie's opinion that Alfred is Anna's killer, Agazzi insinuates that Alfred's complicity extends beyond this crime. As a highly symbolic male figure in a suffocating patriarchal culture, Alfred is guilty of perpetuating the social and psychological conditions that negated his wife's aesthetic agency and ensured that her efforts to establish herself independently would fail.

Closure comes in the form of Alfred's death. When the woman seeking answers avenges herself against the supposed perpetrator, what begins as a narrative of investigation ends as a *Täterinkrimi*. The narrative stages an eye-for-an-eye retribution and exculpates Ann-Marie because of the threat to her own life: if she does not kill Alfred, he will likely kill her. In the final scenes of the novel, at Ann-Marie's request, Alfred takes her onto the balcony to show her the courtyard below where his wife's corpse had lain. The rising tension, as a drunk and nauseated Ann-Marie becomes increasingly hysterical and frightened, reaches its climax and resolution simultaneously: "Ein kräftiger Stoß, ein kaum hörbarer Schrei. Ein Körper stürzt in die Tiefe und schlägt Sekunden später auf dem Kopfsteinpflaster des Hinterhofs auf" [A strong shove, a barely audible cry. A body plummets into the depths, seconds later striking the cobblestone pavement of the rear courtyard, 169]. The text constructs the mutual danger for Alfred and Ann-Marie in queerly identifying the victim only as "a body," momentarily leaving the reader in suspense as to its identity. The ensuing phrase from a wedding vow—"*Bis in den Tod vereint*" [Til death do we part, 169, emphasis in original]—seems to indicate that the body is Alfred's, who is joining his wife in death, but it also sustains the possibility that it is Ann-Marie who is being reunited with her lifelong friend and lover. The latter reading is encouraged by a passage directly preceding the death, in which, in one of two short, marked breaks from the narrative mood, Ann-Marie's first-person voice relates an intimate conversation with Anna. Ending with "Sie sagte, daß sie nie aufhören würde, mich zu lieben, daß sie mich lieben würde bis zu ihrem Tod" [She said she would never stop loving me, that she would love me until her death, 169], the segment conveys a declaration resembling a wedding vow. Only in the five short sentences that follow the unidentified falling body at the novel's conclusion does the reader learn which of Anna's loves reunites with her in death.

The final portrayal of Ann-Marie at the airport waiting for her return flight to New York leads us to conclude that she has executed Alfred and not vice versa. Her successful passage through passport control suggests that Ann-Marie gets away with the murder. Ann-Marie takes the law into her own hands and avenges her lover, killing a reprehensible man who destroys the potential of a lesbian romance and utopia. Agazzi reads the murder of Alfred at the end of the novel as more meaningful than self-defense or revenge; rather, this act is about "die Verteidigung gemeinsamer Träume und Projekte, die nur der Frauenwelt gehörten und die Alfred profaniert hat" [defending shared dreams and projects that belong solely within the women's sphere and that Alfred violated, 105]. In her brief discussion of the novel, Wilke too emphasizes that Kneifl's text is the story of a female same-sex relationship and the obstacles that patriarchal society present to its fulfillment, a problem that only finds closure with the death of the man who represents this society.[19] As Agazzi and Wilke both rightly suggest, Alfred's execution is not just about self-preservation or vengeance, but about the establishment and maintenance of a queer feminist sphere; it ultimately protects the female subject from further incursion and oppression on behalf of the patriarchal system.

Is this justice? Are Ann-Marie's actions morally defensible? The answers that Kneifl's text offers to these questions may be indirect, but they are emphatically affirmative. Killing Alfred is a symbolic rejection of and victory over everything for which he stands. Misled, perhaps, by Alfred's performance of gender and class, the Viennese police believe that a hysterical Anna brought her own life to an end; they fail to serve justice with a thorough investigation of her death. Kneifl's narrative uncovers the misogyny and injustice in Austrian society, but it also offers an alternative. However, that alternative entails a recourse to violence: Ann-Marie must become a perpetrator. In so doing, she secures a chance to begin a new life. Ann-Marie triumphs precisely because she resists the dominant order, avenges her friend, and in so doing succeeds in defending her subjecthood and leaving the sphere in which the others are trapped. While Vienna materializes as a destructive, bourgeois, patriarchal environment that breeds victims and perpetrators, the novel's New York emerges as the prodigious land of opportunity, where individuals marginalized elsewhere on the basis of their gender, sexuality, ethnicity, and class can lead independent and fulfilling lives.

This reading of the novel's end is even more compelling if we interpret it as a commentary on Austrian cultural history in general and National Socialism in particular. Ann-Marie's assertion, "Wir können unsere Vergangenheit nicht einholen" [We cannot recover our past, 130], is more than a banal observation that the past is gone. It is an admonishment, a threat to both Anna and the other female subjects in the Austrian literary canon: if they do not confront the past, it will consume them. Kneifl rejects fictional predecessors, like the unnamed narrator in Bachmann's *Malina* and Erika from Jelinek's *Die Klavierspielerin* [*The Piano Teacher*], who fall victim to violence, cannot break out of its cycle, and become complicit in their own oppression.[20] *Zwischen zwei Nächten* asserts that everyday brutalities like Alfred's psychological abuse will find no end unless they meet with violent rebuttals. Indeed, the text stages an intervention into Austrian history in echoing the generation of 1968's philosophy that to stand silent when others are oppressed is in itself a violent act. The combination of cultural pessimism merged with violence, psychological themes, and social critique is one that readers have come to expect not only in the writing of Bachmann and Jelinek; it is visible in the works of other late twentieth-century Austrian authors such as Ilse Aichinger, Thomas Bernhard, and Elfriede Czurda, and persists in the early twenty-first-century work of writers like Wolf Haas, Josef Haslinger, Anna Mitgutsch, and Marlene Streeruwitz. Further even, Kneifl's work suggests that victim-perpetrator dichotomies are not always clearly delineated and that the victims of oppression themselves carry the keys to their own emancipation, even if this emancipation comes at a violent price. Just as Ann-Marie recycles urban garbage into unique works of art, so too can texts such as Kneifl's turn the burdens of Austrian guilt, pessimism, and decay into productive self-critiques, opening up spaces for negotiation and possibly even liberation.

Kneifl's debut novel lays bare the high stakes of social injustice in late twentieth-century Austria and concludes with a departure from the ancestral *Heimat* [homeland]. Its female subjectivities and sexualities are formed, threatened, and meet their demise through violent struggles for narrative authority, agency, approval, success, money, ownership, and power. At the same time, Kneifl's text is open-ended and withholds concrete closure, a trope common to queer crime stories. This reading of the murder and ending of *Zwischen zwei Nächten* may seem somewhat optimistic, but the text supports such a reading. Despite the "Ausdruck einer pessimistischen Weltdeutung" [expression of a pessimist world view, Tielinen 63] in Kneifl's work, *Zwischen zwei Nächten* concludes by delivering Ann-Marie from harm and placing her in an airport, a highly symbolic architectural space that promises freedom, mobility and adventure. The openness of the airport stands in sharp contrast to the insularity of Viennese society and the architectural profession that caused Anna's downfall. As the return of the repressed, Ann-Marie not only prevails over Alfred and Anna, who are fated to live and die on the Viennese ground that produced them, but her impending departure signals that there is a way out of oppressive social and psychological conditions. She is leaving Vienna.

The Queer Family That Preys Together Stays Together: Ingrid Noll's *Die Häupter meiner Lieben* (1993)

Ingrid Noll's *Die Häupter meiner Lieben* narrates the history of a friendship between two women with distinctly feminist and queer, national and transnational dimensions. By heralding the girls' friendship as the strongest bond of all—above biological kinship and romantic attachments—the text holds it up as a symbiotic feminist model of solidarity that frees them from the tyranny of male lovers and family members and embraces other members in a community of mutual support. Queer desire finds its expression most often indirectly, in the negation of lesbianism but the affirmation of something else, in the murders of men and in triangular erotic constellations. Though much of the action takes place in Italy and the novel features a German artist, an aesthetics of decay, queer elements, and dying men, it has less in common with its literary predecessor, Thomas Mann's *Der Tod in Venedig* [*Death in Venice*, 1912], than it does with the popular contemporary movie *Thelma & Louise* (Ridley Scott, 1991). Like Scott's female-bonding film, *Die Häupter meiner Lieben* narrates the evolution of a friendship, with stations marked by problematic male figures, that solidifies into a partnership in crime when one of the women kills a man who attempts to rape the other. Noll's crime novel brings a transnational dimension to the crime spree in the American road movie: while Thelma and Louise self-destruct before reaching the Mexican border—and therefore never attain the freedom from prosecution that it may offer—Noll's murderous duo perpetrates many crimes abroad, where the authorities never suspect their complicity. This geopolitical dynamic interrogates the evolving relationship between post-unification Germany and the European Union. *Thelma & Louise* set off a heated debate not only because of its representations of reprehensible men and understandably vengeful women, but also because of its lesbian undertones[21]; however, the publication of *Häupter* met with no such controversy. There are indeed pronounced queer facets to the female friendship in *Häupter*, but a queer reading of the text must come to terms with its explicit disavowal of homosexuality. Like spectators of *Thelma & Louise* who read the women on screen for hints of homosexual desire, I interpret the relationships in *Häupter* as meaningful queer constellations, and I bring these into conversation with the novel's transnational setting in Germany and Italy in the early 1990s.

One of the best-read contemporary German crime authors, Noll has become famous for her depictions of murderous women. As one of the very few German-language female crime writers who has written bestsellers, Noll is a recognizable player in the mainstream German crime landscape, an exception among female writers.[22] Her first crime novel, *Der Hahn ist tot* [*Hell Hath No Fury*, 1991], was an immediate hit; the second, *Die Häupter meiner Lieben*, earned her the esteemed Glauser Prize for crime fiction in 1994, making her only the second female author to take this prize after Kneifl; and Noll's third novel, *Die Apothekerin* [*The Pharmacist*, 1994], is now considered a genre classic. All three bestsellers have been made into movies and translated into several languages, and many other novels and short story collections have since followed.

While Noll's stories do not belong to a series in the conventional sense of the term, shared characters form intertextual connections among her books.

For instance, Rosemarie, *Der Hahn*'s first-person narrator, appears in *Die Apothekerin*, though not as narrator; Charlotte, the leading woman in *Kalt ist der Abendhauch* [Cold is the Breath of Evening, 1996], is grandmother to Cora from *Häupter*; and Cora is a central figure in *Häupter* and *Selige Witwen* [Blessed Widows, 2001], both of which are narrated from the first-person perspective of her best friend Maja. Aside from these reappearing characters, Noll's texts also share an interest in the shifting gender and power dynamics in relationships and families, and the tensions and violence festering behind peaceful-seeming domestic facades. Because her novels highlight the first-person experiences of ordinary women who stop at nothing to get what they want, including killing those men (and sometimes women) whom they perceive as obstacles or disturbances, Noll's oeuvre has been classified under labels such as psychological novels, suspense, and thrillers.[23] Nicola Barfoot assigns Noll's stories, alongside other texts that feature women as murderers rather than detectives, to the "confessions-of-a-justified-murderess trend" (72). The texts emphasize the seemingly banal everyday lives and normalcy of bourgeois women who become serial killers for mundane and often selfish reasons—love, money, jealousy—and yet, as Barfoot points out, "manage to retain the sympathy of many readers" (72). Noll's characters succeed on this front not only because of their psychological complexity, but also because their violent actions emerge against the backdrop of neglect and abuse, which are at least partially attributable to structural injustices arising from sexism and gender disparity.

Due to the common understanding of Noll's narratives as psychological novels, much of the available scholarship on her work—as well as the majority of the reviews in popular media—focuses on the interiority of her characters and does not consider their wider political dimensions.[24] However, with its transnational settings and its sustained discussions of finances, migrations, and unions, *Häupter* lends itself especially well to a reading as a commentary on German unification and the changing face and function of the European Union in the early 1990s. The story highlights boundary-crossing alliances between two German girls from different socioeconomic backgrounds, and among these two younger women and an older working-class Italian couple. I read these national and transnational constellations in *Häupter*, which came out a year after the 1992 signing of the Treaty of Maastricht, as political metaphors reflecting contemporary debates about European integration and in particular the establishment of a common currency in the European Union. Following a close reading of the novel's feminist and queer facets, I shall discuss its function as a political and economic allegory in greater detail.

Häupter differs from the other novels I examine in this and the previous chapters because its queer dimensions are less overt. Unlike Kawaters's *Zora Zobel zieht um* and Kneifl's *Zwischen zwei Nächten*, which explicitly depict sexual desire and love affairs between women, and Biermann's *Potsdamer Ableben*, which features an array of gay and lesbian characters, the queer elements of *Häupter* require more unpacking because, like so many of Noll's nuanced texts, the narrative and its characters are rife with ironies and contradictions. On the surface, the two main characters, Maja and Cora, patently deny any and all potential implications of lesbianism, nonplatonic love, or queer desire, but the underlying dynamics of their relationship and the alternate family they form is likely to strike the discerning reader as rather queer indeed. The bond of friendship that ties Maja and Cora together forms the story's narrative axis, and it consistently occupies the gray area between female homosociality and homoerotic desire. This crime novel does not feature a traditional crime investigation; rather, it is the story of a longtime friendship that becomes stronger and more intimate over the years through the collaborative perpetration of crime. In other words, if one can speak of an *investigation* in this text, then the question it asks is what leads these women to commit murder, and its answers lie in social inequalities and patterns of neglect and abuse, while the interpersonal dynamic that emerges as their antidote perpetuates the shared complicity of the main characters in the commission of further murders.

In a first-person narrative from twentysomething Maja's perspective, *Häupter* recounts the journey of a teenager from a broken and abusive family at the beginning to her young adulthood in a balanced and fulfilling domestic arrangement at the end. Details in the opening passage communicate to the reader that Maja's narrative is unreliable: we learn that mendacity, embellishment, thievery and fantasy are all in a day's work for her, but these transgressions are also immediately justified, through flashbacks to her childhood, as survival mechanisms that evolved in the hostile environment of her family home. The reader has no access to events outside of Maja's dark perception thereof and must therefore rely on her version of the story, which, with its emphasis on everyday injustices she endured as a child, takes on feminist contours. Maja reports that, by the age of ten, she was routinely stealing meaningless objects in search of a way to compensate for the emotional warmth she never felt at home, where she was raised by a selfish and depressive mother who doted on Maja's wicked brother Carlo in the absence of Maja's beloved alcoholic father. But in her sixteenth year, the arrival of a new girl in her school brings about a change of tide: "Erst als ich Cornelia kennenlernte, ging es mit mir bergauf" [Only when I met Cornelia did things improve with me].[25] Maja finds all of the affection, devotion and loyalty that are missing in her home life in her friendship with Cornelia ("Cora") Schwab, who ultimately fulfills the functions of both family member and partner. And though Maja describes this friendship as part of a healing process that brings her emotional fulfillment and helps her overcome pathological tendencies (8), in truth the codependent relationship thrives largely on criminal activity, beginning with petty theft and escalating to murder. Their shared complicity in these crimes brings them closer to one another.

Maja and Cora quickly come to embody a queer feminist model of solidarity, and the foundation for their homosocial bond is male blood. The deaths of the men in their lives, beginning with Maja's brother Carlo, the first victim, mark major turning points in their relationship. The killing of Carlo benefits Maja in two ways, both of which have the effect of bringing her and Cora closer together. On the one hand, because Carlo has a sexual interest in Cora, his demise does away with a competitor for Maja's affections. Carlo's murder has queer implications in that it affirms Maja's jealous desire for her friend's love, while also allowing Maja to play the role of Cora's rescuer, because she shoots Carlo in order to prevent him from raping her friend. Fratricide thus both eliminates the attentions of a potential suitor and redirects Cora's desire onto Maja, who protects her from becoming the victim of a sexually motivated crime. With Carlo out of the picture, Maja can fill his place as the lone object of Cora's fondness. On the other hand, because Maja's suicidal mother is consequently institutionalized due to the depression she suffers at the loss of her son, Carlo's death leaves Maja abandoned and open to an invitation to move in with Cora and become a member of the Schwab family. As in *Zwischen zwei Nächten*, the similarity between the names of two figures Cora and Carlo suggests a likeness; in this case, beyond merely implying an overlap between the characters, it culminates in the overt replacement of Carlo with Cora.[26] As a prospective sibling, Cora has everything that Maja lacks and desires: loving, supportive and sensible parents; a trusting relationship with her brother; and the freedom and financial means to follow her whims. If before Carlo's demise Maja and Cora were "ein Herz und eine Seele" [one heart and one soul, 57], after his death they become even closer, for Cora takes Carlo's place and becomes Maja's quasi-sister in a new biological family model. Though they never officially adopt her, the Schwabs view Maja as one of their own—Frau Schwab refers to Cora and Maja as her "Töchter" [daughters, 90]—and Maja maintains a closer relationship to them over the years than does their own biological daughter.

Noll's representation of an affluent family that takes in a needy "relative" with a troubled past could be an allusion to the 1990 absorption of the financially bankrupt GDR into the Federal Republic, the strongest economy on the European continent at the time.[27] Though the novel's German geographies are explicitly Western—the girls live in Heidelberg and visit relatives in Bonn, Hamburg, and Lübeck—its figures' familial and financial circumstances metaphorically situate them on either side of the cultural boundary between

East and West Germany. Maja's depressive mother pines away for her deceased brother Karl, who lived in the West German capital of Bonn: this reference to the pain of German division suggests the loss of contact with family members during the Cold War and looks ahead to the transition of power from the "deceased" capital of Bonn to a new Federal Republic in Berlin. The representation of Maja's mother as a single working-class parent who works long hours to support her two children recalls the *Doppelbelastung* [double-burden] born by many East German women, who earned income outside the home while also performing the bulk of the domestic chores, including childrearing.[28] Frau Westermann, whose name evokes a longing for a Western standard of living that was unattainable for most citizens of the GDR, works as an *Altenpflegerin* [caretaker for the elderly] and later takes a position as a *Schwesternhelferin* [nurse's aide]; these are precisely the kinds of working-class positions that, in both Germanies, would likely have been occupied by women.[29] The Westermann family lives in a cramped apartment and struggles to make ends meet; for Maja, grocery shopping means paying for less expensive staples and shoplifting the items she cannot afford. By contrast, the upper middle-class Schwab family, whose name references a West German region where the standard of living is relatively high, have a spacious home and enough disposable income—Herr Schwab is a sinology professor and Frau Schwab anticipates an inheritance from her wealthy father—that Frau Schwab travels and shops rather than holding a job, their son studies in the United States, and the entire family regularly vacations in Tuscany. The Schwabs are portrayed as generous and caring, if all too stereotypically bourgeois, and the emotionally abused Maja welcomes their affection and support, so a reading of the family as a metaphor for unified Germany might indicate that Noll sought to emphasize West Germany's magnanimity and worldliness and the advantages of financial and political unity for the destitute former East.[30] This perspective resonates with Patricia Anne Simpson's comment about the sociopolitical changes that unfolded in 1989 and 1990: "In retrospect, the political shouts of euphoria and unity drowned out the more skeptical and suspicious voices in both the East and the West with regard to German unification...."[31] At the same time, because Cora enables Maja's criminality and increasing codependency, one could interpret their enduring relationship as suggesting that the Federal Republic's welfare may have raised the quality of life for its new citizens from the East, but nonetheless encouraged financial dependency, moral decline and idleness in the new federal states.[32] There are clearly material benefits to Maja's membership in the Schwab family: for the first time in her life, she has expensive clothing, eats exotic foods and travels abroad. But her joy in losing the baggage of her own blood relations and joining Cora's family, reminiscent of the widespread public euphoria at the fall of the Wall, soon gives way to a sobering reality. Their blissful cohabitation lasts only a few months: Maja gets pregnant and marries her lover Jonas, and her fantasy of creating a happy family of her own quickly dissolves into marital discontent and an unbearably suffocating housewife routine. Maja's experiences of domestic arrangements based on genetic relations are thus, like her troubled childhood and her failed nuclear family experiment with Jonas, unsatisfying, dysfunctional and destructive.

Instead, the only functional family model is one in which lasting alliances are chosen as opposed to genetically assigned (with the exception of Béla, Maja's biological child); they are built not on blood but on bloodshed, with equal doses of conspiracy and trust. Beginning with Carlo's death and concluding with the demise of Maja's father and the disappearance of her husband, the remnants of Maja's broken biological family yield to a long-lived, queer alternative on Italian soil. Solidifying in the final chapters of *Häupter*, this final constellation affirms Maja and Cora's bond, which surpasses all other human relationships, at the heart of a transnational feminist coalition that also includes three other individuals: Maja's infant son Béla, their Italian housekeeper Emilia, and Emilia's lover Mario. Although the household now contains a significant male-gendered contingent, it is still dominated by women, as control remains primarily in the hands of Cora and Maja, with Emilia as their constant ally; baby Béla is too young to play an active part, and Mario, who is mute, aligns his actions with the women's needs and desires. In accordance with the established pattern that the men who stay or live in the home for any length of time—Cora's husband, brother, lover, as well as Maja's husband and father—either die or disappear (or both), a reader might anticipate that Mario's membership in the family would be short-lived at best. However, Mario's collusion in helping cover up the murders the women perpetrate indicates the likely longevity of this relationship.

The killing of Maja's brother Carlo functions as the original crime that cements the bond between the two girls. Emilia's collaboration with them begins later, with her complicity in two brutal murders in their home: the bludgeoning of Cora's wealthy older husband Henning and the poisoning of her New Zealander lover Don. Together with Carlo, these victims share Cora as lover or object of desire; and while Maja kills both Carlo and Henning with her own hands (the latter at Cora's request), a pattern that suggests a queer motive, neither of the two friends is directly responsible for the death of Don, whom Emilia poisons. A fourth man, Maja's father, also dies right after visiting them: although his demise is not a direct consequence of their actions, Maja and Cora wish to kill him but do not consummate this desire due to Emilia's timely intervention. What these four dead men have in common is that their living presence disturbs the peace in the Maja-Cora household and causes tension that only dissipates with their deaths.[33] Though Maja and Cora are cold-blooded killers and by no means fully sympathetic characters, they still emerge as protagonists; as Helga Arend notes, the reader experiences "lediglich eine gewisse Schadenfreude darüber, dass es dem Ermordeten nur recht geschieht" [simply a certain schadenfreude that the crime serves the murder victim right, 281]. The status of *Häupter*'s leading women as murderesses is both affirmative and feminist because their victims represent exploitative, patriarchal obstacles to their independence and happiness: Carlo tortures Maja emotionally and threatens Cora sexually; Henning's insistence that his wife bear a child for him endangers her precious independence; and Maja's father is a parasite who only comes around when he needs money or wants a drink but withholds from Maja the paternal warmth she craves. The final victim, Don, who initially becomes Cora's lover but then sleeps with Maja too, is particularly problematic because he successfully plays the friends against each other in hopes of profiting financially from their conflict. Each of these men's deaths reasserts the primacy of the Maja-Cora bond, while also fortifying it by bringing Emilia into their confidence through her involvement in the fatalities of Henning, Don, and Maja's father.

Killing men represents one problem the women solve; disposing of the bodies is another. The corpse takes on a life of its own, posing a challenge that they must overcome through teamwork and ingenuity, which brings them even closer together. Arend points out that this is one of the ways in which Noll rewrites genre conventions: "Noll verdreht in gewisser Weise die typische Rezeption des Kriminalromans, da normalerweise auf ein Aufdecken des Mordes und die Bestrafung des Mörders gehofft wird, während man hier mit den Tätern gemeinsam auf ein gutes Versteck für den Toten sinnt" [To a certain extent, Noll twists the typical reception of the crime novel, as one normally hopes for the exposure of the murder and the punishment of the murderer, whereas here one seeks, together with the perpetrators, a good hiding place for the dead person, 281]. This process is ongoing, because even after the corpses are buried or discarded, they do not disappear: the dead men's ghostly and embodied presences haunt the narrative, necessitating repeated reckonings with both their legacies and their flesh. The steps involved in the disposal of Don's body become a saga of their own: the trio first leaves him in the Italian countryside, but later retrieves and entombs the decaying corpse in the concrete base of a luxurious new terrace on Cora's spacious Italian villa. Thus the heterosexual male lover's mortal flesh literally becomes the foundation upon which the women build their domestic bliss. In a symbolic answer to the feminist interdiction, "the master's tools will never dismantle the master's house," Cora and Maja do not dismantle but rather renovate the master's house, using a man's dead body as its basis, into a feminist paradise.[34] It would seem here that the only good man is a dead man, were it not for the involvement of a male accomplice in ultimately dealing with Don's body successfully. This feminist foundation ironically comes to fruition through the labor of man, Emilia's lover Mario, a carpenter who builds the terrace by hand and later receives an invitation to move into the feminized household as Emilia's partner.

The queer family roles in this new constellation are not contingent on biological gender. Although Maja holds an uncontested place as Béla's mother, Cora functions as the father figure. When Béla is kidnapped by Sicilian criminals who believe him to be wealthy Cora's child, Cora generously finances the effort to rescue him, suggesting that this is the natural thing to do because he is family: "Ich betrachte Béla auch als mein Kind" [I see Béla as my child too, 246]. Maja's vision of their relationship is similar and genders Cora's parental role in explicitly masculine terms: "Meine leibliche Familie existiert nicht mehr, dafür habe ich mir eine neue geschaffen: Cora ist der Vater, ich die Mutter, Béla das Kind. Unsere Eltern und Bélas Großeltern sind Emilia und Mario. Wie es ihr in dieser Rolle zukommt, sorgt Cora für das tägliche Brot" [My real family does not exist any more; instead, I have created a new one for myself: Cora is the father, I the mother, Béla the child. Our parents and Béla's grandparents are Emilia and Mario. As can be expected from her in this role, Cora provides the daily bread, 265]. But Cora's masculine side comes to expression not only in her ability to pay the bills and support her family; it is also in her gendered and sexualized attitudes and behaviors:

> Wenn ein Außenstehender Cora beschreiben sollte, dann käme eine sehr weibliche Frauengestalt heraus. Aber sie hat durchaus männliche Seiten: ihre Dominanz und kalte Sexualität. Sie kostet ihre Überlegenheit aus, und wenn ich meine depressiven Anfälle habe, rettet sie mich. Ja, gerade diese Retter-Attitüde macht sie zum Vater in unserem Spiel... [265–66].

> [If someone on the outside were to describe Cora, then a very feminine profile would emerge. But she definitely has her masculine sides: her dominance and cold sexuality. She savors her superiority, and when I have my depressive spells, she rescues me. Yes, it is precisely this rescuer attitude that makes her the father in our game.]

This father role constructs Cora as queerly gendered despite her markedly feminine contours. A look back to Cora's teenage years also provides evidence of her penchant for men's clothing and traditionally masculine-coded responsibilities. When she and Maja begin shoplifting together, Cora prefers neckties to Maja's lipsticks. Cora's place as the breadwinner can also be linked to an early episode in their friendship when Cora teaches Maja the finer points in the art of stealing and makes it possible for Maja to purloin an artifact from a museum (21–22).

From the perspective of an older Maja, now employed as a guide on a Florentine sightseeing bus for German-speaking tourists, the novel conveys

its narrator's apparent wariness and weariness of complete economic dependence on her friend. But Maja's income is modest and covers just a fraction of
her expenses: "ich verdiene durch die Touristen auch ein wenig und kann meine
Kleider selbst bezahlen; aber Versicherungen, Steuer, Heizung, Auto, Lebens-
mittel und Emilias Gehalt werden von Cora bestritten" [I earn a little from
the tourists and can pay for my own clothes; but insurance, taxes, heating, the
car, groceries and Emilia's income are covered by Cora, 265]. Maja can literally
afford only the clothes on her back; for everything else, she relies on Cora's
welfare. As the less affluent and feminized half of the partnership, Maja and
her desire to loosen Cora's control by bringing home her own paycheck call
to mind the struggles faced by former East German citizens, especially women,
after the fall of the Wall.[35] In the wake of the GDR's collapse and unification
with the West, many East Germans who had previously been employed and
supported by the socialist state were left without employment, a safety net, or
access to social welfare services. For her part, as a figurative representation of
the financially stable Federal Republic, Cora maintains control not only over
expenditures, but also over household geography and architecture, dictating
both the forms and functions of domestic spaces. And, like Westerners who
made substantial financial contributions to unification with the *Soli* tax [*Soli-
daritätszuschlag*, solidarity surcharge], Cora invests a large amount of money
in the integrated domestic economy.[36] The costly renovations she undertakes
together with her wealthy husband to update their run-down Italian villa, and
again later to entomb her lover in its terrace, are reminiscent of the extensive
Aufbau Ost [rebuilding the East] project, financed largely by federal reserves
and taxpayers in the former West, in which unified Germany invested in order
to modernize crumbling structures and obsolete infrastructures in the new
federal states.[37] However, unlike the West German politicians and citizens
who resented this economic imbalance and bemoaned the toll it took on the
Federal Republic's former financial stability, Cora takes great pleasure in
bankrolling these expenditures, while also deriving power from Maja's dependency.

The female friends are aware of the potential queerness of their codependent relationship, and both girls disavow lesbian identity, but they articulate this denial in ways that still leave open the possibility of same-sex desire.
When a disappointed Carlo seeks an explanation for Cora's rejection, he asks
Maja if she and Cora are perhaps lesbians. Instead of responding directly to
Carlo's question, Maja lashes out by emptying a full ashtray on him, an angry
reaction suggesting that Carlo has touched on a sensitive point. Although the
first-person narrator negates lesbian identity, she also notes that her affection
for Cora and her own schoolgirl crushes on men like her geography teacher
are mutually exclusive, suggesting that these are competing desires (63). Cora

also denies identification with lesbianism in a queerly ambiguous manner. In response to Maja's claim that Cora has never been in love, she says: "Kluges Kind. Vielleicht bin ich nicht wie du. Eigentlich finde ich Frauen viel liebenswerter als Männer, andererseits habe ich leider keine lesbische Ader" [Smart kid. Maybe I'm not like you. I actually find women much more lovable than men, but alas, I have no lesbian blood, 169]. As if she were teaching her a lesson, Cora infantilizes Maja and sets her apart from those (grown) women who are, at least in theory, valid love objects. Cora thus affirms the desirability of the female sex. Like Maja, she explicitly distances herself from homosexuality while simultaneously communicating a more ambiguous relationship to same-sex desire. On one hand, the friends negate any association with the word *lesbian*: Maja asserts that she and Cora are "nicht lesbisch" [not lesbian, 63] and Cora stresses that she has "no lesbian blood." But on the other hand, there is something implicitly queer about an attraction that is "nicht normal" [not normal, 63] and whose object, the female sex, is more attractive than men. By naming and yet negating lesbianism, Maja and Cora's articulations of sexuality shift the focus from identity to desire, affirming a queer homosocial desire for one another (Maja) or for women in general (Cora) that is vested with emotional intensity. There are numerous indications that Maja experiences this desire and devotion more passionately than does her friend—she declares, "es gab kaum etwas, das ich ihr abgeschlagen hätte" [there was practically nothing that I would have denied her, 173]. Maja's refusal to say no to Cora is indicative of codependency and positions her as the submissive and feminized counterpart to Cora's masculinized dominance. This same-sex desire can be mapped at an overlapping point on the continuum between homosocial and homosexual because it refuses to be pinned down as exclusively homoerotic and remains open to the desire for heterosexual objects as well.[38]

As Gayatri Gopinath argues in *Impossible Desires*, female homoeroticism can take on even more telling forms in the absence of characters explicitly identified as lesbians.[39] Relying on the theoretical foundation laid by Eve Kosofsky Sedgwick in *Between Men*, Gopinath demonstrates that erotic triangles often organize same-sex desire between two subjects through a heterosexual proxy.[40] This also happens in *Häupter*: even though no bona fide lesbians appear, same-sex desire is constructed and affirmed indirectly in Maja and Cora's triangular relationships to other men. Each woman becomes involved with the other woman's brother (Cora flirts with Carlo, though it is unclear whether they have sex; and Maja has a passionate affair with Cora's brother Friedrich), and they sleep with two of the same men: Cora's lover Don and Maja's husband Jonas. In fact, the most positive form of expression that this desire takes is in its articulation as mutual sexual attraction to and jealousy over a third person, who serves as a proxy figure to mediate sexual tension between the two women. A triangular structure of homosocial desire also materializes in Maja and Cora's parental relationships to Béla, but their romantic and sexual relationships to their lovers provide even more explicit implications thereof. The first iteration takes shape through Cora's husband Henning, who treats Maja as if she were his second wife and Béla as his own child. But even though he once mistakes Maja for his own wife and, another time, makes both women get dolled up and go out with him "an jeder Seite als schmückendes Beiwerk" [on either side as decorative attachments, 160], Henning does not function as a mutual object of desire, as neither woman is very fond of him. However, the triangular relationship he creates by wanting them both in close proximity to him establishes a pattern that repeats itself, with variations, in other relationships with male partners.

Maja and Cora's affairs with Don and Jonas, the two men they share, provide stronger evidence of queer mediation. With the introduction of the character Don, a hitchhiking tourist whom Cora takes in as her lover, Maja experiences curious emotions: she narrates that the first sight of a tender gesture between Don and Cora "in mir zum ersten Mal ein neues und zugleich uraltes Gefühl erweckte: Eifersucht" [awoke within me for the first time a new and at the same time age-old feeling: jealousy, 191]. It remains ambiguous, however, which person is the object of Maja's emotion: is she jealous of Cora or Don? Unsure of her own intentions, Maja asks herself: "Was war eigentlich mit mir los? Gefiel mir dieser Kerl wirklich?" [What was really going with me? Did I really like this guy? 193]. She attempts to make sense of her feelings by acknowledging that Don resembles her husband Jonas, but her emotional reactions do not involve Don alone; Cora is also the subject of angry and sentimental narrative commentary. Such ambiguity points to the possibility that Don functions not as an outright object of desire but rather as a queer proxy onto which Maja can deflect unacknowledged or unfulfilled desires for intimacy with Cora. Don's penetration into their household forces Maja to consciously evaluate her relationship to Cora: "Auch über Cora dachte ich nach, was ich selten tat. Sie war für mich eine Selbstverständlichkeit und lebensnotwendig, aber sie war auch der beunruhigendste Mensch, den ich kannte" [I even though about Cora, which I seldom did. She was for me a matter of course and indispensable, but she was also the most unsettling person I knew, 194–95]. Maja's acknowledgment of her reliance on Cora, coupled with the concession that her friend has superlatively disruptive potential, suggests an excess of desire. That which unsettles Maja about Cora likely has less to do with Cora than it does with Maja's projection of her own feelings for her friend, which cause her discomfort or anxiety. These feelings repeatedly come to expression, albeit indirectly, appearing, for instance, as an obsession not with Cora herself but rather with her level of intimacy with Don. When Cora, who had, since the death of her husband Henning, allowed Maja to occupy her marital bed, suddenly moves Maja's belongings into another room, Maja foresees Don taking her place: "Also hatte sie vor, ihr Doppelbett mit Don zu teilen" [So she did intend to share her double bed with Don, 194]. And when Maja later notices Don slumbering unclothed in Cora's atelier, she wonders, "Hatten sie nun oder hatten sie nicht?" [Had they or hadn't they? 195]. While Maja's curiosity about Cora's physical proximity to Don could simply convey jealousy over conquering this attractive new man, the intensity of Maja's reaction and her obsession with Cora's relationship to him provide strong indications that she desires more than just Don: she is saddened and confused by the displacement of her unique intimacy with Cora.

The love triangle is consummated when Maja spends a passionate night with Don, a configuration that finds repetition when Cora later seduces Maja's estranged husband Jonas. The morning after Don goes to bed with Maja, Cora catches them together, a scenario that is reiterated with a twist, when Maja finds Jonas in Cora's bed. Both scenes dramatize an exchange of gazes that places the betrayed woman (first Cora, then Maja) at the margins beholding the postcoital nudity of her friend and lover (203, 270–71). However, instead of driving them apart, this queer postcoital gaze serves in each scenario to bring the gazing woman outside and the nude woman inside the bedroom closer and to precipitate the death (Don) or departure (Jonas) of the male lover, ultimately leaving the women alone together (again). Don's seduction of Maja leads directly to his demise: sensing that Don's presence is eroding the women's domestic harmony, Emilia kills him in order to protect the primacy of the female bond in the household. With its final iteration, the erotic triangulation includes a further step, the fantasy of a threesome. Maja imagines herself joining Cora and Jonas:

> Ich konnte mich morgen früh zu den beiden ins Bett legen, entweder im durchsichtigen Hemd oder besser noch als nackte Maja. "Liebe Cora, du wolltest mich à la Goya malen! Lieber Jonas, hier bin ich, deine erwartungsvolle Frau..."
> Mein frommer Mann würde sterben vor Scham, Cora würde lachen [273, ellipsis in original].
>
> [Tomorrow morning I could get into bed with them, either in a translucent top or, better yet, as the naked Maja. "Dear Cora, you wanted to paint me à la Goya! Dear Jonas, here I am, your hopeful wife..."
> My pious husband would die of shame; Cora would laugh.]

This image interrupts a passage that is otherwise filled with violent and bloody fantasies of vengeance, a contrast that highlights its potential significance. What is particularly noteworthy about Maja's daydream is that, while her imagined dialogue suggests that she would offer herself to Cora and Jonas in order to please them both, their hypothetical reactions demonstrate that only Cora would take pleasure from the intrusion. By placing Cora's desires before Jonas's and then concluding with Cora's amusement, Maja's reverie privileges Cora's gratification over her own and suggests that it would be the intended goal of a ménage à trois.

This fantasy vision dissipates into a reality that once again does away with the man and reframes the women in an intimate configuration. Maja's relatively mild vengeful act—emptying Cora's expensive toiletry bottles all over the bathroom—causes the two friends to both slip and fall, landing them side by side in the hospital. The iterations of Maja and Cora's triangular relationships with male lovers culminate in a homosocial image of collective suffering and ultimate harmony: "Im Krankenzimmer lagen wir Bett an Bett und stöhnten uns an" [In the hospital room we laid bed to bed and moaned at one another, 276]. The scene recalls Maja's threesome fantasy by placing them quite literally in adjacent beds at the same time and in a shared room. Moreover, the scene playfully evokes sexual connotations in the nonverbal sounds of the girls' moans, which they direct toward one another. This denouement of the love triangle reaffirms the primacy of the homosocial bond between the two women in a way that carries distinct homoerotic undertones.

If Maja's narrative is to be trusted on this count, the reader is left at the end to believe that she and Cora renounce love triangles for good. When Emilia announces her intention to move in with Mario, Cora invites Mario to cohabitate with them in the spacious villa, which comes as no big surprise, as he has already become an honorary member of the family by helping hide Don's body and rescue a kidnapped Béla. Before accepting the invitation, Emilia stipulates their conditions for cohabitation: the girls must promise never again to sleep with the same man. Affirming Gopinath's claim that "female homoerotic desire and pleasure are often mediated by and routed through heterosexuality as well as class and generational difference" (109), this ending explicitly sets boundaries for the expression of Maja and Cora's same-sex desires while it implicitly predicates the women's domestic arrangement on heterosexual exclusivity, for their own part as well as on behalf of their parental figures, Emilia and Mario. In a visual representation of this new configuration, Maja and Cora collaborate to draw hearts and a cupid figure, together with the names Mario and Emilia, on Cora's cast. This drawing signals that Emilia and Mario have come to embody the fulfillment of the young women's queer desires, offering a route for Cora and Maja to channel their mutual affections. Instead of stealing one another's male lovers and partners, Cora and Maja can now express their love for each other via the newly approved and presumably unthreatening proxy of another heterosexual couple.

The final domestic arrangement, comprised of European citizens of three generations, is also highly symbolic at the level of national and transnational

identity. By 1993, when *Häupter* appeared, Italian and German transnational
economic collaboration was almost half a century old: Italy and West Germany
were among the six founding member states of the European Coal and Steel
Community, a precursor of the European Union created with a 1951 agreement, and the two nations were further linked through postwar West German
labor policies and tourism to Southern Europe. The year 1993 saw the enact-
ment of the conditions agreed upon in the Treaty of Maastricht, a process that
was accompanied by feverish debates among member states of the European
Community regarding membership criteria; a particular sticking point in these
discussions was the amount of permissible fluctuation for national currencies
prior to unification.[41] As a product of this era, the narrative of *Häupter* evinces
a veritable fixation on money, which comes to expression through frequent
references to income, property, theft, inheritance, and blackmail. The novel's
critical negotiations of financial and economic metaphors should not come
as a surprise in a decade that witnessed two economic and monetary unions:
the 1990 unification of East German Mark with its West German counterpart,
and the 1992 agreement on plans for a common European Union currency,
formally introduced in 1999 and completed in 2002. These mergers come to
life in *Häupter*'s domestic coalitions: while Maja and Cora embody German
unification, their cohabitation with Emilia and Mario represents the European
Union. As symbolic German and European federations, Noll's family constellations communicate anxieties about and hopes for unified Germany's role in
the transnational European community.[42]

The interplay among capital, assets, and labor in *Häupter* takes on allegorical forms, critiquing the relationships between the European Union and
its member states. Noll's novel constructs the material foundation for the new
European family as indisputably German: Cora's inheritance, which includes
the Italian villa, is the condition of possibility for the well-being of the family
and the independence and freedom of its members. Cora's lifelong financial
stability, first as a Schwab and then as Henning's wealthy wife and widow,
metaphorically conveys the substantial benefits of German financial hegemony
both prior to and during European unification. Like the robust currency of
the Deutsche Mark and the influential institution of the Bundesbank [Federal
Bank], which became paradigms of resilience and solidity on the European
continent throughout the 1980s, Cora is cautious and resourceful, prudently
controlling household finances with an austerity politic.[43] Maja eventually
seeks employment outside of the home not because Cora obliges her to contribute to the household economy—on the contrary, she repeatedly emphasizes
that her riches are Maja's too—but rather because she fears the potential consequences of complete dependency.[44] Indeed, many if not all economic and
marital unions entail unequal distributions of wealth and power; in Noll's

crime novel, as with the European Union, the greater stability of the whole relies on the stability of its strongest members, which carry the responsibility of subsidizing the smaller member economies embodied by Maja and Béla, and Emilia and Mario, who come from more modest working-class backgrounds. The day-to-day operation of the household enterprise requires not only capital, but also domestic and manual labor, provided here by the Italian contingent: housekeeper Emilia shops, cooks, and cares for the baby, while handyman Mario gardens, renovates, and does carpentry work and odd jobs. Though Emilia and Mario's contributions are substantial and essential, and they actively negotiate the terms of their membership in the domestic community, their labor and even their very presence come about as assets that are bought and sold. Emilia initially joins the family as the villa's "lebendes Inventar" [living inventory, 133]: though this reduces her to the status of a possession—she is purchased as part of the estate—it also gives her the unique right of permanent residency. Emilia is no temporary, marginalized *Gastarbeiter* [guest worker]; she is a resident with inalienable rights who gains in influence and power throughout the course of the novel. The ethnic and economic facets of this relationship—German prosperity and an Italian work force—might be reminiscent of the *Gastarbeiter* phenomenon, but Noll's novelistic version of this collaboration vests the Italian laborers with more agency than migrant workers would have had, even in the postwar era of the *Wirtschaftswunder* [economic miracle] when their labor was necessary for domestic growth. Here, moreover, the migration follows a different path, in line with the typical vacation trajectory of Germans who go on holiday in the sunnier Southern European countries of Italy and Spain. The novel's Germans characters seek the capitalist dream in Italy, an irony that Henning jokingly references when he calls Maja and her husband and son "die Asylantenfamilie" [the asylum family, 155]. We can view Henning and Cora—and perhaps Maja too—as late twentieth-century colonizers who capitalize on economic opportunity abroad.

As the new head of this transnational household, Cora invests in Italian assets that yield over time. She purchases loyalty and the promise of a future together from the Italian housekeeper: in exchange for her silence and later conspiracy in murder, Cora buys Emilia a dog, clothing, and driving lessons; as a final investment in Emilia's membership in the household, she even purchases Mario's companionship. Under the pretense of needing a gardener, Cora hires Mario in hopes that he might become Emilia's lover; he thus enters this domestic sphere as another incidental asset that becomes increasingly valuable. Like Emilia, Mario turns out to be a wise investment, one that greatly benefits all members of the enterprise. Are these representations critical or celebratory, or perhaps even optimistic? Does Noll's novel imply that the EU is nothing more than a German purchase of material European assets, a long-term investment from which it might later profit? Though the transnational alliance in *Häupter* seemingly offers obvious benefits to all of its members, the narrative comes from a distinctly Germanocentric perspective; this is then less a positive representation than it is a sarcastic commentary on the dynamics of migration and labor.

Transnational migrations also present financial challenges, both for travelers and for locals who earn a living in the tourist industry. The novel's opening passage begins with a simple anecdote about the difficulty of calculating the high numbers of Italian lire in conversions and the obstacles it poses; as a tour guide, Maja compensates for the resulting small tips she receives by convincing her tourists to donate to a phony cause and pocketing the money (7). Illustrating how both tourists and the workers whose livelihood depends on them stand to lose from currency conversions, this scenario suggests that a single European currency has clear advantages. At the same time, the problematic role that the calculation of lire plays for these characters metaphorically recalls the instability of the lira and its potential implications for the European market, especially in view of the rapid fluctuation of Italian currency in the early 1990s.[45] But while the novelistic figures ultimately hurt only themselves with their miscalculations, the collapse of an entire currency has devastating consequences beyond a nation's borders. Concerns about the strength of the Italian economy still reverberate two decades after the publication of *Häupter*, and twenty-first-century readers of Noll's novel have the opportunity to interpret its portrayal of money as an eerie foreshadowing of the challenges that the European Union has faced in the wake of the global financial crisis of 2008 and the ensuing European sovereign debt crisis. Though the crisis became especially acute in other Southern European countries in the 2010s, it also affected Italy to such an extent that it appealed to the euro zone for aid.

Within the novel's Italy, Sicily embodies a further economic threat to travelers. The jobless and indebted Sicilian kidnappers of Maja's son, a likely reference to the high rates of unemployment and bankruptcy on the island, justify their crime as a means of earning vital income (251). Though the kidnappers in the novel act alone and are not linked to any larger criminal organization, the parallels to Mafia corruption are clear, as are the obstacles they pose to maintaining social order and European financial stability. The kidnapping scenario posits a hierarchy of crime: it may be defensible, in the logic of the novel, to kill a sexually abusive suitor, an annoying husband, or a blackmailing lover, "aber Kinder klauen geht zu weit" [but stealing children is taking it too far, 262]. It also raises the specter of human trafficking, which some authorities feared would increase with the free movement of people and goods in the EU, as particularly problematic. Cora's fear of reporting the kidnapping to the potentially corrupt Sicilian police conveys anxieties about Italy's coop-

eration with EU policies on human rights and the rule of law, and thus calls
into question the sunny nation's capacity to protect the rights of its residents
and visitors. When Béla is rescued by Emilia's detective work and a family
reconnaissance mission before the ransom money changes hands, the group's
unity in combating a human trafficking crime not only succeeds in saving a
life, but also represents a financial recovery.[46] The kidnapping episode finds a
happy end with an economic metaphor: "'Jetzt haben wir aber viel Geld ges-
part,' sagte Cora, 'wir sollten uns etwas Gutes gönnen'" ["We just saved a lot
of money," said Cora, "we should buy ourselves something good," 264]. This
conclusion celebrates the freeing of assets from a financially and morally bankrupt cause and reallocates them to reward the transnational queer family for
successful collaborative work.

Beyond its roles as longtime partner in the European common market
and as supplier of migrant labor for the postwar German economy, Italy has
also, since the economic miracle years of the 1950s and 1960s, held a special
position in the West German imagination as a vacation paradise.[47] In Noll's
novel, too, Italy represents a panacea for the troubled German soul: Maja's
first trip abroad, which takes her to Tuscany, entails a liberation from the financial and cultural limitations of her working-class childhood; and later, relo-
cating to cosmopolitan Florence is a stimulating alternative to her provincial
existence as a farmer's wife and homemaker. Maja rationalizes her self-imposed
exile as a centuries-old Germanic tradition: "Selbst Goethe ist vor Frau von
Stein nach Italien geflohen" [Even Goethe fled Mrs. von Stein to go to Italy,
151].[48] The novel thus takes up the long-standing trope of cooler Northern
Europe as the embodiment of aloofness and alienation, while the warm and
sunny South offers a culturally enriching experience and symbolizes physical
and emotional health and opportunity.[49] Even as they leave the Teutonic homeland behind, however, the women in Noll's text exhibit a remarkable tendency
to take lovers with German ancestry instead of falling for Italian men. While
Maja has her most passionate encounters with men she meets in Italy, both
Jonas and Friedrich are German and only stay in Florence temporarily. Even
Don, who identifies himself as New Zealander, turns out to be half–German;
he lies about his heritage so that he can gather ammunition to blackmail Maja
and Cora from private conversations in their mother tongue, which they
believe he cannot understand. Indeed, few Italian men receive repeated mention in the text at all, aside from the fatherly Mario, who is not romantically
attached to Cora or Maja, and one fleeting romantic interest, Ruggero, a carpenter with whom Cora has a brief affair. Italy may well be exoticized, represented as the land of sea, sex, sun, and most importantly, opportunity, but
neither are its male citizens eroticized, nor do they pose a specifically gendered
threat.[50] On the contrary, it is the women and their homosocial relationships

and alliances that are of greatest significance; men only matter to the extent that they personify obstacles to the women's cohabitation and control over their space, or, in the case of Mario, as potential collaborators. Indeed, aside from the menacing embodiments of German men in Italy and unemployed men in Sicily, Italy is constructed as an ideal site for female expatriates to find self-fulfillment and to establish a sphere of control outside the parameters of male-dominated structures or patriarchal roles.[51]

Literally and symbolically, the multilingual, multiethnic family in *Die Häupter meiner Lieben* is an example of successful transnational migration and cooperation. Maja, who is first introduced in her tour bus, wearing the colors of the Italian flag and giving her German-speaking guests a primer on Italian culture, epitomizes the opportunities available to workers with intercultural competence on the global market. Similarly, Emilia's successful integration into the queer Maja-Cora family is made possible by language skills—she understands Italian, German, and English—and she transmits her knowledge to future generations by teaching Maja Italian and helping her raise Béla bilingually. Transnationalism, multilingualism, and multiculturalism are likely also the source of the family's material well-being, Henning's riches: the German-Brazilian entrepreneur began his career with a move from Hamburg to Rio, where he started his business.

In the final chapter, Noll makes reference to "12 Miniatursäulen" [twelve miniature pillars, 279], a symbolic portrayal of the European Union, which had twelve member states in 1993 when *Häupter* went to press. These pillars evoke the EU on another level too, by recalling the three-pillar model of European cooperation established with the 1992 Treaty of Maastricht.[52] In the text, the twelve posts have structural significance because they hold together a shelf for Maja's souvenir collection by forming a base for glass display plates, "die auf den flach abschließenden Marmorsäulen sicher ruhen" [that rest safely, flush against the marble pillars, 279]. The figurative EU pillars thus preserve the past while providing a firm foundation for the future expansion of Maja's collection to include new "Schätze" [treasures, 279]. The novel's conclusion with metaphors of collecting and familial unity suggest an understanding of the European Union as a whole that is greater than its parts, an expanding community that values the treasured contributions of its member countries and offers them strength and security.

The novel's leitmotif, color, also comes into play at its conclusion to convey an optimistic outlook for transnational Germany. Each of the seventeen chapters carries a color in its title that is doubly meaningful, referencing both a symbolic object and a stage in the narrative. For example, "Elefantengrau" [Elephant Gray] is an amalgamation of Maja's childhood nickname and the drab cloak she wears during her miserable adolescence; and "Rot wie Blut"

[Red Like Blood] alludes to Maja's adoration of her father, who works for a blood bank, and whose anguished, red-spattered paintings are clues of his murderous past. Among the colors and ranges of connotations Noll accentuates, many of the hues are meaningful at the level of nation, race, and ethnicity: in addition to the aforementioned red and grey, these include pearl, pink, and green. I read these as yet another layer of commentary referring to Germany and to its past and future in the European Union. The final chapter, which celebrates the color "Perlmutt" [Mother-of-Pearl], plays a special role in this constellation by signifying diversity and unity: Maja explains that it is her favorite because "alle Farben sind in Perlmutt enthalten, die ganze Skala des Regenbogens" [all colors are included in mother-of-pearl, the entire scale of the rainbow, 278]. Mother-of-pearl becomes emblematic for the transcendence of singularity and the integration of individual colors into a larger whole: "Diese Vielfalt kommt mir wie ein Symbol für die Reichhaltigkeit des Lebens vor" [This diversity strikes me as a symbol for the richness of life, 279]. This recalls discourses heralding multiculturalism in Germany, a galvanizing catchword in the early post-unification era of the 1990s, in response to rising rates of right-wing violence. Multiculturalism comes up in the text's allusion to Muslim burial practices, which are said to include the use of shells (279). As a signifier of transethnic unity, mother-of-pearl contrasts with the racialized hue that dominates an earlier chapter, "Inkarnat" [Flesh Color], the pinkish tone Cora uses to render Don's portrait before his skin pales from poisoning. Other colors representing familial traumas of the past—such as the trichromatic palette Maja's father uses for painting (red, black, and white) and the secondhand grey cloak Maja's mother forces her to wear—become significant at the level of nation too, evoking the Nazi flag and the single-party socialist state of the GDR. When mother-of-pearl ultimately supersedes colors evoking historical crises and totalitarian regimes, the novel suggests that diversity and transnational unions are key to overcoming past traumas and to redefining the German nation. The closing passage of *Die Häupter meiner Lieben*, which portrays Maja, with son Béla in tow, leaving her father's grave and hoping to forgive her parents, reads as a commentary on the relationship between past and future. As Simpson notes, in post-unification literature, "some aspects of German normality rely on a kind of forgetting, underwritten by the aesthetics of the moment" (78). In Noll's novel, this "aesthetics of the moment" is a release that takes colorful forms, like in the multicolored shell Maja leaves on her father's grave. The final hue to appear in the text, the light green of the foliage in a garden on Maja's route home from the cemetery (280), suggests a brighter future: it emerges as that optimism and release that might follow death, a sensual signifier of fertility and rebirth, freedom and safety, and hope.

In the early 1990s, the representation of two women on a crime spree in *Thelma & Louise* made waves by feminizing the formerly male-dominated genres of the road movie and the buddy film. Noll's *Die Häupter meiner Lieben* follows in the footsteps of its cinematic predecessor in embodying mobility in female characters who challenge gendered notions of domesticity and commitment, violence and pleasure, and economic control and dependence. Like Ridley Scott's award-winning film, Noll's novel critically engages generic traditions by drawing on various conventions, including crime fiction, the psychological novel, and the *Familienroman* [family novel], to formulate its perspectives on murder, marriage, and the family, which provide unique insights into the forms, fictions, and fantasies of female agency. I propose that we allow the categorization of *Thelma & Louise* as a road film to inspire us to view *Häupter* as a road story too, specifically as a historical allegory about the journeys toward German unification and European integration. In the early post-unification era, critics and scholars feverishly anticipated the appearance of the elusive *Wenderoman* [unification novel], the definitive novel about the fall of the Wall and German unification. While I suggest that Noll's crime story can be read as a unification novel, it should come as no surprise that it has not yet been identified as such and is infrequently, if at all, compared to the likes of other contenders by East German writers such as Thomas Brussig, Volker Braun, Reinhard Jirgl, and Christa Wolf, or socially critical texts by the West Germans Günter Grass and Thomas Hettche. As a West German woman who writes in a crime genre that appeals to a primarily female readership, Noll is perhaps an unlikely suspect for authorship of the *Wenderoman*. Weightier factors, however, are the temporal and geographical settings in *Häupter*, because even though the narrative contains many of what Katharina Gerstenberger identifies as "the plot elements common to most *Wende*-novels: unemployment, disorientation, decline of personal relationships, and vulnerability to crime,"[53] it is lacking one defining aspect of the genre: overt references to unification itself. The transitions *Häupter* narrates are metaphorical rather than literal allusions to the historical *Wende* [unification], and these doubly allegorical representations extend beyond the borders of the German nation to embrace revisions of individual and familial identities in a second *Wende* [turning point], the process of European integration. Noll's queer transnational protagonists actively negotiate their positions and alliances in the new Europe and ultimately emerge as successfully integrated transnational citizens. Rather than defiantly ensuring their own annihilation like Thelma and Louise, Maja and Cora build lasting, boundary-crossing coalitions and look ahead to the future of the global nation.

Conclusion: Reading the Criminal

The character of the murderous woman as an embodiment of cultural critique figures prominently in German-language literature of the twentieth century. In a wide range of works from canonical Weimar writers like Alfred Döblin to recent *Frauenkrimi* authors Sabine Deitmer and Thea Dorn, narratives about women killing men actively intervene into contemporary discourses about femininity, marriage, family, and the political stakes of women's professional and sexual lives. Such texts often thematize violence against women—in overt as well as more subtle forms—as the underlying cause for the emergence of the female perpetrator: she kills to avenge transgressions committed by men against her or her loved ones. When women take violence into their own hands, these interventions confront everyday imbalances of power, control, and influence in heterosexual relationships and male-dominated institutions. In the texts discussed here, men's incursions into feminized spheres of control and influence are more often figurative, imagined, and hypothetical than really existing within the diegesis, while the female perspectives from which these events are narrated are unreliable at best. Nonetheless, the fantasies of female vigilantism and collusion they narrate open up possibilities for mitigating cycles of violence and abuse and offer celebratory visions of women's friendships and partnerships.

The texts discussed in this chapter approach this critique through the dual themes of same-sex intimacy and transnational migrations. Kneifl and Noll's psychological thrillers from the early 1990s investigate lifelong female friendships and uncover the secrets, desires, and traumas hidden behind the facades of ordinary couples and families. These works rely heavily on metaphors of space and geography to convey their cultural critiques: institutions like architectural firms, and architectural structures such as balconies, terraces, apartments, and villas carry great symbolic weight in transmitting commentaries on the multiple connections among ethnicity, nation, mobility, and cultural politics. While Kneifl's *Zwischen zwei Nächten* employs the trope of transatlantic travel to expose the devastating consequences of Viennese provincialism and bourgeois closed-mindedness, Noll's *Die Häupter meiner Lieben* explores the opportunities and collaborations made possible by German unification and the opening of borders in the European Union. Both texts imagine German-speaking women establishing their independency and finding self-fulfillment outside the boundaries of present-day Austria and Germany.

In his analysis of the mafia family narrative as emblematic for the crime genre, Cawelti contends that "contemporary crime literature feeds upon the image of a hidden criminal organization, so closely knit that even to reveal its existence is certain death for the informer" (64). Indeed, Kneifl and Noll's stories take the representation of a familial crime organization that is closely knit to the extreme: a boundary-crossing same-sex relationship between two women so intimate that Kneifl's reader cannot determine with certainty whether the two characters are one and the same person, and Noll's reader cannot be sure where platonic friendship ends and queer desire begins. There is something profoundly troubling—and fascinating—about women so loyal and devoted to one another that they will kill to protect their relationship and to avenge violence done to their loved ones. As Cawelti points out, crime literature "expresses a deep uncertainty about the adequacy of our traditional social institutions to meet the needs of individuals for security, for justice, for a sense of significance" (79). That these novels by Kneifl and Noll, unlike Döblin's *Die beiden Freundinnen,* conclude with scenarios of liberation and hope suggests that the era in which they were produced witnessed a growing belief in the possibility of change beyond the otherwise pervasive pessimism in crime fiction regarding the interface between social institutions and individual agency. Ultimately, the reader is likely to celebrate the lack of legal repercussions for Noll and Kneifl's queer female murderers and to read their successes as victories of feminist coalitional justice. These texts from the early 1990s attest to the increased representation of powerful women and queer figures as agents of the tremendous social changes that continued to unfold throughout the last decade of the twentieth century.

CHAPTER 3

When a Woman Loves a Man: The Politics of Desire in Romance and Crime Fiction

Meiner Meinung nach sollten die Frauen in die Weltpolitik und die Heteromänner schwul werden. Das wär der einzige Weg, diese Welt zu retten...

—Ralf König, *Der bewegte Mann*[1]

[In my opinion, women should go into world politics and straight men should become gay. That would be the only way to save this world...]

"Can a man be too desirable for his own good?"[2] This tagline on the North American release of Sönke Wortmann's blockbuster hit *Der bewegte Mann* [*Maybe ... Maybe Not*, 1994], one of the most successful German films of the 1990s, introduces its main theme as a crisis of attraction. The film, like the books it is based on—Ralf König's 1987 graphic novel by the same name and its sequel *Pretty Baby* [*Maybe ... Maybe Not Again!* 1988]—foregrounds the politics of sexual desire: the main character, a gay man, falls for a macho heterosexual male whose sexuality may or may not be in flux.[3] The story highlights the processes of reading, interpreting, and reacting to sexual identity, posing questions about the social implications of misreading desire. How do representations of sexual desires, practices, and positionalities constitute political interventions? Taking up contemporary discourses about the politics of sexuality, both the original graphic novels and the filmic adaptation of *Der bewegte Mann* gained cult status in an era that saw increasing social acceptance of diverse sexual desires and practices and the passing of legislation to recognize homosexuals, protect gays rights, and decriminalize homosexuality.[4] Like other texts of its time, *Der bewegte Mann* invited readers and spectators alike to draw connections among the increasing visibility of gays and lesbians in mainstream media and popular culture; the status of feminist and queer rights movements in Germany and abroad; and the fall of the Wall, European integration, and the liberalization of politics in the unified Federal Republic of Germany. For instance, the first romantic same-sex kisses on prime-time television, which appeared on the soap opera *Lindenstraße* [Linden Street] in 1987 and 1990,[5] bookended parliamentary debates over the most appropriate terminology for identifying gays and lesbians in official governmental records.[6] As several *Bundesländer* [federal states] passed anti-discrimination laws protecting homosexuals[7] and the German gay marriage movement gathered momentum in the early 1990s, media firestorms flared over the outing of public figures such as Cornelia Scheel, Hella von Sinnen, Hape Kerkeling, and Alfred Biolek.[8] Similarly, the discussion elicited by the coverage of a 1994 Ikea commercial featuring two men shopping for furniture together[9] coincided with a landmark victory for the gay rights movement: the last remnants of Paragraph 175, a century-old Prussian law illegalizing homosexuality, were struck from the post-unification German legal code. These examples attest to the many correlations among popular culture, politics, and social change.

Der bewegte Mann was not alone in reflecting these evolving politics of identity and desire. The immense successes of König's graphic novels and Wortmann's film were part of a wider trend involving shifting discourses of gender and sexuality in the final decades of the twentieth century. These issues also found their way into other popular cultural texts of the era, including crime fiction, where they resonate deeply with a genre that stresses questions of identification and identity. This chapter reads three queer detective stories from the 1990s—Gabriele Gelien's *Eine Lesbe macht noch keinen Sommer* [One Lesbian Does Not Make a Summer, 1993], Christine Lehmann's *Training mit dem Tod* [Working Out with Death, 1998], and Martina-Marie Liertz's *Die Geheimnisse der Frauen* [The Secrets of Women, 1999]—as commentaries on contemporary politics of gender and sexuality. These three mysteries feature female-embodied protagonists who identify as lesbian or bisexual, and they share with König's comic and Wortmann's relationship comedy a preoccupation with masculinity and especially with the destabilizing potential of male objects of desire. Like *Der bewegte Mann*, detective fiction by Gelien, Lehmann, and Liertz shakes up notions of sexual identity, but it does so by portraying queer female investigators who desire, fantasize about, or fall in love with men. In the contexts of crime narratives, these attractions become intertwined with other intrigues that must be resolved before the narrative ends. Each mystery couples the closure of the crime investigation with closure on the question of the desired man's identity, revealing the male love object's own queerly gendered or sexualized positionality. These discoveries work to reaffirm the investigators' queer desires and to advocate for the recognition and rights of LGBT populations.

Gelien, Lehmann, and Liertz explore the implications for feminist, lesbian, and transgendered politics when a self-identified queer woman becomes the subject of romantic or erotic desires for a male object. Gelien's and Liertz's heroines describe themselves as lesbian, while Lehmann's amateur detective is bisexual with a preference for women, but all three queer protagonists enter into ostensibly heterosexual relationships with men. The female main characters are first-person narrators who undertake two intertwined investigations, attempting to decode the enigmatic men they desire as they solve crimes. The male love objects are intimately involved in the crime intrigues but play different roles in the investigations: they are victims, witnesses, suspects, and co-investigators; and they take on multiple such roles as the stories develop. Each of the texts offers a unique solution to the question of the attractive man's identity: the man in Gelien's novel is homosexual and the love object in Lehmann's mystery is a transgendered male, while the masculine character in Liertz's story is a cross-dressed woman. The framing and resolution of these riddles convey critical commentaries on the social significance of heterosexual and queer romance and eroticism. Through the shifting positionalities of their female and male characters, the books intervene into contemporary debates about gender and sexuality in the 1990s, confronting issues from sexism, heterosexual privilege, and homophobia; to gay marriage, transsexual rights, and the politics of gender reassignment.

Feminist crime fiction scholars such as Gill Plain assert that the depiction of queer characters and desires is a political gesture in and of itself, especially in the traditionally male-dominated genre of crime fiction.[10] Gelien, Lehmann, and Liertz take additional steps toward politicizing their narratives by mobilizing their queer investigators to expose social inequalities and participate in theoretical negotiations of gender and sexual identity. These mysteries support Paulina Palmer's 1997 claim that lesbian crime fiction "has by no means lost the political vigour which characterised the genre in its early stages but continues ... to successfully interrelate sexual politics with entertainment" ("Lesbian Thriller" 108). The extent to which these stories engage in political critique varies and is in direct contrast with the degree to which they incorporate elements of the romance genre and encourage reader identification. All three texts fulfill the generic expectation, theorized by feminist scholars of crime fiction, that lesbian mysteries are a hybrid genre because they typically feature romance and the erotic.[11] As Phyllis Betz points out, they thus deviate from detective genre conventions: though the classic detective story may include some element of romance, "rarely is the development and pursuit of a romantic attachment by the primary detective the centerpiece of the narrative" (*Lesbian* 41). Plain argues that this also sets lesbian detective fiction apart from mainstream (straight) feminist texts, in which sexual conquests may play a role but the detectives typically sacrifice romantic interests in favor of closing the crime investigation (206). In her landmark study of lesbian detective fiction, Betz posits that the texts belonging to this category can be mapped out along a wide continuum of crime and romance: "While some lesbian detective novels strictly adhere to the convention that positions romance to the periphery of the narrative, the larger percentage can only be said to deliberately incorporate a second, romantic, narrative impulse into the text" (*Lesbian* 41). All three of the novels analyzed here engage both traditions, with Liertz's *Geheimnisse* aligning itself most closely with romance, while Lehmann's *Training* can be located firmly in the category of crime fiction, and Gelien's *Lesbe* falls somewhere in the middle. One could certainly argue, however, that Lehmann's and Gelien's novels incorporate a heavier touch of the erotic than the romantic, celebrating sexual practices over identification and emotion. The following sections follow a trajectory from romance to crime fiction, beginning with the least overtly political, most romantic, and most identificatory of the three narratives (Liertz's *Geheimnisse*), and concluding with the most politically explicit, least romantic, and least identificatory mystery (Lehmann's *Training*).[12] Though this trajectory does not correspond to the chronological order in which the texts appeared, it brings into relief the contrasts among the texts. Whereas the first story I analyze offers visions of relatively stable sexualities, the last one I shall discuss playfully manipulates and deconstructs concepts of identity altogether.

Lesbian Desire: Romancing the Cross-Dresser in Martina-Marie Liertz's *Die Geheimnisse der Frauen* (1999)

Martina-Marie Liertz's *Die Geheimnisse der Frauen* consists of three romantic intrigues that share a first-person narrator and thematize lesbian desire, mobility, and Berlin geographies. Though Liertz's book is marketed as a *Roman* [novel], it is best described as a novella trilogy or a composite novel, as each of its three parts is self-contained but has narrative and thematic connections to the others. Liertz, a Berlin-based writer of short stories, has gained less recognition than authors like Gelien and especially Lehmann, but has received exposure to a mainstream readership through *Brigitte* magazine.[13] The stories in *Geheimnisse* are part romance and part crime fiction, laying heavy emphasis on the exploration of passion and eroticism, while the work of detecting and solving crime play secondary roles.[14] This is all the more true for the third and final story, which focuses almost exclusively on the gender and sexuality of an attractive yet puzzling character. This story, the book's "Dritter

Teil" [Part Three], borrows its title, "Belle nuit d'amour" [Beautiful Night of Love], from an aria in Jacques Offenbach's *Les contes d'Hoffmann* [The Tales of Hoffmann].[15] My analysis of this cross-dressing mystery examines the ways in which the text theorizes the performativity of gender and reads its representation of a seemingly heterosexual seduction as a critique of heteronormativity.

Geheimnisse is narrated in the first person by amateur detective Deborah Gronwald, a lesbian accountant living in West Berlin. In the book's first two stories, Deborah falls in love with seductive women, each of whom is connected to a mystery she investigates. The third story in the cycle deviates from this pattern in that Deborah develops a crush on a man, the countertenor Sascha Fanesini. At the story's end, Deborah learns Sascha's carefully guarded secret: he is Alessandra, a cross-dressing woman for whom passing as a man opens up professional opportunities otherwise unavailable to female singers.[16] Rather than struggle to achieve stardom as an ordinary mezzo-soprano, Alessandra becomes the countertenor Sascha in order to sing in an uncommon vocal range.[17] So convincing is the cross-dresser's performance of masculinity that his lesbian admirer is unaware of his biological gender until the end of the story, when he reveals himself as Alessandra in the boudoir and beds the detective. Until this moment, however, Deborah struggles to reconcile her homosexual identity with the belief that she is falling in love with a man. Sascha is an attractive performer whose success is due not only to his singing talent, but also to his charisma and acting skills, which serve him both on and off stage. Sascha/Alessandra is constantly performing some variant of maleness and masculinity, playing Sascha as a private individual and star persona, and also playing masculine roles on the operatic stage. The two performances are intricately linked and combine to seduce the opera-loving Deborah, who is initially intrigued by the singer's enchanting embodiment of Orfeo in Christoph Willibald Gluck's opera *Orfeo ed Euridice* [*Orpheus and Eurydice*]. As she becomes acquainted with Sascha and their romance develops, Deborah is all the more fascinated by his quirkiness: at times charming and engaging and at others guarded and aloof, Sasha is especially hesitant to discuss his personal life or be seen in the nude.

Crime and romance intertwine with the common object of Sascha, whose identity is at stake. Crime enters the story when malfunctioning special effect machinery repeatedly threatens Sascha's life during operatic performances, terrifying the singer so greatly that he considers early retirement. Behind these threats is Sascha's bitter mother, a fading glory of a mezzo-soprano who hires an assassin because she is envious of her daughter's success and embarrassed by her gender masquerade. The progression of the romance plot and crime subplot entails two investigations of gender and sexuality: the narrator's examination of her own desires, and the inquiry into the mystery behind Sascha. Through these explorations, Liertz's narrative develops a theory of identity that queers gender and yet essentializes sexuality: on the one hand, the text theorizes gender as a malleable and contextually contingent positionality; and on the other hand, though sexual desire initially appears to be shifting and negotiable, it is ultimately affirmed as a stable and unchanging dimension of identity.

Liertz's story offers lesbian readers the pleasure of a heterosexual fantasy and the vicarious experience of heterosexual privilege, all the while maintaining the homosexual identity of the identificatory detective figure.[18] Though neither Deborah nor any other queer character in the novel is a target of outwardly homophobic sentiments or violence, the text points up heteronormativity and heterosexism by calling attention to the public recognition of Deborah and Sascha as an implicitly heterosexual couple.[19] In emphasizing this point, the text takes a step toward social justice: examining not just discrimination and violence, but also privilege, in order to understand the workings of oppression.[20] In an analysis of heterosexual privilege in the same-sex marriage debates, Erika Feigenbaum describes privilege as "a terrain of largely unexamined invisible perks and protections" that subtly oppress sexual minorities by making heterosexuality a socially and politically advantageous positionality (5). Feigenbaum emphasizes the role of vision on two levels that come into play in Liertz's story: the public recognition of heterosexuals as such, and the detection of the inconspicuous workings of privilege. Because she is excluded from participating in the benefits of heterosexual privilege, Feigenbaum—like Deborah, and presumably also Liertz's lesbian readers—has a heightened sensitivity to the sight of privilege at work. Deborah observes that because she and Sascha go out regularly together in public, people assume that they are a heterosexual couple, and she concedes that this assumption can literally open doors for her. When Sascha is nearly injured during a performance, the security guard's reading of Deborah's identity within a heteronormative framework make it possible for the detective to quickly enter a restricted area backstage: "In diesem Fall half es, daß die Welt im allgemeinen heterosexuell und paarweise gestrickt ist. [Die Schließerin] hatte uns einige Male zusammen durch diese Tür gehen sehen und nahm wahrscheinlich an, wir hätten was miteinander" [In this case it helped that the world is generally structured heterosexually and in pairs. The guard had seen us go through this door together a few times and probably assumed that we had something going on, 351]. Presumably, Deborah would have been unable to pass if she were running to a woman's rescue.[21] But because she appears to be Sascha's girlfriend, Deborah has the opportunity to participate in "a particular power and authority granted by systemic forces" (Feigenbaum 5). Several heterosexual privileges come into play in this scene: public recognition of the relationship, access to a restricted area, and presence as a support person in an emergency situation. These evoke a host of additional liberties and protections available to heterosexual couples but not to gay couples, such as the rights to marry, make medical decisions, and inherit property, as well as entitlement to healthcare and retirement benefits and the option to adopt children. In the novel, Deborah's experience of heterosexual privilege also advances the plot: it is precisely because the guard opens the backstage door for Deborah that the amateur detective later catches the criminal in the wings and successfully closes the investigation. Access to the theater's backstage area and the ability to bring closure to the puzzle of crime are both effects of heterosexual privilege. This scenario, which pointedly brings to mind the many ways in which sexual identity can enable or limit mobility, invites readers to recognize and vicariously experience heterosexual privilege in action. The representation of a same-sex couple that could benefit from the rights granted by heterosexual privilege in the late 1990s calls to mind the debates about gay marriage, which escalated in Germany in the last years of the twentieth century and culminated in the legalization of same-sex partnerships in 2001. Liertz's story offers a fantasy of heterosexual passing, of becoming invisible in mainstream culture and taking advantage of rights such as marriage, that could potentially play a role in the future of Deborah and Sascha's relationship, especially if Sascha fulfills his declared intention to continue living as a man. In this sense, *Geheimnisse*'s "Belle nuit d'amour" offers its lesbian readers a form of tourism through heterosexuality, providing them with an experience not unlike the one Wortmann's film, *Der bewegte Mann*, offers straight spectators: both texts invite audiences to take a sightseeing tour through social practices and romantic cultures on the other side of the proverbial sexuality fence, but safely restabilize the identificatory figures of Deborah and Axel by restoring their "original" sexual identities at the close of the adventure.

But even as Liertz's narrative invites its readers to participate in the heterosexual fantasy, it also provides numerous clues that trouble a coherent reading of the leading man as a heterosexual male. Readers can thus simultaneously take pleasure in seeing a lesbian love story unfolding beneath the façade of heterosexual seduction.[22] Marjorie Garber, whose book-length study of crossdressing in popular culture features a chapter on the narrative function of transvestism in detective stories, maintains that, "in order for the mystery to play itself out, for the suspense to be prolonged, it is crucial for both the reader and the detective to fail, at first, to recognize the existence of the transvestite in the plot" (187). The double gesture of looking at and yet overlooking gender masquerade, Garber argues, "is in the detective story an absolutely foundational move" (187). But the romance and crime plots in Liertz's story require a slightly revised version of Garber's double gesture that, like a Shakespearean comedy of errors, encourages reader awareness of the deception. *Geheimnisse* invites us to read Sascha as a man and at the same time see his identity as a well-orchestrated performance. The reader sees Deborah seeing and not seeing when she encounters a mysterious and attractive woman in a lesbian bar who resembles Sascha (and in fact is Sascha's female identity, Alessandra, out of masquerade) but willfully refuses to have a closer look: "Das T-Shirt war enganliegend, ich sah lieber nicht so genau hin" [The T-shirt was tight-fitting; I preferred not to look too closely, 280]. By inviting the audience to align its gaze with Deborah's while also pointing out Deborah's denial of apparent evidence, the text calls upon a trope that traces back to Edgar Allan Poe's early detective story "The Purloined Letter" (1844), in which the sought-after letter is hidden in plain sight and thereby becomes invisible. When Sascha/Alessandra finally reveals her secret to Deborah, the singer expresses disappointed surprise that the detective did not see the obvious: "es ist so naheliegend, daß du eigentlich längst hättest darauf kommen müssen" [it is so obvious that you really should have figured it out long ago, 406]. Prior to Sascha's revelation of her femaleness, Deborah is unable to solve the mystery of the backstage crimes attempted on Sascha because she has evidence that the target of the threats is a female performer, and so she believes Sascha to be merely an accidental victim of a murder attempt directed at someone else. Sascha's coming out at the story's end doubles as a solution to the crime riddle—as Garber notes, "When he or she [the transvestite] is 'found,' or discovered, the mystery is solved" (187)— and substantiates Deborah's theory that a woman was the real target of the murder attempts in the theater. One of the readerly pleasures that the narrative offers is the gratification of cracking the gender code, which is a crucial step in solving the crime. As Phyllis Betz indicates, the portrayal of transvestite and transgendered characters in crime novels is intimately linked to the pleasure of reading between the lines: "Seeing one gender beneath the other calls forth appreciation for the artifice and the reality of the representation."[23] Though it does not take a discerning reader to grasp the cross-dressing ruse in Liertz's story, the reader can congratulate herself for solving the intertwined gender and crime riddles before the detective does. Thus, while readers can see heterosexual privilege at work in the ways in which Deborah and Sascha are treated, they can still identify with Deborah as a lesbian protagonist, examine Sascha's gender performance, and appreciate the development of the lesbian romance.

The text theorizes the constructedness of gender identity through the parallels between Sascha/Alessandra's dramatization of maleness and the singer's performance of trouser roles. Indeed, the character of Sascha is a literary trouser role, confirming in form the claim in the text that the singer has an exclusive preference for playing trouser roles in the opera. Trouser roles, also called breeches roles, are typically sung and acted by female performers with low vocal ranges appearing in men's clothing. Perhaps the most famous trouser role in the operatic tradition is Cherubino in Mozart's *Le nozze de Figaro* [*The Marriage of Figaro*]; other well-known examples include Octavian in Richard Strauss's *Der Rosenkavalier* [*The Knight of the Rose*], Orlofsky in Johann Strauss's *Die Fledermaus* [*The Bat*], and Orfeo from Gluck's *Orfeo ed Euridice*, the last of which Sascha plays with resounding success in Liertz's story.[24] Just as the trouser role interpellates its audience in the construction of the character's gender—operagoers actively suspend disbelief and accept the character as male even though they know that the performer is female—so does *Geheimnisse*, too, ask its reader to pretend to see a man where it can see that there is really a woman in men's clothing.[25] In both cases, gender identity is radically de-essentialized as an effect of performance and interpretation. Judith Butler's account of the discursive constitution of gender resonates with Liertz's stage metaphor, which reveals identity as "a compelling illusion, an object of *belief*" (emphasis in original).[26] The critical difference here is that, with Liertz's narrative, the reader, much like the real-life operagoer, knows that identity is an illusion and consciously subscribes to it, whereas in Butler's theory of gender identity, the "audience" is unaware of its necessary participation in the illusion. Neither does Butler suppose that the "performer" is aware of the performance; rather, the process is part and parcel of social existence. Butler mobilizes theatrical metaphors when she likens participants in the collective drama of identity to performers and spectators, theorizing gender as "a constructed identity, a performative accomplishment which the mundane social audience, including the actors themselves, come to believe and to perform in the mode of belief" ("Performative" 520). Liertz's text develops a similar notion of the staging and reception of identity by connecting and contrasting Deborah's passion for operatic trouser roles with her attraction to the countertenor. The investigator discusses the pleasure she derives from trouser roles when she chooses not to participate in the illusion—and thus reads the performance against the grain—because knowingly seeing "zwei Frauen auf der Bühne in einer Liebesszene" [two women on the stage in a love scene, 287] provides her greater gratification as a lesbian spectator.[27] Ironically, however, she takes Sascha's gender performance at face value, reading the costume as identical with the figure, and buys into the illusion of his maleness. In dramatizing Sascha's stage and star personae as carefully crafted accomplishments, Liertz's crime romance invites its audience to consider the naturalized construction of identity while simultaneously enjoying the pleasures of believing and disbelieving.

    Language also provides meaningful clues about the workings of masquerade, invisibility, performance, and misreadings of identity in mystery fiction.

In Liertz's text, the erroneous couplings of feminine indefinite articles with masculine nouns imply the telling incongruence between the countertenor and masculinity and point to the gender trouble at the heart of the mystery. In this specific case, however, the utterance comes from a non-native speaker of German who inadvertently articulates the secret that remains otherwise unspoken, though his grammar errors may not seem especially noteworthy because they are neither singular nor isolated to the discussion of Sascha. At the beginning of the story, Sascha's American director Henry Gould explains his unconventional choice to cast the countertenor in traditional trouser roles: "schon der Gesangstechnik ist ja ein ganz andere. Und die Stimmen von die Kastraten haben ganz anders geklungen als eine Countertenor. Die Kastraten-stimme ist neutral, wie eine Musikinstrument. Bei die Countertenor ist immer zu horen [*sic*], daß es ein Mann ist, und zwar eine ganze" [alone the singing technique is completely different. And the voices of the castrati sounded very different from a countertenor. The castrato voice is neutral, like a musical instrument. With the countertenor you can always hear that it's a man, namely a whole one, 268]. Gould's description includes numerous errors, particularly in noun and article gender agreement—*der* Gesangstechnik, *ein* ganz andere [Gesangstechnik], *eine* Countertenor, *eine* Musikinstrument, von *die* Kastraten, bei *die* Countertenor, *eine* ganze [Mann]—and three of these resonate with special significance because they combine the feminine articles *eine* and *die* with the masculine nouns *Countertenor* and *Mann*, which could refer not only to the gendered vocal range but more specifically to the figure of Sascha. The director's grammatical mistakes evoke Garber's claim that "linguistic, orthographic, or grammatical cues appear time after time as counterparts to literal acts of cross-dressing within detective texts" (190). As Garber points out, grammatical slippage in the misuse of indefinite articles, especially in foreign languages with gendered nouns, can be linguistic clues about gender masquerades. Although Gould's description of the countertenor seems to point to Sascha's gender trouble, Gould does not suspect Sascha's secret. Himself a homosexual, Gould wishfully misreads Sascha as a gay man: he is attracted to him and attempts to seduce him.

Gould evokes the countertenor's genderedness as troubled terrain by calling attention to the overlaps among the vocal ranges and operatic roles embodied by castrati, mezzo-sopranos and countertenors,. The countertenor is neither a castrato—a male-bodied singer who never reaches sexual maturity—nor a mezzo-soprano—a female-bodied performer who often plays masculine trouser roles. In contrast with these other singers, the countertenor is, to use Gould's words, *eine ganze Mann* [a whole (feminine) man]: a conundrum of feminized maleness whose gender, like Sascha's, is an enduring subject of debate. Garber describes the vocal range of the contralto (an equivalent of the countertenor) as "a sign of [the] capacity for crossing gender boundaries" (192); and Sascha, the "Tenor mit der weiblichen Gurgel" [tenor with the feminine throat, Liertz 269], further troubles the gender binary by singing parts historically assigned to castrati or women. When Deborah begins to flirt with Sascha and her gay friend Arno cautions, "Countertenöre sind in den allermeisten Fällen männlich" [countertenors are in most cases male, 323], he evokes a history in which there have indeed been exceptions to this rule and indirectly signals the gap between Sascha's masculinity and his presumed manhood. Other coworkers from the opera also believe that there is something queer about Sascha: his unusually versatile singing voice, his coyness about his private life, and a three-year gap on his résumé lead them to muse that he could be gay or transsexual (296–97). Sascha's make-up artist Marion takes this inference a step further when she declares, "Sascha ist nämlich kein Mann!" [Sascha is not a man! 350]. The pronouncement promises an outing but falls short in its delivery: when pressed to elaborate, Marion only states that he is instead a countertenor (350). This declaration parodies a homosexual outing, but with a comical (and, for Deborah, disappointing) conclusion. In playing with the rhetoric of decloseting but withholding the gratification of discovery, Marion reveals everything and nothing by shifting the emphasis from Sascha's gender to his vocal performance: in so doing, she tellingly indicates that the figure of Sascha is no more and no less than a performance of the role of countertenor.

Although Liertz's "Belle nuit d'amour" pointedly and playfully represents gender identity as an effect of performance, it offers a more ambivalent model of sexual identity. As Garber notes, in detective stories cross-dressing demonstrates "the conjunction of sartorial gender and the un-knowability of essences or identities, the ways in which clothes can, quite calculatingly, make the man (or woman)" (187–88). While this claim rings true with the treatment of gender in Liertz's text, it does not resonate with the construction of sexuality, which is portrayed as contingent on gender and yet also essentialized as stable and unchanging. This occurs most explicitly with Deborah, who questions her lesbian identity when she falls in love with a "man," but whose homosexuality is ultimately affirmed by Sascha's coming out as a woman. But a similar move also occurs with Sascha/Alessandra, whose lesbianism the text produces in the only two scenes in which the character does not appear in male masquerade: first in the public space of the lesbian bar and again at the end of the story in her bedroom with Deborah. Though Deborah sees Sascha early in the narrative in a women-only bar called La Belle, she is unaware that the eerily familiar "Lady" who resembles Sascha is in fact another role in his dramatic repertoire (280–82).[28] The mysterious woman's feminine gender and queer sexuality are constructed as effects of performance and interpretation: passing the bouncer's inspection to enter the women-only space performatively constitutes her femininity, while dancing seductively and picking up a young woman with whom she eventually leaves produce her desires as lesbian. Watching the attractive patron at the bar provides fodder for Deborah's fantasies of Sascha, in which she transforms him into a female object of desire: "Ich wollte keinen Mann im Bett. Ich wollte eine Frau! Und diese Frau sollte Sascha sein" [I did not want a man in bed. I wanted a woman! And this woman should be Sascha, 344]. Deborah convinces herself that the woman from La Belle is Sascha's sister and sets off in search of her. This quest allows Deborah to maintain her self-definition as a lesbian. Neither queer lesbianism nor bisexuality crystallizes as a viable sexual positionality for Deborah, who yearns for a female version of Sascha and does not actively desire Sascha as a man. Deborah's homosexuality receives confirmation when Sascha reveals that he was indeed the woman in the lesbian bar: "manchmal muß ich etwas tun, damit es hier drinnen wieder stimmt. Dann spiele ich meine Zwillingsschwester und gehe in den Sub. Damit ich nicht irgendwann, wenn ich abends aus den Hosen steige, vergessen habe, daß ich eine Frau bin" [sometimes I have to do something so that I feel right again, here on the inside. Then I play my twin sister and go into the gay subculture. So that, when I take my pants off in the evening, I won't have forgotten that I am a woman, 411–12]. Though he describes masculinity and femininity as roles he plays, Sascha's occasional performance of femaleness and homosexuality are naturalized as a conscious return to an inner or biological essence that, even though it can be temporarily forgotten, requires occasional release through outward expression. While the story's denouement comes just as Deborah accepts Sascha's maleness and the potential implications of her desire as a destabilizer of lesbian identity, its conclusion ironically reassures both Deborah and the reader that her attraction to Sascha has actually affirmed her lesbianism.

Closure for both the romantic drama and the crime subplot comes in the revelation of the cross-dresser's gender masquerade, which concludes the concurrent and interconnected investigations of Sascha's gender and Deborah's sexuality. The narrative curtain falls on Sascha undressing and inviting Deborah to become acquainted with his female side, an encounter that is portrayed as a staged performance but in the private space of the performer's boudoir, where the two actors are also the audience.[29] Garber's assertion regarding the intimate geographies of the denouements of cross-dressing intrigues in film resonates with this written text: "'Truths' about gender and sexuality in cross-dressing narratives are likely to be revealed in bed, which is one reason why bed scenes occur so frequently as moments of discovery" (202). Prior to this bedroom scene, all forms of sexual contact have been avoided, both by Sascha, for fear of revealing his femaleness, and by Deborah, for fear of destabilizing her homosexuality. The conclusion reveals lesbianism as the truth of identity beneath the cross-dresser's garments and also as the truth of Deborah's desire. Liertz's story ends with the promise of intimacy, though the details of the lesbian couple's first sexual encounter are left to the reader to imagine.

Liertz's story theorizes sexuality as innate and unchanging, indicating that its primary political goal is to affirm lesbian relationships and not to trouble social norms. *Geheimnisse* is perhaps best described as a lesbian romance novel with crime subplots that serve to drive forward the romance narratives. To be sure, in providing readers with representations of—and especially assumptions about—homosexual desires and practices, the novel does reference the everyday workings of heterosexism. Sexism also receives attention in the story's representation of the opera world as a male-dominated profession.[30] But this is not an overtly political text, and unlike other specimens of the crime genre, which tend to be more socially critical, Liertz's *Geheimnisse* stresses identificatory pleasures over outright social commentary.

The politics of Liertz's "Belle nuit d'amour" come into greater relief, however, when compared with those of Mickey Spillane's *Vengeance Is Mine!* (1950), another mystery in which a narrator-investigator falls for a transvestite whose performance of gender is sustained and convincing. Liertz's narrative bears a number of similarities to Spillane's hardboiled classic: both thematize the detective's inability to see through the cross-dresser's masquerade and end with a revelation of the transvestite's biological gender that doubles as the solution to the crime investigation. But Spillane's *Vengeance Is Mine!* concludes with macho detective Mike Hammer killing Juno Reeves, the seductive male-to-female transvestite that Hammer finally identifies as the sought-after murderer, an ending that exposes the fundamental conservatism of the hardboiled genre that took shape in the early part of the twentieth century. Despite her biological maleness, Juno is a quintessential femme fatale: she is disruptive because she is not only powerful, rich, and single, but also because her sex appeal poses an obstacle to the investigation, and the threats she represents must be contained in order for the detective to solve the crime and restore order. Juno thus functions like other femmes fatales of her era as a means for the conventional detective novel to confront the challenges feminism poses to male authority by conquering the woman who steps out of her traditionally-defined role as subservient to men. Juno is "a real, live queen,"[31] a gay male transvestite who brings an extra level of danger to the femme fatale role by embodying not only femininity but also homosexuality: this conflation emphasizes the homophobia typical of the hardboiled genre, as Gabriele Dietze points out in her study *Hardboiled Woman* (309, note 135). And Juno is particularly menacing because her performance of femininity is so very convincing that it deceives a robust and experienced heterosexual man.[32] When Hammer reduces Juno to a "lifeless lump" by repeatedly shooting her with his "rod" (512–13)—

a symbolic penetration and emasculation—he rescues his masculinity and heterosexuality from the menaces Juno embodies and secures his own survival. Spillane invites his reader to share in the detective's amused disgust at the spectacle of the unmasked transvestite: "It was funny. Very funny. Funnier than I ever thought it could be. Maybe you'd laugh, too. I spit on the clay that was Juno, queen of the gods and goddesses, and I knew why I'd always had a resentment that was actually a revulsion when I looked at her" (513). Spillane's portrayal of homosexuality and transvestism as unnatural affirms violence as an appropriate means of disarming the threats they pose, together with aggressive feminine sexuality, to dominant masculinity.

By contrast with Spillane's novel, Liertz's story invites the reader to enjoy the gender revelation as a celebration of queer positionalities. The transvestite in *Geheimnisse* is only disruptive insofar as he causes the detective to temporarily question her own homosexuality, and this irritation is neutralized by the confirmation of both characters' lesbianism at the story's end. Whereas Spillane's narrative pathologizes the cross-dresser as an artifice with no redeeming substance, an embodiment of "the evil of murder" (512), Liertz's mystery affirms the transvestite as a master of disguise who harnesses cross-dressing as a successful means of securing advancement in a male-dominated world. Moreover, the transvestite's relation to Liertz's crime plot positions her as a sympathetic victim of murderous envy, a scenario that pathologizes not the crossdresser but rather her mother, who is unable to come to terms with her daughter's decision to live as a man. Instead of killing off the gay transvestite as Spillane does, Liertz delivers him/her from persecution by having the lesbian detective capture the criminal before learning about Sascha's gender identity; this affords the transvestite the liberty to reveal herself in an environment free of homophobia and transphobia, where the only risk she runs is rejection on behalf of her lover. Such a conclusion asserts the naturalness and primacy of homosexuality as an innate desire that leads Deborah to fall in love not with a man, but with the lesbian beneath the masquerade.

Liertz's turn-of-the-twenty-first-century romance-crime story reveals the stakes of male heterosexual privilege, suggests the devastating potential of transphobia, and, above all, affirms lesbian desires. Though the story is not overtly political, it espouses a gay-positive agenda that calls to mind contemporary discourses of gay emancipation. As the next two sections demonstrate, these critical interventions become more explicit in two other mysteries from the 1990s, Gelien's *Eine Lesbe macht noch keinen Sommer* and Lehmann's *Training mit dem Tod*, that openly engage with the hot topics of the era: Paragraph 175, gay marriage, and transgender rights.

Gay Attraction: Queer Lesbians and Gay Rights in Gabriele Gelien's *Eine Lesbe macht noch keinen Sommer* (1993)

Gabriele Gelien's 1993 novelistic debut, *Eine Lesbe macht noch keinen Sommer*, was among the first three German books to appear in the popular feminist series Ariadne, established in 1988 by the leftist press Argument.[33] Now out of print, *Lesbe* has attained cult status and is perhaps one of the best-known lesbian crime stories written originally in German. Despite the popularity of her debut, Gelien has published no further crime novels, though an afterword to *Lesbe* by feminist scholar Frigga Haug claims that, at the time of its appearance, Gelien was already at work on a sequel.[34] Gelien has, however, published children's literature, notably the fairy tale novel *Der Güldne Baum* [The Golden Tree, 1994], also with Ariadne. Having worked for a number of years as a kindergarten teacher and caretaker for children and the elderly, Gelien infuses her writing with advocacy for the rights of minors and senior citizens. The sexual abuse of children is a common theme in feminist crime literature and plays a central role in other Ariadne texts of this era, such as Ann Camones's *Verbrechen lohnt sich doch!* [Crime Does Pay! 1995] and Lisa Pei's *Die letzte Stunde* [The Final Hour, 1995], as well as later novels like Christine Lehmann's *Harte Schule* [School of Hard Knocks, 2005]. *Lesbe* takes part in this discourse, bringing a concern for the welfare of young people together with compassion for the elderly: the story focuses on an amateur investigator's efforts to interfere with the criminal activity of an international child pornography ring while she also attempts to keep up with her regularly scheduled visits to a retired blind neighbor whom she cares for. These humanistic commitments interface with the book's overall politics, which at once ridicule the rhetoric of lesbian identity politics, critique heterosexual privilege and heteronormativity, and support the decriminalization of homosexuality.

Gelien's witty novel mobilizes genre, identity, and narrative voice in parodic ways. *Lesbe* foregrounds the enigma of identity within and beyond the text by conflating the author with the first-person narrator-investigator, whose name is also Gabriele Gelien.[35] The narrative thematizes overlaps between the fictional and the real through a framing device that positions narrator Gabriele as an author too: while in prison serving a three-month sentence for involuntary manslaughter, she writes a book about the crimes that culminated in her incarceration, hoping that the story will earn enough money to defray the costs incurred by her transgressions. The portrayal of Gabriele as a struggling artist rises to the level of irony when she considers giving up writing for a more lucrative job as a porn actor, even though her crime investigation focuses on the exploitative dimensions of the porn industry. Though the prison narrative is likely pure fiction, Gabriele shares a number of biographical features with author Gelien: both hail from Munich; have adoptive mothers and blind veteran father figures; live in Berlin; work as educators; and are activists for the prevention of the sexual abuse of minors. In the afterword, Haug provides a possible extratextual reason for the author's choice to model the main character after herself:

> Als Motiv gibt sie an, daß ihre Liebste schon seit geraumer Zeit im Bett neben ihr allnächtlich Ariadne-Krimis verschlang, die sie erotischer fand als die lebende Person neben sich. Diese nahm das Problem wörtlich und erotisierte sich, indem sie selbst zum Krimi wurde bzw. ihn schrieb [249].[36]

> [She claims her motive was that, for some time, her lover had been lying in bed next to her every night, devouring Ariadne crime novels that she found more erotic than the living person next to her. She took the problem literally and eroticized herself by becoming a crime novel, or rather by writing one herself.]

This justification intertwines crime with eroticism, just as the book does. In writing herself as and into a crime novel, Gabriele Gelien becomes subject and object of a narrative that balances the identificatory pleasures of romance with the critical distance of the crime genre, linking the two with a strong dose of humor.

Aside from the author-narrator, a number of other real-life figures and locales play important roles in *Lesbe*. These include Else Laudan, editor of the Ariadne series, whom the first-person narrator regularly addresses in the second-person familiar register, using the informal pronoun *du*, with asides on the story's form and content. These breaks in the narrative voice interpellate readers in the process of critical reception by inviting them to evaluate the writer's aesthetic and political choices. Several real-life institutions also appear: pivotal information emerges through and about Berlin institutions such as Wildwasser [Wildwater], a women's coalition that educates about sexual violence against girls and advocates for victims of abuse; and the Schöneberg locales Pour Elle, a lesbian bar (called "Pour eL" in the novel, which Gabriele mockingly suggests stands for "Pur Lesbisch" [Purely Lesbian]),[37] and Sexyland, a strip club widely rumored to promote prostitution, particularly that of minors. The challenges of distinguishing between authorial and narrative voices and between real and fictional worlds encourage the reader to consider the tangible political stakes of a mystery whose protagonist crusades for social justice. The author's parodic approach to storytelling, which Haug characterizes as "niemals ganz ernst, aber immer subversiv" [never entirely serious, but always subversive, 250], mocks literary clichés while also manipulating these trends to issue harshly critical commentaries on contemporary society.

Unlike the other two stories discussed in this chapter, in which either the element of romance dominates over the crime plot (Liertz's *Geheimnisse*), or crime takes precedence over romance (Lehmann's *Training*), Gelien's *Lesbe* does not clearly privilege the conventions of one generic category over the other. Rather, it intertwines the two on multiple levels, developing them simultaneously in various intrigues throughout the course of the novel. Riddles and humor about identity become the glue that binds the narrative. Gill Plain's assessment of Barbara Wilson's queer American crime novel *Gaudí Afternoon* (1990) as "less concerned with the solving of a crime than with the detection of the enigma that is sexuality and desire" (210) is an apt description of Gelien's book, in which investigations of identity take central stage, even when they are unrelated to solving crime. *Lesbe* stresses the construction and significance of gender and sexuality at every stage of the story.

Gabriele, the "lesbische Heldin des Krimis" [lesbian heroine of the crime novel, 5], is a struggling continuing education student who takes in gay roommate Boris to help pay the bills (though she sardonically implies that living with a man could endanger her status as a bona fide lesbian). She has a rocky relationship with beloved girlfriend Lisa, a feminist activist who criticizes her politically naïve rhetoric and chaotic lifestyle. Gabriele's downfall, and the reason that she is unable to focus on her schoolwork or her relationship, is an escalating postal neurosis: she becomes obsessed with the idea that that someone is stealing her mail. She seeks psychotherapy for her paranoia but ascribes her therapist Eva-Maria's failure to understand or treat her to sexual identity: because Eva-Maria is a "Heteraschnalle" [hetero-hoochie, 5], she and Gabriele have different concerns. Gabriele resolves to unravel the mail mystery herself and begins to shadow her postal carrier on his Berlin route, which brings her into contact with his roommate Kunz, "der erste männliche Darsteller mit Sympathiegehalt" [the first male cast member with sympathetic qualities, 5]. Kunz, who happens to be the attractive math instructor Gabriele secretly fantasizes about, causes the narrator to ponder the stability of her lesbian identity, and when she discovers that she and Kunz are being watched, she takes pleasure in pretending to be his lover. Meanwhile, Gabriele has several bizarre encounters with a group of radical lesbian feminists who are somehow involved in the mail mystery but warn her against pursuing the investigation. After defending herself against assault by a stalker she leaves behind for dead, the amateur detective flees to Munich. Her cross-country adventure brings her into contact with the people she identifies as the mail thieves, a covert ring of pornographers who are using Gabriele's Berlin address as part of a codified system for distributing illegal home videos of pedophilic sex. In Munich, where Gabriele stays in the parental home, a family drama and a romance unfold as the crime plot thickens. Gabriele must care for her five younger siblings while her mother and father prepare for the impending birth of yet another child. In the course of her daily adventures in childcare and crime-solving, Gabriele falls in love with Hanne, a butch lesbian who is coming out of the closet. Their budding romance is interrupted when Gabriele is sentenced for the involuntary manslaughter of the stalker who had assaulted her—and who is revealed to be a porn trafficker. While incarcerated, Gabriele has two crucial breakthroughs: she learns that Kunz is gay and that her amateur detective work interfered with an undercover investigation of organized sex crime. At the end of her sentence, Gabriele learns that she has inherited her grandmother's Bavarian estate. The story ends with Gabriele living with Hanne in her grandmother's country home, where they receive a visit from the mysterious radical lesbians, who reveal that they are undercover detectives in pursuit of the masterminds behind the international pornography ring, and request Gabriele's assistance in the ongoing investigation.

As this brief summary demonstrates, Gelien's convoluted story is rife with boldly irreverent figures and emphasizes political satire over narrative coherence, taking an uncompromisingly critical approach to any and all forms of ideology. The most consistent objects of critique are separatist feminist and lesbian identity politics, which the narrator openly rejects; her unapologetically apolitical stance sets her apart from her lover Lisa, the undercover lesbian detectives, and the many other engaged feminists in her social environment. This critical distancing from lesbian identity places Gelien's novel in direct contrast with the affirmative representation of lesbianism that we find in Liertz's *Geheimnisse*. Although Gabriele is introduced both by the book's title and by its first lines as a lesbian, she clarifies in the opening passage that she is no stereotypical gay woman, and she illustrates this claim by ridiculing a number of clichés. One object of her mockery is the *Urlesbe* [primal lesbian]— Gabriele instead identifies as a *Junglesbe* [young lesbian][38]—who knows at an early age that she is gay, has never been in a heterosexual relationship, hates men, loves cats, is a die-hard feminist, and inflects her speech with feminist rhetoric, such as the pronoun *frau* [woman], a feminized alternative to the third-person impersonal pronoun *man* [one; literally, man]. The narrator goes to great pains to set herself apart from these stereotypes: she enjoys the company of men, despises cats, and proudly declares her apathy toward feminist politics and activism. The novel's send-up of misandry and feminist clichés begins on page one, where it introduces the main characters in a "Vorstellung des Krimipersonals" [Introduction to the Crime Personnel, 5] reminiscent of a legal protocol or a dramatis personae. This list initially categorizes most of the characters by their gender and sexuality, announcing the narrative's parody of the tendency in feminist and lesbian literature to heroicize women and to characterize men as inherently suspicious, if not outright dangerous and violent. Gabriele claims affiliation with a lesbian "Liberalfraktion" [liberal faction, 12] because she breaks rules of feminist political correctness by living with a man and refusing to purge her speech of patriarchal language. The only men to appear in the list of characters, Kunz and Boris, are both homosexual (though Kunz's homosexuality is not revealed until much later), and are, with the exception of Gabriele's father, the only positive male figures the novel offers. By contrast, the bad guys are not just men but also implicitly straight: the list of characters mentions "unzählige Verbrecher, selbstverständlich alle männlichen Geschlechts und teilweise tot" [countless criminals, naturally all of the male gender and partly dead, 6]. The stereotyping of men as enemies, especially heterosexual men, evokes the feminist separatist cliché that the only good man is a dead one, a gesture that recalls early feminist crime fiction such as Sabine Deitmer's short stories in the collection *Bye-bye Bruno* (1988), which features male victims of violence and murder at the hands of justifiably angry or vengeful women.

Gabriele's most overt transgression against lesbian identity politics, however, is that she experiences desire for a man. Prior to her encounter with Kunz, the narrator is already concerned about the possibility of losing her lesbian status on account of her political incorrectness: she jokingly comments that feminist watchdogs could, at any time, revoke her standing as *Lesbe* and her membership in the *Liberalfraktion*, thereby invalidating her application for retirement in a lesbian community (12). This possibility becomes all the more real when Gabriele begins to fantasize about a man. By evoking sexual identity as an affiliation that requires periodical renewal and policing by an outside party, the narrative calls to mind debates from the 1970s and 1980s about whether non-lesbian women have a place in lesbian feminist movement. But Gabriele quickly writes off these political implications, declaring to her therapist that having erotic dreams about a man is "aus mehreren Gründen ganz normal" [completely normal for several reasons, 17]. The justifications Gabriele provides and the pleasure she takes in exploring her desire for her tutor expose heterosexual privilege and take up contemporary political debates about gay rights. Firstly, as a *Jungleshe*, Gabriele has had more male than female sexual partners, and so she dismisses her experience of heterosexual desire as simply a repetition of a well-rehearsed performance. Secondly, Gabriele rationalizes her attraction to Kunz as a means of assimilating to her cultural environment; she does, after all, live in a heterosexist world (17). For lack of alternative role models, she manipulates her behavior to conform, at least externally, to heteronormative standards. Whether she wishes to or not, Gabriele subconsciously comes to identify with the ubiquitous forms of heterosexual desire and coupling performed in everyday public spaces and projected by the media as healthy and deserving of life (17).[39] In other words, Gabriele's desire for Kunz is simply a deflected desire to feel like—and be perceived as—a normal, healthy, valid human life form, or, as Butler might say, as a "body that matters."

The text's alignment of the term "normal" (quoted above) with heterosexual desire and privilege evokes the various ways in which queer critiques of homophobia and heteronormativity have mobilized the concept of normalization as a goal for gay rights activism, or, conversely, as counterproductive for queer politics.[40] I shall return to the connection between Gelien's novel and critiques of normativity later in this section in the discussion of gay marriage.

The lesbian investigator's attraction to her male instructor provides her with a safe scenario in which to temporarily experience the benefits of heterosexual privilege, one of which is invisibility. Like her classmates, who come to the consensus that Kunz is gay, Gabriele also strongly suspects that there is something queer about this sensitive man, a suspicion that is later confirmed when a prison psychologist diagnoses Kunz as "latent schwul" [latently homosexual, 198]. Gabriele's attraction, which she reads as proof of Kunz's homosexuality, makes it possible for her to experiment with the pleasures of flirtation without having to face the potential threat of reciprocal desire—and the consequences such desire could have if its male object were heterosexual. One of the heterosexual privileges this flirtation offers Gabriele is inconspicuousness: even though Gabriele's gay classmates deem her flirtation with Kunz noteworthy, mainstream society does not perceive these ostensibly heterosexual interactions as remarkable and they thus fall under the radar. The dramatization of invisibility in and of itself as a perk of heterosexuality recalls Feigenbaum's description of heterosexual privilege as "a terrain of largely unexamined invisible perks and protections" (5). The amateur detective mobilizes heterosexual invisibility to her advantage at the beginning of her investigation, when she and Kunz pretend to be a couple in order to observe and mislead the men they believe to be following them. This scenario in which two homosexuals pretend to be straight in order to disappear brings to mind the various social pressures that can persuade queer people to attempt to pass as straight or fit in by living according to heterosexual standards. Gabriele's theatrical rendition of a distraught woman having an emotional reunion with her scorned lover reveals heterosexuality as a performance—one that, in this case, even has an audience. Flirting with a man also gives the lesbian investigator an opportunity to express affection in public without first having to assess her surroundings for homophobic threats, an experience Gabriele asserts is unavailable to same-sex couples (35). The text confronts heterosexual privilege by revealing the ways in which the experience of a marginalized sexual positionality can influence an individual's interactions with his or her social environment: heterosexism and homophobia shape the lives of queer people in indelible ways, affecting how they relate to others and what they disclose, how they perform their desires, when they remain closeted, and when they come out.[41] The revelation that the neurotic Kunz is indeed a closeted homosexual highlights the dark side of heterosexual privilege, implying that internalized homophobia and gay shame are the source of his inhibitions and anxieties.[42] Gabriele, too, has experienced the painful effects of homophobia in her own life, having grown up in conservative Bavaria. Imagining herself as Kunz's lover further allows the queer narrator to fantasize about fulfilling her family's wishes that she be cured of what they hope is a momentary sexual aberration: Gabriele suspects that her mother and grandmother would be thrilled to see her with any man at all, even Kunz, who is some fifteen years her senior (36). This representation both aligns Bavaria with homophobia and highlights another dimension of heterosexual privilege, the premise that one's choice of partner will not be rejected by one's parents on the basis of gender alone.

Lesbe provides an alternate account of contemporary German-German difference, one in which the two Germanies are represented not by the cultures and politics of East and West Germany, but rather by the North and the South, specifically Berlin and Bavaria.[43] Gelien's story unfolds between December 1989 and November 1990, the era immediately following the fall of the Wall, during which the German Democratic Republic ceased to exist and became part of the Federal Republic. But for the Bavarian-born narrator who resides "im Exil" [in exile, 48] in West Berlin, it is her home state—and not the former East—that symbolizes the other Germany, the foreign culture. This ethnicized dichotomy pits socially progressive Berlin, in particular the Schöneberg district where Gabriele lives in the midst gay bars, women's cafés, and feminist activists, against the social conservatism, Catholicism, and bourgeois values embodied by Gabriele's family in Munich. Even though the Wall that divided two Germanies for over two decades has fallen, regional and cultural divides still characterize North and South Germany as radically different universes. These boundaries extend far beyond the sociopsychological vestiges of the Cold War, which manifest themselves in the much-discussed *Mauer im Kopf* [wall in the mind].[44] Indeed, they take very real forms in the state lines and policing mechanisms that travelers and migrants must contend with: "Bayern wird, auch wenn wir seit Jahrhunderten vereinigt sind, immer Grenzen haben" [Bavaria will, even after we've been unified for centuries, always have borders, 88]. Gelien's novel indicates that these boundaries do more than merely define Bavaria as an administrative territory; they also insulate the southern state from external influences and preserve its traditional values, priorities that became all the more pressing for socially conservative Bavarians as unification with the former East threatened to shift the nation's political profile to the left. In a persuasive writing assignment for school, Gabriele argues that Bavaria, whose full state name includes the 1919 designation *Freistaat* [republic; literally, free state] that originally signified its independence from the German Reich, still merits special status as a "free state" due to its outdated antidemocratic standards (50–52). Gabriele supports her claim with evidence of Bavarian exceptionalism: the continued representation of the CSU [*Christlich-Soziale Union in Bayern*, Christian Social Union in Bavaria] state party, which represents Bavaria alone, at the federal level[45]; residency stipulations for new voters that are more stringent than in any other state; and special laws applying only to people with HIV and, by extension, primarily homosexual citizens (50–51). Gays, lesbians, "asoziale[s] Gesindel" [asocial vermin, 51], and other "unangepaßte[] Elemente" [unassimilated elements, 51]: these populations tend, like Gabriele, to leave Bavaria, often for Berlin, a diasporic movement that perpetuates the state's social conservatism.[46] Gabriele's experiences in Bavaria provide poignant examples of the oppressiveness of social conservatism, particularly through the invisibility of women and gay life in the public sphere.[47] Conservative attitudes also dictate the mistaken perception of Gabriele as a young mother when she takes her siblings on excursions in Munich. More than any other character in the book, however, it is Gabriele's homophobic mother who embodies bourgeois Bavarian ideals: a devout Catholic, Gisela embraces procreation as a value in and of itself and proselytizes about the merits of heterosexuality. Gabriele's mother and grandmother, who repeatedly try to convince her to abandon her queer lifestyle and partner up with a man, are emblematic of closed-minded provincialism and its offensive approach to social difference. In the final count, the narrator declares, Bavaria's *Freistaat* status is not without irony, as it literally and forcefully divests itself of all forms of progressive thought and thus emancipates itself from any obligation to acknowledge competing ideologies (52).

Published in 1993, Gelien's *Lesbe* tackles a matter of sexual politics that became more urgent in the process of German unification: the debate over Paragraph 175. While serving time, Gabriele attempts to further her crime investigation by mining the prison library's resources to learn about the sexual exploitation of minors. She is disappointed, however, to discover that all of the available literature equates pedophilia with homosexuality. Having encountered only heterosexual pedophilia—grown men desiring young girls—in her own adventures in crime-solving, Gabriele finds the implicit conflation of child sex abuse with homosexuality both counterintuitive and counterproductive (99). Such alignment constructs homosexuality as a catch-all category for any form of criminal or sexual deviance[48] and indirectly justifies the enduring existence of Paragraph 175, which remained in the *Strafgesetzbuch* [Criminal legal code] of the Federal Republic until 1994. Paragraph 175 became a pivotal issue for German politicians and citizens after 1989, as it was one of the discrepancies between East and West German legal codes that unification brought into relief. Dating back to a Prussian law of 1871, this infamous clause criminalizing homosexuality had been abolished in the GDR in 1988, but remained on the books in the FRG, albeit in an abbreviated form that applied exclusively to sex with minors.[49] In *Lesbe*, Gabriele's research on Paragraphs 175, 176, and 182 affords her insights into the double standards that underlie her nation's definitions of legal and illegal sex acts: the age of consent for sex acts between men is 18 (Paragraph 175); but if the younger participant is female, then the age of consent is 16 (Paragraph 182); and as long as the girl is over 14, then the penalty for her male partner is more modest than if she were under 14 and therefore classifiable as a child (Paragraph 176; Gelien 99–102). The summary of these laws places into relief the varying standards they set for men and women, and for homosexuals and heterosexuals. Gabriele quips that women "ja eh keine Sexualität [haben]" [have no sexuality anyway, 100], which explains why they only appear in legal statutes as sexual objects. The absence of lesbians in such legislation altogether indicates that they do not qualify as sexual beings but rather persist in the popular imagination as merely antisocial (102).[50] Gabriele implies that homophobia even affects the rhetoric of the pedophile rights movement, which does not advocate for the repeal of laws applying to same-sex acts because this, ironically, would no longer be "akzepta- bel" [acceptable, 100]. Though *Lesbe* does not explicitly plead for the abolition of Paragraph 175, its exposure of the inconsistencies in German legislation attacks the validity and necessity of such antiquated regulations. In taking to task segments of the criminal code that stipulate the differentiated treatment of homosexuality, Gelien's mystery participates in contemporary debates over the status of Paragraph 175 in the unified German state. Though Gelien's nar- rator herself personifies something of a political double standard—she dis- tances herself from lesbian politics and yet her account repeatedly uncovers the subtle workings of sexist and homophobic discrimination and emphasizes the benign forms of violence they entail—she takes an unmistakably pro-gay liberation stance in critiquing a law that galvanized contemporary gay rights activism.

While the novel tacitly supports the emancipation of homosexuals from the historical burdens of Paragraph 175, it refrains from embracing another pivotal issue for gay liberationists of the same era: the fight for the legalization of same-sex marriage. *Lesbe* appeared just as public debates over gay marriage escalated in the wake of the nationwide August 1992 protest *Aktion Standesamt* [civil registration campaign], organized by the SVD [*Schwulenverband in Deutschland*, Gay Federation in Germany], when some 250 same-sex couples, including lesbian media darlings Hella von Sinnen and Cornelia Scheel, demanded the right to a legal wedding in municipal offices across the country.[51] Though I argue above that *Lesbe* uncovers heterosexual privilege and depicts Gabriele as wishing to benefit from some of the protections it offers, partic- ularly invisibility and tolerance, the novel provides no evidence that she desires to participate in the specific privilege of marriage. In fact, the text's stance toward marriage is at best ambivalent. One could make the case that this is symptomatic of a wider hesitancy toward marriage among young Germans: young couples often live in long-term monogamous relationships without entering into a legally sanctioned bond of wedlock.[52] But the cynicism with regard to marriage in *Lesbe* goes beyond this cultural trend: it is part of a broader rejection of the bourgeois mores that Gabriele's biological family epitomizes. Haug notes that author Gelien is uncompromisingly critical of bourgeois lifestyles, which she views "als unlebbare Form, als Zerstörung" [as an unlivable form, as destructive, 250]. This critique is palpable in the characterization of Gabriele's family, whose home is suffocatingly devoid of private space, and especially of her mother, who seemingly bears children incessantly and repeatedly attempts to force Gabriele into the mold of the middle-class daughter, wife, and mother. Though Gabriele is an attentive caretaker of her younger siblings and eventually enters into a committed relationship with Hanne, she expresses no desire to follow in her mother's footsteps by marrying or starting a family. The narrator does mention same-sex marriage once in the novel; here, however, it serves not to promote the institution but rather to provoke her mother, who is uncomfortable with the idea of being a mother-in-law figure to her daughter's girlfriend:

> Seit ich ihr von dem Würzburger Pfarrer, also zum einen Bayerisch (sorry: Fränkisch natürlich!) und zum anderen Katholisch, der zwei Lesben getraut hatte, erzählt habe, befindet sie sich in einem schwierigen Zwiespalt. Mama kann sich einfach nicht entscheiden, ob sie es der Kirche anlasten soll oder nicht [92].
>
> [Ever since I told her about the priest from Würzburg—not only Bavarian (sorry: Franconian, of course!) but also Catholic—who had wedded two lesbians, she has been having a difficult inner conflict. Mom simply cannot decide whether she should bring charges against the church or not.]

The anecdote suggests that Gabriele uses the lesbian wedding to bring her devout Catholic mother to question the church—and, by implication, perhaps even her religion. Gay marriage is therefore simply a tool in Gabriele's rebellion against the conservative ideologies that her ancestors espouse.

Gelien's novel attests to the emerging and increasing influence of queer theory and politics in the arena of gay rights activism in Germany of the early 1990s. Central to these debates are notions of normalcy and normativity, in particular heteronormativity, which are bound up with traditional heterosexual institutions like marriage. In rejecting the bourgeois values of marriage and procreation, Gelien's *Lesbe* takes a stance similar to that of other queer scholars and activists of the 1990s, such as Michael Warner, who in his polemical monograph *The Trouble with Normal* contends that the fight for marriage rights is undesirable and even counterproductive for queer politics. Lisa Duggan similarly maintains that lobbying for same-sex marriage and other rights under a banner of gay equality "does not contest dominant heteronormative assumptions and institutions, but upholds and sustains them."[53] Gelien's approach to this critique is not through the institution of marriage per se, but rather by manipulating notions of normalcy in such a way that their heteronormative connotations are ultimately displaced—as Haug affirms, Gelien's writing "dekonstruiert unaufhörlich Normalität" [constantly deconstructs normalcy, 250].[54] Normalcy, defined in *Lesbe* according to Gabriele's mother and grandmother's expectations, would appear to be cohabitation with a man. When the Franconian grandmother dies and leaves Gabriele her estate, her inheritance carries with it the stipulation that she inhabit the home "mit einer männlichen Bezugsperson" [with a male companion, 221]. One of the ironies of this condition is that Gabriele already lives with a man, her gay roommate Boris, in her Berlin apartment. But though Gabriele initially struggles to think of a man with whom she could cohabitate long-term (Boris, a slob and a cat owner, is not an ideal roommate), the book's last chapter, beginning with the subheading "Omas späte Rache" [Grandma's late revenge, 215], narrates Gabriele's gratifying post-prison lifestyle in the Franconian country estate she shares with Hanne and another lesbian couple.[55] *Lesbe* prolongs the revelation of the male cohabitant's identity until its final lines, privileging this disclosure as the final mystery to be solved. The man inhabiting the otherwise lesbian household is ninety-four-year-old Opa Müh [Grandpa Trouble], a blind neighbor Gabriele cared for in Berlin. Though Gabriele's relationship to Opa Müh does not resemble a traditional marriage—he has his own living quarters and bathroom, and she treats him with the respect and affection that usually mark interactions with older relatives—it fulfills some of the roles typically played by married couples: they live together, enjoy one another's company, and Gabriele cooks and cares for him. Queer scholar Sara Ahmed employs a rhetoric of alignment in suggesting that gay marriage could reinforce conservative values by "'extend[ing]' the straight line to some queers, those who can inhabit the forms of marriage and family, which would keep other queers, those whose lives are lived for other points, 'off line.'"[56] Instead of extending the "straight line" by depicting or even advocating gay marriage, Gelien's novel pushes the "off line" with an ostensibly heterosexual domestic arrangement that may, on paper, look like a traditional coupling, but that facilitates the establishment of a lesbian-dominated household. By presenting the membership of a man in the household as the condition of possibility for this otherwise all-female domestic sphere, the ending of Gelien's mystery parodies an utopian cliché found elsewhere in lesbian literature, such as the contemporary Ariadne crime novel by Kim Engels, *Zur falschen Zeit am falschen Ort* [In the Wrong Place at the Wrong Time, 1991], which concludes with the four main female characters living together in a communal arrangement without men. Gabriele mobilizes the model of heterosexual cohabitation, which fulfills her grandmother's condition, to accommodate her own same-sex relationship and to provide care for a person in need. Gabriele's household thus goes some distance toward fulfilling Warner's call to contest heteronormativity: "Even when coupled with a toleration of minority sexualities, heteronormativity can be overcome only by actively imagining a necessarily and desirably queer world" (Introduction xvi). The conclusion of *Lesbe* thus subverts both the notion of bourgeois heterosexual monogamy and the separatist feminist ideal of a women-only community.

Another unification era issue that *Lesbe* confronts is the pornography debates. Geography and pornography are aligned in a secret code that Gabriele finds in her mail and must decipher in order to locate the criminals. Gabriele misreads the abbreviation "SL" in the child pornographers' code language as referring to the Berlin strip club Sexyland when it actually signifies Schleswig, the region in northwestern Germany where the criminals have their headquarters. This confusion evokes the cliché that what East Germans loved most about the West was the sex industry. Despite the implied association of porn production with the West (Bavaria and Schleswig) and its distribution and consumption with the East (Berlin), the porn industry materializes in the novel as neither a West German nor an East German phenomenon but rather a pervasive problem in and beyond the unified state. Gabriele's investigation implicates the entire unified Federal Republic, from Saarbrücken to Dresden, in the trafficking of child pornography. The representation of diverse cities and regions emphasizes the ease of passage, for people and goods, between formerly divided parts of the nation. The amateur detective suggests that German unification and European expansion have only facilitated the growth of the international porn industry and the concomitant exploitation of minors by opening up new trade routes and markets: "Die EG '92 fiel mir ein, und damit die Vermutung, daß der Verbrecherring sicher international 'arbeitete'" [The '92 European Community agreement crossed my mind, together with the suspicion that the ring of criminals surely "operated" internationally, 133]. Such economic reorganization brought about an administrative decentralization that posed new challenges for the investigation of international crimes and prosecution of the criminals. Gabriele seems to take the side of anti-pornography feminism when she claims to repudiate all forms of pornography, going so far as to propose that everyone involved in the industry belongs behind bars. This includes the infamous "Frau Uhse" [Mrs. Uhse, 143], a reference to entrepreneur Beate Uhse, whose name is synonymous with the eponymous German sex shop empire. But the narrative delivers this, like much of its commentary, with a good dose of sarcasm, and its stance toward porn is more ambivalent than such statements imply.

The novel does, however, take an uncompromising stance against pedophilia and the sexual exploitation of minors, but because it does so by means of an attack on a video industry that capitalizes on the sexual abuse of young children, this representation can be read as casting a critical eye to pornography altogether. *Lesbe* implies that the distribution network for such exploitative media extends far beyond the boundaries of Germany or even Europe: the worldwide venture is implicated in child prostitution in Southeast Asia (163). The problem proves to be too large to solve within the limits of this narrative, and the lack of closure on this count underlines the gravity and ubiquity of such crimes. At the end of the story, only the good guys have been convicted and served time, while the bad guys remain on the loose: amateur detectives Gabriele and Kunz complete prison sentences for the involuntary manslaughter of a pornographer, even though they are innocent, and the investigation of the real criminals, the porn kingpins, is left pending. The case remains open, a narrative element that subverts the generic demand that crime narratives conclude with the closure of the mystery.

Gabriele Gelien's *Eine Lesbe macht noch keinen Sommer* reveals that existing categories for sexuality and desire are approximate and contingent at best. It does this in part by exploring a self-identified lesbian investigator's desire for a man and rejecting lesbian feminist identity politics, while embracing certain aspects of gay emancipation and queer theory. Although the novel places labels for gendered and sexualized positionalities under the microscope, it concludes with a confirmation of lesbian desire: the titular lesbian is madly in love with a woman and safely lodged in a stable same-sex relationship. The term *queer* does not appear in the narrative, likely because it had not yet become common in German usage at the time of this novel's publication in 1993.[57] But the text exposes other available categories as limited and limiting, and ironically, it is Gabriele's conservative mother who speaks the words that resonate most forcefully with the novel's overall take on identity: she declares that "menschliche Realität vielfältiger ist als homo ODER hetero" [human reality is more multifaceted than homo OR hetero, 118, capitalization in original]. Gabriele's desires destabilize the very category to which she assigns them, on the one hand constructing *lesbian* as a chosen term of affiliation, while on the other hand highlighting its incapacity to represent boundary-crossing subjects. This is also true for Kunz, who professes to have heterosexual desires and shows affection for Gabriele, but turns out to be gay, as well as for Gabriele's best friend Suse, who identifies as an unfulfilled heterosexual but finds her life partner in a woman. One can infer from these characters' developments that their desires might be classifiable as shifting or bisexual, and that the labels they choose are subjective and strategic. Gabriele's identification with lesbianism and the simultaneous destabilization of the category of lesbian resonate not only with the book's representations of sexual practices but also with its politics, offering decidedly queer answers to contemporary debates about identity in post-unification German society.

Animal Magnetism: Investigating Transgender Representation in Christine Lehmann's *Training mit dem Tod* (1998)

> Wann ist ein Mann in der Lage, die Klobrille runterzuklappen? Nach einer Geschlechtsumwandlung.
> —"Die besten Männerwitze," *Emma*[58]
>
> [When is a man capable of putting down the toilet seat? After a sex change.]

Christine Lehmann's *Training mit dem Tod* is the second installment in an ongoing detective series featuring the bisexual reporter Lisa Nerz. *Training mit dem Tod* belongs to the original Lisa Nerz trilogy published in the popular Rowohlt crime series in the late 1990s, beginning with *Der Masochist* [The Masochist, 1997] and concluding with *Pferdekuss* [Horse's Kiss, 1999]. Lehmann continued the series with the feminist publisher Ariadne, starting with the fourth installment, *Harte Schule* [School of Hard Knocks, 2005]. The republication of the first three Nerz books with Ariadne in the 2000s attests to the enduring appeal of the series, which now consists of ten novels.[59] The prolific writer has also achieved mainstream success with her love stories, in particular *Der Bernsteinfischer* [The Amber Fisher, 2000], which was adaptated as a television film for ARD (Olaf Kreinsen, 2005). Other romances followed, including *Die Racheengel* [The Vengeful Angels, 2003] and *Die Liebesdiebin* [The Love Thief, 2005], the latter of which has reached an international audience through translations into Russian and Ukranian. In addition, Lehmann writes historical novels, under the pseudonym Madeleine Harstall, and romance-thrillers for young adults.

The Lisa Nerz crime series, which accounts for approximately half of Lehmann's novelistic production, takes up several conventions of American hardboiled detective fiction of the early and mid-twentieth century but with a queer feminist inflection.[60] First-person narrator Lisa Nerz is a physically and emotionally tough detective whose encounters with corruption in public institutions have equipped her with a cynical outlook on violence and social order. Lisa's performance of macho masculinity locates her in the tradition of the hardboiled hero: she is strong, quick to resort to violence, and, though she embodies an andogynous gender aesthetic, she would likely identify more closely with masculinity than femininity. Described by one critic as "gendermäßig oszillierend" [oscillating gender-wise][61]—a description that author Lehmann has enthusiastically adopted—Lisa performs both butch and femme identities in different spaces, depending on her mood and the context. Though Lisa occasionally enjoys playing up her feminine side with short skirts and makeup, she typically prefers to dress in men's clothing and takes particular pleasure in being perceived, in the lesbian scene, "als harter Bursche" [as a tough lad],[62] or mistaken for a "Bube" [boy].[63] Lisa appreciates the benefits of being able to play various gender roles, which also serve different purposes: she performs femininity more for personal amusement and as an expression of her deviance from a unified gender identity, while the macho-inflected roles she more often plays have a greater tendency to serve the needs of her work as an investigative reporter and crime solver. Like the hardboiled sleuth, for whom seduction goes hand in hand with solving crime, Lisa frequently finds herself in compromising positions with suspects, victims, and even colleagues. She is also queerly sexualized: in *Training* Lisa claims that she prefers to romance the fairer sex—"Ich habe eigentlich mehr für Frauen übrig" [I'm actually more interested in women, 21]—but several novels portray her flirting and sleeping with men too. Her only sustained romantic interest, however, is in a man with whom Lisa plays the more dominant, traditionally masculine, role. Lisa marries her performance of hard masculinity with a professional commitment to feminism and women's issues: in *Masochist*, she writes for a feminist journal called *Amazone* [Amazon], and as a reporter for a Stuttgart newspaper in *Training* and its sequels, she specializes in the rubrics women, society, and modern living. A journalist by trade, Lisa calls on the talents and assets that have brought her professional success, especially her research skills and useful contacts in law enforcement and the justice system, to investigate crimes in Stuttgart and surrounding Swabia; and, in turn, her amateur crime-solving work gives her access to salacious details for breaking stories.

Training is especially significant among the Nerz novels because it narrates Lisa's first encounter with Richard Weber, a post-operative transgendered man who works as a public prosecutor and plays a pivotal and ongoing role in the series. While Richard is a reappearing figure as Lisa's occasional collaborator in investigations and on-again, off-again lover, *Training* is unique among the ten Nerz books in referencing Richard's pre-operative life as a woman; later installments simply identify Richard as a man and neither mention his transgender identity nor problematize his gender. The titular term *Training*—referring specifically to working out—evokes an emphasis on the body that comes into play both generally in the crime story, which involves three mysterious deaths and the trafficking of illegal drugs in a fitness center aptly named the *Schlachthof* [Slaughterhouse], and in particular with the physically toned and gendered representations of Richard and other patrons and employees of the same gym. Lisa's investigation of the *Schlachthof* deaths positions Richard as both object and subject: she meets him on her first visit to the fitness center, and his dubious, long-standing ties to the fitness center make him a prime suspect, but despite this, Lisa enlists his help to solve the crimes. The prosecutor's past life, which he keeps secret, begins to surface when the journalist unearths an article about a traffic accident involving his former female identity, Karoline Weber, in the newspaper archives. Lisa initially believes that Karoline is Richard's sister, a misreading that recalls Liertz's *Geheimnisse*, in which Deborah misinterprets the first visual evidence of Sascha's female identity as an indication that the mysterious man has a sister. Though Lisa initially finds Richard repulsive—she dislikes his impeccably businesslike demeanor and is suspicious of his contact with a clique of judo enthusiasts—she becomes increasingly interested in him as the investigation continues. Richard's coming out to Lisa as a transsexual marks a turning point in the crime plot and in their relationship, after which the various strands of the murder investigations come together, exculpating Richard, and Lisa ceases to flirt with women, focusing her attention on Richard. The journalist and the prosecutor become a team, not only working together to solve the murders, but also protecting one another from harm. Lehmann's novel also concludes similarly to Liertz's story, with the physical unveiling of the transperson and the promise of coupling: as Richard reveals to Lisa the details of his past involvement with the fitness studio, he slowly undresses, and any remaining tension, the narrative implies, will be resolved in bed.

Lehmann's text makes an explicit political intervention not only by depicting a transgendered person at the heart of the mystery, but also by developing theories of gender identity and commentaries on transgender rights throughout the narrative. Betz notes, "Since the outcome of any detective novel is the restoration of normalcy—or, at least, a return to order—the inclusion of transgendered characters in that order encourages the relaxing of the fear and bias that kept them outside" ("Re-Covered" 31). Indeed, Lehmann's second Nerz novel makes a radically democratic move by positioning a transgendered figure as the detective's love interest, a stance that subsequent books uphold by maintaining Richard's centrality in the series. But its intervention is also overt: *Training* addresses contemporary discourses about transgenderism by confronting social and legal problems such as prejudices against transpeople and the limitations of German legislation in the 1990s. I shall discuss this context in further detail as I flesh out my reading of the novel's social critique.

At the thematic level, Lehmann's novel develops a critique of social attitudes toward transgenderism by contrasting two different kinds of bodily manipulation. On the one hand, the text emphasizes the ubiquity of physical and chemical measures undertaken by many of its characters on a daily basis in order to achieve and maintain the desired physique through weight loss and muscle gain. On the other hand, the transgendered character personifies the less common legal and surgical changes transgendered people undergo in order to bring their official documents and biological bodies into alignment with their gender identities. Virtually every patron and employee of the *Schlachthof* engages in some kind of excess in order to become fit and thin, and though these measures can take life-threatening forms, they are socially accepted and largely unquestioned. The novel underlines the deadly risks of fitness fanaticism in the three fatalities it narrates: aerobics instructor Anette starves to death after taking weight-loss pills; trainer Fritz Schiller strangles himself while bench-pressing; and gym employee Horst Bleibtreu is killed by owner Gotthelf Schenk after attempting to traffic in weight-loss drugs. Schenk, whose nebulous past suggests he has been using the gym to launder money and evade taxes for years, is also a producer of fitness pornography and fat-burning pills; he is thus multiply complicit in profiting from an industry that exploits desires for beauty and physical enhancement. Even Lisa almost perishes due to excessive, albeit unwanted, bodily manipulation: femme fatale Gerda, Schenk's wife, attempts to protect her husband by strapping Lisa to a tanning bed on maximum strength and leaving her to burn to death.

By contrast with these dangerous interventions, *Training* portrays gender reassignment surgery as a life-affirming measure. Acquiring a male body unfetters Richard from the physical and psychological burdens of a gendered embodiment with which he does not identify. Richard's account of his preoperative past indicates that he has felt masculine since childhood, and that this gender identification only intensified as he grew older. Unlike the bodily manipulations made by the fitness fanatics, gender reassignment surgery does not put his life at risk; rather, surgery liberates the transgendered man from the constraints of living in female body. As a man, Richard also gains access to the benefits of male privilege in pursuing his career. Gender reassignment delivers Richard from the sexual vulnerability and professional limitations that he experienced as a woman: he recounts that, during his law school and internship years, he was the victim of repeated sexual harassment and rape at the hands of male colleagues who apparently perceived the subjugation of their female counterparts as a job requirement (141). Alcoholism and depression ensued, and Richard relates that he only found a way out of this destructive cycle when he began to live as a man and underwent the sex change process. By contrasting the fitness fanatics with a transgendered figure, Lehmann's novel proposes that the more widespread and socially acceptable means of pills and exercise can have far-reaching insidious effects, while the less commonly accepted practice of gender reassignment endangers no one and has the potential to enrich and even save human lives.[64]

Lehmann's novel can also read as a critique of the use of performance-enhancing substances in sports. The textual connections between exercise and illegal medications in *Training* recall the pervasive and highly publicized use of anabolic steroids and blood doping since the 1970s. The consumption of steroids by East German athletes competing internationally was a topic that featured prominently in Western media before and after unification and often served the propagandistic purpose, from a Western point of view, of underlining the manipulative intervention of the socialist state into the lives and bodies of its citizens. Though the practice of doping was by no means exclusive to East Germany, the GDR was unique in instituting doping as a policy and controlling it at the state level. Lehmann's novel offers a diffuse critique that does not explicitly invoke the GDR, as the drug in question is developed abroad by an international team; the text therefore avoids linking the problem with a specific nation and instead represents it as rampant on a global scale.[65] The pills in *Training* are even more dangerous than steroids or blood doping because they contain a virus that literally poisons those who take it. The entire industry that thrives on weight loss and performance-enhancing drugs is embodied in the well-connected, powerful, and corpulent Schenk, who stands in for the doctors, traffickers, medical institutions, and fitness industries that are accountable for distributing substances that destroy human lives.

The novel's most explicit political intervention, however, comes in the representation of the transgendered character, which exposes the limitations of transgender rights in Germany of the late 1990s. Richard's account of his transition process serves a didactic purpose for the story's reader in outlining the state of the law and the protections it provides for and withholds from transgendered people. The critique of transgender rights that crystallizes in Lehmann's story functions as an overt plea for the revision of the *Transsexuellengesetz* [transsexual law] that was originally passed by the West German parliament in 1980 and went into effect in 1981. As Richard elaborates in *Training*, the 1980 law presented two ways for transgendered people to gain legal recognition. The so-called "kleine Lösung" [small solution] allowed for name changes, provided that the petition had the support of two professional opinions; and the seldom-granted "große Lösung" [large solution] made possible a change of gender identity in official documents, albeit only in "Ausnahmefällen" [exceptional cases] and only under the precondition of surgical gender reassignment (141). Feminist and transgender rights activists mobilized in the 1990s to raise awareness about social and political issues that the law did not address and to rally for new legislation. Campaigning for a revision of this law remained a major focus of the trans and queer movements in Germany until the law was revised 2009.[66] Aside from the problematic prerequisite of invasive surgery for legal recognition of transgender status, a number of other aspects of the original law came under fire in the three decades after it was passed. Certain rights and privileges were not available to transgendered individuals, such as marriage and procreation.[67] For instance, legal gender reassignment was contingent on medical sterilization; this provision recalls the forced sterilization campaigns of the Weimar and Nazi eras, a connection that Lehmann's text also implies.[68] The legal stipulation that defines transgenderism as mutually exclusive with childbearing is symptomatic of a lack of understanding of its underlying causes and betrays wide-ranging fear of transpeople.

Training also reveals the chauvinism at work in discourses of transsexuality. This critique tackles the law as well as its social context by highlighting two interconnected issues: the difficulty of gaining access to medical treatment, and the gendered preconceptions that underlie discriminatory attitudes toward female-to-male transsexuals in a male-dominated culture. Both of these problems pose obstacles for Richard when he opts for the "large solution" but is unable to find sympathetic doctors: "Psychologen, die sich mit Transsexuellen auskannten, waren dünn gesät, und es gab buchstäblich keinen einzigen, der verstand, wo das Problem lag, wenn eine Frau sich als Mann fühlte" [Psychologists who were well-acquainted with transsexuals were few and far between, and there was literally not a single one who understood what the problem was if a woman felt like a man, 141–42]. The paucity of medical professionals knowledgeable about transsexuality implies a shared disinterest in researching and treating the condition. Richard's description of this blind spot in the medical profession reveals that access to treatment is just one of many challenges transsexuals face when they wish to begin the legally prescribed transitioning process. Richard must also contend with the widespread refusal, even among medical professionals, to view a biological woman's male gender identification as a sincere expression of personal identity. He describes two psychologists, both men, who deflect his gender identity onto sexual politics (142). Instead of taking female-to-male transsexuality seriously, Lehmann's text suggests, doctors—especially male doctors—misconstrue it as an abstraction of sociopolitical concerns (it is no coincidence that the first doctor to take Richard's gender identity seriously is a woman). Prominent feminist Alice Schwarzer, whose women's magazine *Emma* published a special issue on transsexuality in 1994, describes a similar trend in mainstream attitudes toward female-to-male transpeople: "Es gilt im Patriarchat als 'normal,' aus der weiblichen Enge zu den männlichen Freiheiten zu streben" [It is considered "normal" in the patriarchy to seek an escape from feminine constraint to masculine freedoms].[69] The interpretation Schwarzer cites is symptomatic of a tendency to read a biological woman's attempt to attain the more powerful gender positionality of manhood as merely a "normal" means of accessing authority and agency in a male-dominated society. Though, on the surface, the normalization of identification with manhood implies an acknowledgment of the social inequalities inherent in a culture that privilege maleness over femaleness, it ultimately works to deny female-to-male transsexuals recognition as such. Garber takes up rhetoric similar to Schwarzer's in asserting that a woman's desire to be a man is perceived as "perfectly 'natural'" (45). Garber demonstrates that this dismissal entails a disavowal of female-embodied sexual subjectivity: "women are regarded as having not *sexual* but *cultural* desires—desires that the culture and its doctors understand" (45, emphasis in original). Richard also witnesses this sexism in his medical caretakers' omission of information about the sexual side effects of hormone treatment.[70] As Garber indicates and Richard's experiences confirm, the conflation of a female-to-male gender identity with feminist politics and the concomitant disavowal of female-embodied desire lay bare the chauvinism of both the culture at large and its medical practitioners in particular.

Training further emphasizes this point by calling attention to a double standard in the politics of gender reassignment surgery. Richard undergoes surgery abroad because he is unable to find a surgeon in Germany willing perform the procedure, and though undergoing this kind of operation in a foreign country is not an uncommon narrative, Lehmann's novel suggests that this displacement results from yet another obstacle faced specifically by female-to-male transsexuals.[71] Male-to-female gender reassignment surgery, while more invasive, is a far more common procedure:

> Die Ärzte sehen im allgemeinen kein Problem darin, einen Männerkörper mit weiblichen Merkmalen auszustatten. Doch obgleich es Ärzten bereits in den dreißiger Jahren gelang, nach einem Unfall bei einem Mann den Penis zu rekonstruieren, hielt man die Phalloplastie bei einer biologischen Frau für unmöglich [142].
>
> [In general, doctors see no problem with equipping a man's body with feminine characteristics. But though, as early as the thirties, doctors had success in reconstructing a man's penis after an accident, phalloplasty on a biological woman was thought to be impossible.]

Lehmann's representation of these surgical politics resonates with histories of transsexualism demonstrating that male-to-female surgery was more common and that medical advancements in the process evolved more rapidly than with procedures for female-to-male transsexuals.[72] The text reveals misogyny as the foundation for this surgical double standard: the problem is not the challenge of phalloplasty, but rather the gender of the patient. Doctors deny female-embodied patients access to a procedure that becomes feasible, and in some cases desirable or necessary, when the patient is male-embodied. Moreover,

the presumption that a vagina can be constructed while a penis cannot resonates with traditional yet antiquated theories of gender dimorphism that
align masculinity with nature and femininity with artifice. Garber asserts that
the assumption of male naturalness justifies the medical chauvinism that views
equipping a biological woman with a male sexual organ as impossible: "In sex
reassignment surgery there remains an implicit privileging of the phallus, a
sense that a 'real one' can't be made, but only born" (103–04). A woman's
desire to hold a masculine position of power may well be perceived as rational
and understandable, but her attempt to fully embody masculinity by acquiring
the phallus breaks a taboo. Richard's struggle to become a man exposes the
real stakes of the transsexual double standard: the medical establishment's
resistance to building male genitalia has less to do with the physicality or complexity of the anatomical penis than it does with its symbolic value in embodying phallic power; denying women the phallus means limiting their access to
male-dominated spheres of influence.[73] A biological man who becomes a
woman, by contrast, would more likely be humored and tolerated because her
transition involves a demotion to the lower social status of the feminine—the
subject is therefore less threatening, albeit a greater spectacle, than a female-
to-male transsexual whose transition entails social climbing.

These dynamics underline the often unacknowledged factor of male privilege in the politics of female-to-male transsexuality. For Richard, male embodiment is first and foremost about anatomical alignment and recognition—"ich
träumte davon, als Mann ins Freibad zu gehen" [I dreamt of going to a public
pool as a man, 142]—but it does have the added benefit of giving him access
to male privilege.[74] These effects play out visibly in the attorney's post-operative
professional life, where his unchanged qualities are assessed according to differently gendered criteria: "Intelligenz, Ehrgeiz und Leistungsfähigkeit, die
ihn als Frau eher behindert hatten, erwiesen sich jetzt als karriereförderlich"
[Intelligence, ambition, and productivity, which had if anything handicapped
him as a woman, now proved to be career-enhancing, 143]. In *Training*,
Richard's experience confirms that acquiring the phallus, which demands a
perception of his character and accomplishments in a newly gendered framework, dictates the register of social recognition he receives and makes certain
forms of professional advancement possible.

Richard's seamless performance of robust masculinity resonates with discourses that posit transsexuality not as queering gender, but rather as a confirmation of gender dimorphism—the pre-operative transsexual is simply in
the wrongly gendered body. Though Lisa finds hard evidence of Richard's former female identity in a newspaper article and photo, she is unable to locate
any trace of femininity in his appearance (143). A superficial reading of the
Lisa-Richard coupling at the story's close might also seem to confirm the

notion that the two figures are actually heterosexuals who simply needed to find the right lover of the opposite sex. However, it would be a mistake to conclude that Lehmann's narrative therefore offers dimorphic or heterocentric models of gender and sexuality; on the contrary, it invites its reader to explore a range of queer desires, positionalities, and embodiments. The text repeatedly reminds its reader of Lisa's androgyny and refusal to perform gender coherently: in addition to dressing in men's clothes, she embraces character traits typically aligned with masculinity, such as stubbornness, animal reflexes, and aggressiveness, and she takes distinct pleasure in playing the more active role of initiating sexual contact with the transsexual lawyer. For his part, Richard is all male, but he is not a whole man: with a penis reconstructed from monkey genitalia, he personifies the breakdown of boundaries that Donna Haraway theorizes in her seminal feminist text, "A Cyborg Manifesto."[75] Though Richard does not inhabit the post-gender world that Haraway fantasizes, his body, both at the pre- and post-operative stages, subverts some of the norms she criticizes, particularly regarding integrity and wholeness. Richard's embodiment queers notions of gender and of humanness by manifesting masculinity through an amalgamation of man and animal. When Richard discloses the provenance of his genitalia to Lisa, her first reaction—"Mir wurde anders" [I felt nauseous, 142]—conveys revulsion, a response likely both to facilitate reader identification and to confront readers with the implications of such unease. Lisa's disgust, which quickly turns to desire, expresses what transgender activist Susan Stryker calls "the anxious, fearful underside of the current cultural fascination with transgenderism."[76] The text does not explore whether Lisa is most enthralled by Richard's disclosure of transgenderism, the vulnerability it implies, or the prospect of coming into contact with his animal parts. Nevertheless, her attraction to the public defender, which, in the wake of his confession, precludes her other sexual interests and persists until the novel's end when the two go to bed together, confirms Lisa's pronounced preference for queer objects of desire. The investigator's desire for a transsexual (and his monkey organ, which receives specific mention in the closing scene) in *Training* takes up a trend that begins with the novel's precursor, *Masochist*, when she beds both an effeminate gay man and a female dominatrix. To describe the protagonist as heterosexual or bisexual rather than queer could result in a distortion or oversimplification of Lisa's sexual practices, and the versatile term *queer* better captures the diversity of her desires.

The text also queers identity on the level of the crime narrative with playful representations of signs and spaces like fingerprints and restrooms. When fingerprints collected at the scene of trainer Fritz's death are misidentified as belonging to Lisa, she becomes a suspect in the police investigation. The misread fingerprints destabilize the usual connotations of such traces in crime narratives, where they function as reliable tools in identifying a culprit and as irrefutable proof of identity. The fingerprints belong to Richard, though they do not signal his complicity in the crime—he innocently discovers the body after Fritz's death—but rather expose Richard's secret vulnerability. He touches evidence at the crime scene to steady himself because he feels nauseous, and his fingerprints attest to his weakness, necrophobia (177). Richard seems especially sensitive about this issue, perhaps for fear that it could undermine perceptions of his manly strength and resolve. The misinterpreted fingerprints align Lisa and Richard physically as well as symbolically: by seemingly incriminating them both, the prints bring about an alliance between the detective and the attorney, who collaborate to close the mystery. A climactic showdown pits Lisa and Richard against police investigator Christoph Weininger, with each party erroneously believing in the guilt of the other, in part due to the misconceptions initiated by Richard's fingerprints. Weininger hunts the crime-solving duo in the fitness center, but they outwit him by hiding in the women's restroom: "Kulturelle Hemmungen saßen tief: Weininger würde zuerst bei den Männern reinschauen" [Cultural repressions ran deep: Weininger would have a glance in the men's first, 175]. Since Weininger's gender identity is coherently readable, his movements can be predicted within a specific cultural context. Penetrating the gender-specific space of the women's room has an unforeseen effect on Richard, queering his otherwise stable masculinity. The text demonstrates that spatial contexts can queer gender performances by making the ladies' room the setting for Richard's confession of necrophobia in a discussion that also contains multiple critical remarks aimed at his prowess: Lisa calls him a "Niete" [loser, 175] and insults his "schwache Vorstellung" [weak idea, 175], while Richard refers to himself as a "Feigling" [coward, 177] and an "Idiot" [idiot, 177] as he expresses embarrassment over his necrophobia and regret for his actions. The scene further emasculates the transsexual by positioning Lisa as his protector when she overpowers and topples him, pushing him out of the path of the oncoming Weininger. However, the ultimate insult to Richard's masculinity comes when Lisa reprimands him for attempting to take the lead as they emerge from the restroom: "Hör auf, dich wie ein Mann aufzuführen" [Stop acting as if you were man, 178]. Though Lisa maintains the upper hand in this scene, the power dynamic in her evolving relationship with the public defender begins to level out as they collaborate more closely and the narrative reaches its conclusion. Nonetheless, the intimate space of the restroom and the power flow it frames in this scene foreshadow the novel's closing dynamic, which positions Lisa on top again, throwing Richard into her bed in a judo maneuver.

Lehmann's *Training* is not a romance novel, although my analysis of the narrative might seem to imply that the text prioritizes constructing a romantic conflict around Richard and exploring Lisa's desire for him. On the contrary, this mystery privileges crime and political critique over romance and reader identification, and even the development of the passion between the detective and the public defender remains surprisingly unromantic as the narrative lays greater emphasis on the strategic and the erotic than on warmth or sentiment. Lisa and Richard's businesslike and often impersonal interactions may well leave the reader grasping for evidence of their attraction to one another. Unlike the other two novels discussed in this chapter, in which the romance has the effect of destabilizing the detective's self-perception while also providing a point of reader identification, here it merely functions as another element of the intrigue. Richard is initially introduced as a suspect, and he ultimately coalesces as a curious and unusual object of desire. The two erotically charged scenes, in which Lisa and Richard become intimate, come on the tails of major revelations or discoveries, thereby serving the structural purpose of providing relief from suspenseful, climactic moments. However, such relief is partial and short-lived, as both scenes are interrupted, the first by Weininger's unexpected arrival, and the second by the novel's end. Like Liertz's romance in *Geheimnisse*, Lehmann's mystery concludes in bed, where Lisa, who reminds her reader that she is not accustomed to sleeping with men, welcomes Richard's final revelation, the unveiling of "sein[em] Affe[n]" [his monkey, 208]. But by denaturalizing the body and underlining the foreignness of this sexual interaction, the ending of *Training* thoroughly parodies the crime fiction convention of the detective who beds the love interest at the close of the case.

That Lehmann's book is intended as a sociopolitical critique rather than a romance is also implied through references to *Geschlechtertausch* [Sex Change, 1980], a collection of three East German short stories written by Sara Kirsch, Irmtraud Morgner, and Christa Wolf, and edited by Wolfgang Emmerich.[77] Wolf's "Selbstversuch" [Self-Experiment, 1972], the best-known contribution to Emmerich's volume, plays a special role in Lehmann's novel because it is cited in a passage that introduces Richard's pre-operative past.[78] This reference invites the reader to draw parallels between Lehmann's transgender mystery and Wolf's political allegory about an East German female scientist who undergoes a temporary sex change.[79] Allusions to Wolf's story surface to the level of language in *Training* in the adjective "anders" [other], which appears repeatedly in scenes featuring Richard, and through which Lehmann makes intertextual references to Anders, the name of Wolf's female-to-male transsexual character. Lehmann's novel recasts Wolf's representation of the female other, who becomes a man in order to gain respect in a male-dominated profession, as a transgendered other who fully identifies with maleness. Wolf's and Lehmann's negotiations of the identities of their main characters reveal the far-reaching implications of the politics of gender and sexuality. Though the historical contexts differ, both narratives are set in self-defined democratic states that allegedly embrace gender equality, and in both cases the transgendered character attempts to emancipate herself or himself from the constraints of the feminine by living according to standards of maleness. For Anders, becoming a man is a means of gaining unique insights into the mechanisms of gendered oppression, and once he acquires this knowledge, he relinquishes maleness and re-embraces female subjectivity. For Richard, by contrast, male embodiment represents the fulfillment of gender identification and is the final goal of his transition; and at the same time it serves to reveal the vestiges of sexual discrimination and male privilege in late twentieth-century Germany. Significant differences may set the two stories apart, but they nonetheless articulate comparable political commentaries.

Christine Lehmann's *Training mit dem Tod* indicts the contemporary Federal Republic for failing to protect those citizens who cannot easily be classified in binary-gendered categories, and whose lives are indelibly marked by fear, misogyny, and prejudice. The novel aligns itself with Christa Wolf's critique of the gendered blind spot in a socialist patriarchal state that defines citizenship and humanity as gender-neutral and yet implicitly male, but updates this commentary in mobilizing the transgendered character as a vehicle for exploring transsexual rights. Lehmann's turn-of-the-twenty-first-century murder mystery engages in contemporary discourses and debates by arguing for the social and legal recognition of transsexuals. In taking up the specificity of transgender experience and representing a central figure's desire for a transgendered sex object, the novel poses radical questions about the potential for the emancipation of queerly gendered and sexualized people.

Conclusion: Reading Identity

Queer crime fiction is a hybrid genre that inflects a crime story with an element of romance or, more often even, of eroticism. The extent to which a novel engages generic traditions can have a profound influence on the form and forcefulness of its social critique. The queer detective stories analyzed in this chapter negotiate constructions of gender and sexuality as shifting, malleable, and politically charged, and locate these notions at the center of their intrigues. This comes as no surprise, as questions about identity are at the heart of the crime genre and its commentaries. Masquerades, name changes, and secret identities: these are a few of the building blocks that detective stories employ to develop critiques of social order and imagine viable alternatives. When characters claim specific gender or sexual identities for themselves in the contexts of crime investigations they are leading (or trying to evade), these claims can have wide-reaching implications for textual politics. Whether a text aims to affirm or trouble social norms, to encourage its reader to identify with the story or to maintain a critical distance, identity and desire are meaningful devices, particularly in a genre of fiction in which legality, justice, and life and death are at stake. The dynamics of narrative perspective, development, and closure are intimately linked to the identities of the characters that drive them. When an investigator, a victim, or a criminal identifies as lesbian, bisexual, heterosexual, or transsexual, this declaration has a direct impact on what the crime investigation uncovers and how this is articulated. The queer crime genre demonstrates that claims about gender and sexuality have tremendous social and political force.

When feminist scholar and activist Audre Lorde claimed, "Just because I am a lesbian does not mean that I cannot sleep with a man," she evoked the term *lesbian* as both a descriptor of sexual identity and as a category of political affiliation.[80] Lorde maintained that heterosexual-identified women could identify for political reasons with the word *lesbian* even if the label did not accurately denote their sexual practices; further even, she viewed this as a desirable and effective strategy of advocating for feminist causes. In the sociopolitical context of Germany in the 1990s, affiliations like *lesbian* resonated not only in feminist and gay cultural contexts, but also at the level of the state. In the late 1980s, members of the West German *Bundestag* [Parliament] engaged in heated arguments over language and censorship, deliberating whether it was appropriate to use the more casual terms *schwul* [gay] and *lesbisch* [lesbian] instead of the word *homosexuell* [homosexual] in the legislative body's official records.[81] The discussion concluded in 1990 with a victory for the Green Party, which succeeded in pushing through the official acceptance of the terms *schwul* and *lesbisch*, which were in common use in the gay and lesbian community. Around the same time, philosopher Judith Butler drew a similar parallel between politics and identity when she proposed that "the assertion of 'queer' will be necessary as a term of affiliation, but it will not fully describe those it purports to represent" (*Bodies* 230). Queer crime stories of the 1990s by Gelien, Lehmann, and Liertz support Butler's claim and provide further evidence that descriptors of gender performances and sexual practices have distinct political implications. Together, these various theoretical, literary, and cultural texts illustrate that, despite the slippage among overlapping categories of gender and sexuality like *lesbian* and *queer*, such terms become politically meaningful and necessary in varying contexts, as do shifts within and movements among them.

The blockbuster film *Der bewegte Mann* [*Maybe ... Maybe Not*; literally, The Moved Man] reveals that fluctuation and uncertainty about identity were popular fixations in the 1990s. Like Axel, the film's titular "moved" man, the male and female characters in the novels analyzed above are *bewegt* in ways that have significant implications not only for other characters within their narratives, but also for the texts' politics, serving as vehicles for social critique. Though the queer female figures in *Lesbe*, *Training*, and *Geheimnisse* fantasize about, fall in love with, cohabitate with, and sleep with male-gendered characters, Gelien's, Lehmann's, and Liertz's texts resist describing or identifying their protagonists as heterosexual. Instead, the heroines Gabriele, Lisa, and Deborah embrace queer positionalities that call attention to the constructedness and malleability of gendered and sexualized performances. These performances not only highlight the incongruences among naming, desiring, practicing, and identifying, but also work to expose sexism, homophobia, and transphobia. Through such representations, queer mysteries of the 1990s participate in contemporary discourses about the possibilities and limitations of identity-based and queer movements in the late twentieth century.

CHAPTER 4

Transnational Narrators Undercover: Queer Feminist Critiques of Globalization

> He knew danger was close at hand. And yet he never suspected *me*.
> —Agatha Christie, *The Murder of Roger Ackroyd*[1]

Detective literature thematizes the concealing and revealing of identities by manipulating reader expectations, but even these playful gestures intrinsic to the genre often fall in line with recognizable traditions. Readers of detective fiction gain access to a story through the narrative voice and through the detective's perspective, which become aligned when the first-person narrator and the investigator are one and the same character. A reader is thus doubly dependent on a narrator-detective for a reliable description of the crime and its circumstances, which, it is expected, will supply the reader with the clues necessary to unraveling the story's riddles.[2] Agatha Christie's classic mystery *The Murder of Roger Ackroyd* (1926) shocked fans and critics by breaking long-accepted rules of detective fiction: the sought-after murderer cannot, at the end of the investigation, turn out to be the very narrator on whom the reader relies for a faithful account of events.[3] Christie's narrator, Dr. James Sheppard, is the first person to "find" the murder victim, and thus appears to be an innocent witness who then assists the detective, Hercule Poirot, in conducting the investigation. It is only in the novel's final chapter, aptly titled "Apologia," that the reader learns the truth when the narrator, having been accused by Poirot of killing Ackroyd, confesses and admits that he intentionally gave an incomplete account of his involvement in the crime.[4] Sheppard congratulates himself on his craftiness as a storyteller, particularly his choice of ambiguous phrases—such as "I did what little had to be done" (52, 305)—to deliberately obfuscate his complicity. Breaking the rules of fair play made Christie's novel one of the most controversial works of its time and profoundly influenced the genre of the detective story. By creating a duplicitous narrator, Christie expanded the scope of the crime investigation in her book: no longer a trusted subject, the narrator became an object of critical inquiry, a potential suspect with motives of his own. Indeed, a first-person narrator necessarily provides a limited perspective on the crime and its investigation; a coherent reading of a mystery's meaning must therefore consider the ways in which the text constructs the narrator's character, perspective, and voice as means of concealing or revealing specific elements of the story. Christie's novel altered the stakes of detective narrative politics as well as those of reading. More than half a century later, her innovative approach to detection and storytelling in *The Murder of Roger Ackroyd* still resonates with crime fiction today.

Many queer mysteries take a similarly playful approach to the narrativization of criminality and its investigation, while also extending it to the depiction and sublimation of sexual desire. Queer crime novels thus link a standard element of detective fiction—the work of reading codes to solve mysteries and identify perpetrators—with the metaphor of the homosexual closet.[5] Such texts further dramatize the work of revealing and concealing identity by intertwining it not only with the status of the narrator and the negotiation of sexuality, but also by locating such endeavors in a larger political context, in which sexual desires and practices carry additional meaning as allegories for national and transnational discourses. This chapter examines the interface between the voices of queer narrators, who relate the details of the criminal and romantic intrigues they investigate, and the overt political engagements of the narratives in which they appear. Susanne Billig's *Sieben Zeichen: Dein Tod* [Seven Signs: Your Death, 1994] and Katrin Kremmler's *Die Sirenen von Coogee Beach* [The Sirens of Coogee Beach, 2003] mobilize the trope of the closet in order to convey unease about contemporary transnational developments within and around post-unification Germany, examining migrations and cultural trends on a global scale. Both novels dramatize the narrative structure of the closet by revealing or affirming one "hidden" facet of the narrator's identity in order to distract readers and diegetic characters from another, closeted, identity that has direct bearing on the crime investigation and that resonates symbolically with the narrative's social commentary. In Billig's *Sieben Zeichen*, the closeting of a journalist who goes undercover to research an Anglo-American cult invites a critique of globalization, cultural imperialism, and the exploitation of inequities between former East and West German societies in the early post-unification era. In Kremmler's *Sirenen*, the narrator's secret participation in an international conspiracy develops the notion of global citizenship as an imperative by exposing the shortcomings of asylum policies and human rights protections in Germany and Australia. These novels offer visions of the devastating, or, conversely, vital potential of the transnational flows of ideologies and migrants that become possible with the end of the Cold War, German unification, the opening of European borders, and revisions of immigration laws at the turn of the twenty-first century.

Billig's *Sieben Zeichen* and Kremmler's *Sirenen* can be assigned to a wave of queer feminist crime novels that examine the stakes of national belonging as they play out within and beyond the boundaries of the German nation. Like other such novels, including Maria Gronau's *Weibersommer* [Women's Summer, 1998] and *Weiberschläue* [Women's Shrewdness, 2003], Uta-Maria Heim's *Ruth sucht Ruth* [Ruth Seeking Ruth, 2002], Karin Rick's *Furien in Ferien* [Furies on Vacation, 2004], Thea Dorn's *Mädchenmörder* [Girl Killers, 2008], and Corinna Waffender's *Tod durch Erinnern* [Death by Remembering, 2009], these texts position their crime stories in a transnational arena, a setting that allows them to scrutinize contemporary discourses about the many facets of globalization: nationalism and multiculturalism; colonialism and domination; international justice; and tourism, immigration, exile, and repatriation. Billig's and Kremmler's contributions to the queer feminist crime genre stage overt literary interventions into discourses of political and cultural globalization by mapping interpersonal narrative conflicts along the fault lines of ethnicity and nationality in a historical context that personalizes specific dimensions of German cultural identity. Although Billig's and Kremmler's narrator-protagonists, journalist Helen Marrow and adventurer Gabriella Müller, do investigative work, it is significant that neither of these figures is the police officer, professional detective, or private investigator often found in mystery fiction. Their participation as ordinary citizens in the perpetration and investigation of crime metaphorically conveys the novels' democratic visions; these texts thus argue for political action and activism, suggesting that it takes more than bureaucrats or legislation to bring about political reform, even beyond the boundaries of the nation.

The Undercover Investigator: Drowning in Queer Waters in Susanne Billig's *Sieben Zeichen: Dein Tod* (1994)

By profession a reporter and commentator for radio, television, and print publications, Susanne Billig has found success as a crime novelist with a mystery series featuring amateur investigator Helen Marrow, who is a journalist like her creator Billig. The Marrow series began in the 1990s with *Mit Haut und Handel* [Hawking Hides, 1992] and three further novels published with Rowohlt. *Sieben Zeichen: Dein Tod* is the second installment featuring reporter

Helen, who occasionally takes on private undercover assignments to unearth salacious stories and supplement her income. The Marrow series also includes *Im Schatten des schwarzen Vogels* [In the Shadow of the Black Bird, 1995] and *Die Tage der Vergeltung* [The Days of Retribution, 1997]. The first three installments were republished in the early 2000s with Orlanda Frauenverlag [Orlanda Women's Press].⁶ Billig has published short fiction, including the crime story "Dora," which appeared in the collection *Queer Crime* (2001), and a popular lesbian novel, *Ein gieriger Ort* [A Greedy Place, 2000], a social portrait of the intertwined lives of seven women living in Berlin. Billig has also gained fame as the author of the award-winning screenplay for the film *Verfolgt* [*Hounded*, 2006], directed by Angelina Maccarone. Billig's interests in environmentalism, human rights, and feminism permeate much of her fictional and journalistic work.

Billig's *Sieben Zeichen* narrates journalist Helen Marrow's undercover investigation of an Anglo-American water-worshipping cult that seeks to expand its influence in Eastern Europe after the fall of the Iron Curtain. Numerous facets of the book's portrayal of a secretive sect in this particular historical and geographical context recall the controversy surrounding the Church of Scientology, and the novel may be read as a polemic against cults at a time when Germany—in particular in the territories of the former German Democratic Republic, as well as other former Soviet satellite states—witnessed the importation and rapid proliferation of religious groups. When Billig's narrator-protagonist Helen accepts an invitation to join a religious commune and help build a new facility for the Society for Aquatic Lifestyle (hereafter referenced as the S.A.L.), she has two explicit aims: first, to find her roommate Marianne's missing son Michael, whom she believes to have joined the sect, and second, to use her insights into the group as the basis for an insider report for publication in a popular magazine. The novel thus doubles as a crime story about the search for a missing person and as a chronicle of religious indoctrination and of the evolution of a totalitarian community. Billig's portrayal of manipulative water worshippers warns of the devastating effects of expansionism and globalization. By depicting the cult as the locus of illegal activities and a destroyer of human lives, *Sieben Zeichen* develops a potent commentary on the abuse of religious freedoms and the exploitative potential of foreign cultural influences within a specific set of social and legal circumstances.⁷

Sieben Zeichen also offers another level of encoded meaning, one that employs the cult parable to rehearse a sexual closeting and coming out. References to undercover identities, water rituals, drowning, and closeting frame a story about a woman awakening to queer desire. Helen's name, recalling the Trojan horse of Greek mythology, suggests to readers that something lies hidden beneath the surface, something that in this text only partially comes to expression. Helen's acceptance of the S.A.L.'s teachings and her entry into the commune are red herrings for both narrator and reader, distracting them from Helen's attraction to Edna, the cult's head priestess and the group member most closely associated with the water. The following pages provide a multi-faceted reading of Billig's text that develops these two interpretive positions—viewing *Sieben Zeichen* as a critique of cults and as a coming out story—and combines them in an analysis of the narrative's overall meaning. While the novel intertwines allegories about globalization and queer desire, these two subjects do not receive the same critical treatment. Against the backdrop of *Sieben Zeichen*'s censorious depiction of global religion and the colonization of former East Germany, the text celebrates the liberating potential of acknowledging same-sex love. Even though the story sublimates the expression of its narrator's nascent queer desires, its queer-friendliness finds articulation in the sympathetic treatment of the three main queer female figures—Helen, Edna, and Edna's lover Margarete—as resilient protagonists who ultimately rise above the violence and power-mongering that cause the downfall of the S.A.L. commune. The novel's embracement of queer figures and its mediation of queer romance—if one can call such a subdued theme "romance"—provide readerly pleasures that counterbalance its more explicit social critique. These narrative axes also create points of identification for the presumably female reader, who may more readily identify with feeling romantic interest in women than with the experience of joining a cult.

Billig's second Helen Marrow novel diverges from most queer crime stories in its treatment of eroticism, for the narrative contains no sex scenes and the protagonist's attractions remain at the level of subtext. Its overt focus is not the development of a romantic relationship, but rather the susceptibility of even the greatest skeptic to ideological seduction. But despite the sublimation of the romantic storyline, *Sieben Zeichen* provides ample evidence to support a multifaceted queer reading, because an understanding of the main character as having queer sexual desires has implications for the overall interpretation of the novel's social commentary. In formulating a queer reading of *Sieben Zeichen*, I do the work of a detective, looking for fissures and cracks in the constructions of Helen's feigned spiritual devotion and implicitly heterosexual identity, and fashioning an interpretation of the text based on this evidence. One might say that I am outing Helen Marrow and Billig's crime series, and this is indeed the case—on more than one level, for I am outing *Sieben Zeichen* not only as a queer crime novel, but also as a commentary on Scientology and as a parody. But my understanding of Helen's sexuality as queer is an effect of interpretation, because her desires are conveyed in subtle and symbolic ways that may go unnoticed by a reader who is not looking for codes of queer sexuality. Billig's narrator does not explicitly identify as lesbian or queer; if, however, one were to attach a narrower label to Helen's queer desires, they could be located somewhere on a continuum between queer heterosexuality and bisexuality.

Though a women's press issued the 2003 version of the novel, *Sieben Zeichen* initially came out with the general interest publisher Rowohlt in a high profile crime series that was marketed in mainstream venues. The volume has appeared in bookstores under the rubric of crime fiction, and there is no mention of sexuality on the jacket or in the publicity for *Sieben Zeichen*; it is therefore fair to assume that some readers may neither expect nor find a queer narrative between its covers.[8] However, a reader familiar with Billig's biography and her other publications is more likely to seek and perceive the queer elements of the text.[9] Narrator Helen is divorced and by all appearances heterosexual; in the background is British ex-husband Edward, who receives occasional mention but plays no major role in any part of the series. Of far greater significance for Helen's characterization than her past with Edward is Nancy, the only child their marriage produced, who died young in an accident and whose loss Helen still mourns. Although in both *Sieben Zeichen* and its sequel *angstherz* [Fearheart, 2004, originally published under the title *Im Schatten des schwarzen Vogels*, 1995], Helen mentions previous liaisons with and has fleeting crushes on men, she has no romantic heterosexual relationship in either narrative. Indeed, *Sieben Zeichen* highlights Helen's very lack of feeling toward the men who do flirt with her, while it describes her growing interest in Edna, a charismatic and devoted spiritual leader who has a magnetic pull not just on Helen, but on other cult members too. Helen's interest in the priestess goes beyond that of the other characters because it can be read as both spiritual and romantic. Because Helen overtly denies attraction to Edna, a queer reading of the main character based on one novel in a series might seem problematic were it not supported by evidence from the sequel *angstherz*, in which narrator Helen identifies Edna as her first female love interest. At the same time, Billig's crime series depicts Helen's desire for Edna as exceptional; her intimate and often tense attachments to other women never explicitly exceed the boundaries of conventional friendship. These include domestically, financially, and emotionally codependent relationships with female roommates, clients, and victims throughout the series.[10] *Sieben Zeichen* is unique in suggesting parallels among the narrator's performances of an undercover identity for the purposes of the investigation, the psychological processes she undergoes in joining a sect, and her inner experiences in the queer closet.

Sieben Zeichen opens with Helen's return to her native Germany after living and working in London for twenty years. She accepts a job offer as foreign correspondent for an influential British magazine and rents a room in

Berlin's Schöneberg district from psychologist Marianne Nowak, a flighty single mother of two. Workaholic Marianne is always busy with patients and rarely available to care for her children, but journalist Helen works at home and becomes an unofficial surrogate parent to seventeen-year-old Michael and five-year-old Feli. The crime story begins with Michael's bizarre and increasingly alienating behavior: an obsession with the ocean and a loss of interest in school, family, and friends culminate in unexplained disappearances for days at a time. After one of Michael's mysterious absences, Helen spots him on a nearby street arguing with an older woman, identified much later as the water priestess Edna. Weeks later, Michael returns home for the last time, disheveled and accompanied by a frightened girl named Johanna. The two teenagers are in the apartment only briefly before Johanna jumps from a window to her death and Michael vanishes again, together with his female companion's corpse. Terrified by these events, Helen follows clues that lead her to the water worshippers. She goes undercover and infiltrates the group, and after attending a series of free and then paid meditation courses, she officially joins the Society for Aquatic Lifestyle. Though Helen's frightening initiation involves a near-drowning experience, she continues the investigation and feigns dedication to the S.A.L.'s mission by performing regular devotionals in the group's Berlin meeting space and by doing missionary work around the city. Several weeks into this routine, Helen accepts an invitation to help establish a religious educational center in rural Brandenburg for S.A.L. worshippers from around the world. As the investigation progresses, Helen not only unearths information about the cult's troubled past and the conflicts dividing its members, but she also becomes unwillingly enamored with its philosophies and begins, under Edna's tutelage, to find a sense of inner peace through water worship. This is ostensibly why Helen is identified on the novel's first page as a figure that "so tief in eine Sache ein[taucht], dass ihr die Luft wegbleibt" [dives so deeply into a case that she loses her breath, 3]. Over time the superficially harmonic coexistence of the commune's inhabitants dissolves into a power struggle between two leaders, Edna and an American named Roy,[11] while a series of increasingly violent transgressions indicates that a dangerous traitor lives among them, and, unwilling to involve the police, the cult leaders resort— unsuccessfully—to interrogation and intimidation to identify the perpetrator. Helen must strike a balance among her growing fear and depression, her personal and spiritual allegiances in the S.A.L., and the need to stay close to the information sources that might lead her to the still-missing Michael. Because Helen continues to hide her identity and plays the part of a devoted follower so well, she is entrusted with an office job organizing the sect's financial records; she thus gains access to hidden files and learns that the S.A.L.'s child members were forcibly deported to another commune in Wales. Having finally solved the mystery of Michael's whereabouts, Helen resolves to leave the Society, travel to Wales, and bring the boy home, but not before devastating tragedies occur, including a violent attack by neo–Nazis that leaves Helen in a coma and a triple murder-suicide among the commune's members. The novel concludes with Helen's journey to the British Isles, accompanied by Edna and her longtime lover Margarete. Helen is relieved to find Michael not only alive and well, but also willing to go back to Berlin with her, and after a poignant yet awkward farewell from Edna, she and Michael embark on the return voyage.

The story's historical setting is the early 1990s, and a normative reading of the novel provides a socially critical commentary on globalization in the wake of the fall of the Wall that is readily available to readers not looking for the more oblique queer structures in the text. Billig's fictional Society for Aquatic Lifestyle bears numerous similarities to the real Church of Scientology, which gained influence so rapidly in Germany in the early 1990s that it alarmed bureaucrats and set off a heated public debate about Scientology's presence in the newly unified country and its status as religion.[12] In 1991, allegations that the Church of Scientology was attempting to infiltrate German political parties culminated in a ban against the membership of its adherents in the Social Democratic Party and the Free Democratic Party.[13] While Scientology gained official recognition as a religion—and tax-exempt status—in the United States in 1993, the German government denied Scientology legal recognition as a church and classified it as a *Sekte* [cult] to be kept under observation.[14] *Sieben Zeichen*'s representation of a powerful religious group with distinctively totalitarian dimensions develops a critique of globalization that projects East Germany after the disintegration of the Soviet Bloc not as a postcolonial territory, but rather as neocolonial space: instead of opening former socialist countries up to the possibility of self-determination, the GDR's liberation from Russian control leaves its beleaguered and destitute population susceptible to other forms of dominance.[15] Antiforeigner violence, right-wing extremist activity, unemployment, real estate speculation, and large-scale construction and renovation projects in Berlin and the surrounding area of Brandenburg: these details in Billig's narrative highlight the transformative confrontations with disparities between East and West German infrastructures and standards of living as the two nations underwent the unification process. This transitional economic and political landscape sets the stage in *Sieben Zeichen* for the arrival of unprecedented numbers of spiritual groups seeking converts: as Helen describes it, "Die Gurus stürzen sich wie ein Schwarm Fliegen auf den Osten" [The gurus are descending on the East like a swarm of flies, 63]. It is no coincidence that the newly arrived cultural form clamoring for power and influence is Anglo-American (though Scientology is an American invention, the novel's

S.A.L. was born in Britain and then brought to the United States): the cult epitomizes capitalism, thus representing the ideological antithesis to the Soviet Union, and by extension the GDR. Like the Church of Scientology, which undertook a large-scale recruitment effort in the former socialist territories in the early 1990s, the S.A.L. seizes the fall of the Wall and the resulting social unrest as an opportunity to tap new resources of labor and finances, strategically choosing locations in Berlin for missionary activity and in Brandenburg for its headquarters. One of the S.A.L.'s leaders phrases it thusly: "Wir sitzen hier mitten im Osten. Tausende von Menschen um uns warten buchstäblich darauf, dass ihnen jemand einen Weg aus ihrer Misere zeigt!" [We're sitting in the middle of the East here. Thousands of people around us are literally waiting for someone to show them a way out of their misery! 158]. With such rhetoric, the Society casts its mission as the fulfillment of a social need and glosses over its capitalist aims. Renate, who is assigned to Helen as a "Symbiontin" [symbiote] and guides her through the S.A.L.'s initiation process, is exemplary of the vulnerable former East German citizen such enterprises might target for conversion: an unemployed twenty-one-year-old victim of abuse and the embodiment of provincialism and poverty, Renate uncritically adopts the sect's philosophies and buys into the promise of liberation from her suffering and the tyranny of her upbringing. Though other converts, including Helen, are presumably West German, the S.A.L.'s explicit focus in establishing the Brandenburg commune is to make its mark in the region by attracting people like Renate and her former socialist comrades.[16] Symbolically, the process of ideological indoctrination further functions as a metaphor for German unification. A reading of the text along these lines suggests that East Germans were duped into joining the "cult" of capitalism; brainwashed into believing that this would offer a better way of life, they did not foresee the violence that it could bring about through the eradication of their own culture.[17]

One might ask why, in a cultural context where Scientology was the subject of intense debates, Susanne Billig would invent the fictional Society for Aquatic Lifestyle and avoid naming Scientology as the object of her critique. Clearly, Billig would not have been alone in denouncing the Church, especially in late twentieth-century Germany. However, journalists, scholars, and former members have also charged Scientologists with mounting vehement attacks against their detractors and defectors, from intimidation to persecution and litigation, allegedly in accordance with an erstwhile official Church rule that ex–Scientologist Kate Bornstein identifies as the "Fair Game policy."[18] Billig may have sought to mask her representation of the reputedly secretive Church under the name of an imaginary organization in order to avoid direct confrontation with its adherents or its legal arm. In view of these circumstances, the reader can interpret Helen and her undercover research for an insider exposé on the S.A.L. as emblematic for Billig, herself a journalist by profession, whose second crime novel conveys an oblique commentary on Scientology and its social and psychological effects. This adds another level to Billig's narrative of interconnected investigations that the reader must decode: it would appear that encoding her critique in a crime story was the author's way of distancing herself from the novel's subject, thereby protecting both herself and her professional reputation. This is one possible interpretation of a complex web of textual and extratextual details, and the book can also simply be read as an inquiry into the spread of religion through indoctrination. Overtly, *Sieben Zeichen* expresses skepticism toward organized religion in general and cults in particular: the text compares the S.A.L. to controversial sects such as the Jehovah's Witnesses and Jonestown, and even suggests that the S.A.L.'s water-worshipping mythology is no more bizarre or irrational than some Judeo-Christian beliefs.[19] Only once does Scientology receive explicit mention, in a passage that calls upon the Church as the incarnation of a powerful and ruthlessly exploitative organization. Concerned about the S.A.L.'s growing control over Helen's life, roommate Marianne warns about the challenges Helen could face in defending herself against such an influential institution: "Irgendwann endest du mit ungedeckten Krediten und Schuldenbergen wie die Anhänger der Scientology-Kirche. Diese Leute haben Rechtsanwälte, gegen die kommst du nicht an" [Eventually you'll end up with unsecured credit and mountains of debt like the followers of the Scientology Church. These people have lawyers; you're powerless against them, 62]. The parallels between the fictional Society and the real Church are so numerous that a discerning reader is likely to detect them: like Scientology, Billig's S.A.L. recruits with missionaries and brochures, encourages newcomers to register for a series of courses with steadily increasing prices, describes payments from members as donations, claims to cleanse people of negative thoughts and emotions, aims to world domination, and uses doomsday rhetoric about saving humanity and the earth. These parallels extend to the fictionalized events, conflicts, and names in *Sieben Zeichen*. For instance, Helen's investigation begins after Michael's friend and fellow S.A.L. member Johanna kills herself by defenestration, a death that recalls the real-life suicides of victims who had reportedly spent large sums of money on Scientology courses and counseling: Patrice Vic, a married father of two who jumped from his apartment balcony in Lyon, France, on March 24, 1988; and Noah Lottick, a college student who jumped out of a hotel window in New York City on May 11, 1990. These suicides led to a lengthy legal investigation and the indictment of several members of the Church in France and precipitated public criticism of Scientology in both European and American mass media.[20] Scientology's long-standing war against psychology is personified in Billig's text by an ever more brainwashed Helen and her heated arguments with psychologist Marianne, the latter of whom uses psychoanalytical rhetoric in expressing disapproval of her roommate's ideological reprogramming. In addition, *Sieben Zeichen* features names strikingly similar to those associated with Scientology: in charge of the S.A.L. commune in Brandenburg is Roy, an imposing American ideologue whose portrayal recalls Scientology's founder and longtime leader L. Ron Hubbard; and the name and location of the S.A.L.'s first home in the coastal town of Seaford are reminiscent of the Sea Org, originally an elite oceangoing flotilla established by Hubbard that still serves as the Church's primary religious division.[21] There are also many details of Helen's experiences in the S.A.L. commune, too numerous to list here, that bring to mind various allegations made by critics toward the Church of Scientology.

More than simply constructing an allegory about a religious cult that resembles Scientology, however, Billig's narrative depicts the dangers of such organizations through the progressive indoctrination of her main character and the threats she and other members face. Initially, Helen must work to hide her skepticism about the S.A.L.'s doctrines and the lack of transparency in its leadership as well as her distrust in the genuineness of its most overtly devoted practitioners. But the longer she remains a member, the more readily Helen accepts its tenets. The text portrays the indoctrination process in great detail, a process that is neither unfamiliar to Helen, who vividly remembers losing her teenage best friend to Jehovah's Witnesses, nor unacknowledged by the journalist, even though such awareness alternates with denial as she gradually comes to a genuine appreciation of the faith. Helen becomes a devoted water worshipper despite her initial reservations, which do not dissipate but rather intensify over time. No one in the S.A.L. escapes harm in the increasingly violent episodes that unfold throughout *Sieben Zeichen*. In addition to Michael's friend Johanna, who commits suicide in order to avoid deportation to the children's commune, other devotees fall victim to life-threatening infections and injuries or meet with death: several hospitalizations result from food poisoning and physical attacks, and three casualties are caused by the explosion of a boat during a dramatic power struggle. A psychologically scarred Helen manages to leave the commune in one piece, but notes as she departs, "dass die vergangenen Monate meine Sinne mehr als abgestumpft zurückgelassen hatten" [that the last few months had left my senses more than numb, 250–51]. Despite this implied emotional damage, Helen suggests at the story's end that some elements of water worship may stick with her even as she rejects the S.A.L. and returns to her previous secular existence. These dimensions of the narrative come together in an unmistakably unfavorable portrait of the bleakness of cult life and the devastating and potentially fatal consequences of unchecked religious absolutism. The novel both argues for an increased awareness of cult machinations, articulating a fantasy of eradicating the S.A.L. in Germany, and concedes that monitoring or curbing cult activity can present tremendous challenges, especially for nations in transition like Germany of the 1990s.

Billig's S.A.L. also serves as a vehicle for the critique of American cultural imperialism and German totalitarian mindsets. Founded in England, exported to the Western United States, and ultimately widening its sphere of influence to include much of Western and Eastern Europe, Billig's S.A.L. follows a path of historical colonialism. Likened to an invasion, the eastward growth of the cult in *Sieben Zeichen* comes across as a parasitic movement for the primary purpose of financial gain, which resonates with the discourse of German unification as a colonization of the East by the West and with the notion of exoticizing the GDR as a new Oriental frontier.[22] With characteristic colonizing practices, the S.A.L. epitomizes capitalist globalization at its worst: it identifies an untapped market in a developing area; exploits economic, political, and social inequalities; and promotes an intangible ideological product under the guise of psychological transformation and a more highly evolved life. These developments are recognized by scholars such as Ulrich Beck and Jan Aart Scholte as among the signifiers of globalization.[23] Here we see cultural flows working in extremely destructive ways that are reminiscent of the equation of globalization with cultural imperialism.[24] The narrative of the fictional S.A.L. can be understood, like Janet Reitman's description of Scientology, as "a story about the buying and selling of self-betterment: an elusive but essentially American concept that has never been more in demand than it is today" (xiv). In taking its doctrines abroad, the S.A.L. imports the American myth into underprivileged cultural contexts where it further subjugates its converts, displacing other belief systems and encouraging the dependency of its followers. The cult manipulates adherents into giving over any resources they can provide: forced to liquidate their bank accounts before moving to the commune, members are overworked, underfed, and sleep-deprived, a routine sect leaders portray as the only means to spiritual cleansing and salvation. Repeatedly depicted in financial metaphors, the S.A.L. is driven by the capitalist greed of its administration: Helen's work on the organization's financial records reveals widespread corruption and money laundering that benefits only its most highly ranked leaders, both on location in the Brandenburg commune and behind the scenes in its American headquarters in Portland. The narrative perspective is sympathetic to the sect's disenfranchised work force, its German converts whose devotion, manual labor, and self-annihilation drive the group's large profits, and who are denied participation in the returns on their investments.

At the same time, the effectiveness of the S.A.L.'s indoctrination techniques, which recall strategies of social control mobilized by the Gestapo in the Third Reich and the Stasi in East Germany, also warn of the danger of repeating patterns in the twentieth-century past.[25] This critique provides yet another link to Scientology, which German officials have described as antidemocratic and totalitarian.[26] While the targeting of East Germans for conversion in *Sieben Zeichen* might suggest that citizens of the former Soviet Bloc are perceived as especially open to assimilation because they are accustomed to being told what to do, the novel in fact demonstrates that anyone is susceptible; furthermore, it charges adherents of oppressive ideology with complicity for the transgressions it inspires. Even as she becomes more devout, Helen condemns the follower mindset that keeps her fellow disciples from taking action to stop the violence plaguing them: "Sie *tolerierten* es, dass ein Mensch so zusammengeschlagen wurde, mindestens das, und niemand machte eine Ausnahme" [They at least *tolerated* a human getting beaten up so badly, and no one made an exception, 182, emphasis in original]. Roy takes on the contours of a dictator, enlisting his followers to interrogate and surveil one another, and no one speaks out against these intimidation tactics. The danger of fascism is present not only in the cult, but also threatens it from the outside: Helen fails to heed the warning of a swastika she finds graffitied on commune property, and Tilman, a high-ranking member who believes he is the chosen one and seeks to destroy the others, enlists local neo–Nazis to commit terrifying assaults on his brethren. Revelations about what happened to the children that once lived on the commune are redolent with Nazi euphemisms: the children were "abtransportier[t]" [transported away, 252] in a "Nacht-und-Nebelaktion" [Night and Fog campaign, 215] and sent to a children's commune to receive a special education so that they would embody the group's "Mission in Fleisch und Blut" [mission in flesh and blood, 215]. These metaphors recall the notions of youth indoctrination so central to the Nazi and East German propaganda machines, and the practice of *Kinderlandverschickung* [relocating children to the countryside] to evacuate German children from metropolitan areas susceptible to aerial bombing during World War II.[27] The novel is unwaveringly critical of totalitarianism and its tacit supporters, arguing that to do nothing in the face of injustice is itself unjust. Unlike Pieke Biermann's *Potsdamer Ableben*, which is analyzed in chapter 1 of this study and which, as Katrin Sieg demonstrates, not only delivers a critique of globalization but also develops counterstrategies ("Postcolonial" 153), Billig's novel simply asserts that resistance is necessary and stops short of exploring oppositional approaches. The commune self-destructs, but a few leaders express intentions to rebuild; this development implies that patterns of injustice and oppression will simply repeat themselves if no one intervenes—and Helen's departure clearly indicates that she views her work there as finished. The novel's representation of the process of globalization links capitalism with fascism by depicting a parasitic corporation that becomes a breeding ground for fascist tendencies. In exposing these mechanisms, Billig's mystery delivers an unmistakably antiglobalization commentary.

Beyond its critique of religious totalitarianism, *Sieben Zeichen* opens up to readers another hermeneutical possibility, mobilizing the cult's imagery, together with the plot structure, as performing a symbolic queer outing of its main character. A focal point in Helen's investigation of the religious society is the search for and the attempt to decode a mysterious woman, the high priestess Edna, with whom the undercover reporter becomes more and more enchanted as the narrative progresses. By contrast with the misguided and superficial piety of the commune's other leaders, Edna's devotion is sincere; as a founder of the religion, she is disheartened to witness the sect's evolution away from its spiritual origins and into a mind-controlling capitalist industry. The reader might be tempted to interpret the portrayal of the benevolent Edna, together with her small circle of compassionate and committed followers, as Billig's way of indicating that there are exceptions to the otherwise overwhelmingly unfavorable representation of religious fanatics as driven by negative emotions, coercion, and malicious intentions—and this is indeed a valid reading of the text. However, the sympathetic and clairvoyant priestess also serves an allegorical purpose as the personification of water, an embodiment of spiritual unity with nature. Edna is the cult member most closely associated with the oceans she worships, and she is often seen near the water, meditating by the fountain where the S.A.L.'s holiest rites take place. This alignment is not coincidental: nature in general, and water in particular, is a classical symbol for femininity and female sexuality.[28] If we read the water priestess as a metaphor for feminine sexual allure and power, then Helen's interest in Edna and openness to her influence can be understood as an intoxication with the feminine and a willing immersion into same-sex attraction.

On the structural level, Billig's narrative structures Helen's investigation as the search for a woman, despite her own conscious rationalization of this mission as rescuing her surrogate son, Michael. As if to confirm the mandate that drives many a conventional male-dominated detective story, *cherchez la femme* [look for the woman], the crime plot begins by evoking a feminized mystery: Michael explains his long absences from home by proclaiming that he has met a woman, but provides scant information, leaving Helen little to go on aside from a gendered enigma. "Cherchez la femme," a phrase that in modern usage articulates an imperative to look beyond surfaces for the real cause of a crime, originally indicated a deep-rooted suspicion of the female sex: where there is mischief, murder, or mayhem, one does best to look for a woman at its origin.[29] In conjuring up the stereotype of the femme fatale as the root of evil, however, *Sieben Zeichen* parodies and queers the gender politics of the traditional detective story. Although here the woman Michael references is indeed at the heart of the mystery, she will later be revealed as a positive figure. The teenager's declaration ironically suggests that romance is the cause of his strange behavior, but this story holds no romance for him; instead, the clue he provides sets off Helen's discovery of queer desire. When she first encounters Edna, Helen is captivated by the woman's glowing eyes: this vision draws the reporter into the investigation. Helen's research into Michael's whereabouts develops into an obsession with Edna: "Immer häufiger kam es dazu, dass ich mitten in der Arbeit innehielt, auf mein Papier starrte und einem Gedanken nachhing. Die Frau, die hellen Augen. Edna. Ein Name, der glatt und angenehm im Mund lag" [More and more frequently it would happen that I'd pause in the middle of my work, stare at my paper, and get caught up in a thought. The woman, the bright eyes. Edna. A name that felt smooth and pleasant in the mouth, 40]. These moments highlight the sensory dimensions of desire, with Edna's name literally leaving a pleasant aftertaste, an effect with distinctively erotic undertones. Edna even invades Helen's dreams, where she also brings pleasurable sensations. In order to answer the questions raised by Michael's absence and Johanna's death, Helen must find the enigmatic woman and come to terms with the feelings she arouses. *Cherchez la femme* becomes a driving force behind Helen's investigation, but her desire for intimacy with Edna is sublimated as a commitment to solving other mysteries.

Helen's immersion into the waters is literally and symbolically connected with the image and influence of the elusive Edna. Subsequent sightings, each signaling a transition in Helen's status in the Society, follow the initial encounter with Edna that draws Helen into the cult. She catches fleeting glimpses of Edna twice in Berlin before moving to the commune: first in a crowded plaza where Helen meets S.A.L. missionaries who recruit her to join a meditation group; and again during her initiation ceremony, just before Helen gets trapped underwater, loses consciousness, and almost drowns. The link between the vision of Edna and the near-death experience suggests that Helen is as much in danger of drowning in her fascination with Edna as she is of being engulfed by the religion itself. Water worship becomes conflated with surrendering to the influence of the priestess: after participating in Edna's religious services at the commune, Helen narrates, "ich [wusste] nicht mehr, wie ich mich ihrer Macht entziehen sollte" [I no longer knew how I was supposed to extract myself from her power, 129]. The undercover investigator attributes her incapacity—or lack of desire—to resist the pull of the oceanic philosophy neither to the cult nor to the waters, but to the powerful priestess. Physical contact with Edna, though it occurs almost exclusively during ceremonies, has noteworthy effects on the queer narrator. "*Watch it*" (161, emphasis in original), Helen tells herself, when a nude Edna holds her hand during a group immersion ritual. Her baptism takes place alone with the priestess in

the sacred fountain, a sexually charged event that Helen perceives as the breaking of a taboo: "Ich hatte noch nie gesehen, dass es jemandem von ihr erlaubt
worden wäre, so wie ich jetzt in das Heiligtum zu steigen. Und ich staunte, als
sie hinter mir herkam...." [I had never seen her allow anyone to climb into the
sanctuary, as I now did. And I was astonished when she came in behind me,
200]. If we give this citation a queer reading, the implications of the expression
"climb into the sanctuary" coupled with forms of the verb "astonish" and
"come" are that Edna seduces Helen, who readily takes in the experience, and
that both participants take pleasure in this sensual moment. The baptism
involves Edna holding Helen from behind and repeatedly falling backward
into the water, aligning a spiritual transition with close physical contact
between two women. Though the narrator describes the scene from an emotional distance as "Fast unaufregend" [Almost unexciting, 201], this formula-
tion acknowledges that the experience still somehow excites, even if only
slightly. Afterward, Helen's remark that she feels "von Liebe durchströmt"
[love flowing through her, 201] indicates a profoundly emotional reaction.

By coupling religious faith with queer desire, such parallels evoke an antiquated euphemism for homosexuality: gays surreptitiously described themselves as "going to the same church." Helen's experience is a playful reversal of
the metaphor: her literal entry into the cult doubles as a figurative introduction
to queer desire. This comparison seems all the more fitting because Edna is
unveiled as a lesbian in a long-term relationship with Margarete, another member of the commune, and so Helen's attraction to Edna can read—outside of
its spiritual connotations—as both a yearning for her companionship and as
admiration for a queer woman who has already come out of the closet. As the
novel approaches its conclusion, the narrator consciously registers Edna's
queerness for the first time when she sees her holding hands with Margarete
and expresses surprise that she did not notice their attachment earlier. In failing
to detect clues pointing to Edna's involvement in a lesbian relationship, Helen
functions as a foil for the reader, who may also overlook evidence of the narrator's queer desires. The scene in which Edna and Margarete signal their relationship features another coming out that serves to distract from the question
of Helen's sexuality: Helen discloses her identity as Michael's friend, divulging
that his disappearance motivated her to join the Society. The coupling of these
two simultaneous decloseting gestures—Edna and Margarete's, and Helen's—
resonates with Eve Kosofsky Sedgwick's theory that structures of the closet
and coming out, even those that appear unrelated to sexuality, still carry with
them the weight of connotations of the gay closet (*Epistemology* 71–73). *Sieben
Zeichen* dramatizes this connection, on the one hand by linking the two coming out processes, and on the other hand through the prolonged closeting of
Helen as an undercover reporter and as experiencing same-sex attraction.

Only in its final pages does the text overtly address the question of the undercover investigator's closeted sexuality, but this delayed confrontation with the unspoken queer desire that permeates the entire story serves to outwardly dismiss it. Helen's closet escapes language but surfaces to the level of metaphor, thus resembling the closetedness Sedgwick describes as "a performance initiated as such by the speech act of a silence—not a particular silence, but a silence that accrues particularity by fits and starts, in relation to the discourse that surrounds and differentially constitutes it" (*Epistemology* 3). Michael, it seems, is alone in reading Helen's silence as meaningful, but when he accuses her of having fallen in love, she reacts with such surprise and denial that she appears to be in the closet even to herself. Though Michael does not name the person whom he believes Helen fancies, she concedes, "Ich ... schätze Edna sehr. Das ist alles" (I ... hold Edna in high regard. That's all, 255, ellipsis in original): on the surface, this is a denial of romantic desire, but the pause and the subsequent acknowledgment that Edna is the presumed love object betray an awareness that something more is at play. A reading of the symbolism in the closing passage suggests a sublimated affirmation of homosexual attraction. As she gazes at the ocean, Helen contemplates her relationship to the water philosophy:

> Da hinten irgendwo, weit von mir, durchkreuzten sie die Wasser, unsere Brüder, die Wale und Delphine, unsere Schwestern, die Seejungfrauen. Ich wäre in diesem Moment gern bei ihnen gewesen, hätte das Blau mit ihnen geteilt, anstatt hier zu stehen, am Rand, und zu frieren. Edna schickte ihr Herz gerade zu ihnen, vielleicht... [255].
>
> [Somewhere out there, far from me, they were traversing the waters, our brothers, the whales and dolphins, our sisters, the mermaids. I would have liked to be with them in that moment, sharing the blue with them, instead of standing here, at the edge, and freezing. Edna was sending her heart to them now, perhaps.]

The narrator indicates that water worship still holds sway over her, and that this feeling is linked to its enigmatic priestess. Imagining herself as part of a community to whom Edna sends her heart, Helen not only expresses a desire to share in this devotion, but also positions herself as a part of a group to which Edna's love rightfully belongs. References to brothers and sisters in the passage recall the colloquial usage of the term *family* to refer to the homosexual community.[30] This imagery answers the question that receives only vague and incomplete answers through Helen's spoken words. This is by no means a traditional coming out, for Helen remains in the closet—partially, at least—because she does not acknowledge queer desire unambiguously. The novel withholds closure on the issue of her sexual positionality, leaving it an unsolved mystery.

The answer to this riddle is postponed until the novel's sequel. In *angst-*

herz, queer identities play a central role; although here, like in *Sieben Zeichen*, Helen is not involved in romantic or erotic relationships, the text explicitly thematizes queer sexualities by including openly homosexual characters such as Tanja, a lesbian who shows interest in Helen.[31] In a sentimental moment, Helen gives the reader a brief overview of her romantic history, which includes her ex-husband Edward and several other men. Almost as an afterthought, she admits that one woman also figures among these love interests: Edna. While the text finally delivers confirmation of Helen's attraction to Edna, it does so by simultaneously making several gestures that defuse the potentially destabilizing effect of same-sex desire on the narrator's sexual identity. First, the female love object is marginalized in relation to the handful of men who receive mention: she comes last, and does not count as one of the three romantic interests who were most important to Helen. Second, narrator Helen downplays the meaning of her attraction to Edna because she is unsure what to make of it: "Dass es auch mindestens eine Frau gegeben hat, die mir wichtig war, schiebe ich ein bisschen beiseite, weil ich mich dazu nicht zu verhalten weiß" [I'm setting a little to the side the fact that there was at least one woman who was important to me because I don't know what to make of it].[32] Though the admission that there was "at least" one woman hints that there could have been others too, the statement suggests that she is still in the process of coming to terms with her closeted desires. And third, Helen further minimizes Edna's significance due to her romantic unavailability, claiming that Edna's long-term relationship status forecloses the question of what consequences this attraction could have: "Deswegen führte mich das Ganze nicht weiter in Versuchung, und ich beließ es bei einem vagen Eingeständnis vor mir selbst" [That's why the whole thing led me no further into temptation, and I let the matter rest with a vague confession to myself, 157]. This declaration uses Christian rhetoric reminiscent of the Lord's Prayer, which aligns Helen and Edna with spirituality, and doubles as a confession, thereby metaphorically cleansing Helen of any threat her desire could pose. It also indicates an understanding of sexual positionality as a function not of desire but rather of acts: because Edna already has a lover, Helen's desires do not translate into actions or even into temptation, thus circumventing any confrontation with same-sex eroticism. But Helen ultimately affirms her attraction to a woman, even if she dismisses its implications. If she does not come out of the closet to anyone else, she nonetheless confesses to a small audience consisting of herself and her reader. What remains below the surface in *Sieben Zeichen* thus finds clearer articulation in *angstherz*, but the closet remains a powerful force in Helen's life and in the text.

Though this analysis has emphasized two different interpretive positions toward Susanne Billig's *Sieben Zeichen*, they are compatible. Indeed, we can combine these two readings—the critique of cults and the coming-out story—

in a holistic interpretation of the text as a parody of homophobic views about gay culture and identity. By linking religious brainwashing with a woman's awakening to queer desire, Billig's novel sends up homophobic fears of "homosexual indoctrination." This expression, typically associated with social or religious conservatism, denotes the idea that homosexuals brainwash children and other vulnerable individuals in order to recruit and convert them.[33] According to this theory, such indoctrination can take the form of advocacy for tolerance of homosexuality and gay culture, which ultimately serves the purpose of spreading homosexuality. *Sieben Zeichen* playfully addresses this parallel by depicting the priestess Edna as a queer woman in a position of power and assigning her a central role in Helen's religious conversion as well as her sexual awakening. It is, however, difficult to read Edna as brainwashing Helen into accepting homosexuality or even embracing her own same-sex desires, especially since Edna does not overtly come on to Helen, nor does she come out until long after Helen begins to experience desire for the priestess; and when Edna does finally come out, it is by means of a nonverbal and unthreatening expression of love for someone else. Nonetheless, as the object of queer desire, Edna does serve as a vehicle for Helen's awakening, even if this is unintentional. Originally published in 1994, just as the gay marriage debates were coming of age and political discussions about Paragraph 175 culminated in the abolition of special laws governing homosexual sex, *Sieben Zeichen* can be read as a poignant social commentary on these themes, which are covered in more detail in chapter 3 of this study. Billig's novel displaces the negative stereotype of homosexual indoctrination by reverently holding up the queer priestess as a love object and potential role model for Helen. Edna is an unmistakably positive figure: although she seems suspicious at first, by the story's end it is clear that she is a sincere and loyal leader whose only shortcoming is having too much faith in the good intentions of others. The mystery's compassionate portrayal of lesbian couple Edna and Margarete normalizes homosexuality, setting it apart from other deviant sexual desires and practices—specifically, incest, rape, and pedophilia—that the text reveals as pathological and destructive. A violent confrontation and explosion at the novel's end sends three members of the S.A.L. commune to their deaths: Tilman, Florence, and Manuel are not only among its most powerful and shady figures, but they are also noteworthy for transgressing the boundaries of normative sexual behavior. Florence and Manuel are brother and sister as well as possessive and jealous lovers, and Tilman's first-person narrative reveals that he has a pattern of violently coercing both male and female partners to have sex with him, while his preference is for underage girls; Tilman's visits to the grave of a girl whose death he caused further imply necrophilic activity. All three of these deviant characters die during a dramatic dispute in the middle of a lake because they cannot control their subversive desires and actions; they can thus be said to drown in the waters of their own sexualities. Unlike them, the queer Helen survives life on the commune and emerges from her romantic intoxication with Edna, with the novel's close subtly affirming same-sex desire and celebrating the completion of Helen's journey through these experiences.

The Undercover Perpetrator: Asylum and Gay Globetrotting in Australia and Germany in Katrin Kremmler's *Die Sirenen von Coogee Beach* (2003)

Multitalented and multilingual globetrotter Katrin Kremmler has made herself an internationally recognized figure in lesbian visual and literary culture. She achieved subcultural fame in the late 1990s and early 2000s with the interactive online lesbian comics *Dykes on Dykes* and *Pussy Rules*; attesting to the enduring popularity of the series, an illustrated anthology chronicling the life of *Dykes on Dykes* in English and German appeared in 1998. In Budapest, where the German-Hungarian author lives and works, Kremmler is a prominent queer activist, working to bring visibility to lesbian life and culture, which remain largely out of sight in Hungary.[34] To this end, Kremmler helped to organize the first Lesbian Festival in Hungary in 2005. In collaboration with the Lesbian Film Collective, Kremmler has written and directed Hungarian-language films, including the transgender short *Puszta Cowboy* (2004), which circulated internationally at gay and lesbian film festivals. In Germany, however, Kremmler is better known as the author of three successful lesbian mysteries published with Ariadne: two novels featuring amateur detective Gabriella Müller, *Blaubarts Handy* [Bluebeard's Cell Phone, 2001] and *Die Sirenen von Coogee Beach* [The Sirens of Coogee Beach, 2003], and the cybermystery *Pannonias Gral* [Pannonia's Grail, 2004]. Unlike Billig's *Sieben Zeichen*, which can be read as a queer text even though it does not openly encourage such labeling, Katrin Kremmler's novels are—like much of her aesthetic production—marketed as lesbian and celebrate their characters' queer genders and sexualities. Together with other lesbian crime novels in Ariadne's feminist series, *Die Sirenen von Coogee Beach* has an odd series number designating a story with queer protagonists, and the drama centers on five gay women who share a house in Sydney, Australia.[35] Kremmler situates her lesbian leading ladies within a larger social context: her narrator and other main characters are politically and socially active in their local gay and feminist subcultures. Set in late 2002 during the Gay Games,[36] *Sirenen* unfolds largely within the city's lesbian milieus, and Kremmler's rendition of Sydney's geographies partially reads as a tourist brochure, offering insider tips for the queer vacationer. The book participates in a discourse of global citizenship, promoting migration by introducing Sydney's treasures and idosyncracies to German readers. At the same time, it warns of the dangers that await adventurers and refugees alike, who may be targeted as victims of crime or find their human rights violated during their journey. These are qualities that *Sirenen* shares with Kremmler's other two crime novels: set in Budapest, both *Blaubarts Handy* and *Pannonias Gral* explore the darker sides of Hungarian society, while at the same time celebrating the pleasures of travel and tourism and portraying their narrators' multicultural backgrounds as assets in crime investigations.

Kremmler's *Sirenen* emphasizes Sydney's cosmopolitan allure, but it also reveals the city's charm as artifice, mobilizing this as an allegory for Australia's attractiveness to refugees despite the nation's pathological obsession with ethnic identity and immigration. Exposing Australia's political, social, and economic underbelly, *Sirenen* reflects on contemporary discourses of multiculturalism, national belonging, and immigration and asylum, but this commentary does not target Australia alone. On the surface, a reader may see few similarities between Australia and Germany—aside from the fact that both are wealthy, stable democratic nations—but Kremmler's mystery draws numerous subtle comparisons between the two developed countries. Though the novel is framed as a critique of the island continent's border politics, pivotal scenes unfolding on planes bound for Frankfurt and at Germany's largest airport broaden the object of the story's critique to include the politics of identity in Germany. The text's post–9/11 settings place special emphasis on national boundaries and transnational mobility, highlighting the ways in which nations define themselves through exclusions justified as security issues, and juxtaposing different types of migrations that are facilitated or hindered by the ethnic identities of individual travelers and the documents they possess. Contrasts among migratory movements for different purposes (tourism and asylum) and among migrants from different economic and ethnic backgrounds (middle-class Western Europeans and destitute Middle Easterners) bring into relief the double standards in the enforcement of immigration policies. The novel's setting in 2002 and publication in 2003 invite readers to reflect on the parallels among the border crossings it narrates and the place of immigration as a contentious issue on both sides of the globe in the 1990s and early 2000s, when debates over Australian border politics raged under John Howard's Liberal-National coalition, and Gerhard Schröder's Social Democratic-Green coalition undertook ambitious revisions of German citizenship and asylum laws.

At the level of character, *Sirenen* plays with notions of ethnicity and national identity by intertwining several narrative threads involving hidden and stolen identities. The text generates tension by alternating mechanisms of concealment and revelation with respect to these mysteries of identity, which include the question of the narrator's relationship to the crimes narrated, the theft of a passport and its use to cross international borders, and other intrigues surrounding immigrants, tourists, and refugees coming to Australia from Germany, Hungary, Ireland, and Iraq. First-person narrator Gabriella ("Gab") Müller personifies multiple border crossings that are further emphasized by the novel's transnational plot: Gab is a German-Hungarian graduate student who lives Sydney, where she has worked semilegally for the city planning bureau on an extended tourist visa for a year; she is also writing a dissertation on the cultural identity of second-generation lesbian migrants in Australia. The crime narrative begins not with Gab's story, however, but with one of several passages in an unembodied third-person narrative voice, a "Prolog" [Prologue] introducing Andrea Hönig, a German-Spanish badminton player in Sydney to compete in the Gay Games, who wakes up in an unfamiliar apartment with a drug-induced hangover and discovers that her passport and return ticket to Frankfurt are missing.[37] Andrea immediately buys into a red herring, suspecting that the thief is identical with the Irish vixen Eve who drugged and seduced her the night before, presumably leaving Andrea tied up in the vacant apartment in order to abscond with her papers. Stranded in Sydney until she acquires new travel documents, Andrea turns to her acquaintance Gab for help; Gab invites the tourist to lodge in her home until she is able to return to Germany. Though Gab narrates much of the story, she withholds important information regarding her own involvement in Andrea's misfortune, but subtle clues about her complicity surface in the narrative. Unbeknownst to the theft victim or to the reader, Gab's sympathy for Andrea is driven by guilt: she pilfered the documents herself—while her roommate Siobhan (written "SHE1" in the text; she uses the pseudonym Eve with Andrea) was drugging and bedding Andrea—in a conspiracy organized together with two other roommates, Meg and Stace, who are refugee rights activists. Andrea, however, mistakenly believes that the robbery is the work of a single perpetrator; she therefore does not see Gab as a potential culprit. To complicate matters further, Gab falls for Andrea, and this romantic constellation becomes a consummate love triangle when Gab's lover Lilli, a German-Hungarian athlete who resembles Andrea, takes interest in Andrea's story and helps with the investigation while also seducing her. After days of searching, to no avail, for the femme fatale who drugged her, Andrea learns of her hostesses' collusion in a scheme months in the making: she became a target in their humanitarian mission to use papers purloined from a Western European tourist to secure safe passage out of Australia for an undocumented Iraqi refugee named Hawa, in hopes that she might gain asylum elsewhere. As Hawa enters Germany with Andrea's papers, Andrea struggles to explain to officials how her passport returned to her homeland without its legal owner. A final twist in the story comes when, after obtaining new documents, Andrea again falls victim to drugging and robbery, just as she boards her return flight to Frankfurt. This time it is Lilli who filches Andrea's passport, swapping it with her own expired visa in order to extend her stay in Sydney and pursue an affair with Gab.

The novel explicitly positions itself as a commentary on immigration and Australian border politics with a metafictional device consisting of two short passages preceding the beginning of the crime story. These two passages serve as clues for the reader, who must make sense of the subtle connections between the fictional mystery of a stolen passport and the larger narrative of cultural critique. The first opening passage about sirens evokes the novel's titular mythological beings as emblematic for Australia's international image: the infamous sirens represent not only the possibilities of survival and safety that entice refugees to undertake perilous journeys, but also the exoticism, promise of adventure, and high standard of living that attract well-heeled travelers. The problem with sirens, Kremmler's text asserts, is that their song is a deception with devastating consequences: "In der Legende zerschellen die Boote der Betörten dann an den Steilklippen" [In the legend, bewitched travelers' boats then shatter on the steep cliffs, 7].[38] This depiction unifies the two facets of popular cultural representations of Australia "as both dramatically beautiful and radically life-threatening," to use the words of Stephen Knight.[39] Here, however, the nation's life-threatening potential is linked not to its rugged natural geography, but rather to contemporary politics and culture. The deceptive "Signale" [signals, 7] that the sirens broadcast recall radio and television transmissions, and broadly construct the mythical creatures as symbolic for cultural imperialism. As Knight and others suggest, crime fiction set in Australia—a nation that is racialized as white and that is "basically an exclusive nineteenth- and twentieth-century society, with a single point of origin and with, because of its geographic location, distinctly limited influences" (Knight 25)—is particularly well positioned to interrogate the legacies of colonial possession that have become part of national consciousness.[40] *Sirenen* participates in this trope of postcolonial crime fiction by juxtaposing Australia's image in the global imagination as a land of mystery and adventure with the enduring tension between politics of inclusion and exclusion. Though Kremmler's novel later tackles the problems of British cultural hegemony and the marginalization of aboriginal history more explicitly, the novel's opening depiction of Australia as threatening seems directed not toward its dispossessed indigenous population, but rather toward twenty-first-century international arrivals. The opening passage of Kremmler's *Sirenen* casually addresses the (presumably non–Australian) reader by repeatedly using the informal second-person pronoun *du*, which simultaneously draws the reader in and interpellates her into the group of pioneers, tourists, migrants, and refugees susceptible to Australia's allure.

In both content and form, this segment conveys an immediate warning about the dangers awaiting travelers, whatever their motives, and positions the novel as critical of the ways in which the nation's spectacular scenery overshadows the ugly realities of impermeable borders, antiforeigner sentiments, and the rejection of multiculturalism. Ending with a reference to silence—"wenn [die Sirenen] schweigen, hast du ein Problem" [when the sirens are silent, you have a problem, 7]—the passage also playfully reveals to the attentive reader the key to deciphering the puzzle of the crime: the solution to the mystery can be found in that which remains unsaid. In her first-person narrative, Gab occasionally makes allusions to information that she withholds from her interlocutors; these telling clues point to her own culpability and recall the narrator's craftiness in Christie's *The Murder of Roger Ackroyd*. Attentiveness to these silences is crucial to appreciating the complex web of intrigue and complicity that *Sirenen* weaves in order to implicate not only its narrator, but also the national state and its conflict-ridden relationships to cultural heritage and ethnic hegemony.

The shipwrecks mentioned in the first opening passage and referenced above provide a symbolic link to the sunken refugee-laden fishing boat that is the subject of the next opening segment. This second passage consists of an excerpt from an Amnesty International report about a real-life event commonly known as the SIEV X incident,[41] which brings the warning signaled by the seductive sirens and their seafaring admirers into a contemporary international political context. The metatextual citation in Kremmler's novel briefly summarizes facts relating to one of the largest maritime disasters in Australian history: on October 19, 2001, an overloaded fishing boat bound southward from Indonesia sank in the Indian Ocean, taking the lives of 353 asylum seekers, many of them women and children (8).[42] News of the boat sinking broke in the midst of a reelection campaign for Liberal Prime Minister John Howard, who advocated a hard line on asylum and immigration; and, occurring on the heels of two other highly publicized maritime incidents involving refugees, the Tampa affair and the Children Overboard affair, the SIEV X incident fueled the flames of an already divisive political firestorm.[43] The sinking of SIEV X was particularly controversial due to numerous allegations that military and governmental representatives colluded in refusing aid and concealing information about the unseaworthy vessel's whereabouts, knowingly allowing the boat to sink and thereby shirking an international obligation to rescue imperiled seafarers.[44] Though *Sirenen* references neither the Tampa nor the Children Overboard affair, it evokes the climate in which the SIEV X incident transpired by alluding to the legal and military measures the governing coalition instituted in the aftermath of these events, profiting from the situation to advance its position on curbing immigration.[45] Prime Minister Howard receives mention elsewhere in Kremmler's text as personifying Australia's lacking recognition of asylum seekers and human rights, and more generally representing a conservative turn in the nation's politics in the late twentieth and early twenty-first century. While the author does not take an explicit stance in this opening passage, by citing Amnesty International she aligns the novel with the organization's mission to defend human rights, indicating disagreement with the Australian Liberal-led government's firm position on border protection, which gained strong popular support in the wake of the 9/11 terrorist attacks in the United States. Moreover, by locating its crime plot in this geographical and historical context, *Sirenen* positions itself to pose compelling questions about national belonging and accountability, engaging post–9/11 discourses on globalization, democracy, and terrorism. These two opening passages introduce several symbols that will come to play crucial roles in the mystery, such as boats, the ocean, and travel documents, which provide concrete links to this wider cultural context. The novel offers a parodic comparative perspective on transnational migrations by juxtaposing the struggles of an undocumented refugee with the misfortunes of a stranded tourist. It also does so by contrasting asylum seekers who undertake dangerous voyages on overcrowded boats with wealthy Australian nationals and immigrants (Gab's duplicitous employer and her affluent friends) who regularly indulge in leisurely junkets on luxury yachts.

Set during the Gay Games, a weeklong event that draws thousands of athletes and spectators from around the world, Kremmler's novel negotiates portrayals of Australian politics of inclusion and exclusion, linking issues of race, ethnicity, and class to gender and sexuality. From the beginning, the narrator differentiates between that which Sydney represents to outsiders and the realities that contradict paradisiacal illusions of the Australian metropolis. With its ethnically diverse population, tourist-friendliness, rich gastronomic culture, and colorful nightlife, Sydney has the appearance of a global city that embraces difference: "Sydney repräsentiert Exotik, Spaß, Sex, Phantasie, Differenz. Es ist ein Ort, wo man sich hinflüchten, in dem man aufblühen kann, ein Hafen für alles Schrille, Exotische, Andersartige, ein Ort, wo alles möglich ist" [Sydney represents exoticism, fun, sex, fantasy, difference. It's a place where one can take refuge, where one can flourish, a haven for everything flashy, exotic, different, a place where anything is possible, 25]. However, opportunities to partake in the city's cultural offerings are not universally available. Terminology such as "take refuge" (the German also translates as "to flee to" or "to escape to") and "haven" (the German word literally means "harbor") in the above description self-consciously evokes the exclusionary politics underlying the conditions for transnational migration. Gab dismisses the much touted myth of tolerance in Sydney, and more generally in Australia, firstly by asserting that its gay culture is less accepted, integrated, and visible than a tourist attending a large, queer-inclusive, and yet transient event like the Gay Games might believe. Secondly, she contends, Sydney's cultural life is heavily stratified along class lines: that gay events are expensive and only accessible to affluent participants signals general economic segregation, symptomatic of a superficial society whose members literally wear their wealth on their sleeves and whose social interactions are dictated by their income levels. And thirdly, despite the obvious ethnic diversity of its citizenry, Australia fantasizes itself as a nation of primarily white, northern European heritage: its politicians and policies deny the legitimacy of aboriginal societies and couch racist views in rhetoric of "Assimilation" [assimilation, 36].[46] Those Australian citizens and immigrants with multiethnic or non–Anglo heritage—that is, residents who are neither light-skinned nor of British descent—fall into the broad category of *wogs*, a racialized and often derogatory term that can include a wide range of cultures from southern European to Middle Eastern (37).

The narrator's interest in examining intersections between race and sexuality coalesce in her dissertation research on lesbian *wogs* and come to life in the character of Zed, an Australian citizen of Hungarian descent who is at the heart of a secondary mystery, a wrenching tale involving sexual abuse, homophobia, persecution, and psychological instability. *Sirenen* provides a counterpart to the account of Hawa, the Middle Eastern refugee who is unable to obtain legal status in Australia, by giving a voice to Zed, a successfully immigrated and assimilated and yet nonetheless dispossessed resident. Zed's sad story also involves multiple lesbian heartbreaks, and the text privileges closure on this front by giving her the last word in a romantic happy end that brings with it a dramatic resolution of her past traumas (184). Kremmler's sympathetic portrayal of a marginalized *wog* comes into relief against its critical representation of a conservative Australian mainstream that celebrates monoculturalism and aims to make itself impermeable to immigrants, particularly Asians, but also, especially since 9/11, migrants of Arabic origins. Hailing from Iraq, Hawa personifies entire categories of asylum seekers who are perceived as threats on the sole basis of their ethnicity: the narrator quips, "die könnten schließlich verkappte Terroristen sein" [they could, after all, be terrorists in disguise, 38]. Such refugees are persistently denied their human rights: once on Australian land, Hawa endures forced separation from the spouse and family with whom she had fled her homeland; long-term detainment in overcrowded camps without access to the media or opportunities to participate in local culture; and repeated deferral of the asylum process, with little prospect for becoming a legal resident. Hawa's two suicide attempts signal that the harsh existence she finds in a land she had hoped would provide refuge holds neither greater safety nor higher quality of life than the oppression she had initially fled. Attempted suicide forms a link between the disaffected characters of Hawa and Zed, both of whom struggle to come to terms with the outsider positions they have been assigned in Australian society. Hawa's despondency arises not only from the miserable conditions under which she lives in the immigration detention camp, but also because she is mourning the loss of her young daughter, who does not survive the arduous voyage from Iraq. Zed, by contrast, attempts suicide in order to escape the clutches of her incestuous Hungarian father, who abused her as a child, refuses to accept her homosexuality, and stalks her relentlessly. Though the two figures try to take their lives for different reasons, both women's suicidal tendencies develop as consequences of persecution. By the story's end, however, both migrants succeed in overcoming the circumstances of their malaise with the help of the novel's other leading ladies. This conclusion brings together feminist concerns with a critique of globalization. While Hawa escapes from the prison of Australian immigration impasses, Zed exacts revenge on her abusive father, and both women—perhaps for the first time in their lives—finally feel safe.

Because Hawa ultimately succeeds in gaining entry to Germany, one might be tempted to read the text's representation of the Western European republic as positive in contrast with its portrayal of the land down under. Indeed, Gab and her cohort target Andrea as their passport theft victim for two reasons: she resembles Hawa and hails from a country where Hawa has better chances of gaining political protection. This depiction resonates with "Germany's image as an unusually liberal asylum country," despite the lagging rates of immigration belying the nation's reputedly generous acceptance of refugees.[47] However, Germany does not escape critique in Kremmler's novel: though the author partially masks her satire of German antimulticulturalism under the guise of her overt condemnation of Australian conservatism, *Sirenen* provides ample evidence for an interpretation of its commentary as implicating Germany in the political and cultural dynamics that it alleges are particularly problematic. The novel's Germany is no more protective of refugee rights or welfare than Australia: Hawa enters both countries illegally, and in both states her safe passage becomes possible only by unlawful means involving the collaboration of activists and members of refugee aid networks who must themselves be careful to avoid arrest. The text makes a direct allusion to Germany's fascist history when Gab's roommate and coconspirator Stace compares Woomera, the immigration center in a remote part of South Australia where Hawa is detained for sixteen months, to a Nazi concentration camp (168).[48] The circumstances of Hawa's detention and escape recall other aspects of Nazi oppression: her internment, persecution, and escape evoke the circumstances under which victims of racist discrimination and political persecution suffered and attempted to survive during the Third Reich.[49] The collaboration of underground organizations to place Hawa in a safe house and to help her enter Germany with stolen documents might also remind readers of covert resistance operations in Nazi-occupied Europe.

Kremmler's depiction of a narrator-perpetrator who conceals her own involvement in the story's crimes draws attention to the interface between dominant narratives and their subtexts and silences, suggesting that other messages may lie hidden between the lines of her novel. The undercover perpetrator, who is half German, serves as a figurative doppelgänger for the German nation; both are complicit in wrongdoings that the text sublimates, though their complicity is not of the same order. By perpetrating illegal transgressions, Gab seeks redress for the kinds of systemic injustices in Germany and other countries with white majorities that privilege white citizens and migrants while marginalizing others. One of many noteworthy parallels between these two kinds of complicity is the ethnic profiling in which Gab engages in search of her passport theft target—"im Idealfall nicht aus dem Mittleren Osten, sondern, sagen wir, der EU oder Kanada oder so" [ideally not from Iran or Southern Asia,[50] but rather, let's say, the EU or Canada or something similar, 170]—which replicates the forms of racial profiling that occur at national borders, but for different purposes. Gab uses racial profiling in order to secure a refugee's safe passage across national borders, while passport controls and customs agents and border patrols use it to identify potential threats to national security. On the flight to Frankfurt, Hawa is subjected to racial profiling by the German passenger next to her, who is irritated to learn that her dark-skinned neighbor holds a German passport. The assumption underlying the German traveler's surprise is that Germanness equals whiteness: "so dunkel, wie sie war, konnte sie durchaus aus einem arabischen Land stammen" [as dark as she was, she was probably from an Arabic country, 69]. The German woman's obsession with Hawa's ethnicity gives way to paranoia about the hidden dangers she could embody—after all, weren't Arabic people "alle abgebrühte Fanatiker" [all hardboiled fanatics, 69]? In assuming that Hawa poses a security risk, it is the German woman who ironically endangers the refugee's safety by reporting her luggage to authorities and unleashing panic over a possible bomb in the airport. These anxieties evoke escalating anti–Islamic and antiforeigner sentiments in Germany following 9/11, in the midst of heated debates about *Leitkultur* [dominant culture] versus multiculturalism; conservative fears about the decline of the German population vis-à-vis increasing numbers of residents with *Migrationshintergrund* [migrant backgrounds]; and the Social Democratic-Green coalition's measures to enact long-overdue reforms to asylum and immigration laws, which were still under negotiation as *Sirenen* went to press.[51] The parallels Kremmler constructs between racism and xenophobia in Australia and Germany charge Germans with intolerance and resistance to change and convey skepticism about the extent and efficacy of German policy reforms. Kremmler, however, does not stop there with her critique; she also attacks the middle class, whose blindness to its own privilege and whose apathy in the face of human suffering can derail attempts to ensure the welfare of asylum seekers. The depiction of a Frankfurt airport employee who is uninterested in helping an obviously distressed Hawa indicates that political change must also target the complacent and disinterested middle class in its efforts to promote human rights and democracy: even nonracist Germans require education regarding the vital importance of refugee assistance and humanitarian aid.

Sirenen is a postcolonial crime novel, offering a scenario in which "social order is no longer restored, but questioned through alternative notions of justice."[52] The specific models of justice that the novel endorses, feminist activism and transnational humanitarian action, aim to undo the injustices perpetrated by state bureaucracies and mainstream conservative cultures; however, the obstacles they face are immense, and their efficacy is thus limited. The novel's protagonists do save one refugee, but they are unable to help countless others who wait for years in limbo, are denied asylum and deported, or meet with worse fates. Rather, the text's power lies in its interrogation of the dominant social order, particularly in its exposure of racism and ethnocentricity as pervasive, antidemocratic, and life-threatening forces. In addition to providing the "morally ambiguous closure" typical of hardboiled crime fiction, Christine Matzke and Susanne Mühleisen assert, postcolonial crime texts explore forms of knowledge and resistance "against the local or global mainstream, past and present, or against potential projections of a dominant group and a (neo-)imperial West" (5). *Sirenen's* anti-imperialist vision of justice challenges legal discourses that define Gab and her coconspirators as criminals; instead, the Western nation-state takes the contours of the ultimate villain. Emerging as an intolerant institution led by bigoted politicians in the interest of a white bourgeoisie, the state, as exemplified by the novel's Australia as well as its Germany, is the perpetrator of the real crimes at the heart of the story: propagating inequality, discriminating against minorities, oppressing refugees and immigrants, and abusing human rights. Gab and her cohort function as the story's heroes, putting their own freedom at risk in order to create the carry out alternative forms of justice. With the tale of Hawa's travails and the activists' efforts to help her, Kremmler's novel aims to educate its reader about the vital function of asylum, the connections between racism and antirefugee attitudes, and the devastating effects of conservative immigration laws on the physical and psychological well-being of people whose lives are already in danger. Globalization, Kremmler stresses, entails an imperative, the obligation to act, to extend the privileges of living in a stable democracy to refugees who desperately need its protection.

Kremmler's novel theorizes a new form of citizenship in the age of globalization that is at once radically democratic and radically individualistic, promoting a notion of global citizenship that is by definition universal, honors the primacy of human rights above all other imperatives, and confers upon its subjects the right of transnational mobility.[53] The text articulates what Stephen Castles and Alastair Davidson call the "crisis of citizenship," a phenomenon that has accompanied the changing form and function of the nation-state in a global context at the turn of the twenty-first century, and that becomes visible, among other places, in the revised citizenship and immigration laws of various nations.[54] In Kremmler's Australia, this crisis finds partial articulation in the foregrounding of women of various nationalities—Australian, German, Hungarian, Iraqi, and Irish, among others, as well as bicultural ethnicities such as German-Hungarian and German-Spanish—who bear few cultural markers aside from the ethnicities the text assigns to them. The collaborations of these diverse women instead offer functional models of global citizenship with their own sets of rights and responsibilities: these characters mobilize the privileges conferred upon them by their own ethnicities, middle-class status, and participation in local lesbian culture to secure the safety and survival of a woman they barely know, but who needs assistance in transcending the national boundaries that limit her mobility and therefore bar her access to life-saving asylum. Hawa's experience represents one of many disjunctures, to borrow a term from Arjun Appadurai, in evolving global flows. *Sirenen* attests to the decreased primacy of the nation in defining the meaning of citizenship in the twenty-first century but also demonstrates the global effects of existing borders and especially the asylum and immigration policies that still rely on categories of national citizenship. Gab and her cohort embody the responsibilities that a changing global context foists upon its only partially postnational citizens by participating in what Appadurai describes as a facet of the imagination, a pivotal axis of the global cultural economy, "a form of negotiation between sites of agency (individuals) and globally defined fields of possibility" (31). The heroines of Kremmler's mystery set out to explore and expand these fields of possibility through their own actions and collaborations, which cross ethnic and national boundaries. In so doing, they project a fantasy of a postnational world society.

Sirenen does this by exposing the limitations of current practices of assigning citizenship and identity. The novel takes the conventional rhetoric of asylum, which is typically described as a right, and recasts it as a luxury—like tourism—only available to the privileged few that can afford it. The drama of stolen documents reveals that the condition of possibility for transnational mobility is, to a certain extent, a function of what one possesses: a traveler's or a migrant's ability to cross borders has just as much to do with the documents she holds as it does with her personal identity. Kremmler's tale contests and destabilizes the traditional concept of citizenship by distinguishing personal from political identity and by revealing the latter as contingent on external confirmation through bureaucracy and paperwork. At the same time, opportunities to hold precious documentation are nonetheless largely dependent on national origins, and personal identity thus plays a pivotal role in determining potential for mobility: the currency with which we purchase these documents is our recognized political belonging, a belonging that the documents in turn prove. Andrea may be temporarily inconvenienced by the theft of her passport, but because she is from Western Europe, it is fairly easy for her to gain access to new legitimate documents and to regain her rightful mobility. Hawa, by contrast, can only cross into Germany because the papers in her hand do not reflect the true identity that has become her prison. Immigration laws and bureaucracies pose obstacles for asylum seekers as well as for tourists, and in *Sirenen* these problems have one and the same illegal remedy. The second passport theft at the end of the novel allows for a reading of Lilli, another German tourist who steals Andrea's papers in order to prolong her own stay in Australia, as the ultimate benefactor of the story's political message. Closure of the passport theft intrigue brings with it a shift toward the politics of desire. Lilli's problem ironically reverses the challenges Hawa and Andrea face when they are unable to leave Australia without proper documentation; instead, Lilli cannot fulfill her wish to stay longer in the land down under precisely because of her papers, as her tourist visa is expiring. When Andrea learns of the conspiracy to which she fell victim, she acknowledges that the situation has opened her eyes and concedes that, in spite of everything, she agrees with the schemers' motives: "Ich finde die australische Flüchtlingspolitik auch nicht gut" [I also think the Australian refugee politics aren't good, 176]. However, it is Lilli who demonstrates that she has not only learned from these events, but that she can put her newly acquired knowledge to use, harnessing what she has garnered from the feminist activists about identity theft to achieve the specific goal of controlling the terms of her own mobility. In contrast with Iraqi refugee Hawa, whose reasons for using stolen documents are political, Lilli's goal is to pursue a romance: she is in love with Gab and, unbeknownst to the first-person narrator, will stay in Australia for the sole purpose of winning her heart. With Andrea's purloined papers and a bottle of hair dye, Lilli is equipped to get what she wants. By narrating this final, unexpected reversal motivated by romantic interests, Kremmler's novel places the lesbian activists' political justifications into even greater relief while reframing the focus of the story on the personal dimensions of desire. In the mystery of the stolen passport, Lilli gets the last laugh — and the reader laughs with her, because the tables have been turned on Gab, who is no longer the agent of dramatic irony, having now become its object.

This analysis has focused largely on the novel's negotiations of transnational politics, but its sexual politics are noteworthy too. The representations of Sydney's queer subcultures in general and Gab's sexual activities in particular are entertaining affirmations of lesbian lifestyles, desires, and practices in a wide range of forms. The text guides the reader through Sydney's lesbian- and gay-friendly institutions, mentioning the names, locations, and peculiarities of women's beaches and bookstores, lesbian bars, and queer parties, giving tips on the best times of year to partake in this subculture. Diverse events and sexual practices are described, from the local to the global—we read about Gurlesque, a monthly lesbian strip party in the queer-friendly neighborhood of Oxford Street, and a concert given by k.d. lang, a Canadian singer who has become an international icon—and from vanilla sex to bondage, live piercings, fecal play, and blood fetishism. At times merely suggestive and at others extremely graphic, Kremmler's depictions of lesbian sex are unabashedly celebratory. The unpleasant and even destructive dimensions of sexuality are not glossed over, however: exploitation, jealousy, heartbreak, abuse, and incest play important roles in the novel's intertwined mysteries, beginning with Andrea falling victim to a crime she terms "lesbian date theft" (24). Andrea's attempts to identify the perpetrator dramatize Sydney as a space where the global and the local collide: it may be filled with thousands of queer foreigners who are there to partake in its sexual culture, but its lesbian community is small, and everyone knows everyone. The locals are highly amused by the wanted posters Andrea and Gab distribute to every lesbian locale in the city, because they all recognize the perpetrator as Gab's roommate Siobhan, a promiscuous member of their community. A reader might be tempted to ask whether this particular subculture is crucial to the crime story, and the answer is that the setting not only lends the narrative a particular flavor, but also colors its development. The intrigue plays on the stereotypical insularity and incestuousness of lesbian communities, where the cliché is that, despite being part of the same metaphorical family, everyone sleeps with—or knows someone who has slept with—everyone else. Kremmler takes this cliché and turns it into the condition of possibility for the sexual and political intrigues she weaves.

Sirenen also challenges and politicizes narrative traditions by playing with reader expectations. In dramatizing the complicity of an unreliable first-person narrator who obfuscates the details of a crime, *Sirenen* recalls the narrative twist at the end of Agatha Christie's canonical 1926 mystery, *The Murder of Roger Ackroyd*. Like Christie's Dr. Sheppard, who narrates the investigation in the first-person voice, Kremmler's narrator-perpetrator ostensibly helps to investigate the crime and thus appears to be free of suspicion. Both novels challenge principles of fair play by casting the narrator as a criminal: the reader, who accesses the mystery through the narrator's account, typically views the narrator's voice as authoritative and is unlikely to suspect that it is selective or untrustworthy. Pierre Bayard, however, argues that texts such as *Roger Ackroyd* do not violate the conventions of detective fiction; rather, they dramatize the constructedness and inherent unreliability of the narrative in a way that is unique to the genre, where the very function of the story is to mislead the reader until the revelation of the mystery's solution (54). Upon learning of the narrator's guilt, which is exposed at the ends of Christie's and Kremmler's tales when other characters identify Dr. Sheppard and Gab as perpetrators, the reader must reassess all available evidence in order to digest this new information. Truth, these stories suggest, is always a matter of context and interpretation. Kremmler makes a direct nod to Christie's text when Gab, pressed by Andrea to explain incriminating evidence, offers an incomplete account that is nonetheless honest: "*Die Wahrheit. Und nichts als die Wahrheit, so wahr mir Gott helfe*" [*The truth*. And nothing but the truth, so help me God, 89, emphasis in original]. Citing the title of the penultimate chapter of *Roger Ackroyd*, "And Nothing but the Truth," in which Christie's detective Hercule Poirot reveals to the narrator the process by which he deduced his identity as the perpetrator (298), Kremmler aligns her work with a literary tradition of subverting reader expectations while also raising its stakes: like Christie, Kremmler theorizes the relativity of truth and reveals the constructedness of narrative, but she further mobilizes this dynamic to develop a pointed social critique.

One of the ways in which Kremmler politicizes the stakes of Christie's plot is by omitting the figure of the professional sleuth: in *Sirenen*, no police officer or detective investigates any of the crimes it narrates. Instead, those transgressions that would typically call for an official investigation—the theft of Andrea's passport and plane ticket at the beginning of the novel and the murder of Zed's father at its end—are officially recorded as a crime of opportunity and an accident. When law enforcement and government officials do appear in the text, their performances are brief and emphasize their inefficacy and misdirected suspicions.[55] Indeed, the representation of bureaucrats as misled, incapable, and hostile (if and when they are at all present) supports the text's larger political message of condemning the Australian state and its policies. In the absence of police or private investigators, the victim of the robbery takes the investigation into her own hands, but mistakenly enlists the help of the very characters who are guilty of the crime, and in so doing, creates the conditions of possibility for her own education about social injustice.

Although, like Christie's Dr. Sheppard, Gab leaves traces of her guilt in the narrative, these are easily overlooked by a reader who is not searching for clues pointing to the narrator's involvement in the transgressions against

Andrea. For there are other transgressions in which Gab openly declares her complicity: she lets the reader in on her participation in schemes to kill one roommate's dog and another roommate's father. Like many detective stories, Kremmler's text begins with a body—two bodies, in fact, though neither is the typical human corpse one might expect in such narratives. The first victim is Andrea, and though she is alive, her wounded body recalls the detective fiction convention of the feminized corpse, with her physique bearing traces of the transgressions she has endured and providing clues for the investigation: she is naked and alone; writing in pain; and tied up and locked into a strange apartment. Although Andrea will attempt to investigate the crimes to which she fell victim, this initial scenario prescribes her position as the object rather than the subject of this inquiry. The second body is a true corpse, fulfilling the oft-cited generic convention that a detective story should begin with a murder.[56] But this is a canine corpse, belonging to Paws, a seventeen-year-old mutt who lived in Gab's household. Assuming that their elderly pet died of natural causes, Gab's roommates do not see the corpse as evidence in a mystery. While her roommates mourn the loss of their four-footed friend, the narrator reveals to her reader that living with an incontinent dog was unpleasant and unsanitary, and that she took control of the situation by giving the dog a merciful and humane death with a lethal dose of calcium chloride: "Es ging schnell und hat ihr nicht wehgetan" [It went quickly and caused her no pain, 16]. The reader learns early on that dramatic irony plays a role in the narrative, and the tension created by the reader's inside knowledge of such details—feeling as though she is in on the joke—adds to the many pleasures of reading this parodic text. However, the reader's awareness of this ironic twist functions as a red herring because it encourages her to trust the narrative voice and to believe that Gab will divulge her transgressions in this first-person account, even if she hides them from other characters. The reader is thus likely to overlook the possibility that this situation offers evidence of Gab's duplicity and willingness to take justice into her own hands. Just as the first body assigns Andrea to the position of unknowing victim, this second body inscribes Gab's role as cunning perpetrator, a structure that hints at her possible responsibility for other crimes. Within this constellation of mysteries both personal and political, *Sirenen* raises a number of ethical questions about ending animal and human lives, when it is permissible to take justice into one's own hands, and what it means to act in the name of humaneness or humanitarianism. Now, ten years later, these questions still resonate deeply with feminist and queer theory, debates about euthanasia and animal rights, and scholarship on globalization and ethics.

The novel's conclusion with a murder reminds its reader of these concerns and locates them as distinctively feminist. The murder victim, Zed's father

Thomas, embodies multiple evils in the eyes of left-wing feminism, from bourgeois entitlement and exploitation to homophobia and sexual abuse. Though Thomas's death is both desirable and just in the novel's logic, it raises unanswered questions about the limits of humanity and humanitarianism. It also puts the story's other crimes into perspective: if murder even represents a form of justice, then how could we object to an identity theft or an illegal border crossing, crimes that cause relatively little no harm but stand to benefit many?

Conclusion: Reading the Closet

Following in the footsteps of Agatha Christie's trailblazing novel *The Murder of Roger Ackroyd*, Susanne Billig's *Sieben Zeichen* and Katrin Kremmler's *Die Sirenen von Coogee Beach* play with reader expectations by closeting important dimensions of their first-person narrators' identities. Billig and Kremmler's stories are, in many ways, almost diametrically opposed, not only in their treatment of the multiple closets that they open up (or keep closed) for the reader, but also in their structures, narrative voices and perspectives, portrayals of the investigators, and approaches to detective fiction conventions. Readers of *Sieben Zeichen* perceive events largely through the perspective of Helen Marrow, the first-person narrator, who also functions as a protagonist. Helen's psychological turmoil and critical processes are therefore available to Billig's reader in an unmediated way, but they are also subject to Helen's own blind spot, her inability or unwillingness to acknowledge her own queer desires. At the same time, the heavy emphasis on Helen's psychological development occasionally takes precedence over the novel's implicit political critique. In *Sirenen*, the narrative perspective favors the first-person voice of perpetrator Gab Müller, who intentionally hides her complicity in the crimes; the reader's blindness to Gab's guilt is therefore a function of a willful omission rather than a blind spot on the narrator's behalf. The narrative voice in *Sirenen* also rotates to include other perspectives, thereby emphasizing the novel's commentary on mobility and democracy. Sex and romance, which play a central role in *Sirenen*, are understated in *Sieben Zeichen*. While Billig's novel lets the reader in on Helen's professional undercover status from the beginning on, it postpones explicit discussion of her desires until the final pages, and even there, it never clearly articulates her sexual identity. Kremmler's mystery, on the other hand, outs its characters as lesbians from the very beginning, but prolongs the play on the narrators' criminal status by gradually revealing evidence of their crimes and outing them as criminals at its end.

These two novels, published at the turn of the twenty-first century, also share several noteworthy qualities. Intertwining the trope of narrative unreliability with their mysteries' transnational critiques, Billig and Kremmler emphasize the reader's role in doing the necessary interpretive work of opening the closet and unveiling their nuanced commentaries on the human stakes of globalization. *Sieben Zeichen* and *Sirenen* require their readers to actively decode the meanings of the multiple connections they construct among gender and sexuality; race and ethnicity; national boundaries and transnational mobility; marginalization and belonging; and power, agency, and complicity. Both novels stress milieu-oriented depictions of small communities, one religious and the other social, in which the central conflict is set into motion by the movement of ideologies or people across international borders. In demanding the reader's involvement in decoding their queer critiques of imperialism and postcolonialism, these crime stories provide voices for the marginalized perspectives of the disenfranchised and explore strategies of resistance. In further combining such critiques with references to the Third Reich and fascist regimes of the past and present, the texts allude to the enduring presence of racism and xenophobia in and beyond Germany. Implying that such structures inevitably lead to devastation, both texts argue for a global vision of humanity that takes into account national and ethnic specificity but confers the rights of self-determination, mobility, and asylum to all.

Conclusions: Writing Queer Crime into the Twenty-First Century

As a child, I was enchanted by Nancy Drew, so generous and enterprising, and with the perfect outfit for every occasion. Nancy's ambition, adaptability, resourcefulness, and collaboration with her friends Bess and George were inspiring examples of feminism in action. Like the original Nancy Drew, each of the investigators and perpetrators examined in this study represents "a moment in the history of feminism"[1] while also embodying a mystery in her own right. The authorship of the series in which Nancy stars is as hard to sort out as some of the enigmas I have explored in this book about her successor sleuths. Planned by a man and produced by a syndicate, the Nancy Drew books were ghostwritten by at least two different women.[2] The original texts, moreover, were later revised in an effort to accommodate changing cultural and political sensibilities. The varying incarnations of the iconic Nancy Drew and the evolving authorial identities of the elusive Carolyn Keene may have in some way prepared me for the present study of sleuthing, culture and politics, identity shifts, and intersecting criminal and sexual ambiguities.

This project is a mystery made in Germany and Austria. By contextualizing analyses of queer crime stories within their geographical and historical settings, it has sought to detect and elucidate the ways in which cultural critique is encoded in the genre. Close readings of novels by German-speaking authors from Kawaters to Kremmler formed the basis for excursions into the overlapping domains of genre fiction, cultural studies, and queer and feminist theory, demonstrating how queer crime narratives negotiate the values, fears, and preoccupations of their times. Crime fiction is intimately concerned with the work of detection and with questions about identity, and queer mysteries adapt generic traditions by linking complex and changing genders and sexualities with the misdeeds and investigations they narrate. Paradoxes of identity cannot always be untangled, and the challenges of interpreting queer desires and embodiments, riveting though they may be, can confound and unsettle. Queer subjects often remain elusive despite our best efforts to pin them down.

In the interest of highlighting cultural discontent and political activism in portrayals of social transgressions, I have doubtless underemphasized the pleasures of reading these books. Those pleasures are multiple: irony, masquerade, defiance, and hope, to name a few. Queer crime stories, like many mysteries, give readers opportunities to test their detective skills and play with identity; readers take part in the processes of decoding language and behavior, assigning meaning to the narratives, and constructing plausible solutions for their riddles. The crime genre as a whole traffics in the fantasy (even if unfulfilled) of seeing justice served, whether through detective work, legal intervention, vigilantism, or further transgressions. In the mysteries featured here, the distinctively feminist and queer dimensions of these fantasies materialize in confrontations with social inequality, structural oppression, and the struggles of individuals and state institutions to address these injustices.

The fictional investigators, rebels, and criminals alike are feminist role models with human dimensions: they are strong, insightful, driven, and loyal, but they are often also—like their readers—fallible, quirky, and misunderstood. While some of the writers whose work I have examined, such as Billig and Liertz, take relatively sober approaches to their subjects, many others, such as Biermann, Gelien, Kremmler, and Lehmann, entertain with wit, sarcasm, and parodies of feminist and queer culture. Wielding humor as a weapon, they tackle social stereotypes and literary clichés, taking to task the status quo. In short, these authors use satire and laughter as forms of resistance.[3] Queer crime fiction thus inspires and incites the feminists within us.

One of the organizing principles of this project has been the types of characters appearing in queer crime novels. The chapters are sequenced as a series of parallel readings of texts whose protagonists share multiple features, the comparative analysis of which helps elucidate the discourses linking popular culture and politics. I began this study by proposing that the detective work undertaken by two of the earliest feminist investigators of the 1980s, Kawaters's Zora and Biermann's Lietze, exemplifies queer feminist practices. The novels examined in chapter 1 seem very different: Lietze is a police commissioner and Zora is an autonomous activist, and Biermann humanizes government officials while Kawaters is suspicious of bureaucracy. Nonetheless, both characters epitomize contemporary feminism in their support of leftist-inspired movements and involvement in coalitional action. The stories of murderesses in chapter 2 diverge from the majority of those analyzed in this study in their portrayal of women as sympathetic criminals and their misdeeds as retribution for the injustices they and their loved ones suffer. Kneifl's and Noll's queer twosomes, Anna and Ann-Marie, and Maja and Cora—like Gab, the investigator-perpetrator in chapter 4—resort to violence as a means of overcoming obstacles to women's autonomy and mobility in Austria, Germany, the European Union, and beyond. The focus shifted in chapter 3 to maleness and masculinity, with emphasis on men who become objects of desire for queer female investigators. The ostensibly heterosexual flirtations of Liertz's Deborah, Gelien's Gabriele, and Lehmann's Lisa resonate with discourses of the 1990s about lesbian identity, gay emancipation, and queer theory. The incorporation of romantic tropes and the revelation near the end of each story that the desired man is himself queerly gendered or sexualized represent playful twists on crime narrative conventions. The novels discussed in chapter 4 also challenge the traditions of the genre by hiding meaningful dimensions of their narrators' identities. The undercover status of their queer protagonists, Billig's journalist-investigator Helen and Kremmler's activist-culprit Gab, allows them to exert influence on politically charged transnational settings. The mechanisms of concealing and revealing in these queer mysteries dovetail with their commentaries on citizenship, oppression, migration, and asylum in an age of rapid globalization.

The last two novels I examined, Billig's *Sieben Zeichen* and Kremmler's *Die Sirenen von Coogee Beach*, are not alone in exploring connections between concealed information and transnationalism. Crime and detective fiction, police procedurals and thrillers: these investigative literary genres all build upon the possibility that something hidden may come to light. More so than other genres of fiction, crime stories highlight the ways in which we gain knowledge by reading clues, and the ways in which access to information affects our behavior. In the increasingly globalized cultures of the late twentieth and early twenty-first centuries, information, whether encoded or not, easily crosses national borders, beyond which its impact cannot be predicted. Like the people who create them, texts and ideas are highly mobile and can evade detection, even the most earnest and ingenious attempts. In mysteries by Kawaters, Kneifl, Noll, Gelien, and Liertz, entities and concepts with foreign origins—ranging from operatic traditions and child pornography to economic practices and diasporas—are crucial to the crime plots. Kremmler's stories in particular, with their foregrounding of technologies of communication such as cell phones, word processing, and the internet, evince a fascination with the shifting ways in which medium influences meaning as it travels. These concerns attest to the local and regional anchoring of queer crime novels along with the global perspectives of their commentaries. It somehow seems fitting, then, that the present study of German-language literature, written by an American who has lived and studied in Berlin, Vienna, and Paris, is being published in the United States.

Queer crime fiction continues to proliferate in Germany and Austria, where it is appearing in series both established and new.[4] Several of the authors discussed in this project are still writing crime novels well after the turn of the twenty-first century: Kawaters, Kneifl, Kremmler, Lehmann, and Noll have all added to their ongoing crime series or created new heroines in recent years. Their latest mysteries extend the trajectories of the critiques developed in their earlier work and make possible future research on how their evolving social philosophies find expression in innovations within the crime genre. Since 2000, queer crime novels and stories have been published by the likes of Annette Berr, Thea Dorn, Maria Gronau, Uta-Maria Heim, Hedi Hummel, Manuela Kay, Barbara Kirchner, Litt Leweir, MAF Räderscheidt and Stephan Everling, Karin Rick, Ursula Steck, Ursula Stocks, and Corinna Waffender, to name just a few. Antje Wagner's queer teen mystery *Unland* [No-Land] attests to the presence of queer discourses in contemporary youth culture. A number of mainstream authors popular with literati, such as Antje Rávic Strubel, who is not typically described as a crime writer, can also be viewed as participating in the topoi of queer mysteries. Recent queer crime novels incorporate in their plots sexual paraphilias such as pedophilia, incest, and zoophilia; a consideration of the representations of these transgressive practices could potentially broaden or subvert the concept of *queer* and notions of queer politics. Related subjects such as child abuse, violence in schools, and animal welfare, which were among the early concerns of feminist crime writers, still figure in queer texts. Coming years may see a rise in novels focusing on cyberbullying, online stalking, child prostitution, and other internet crimes against children that are on the rise due to increased access to electronic media. Gay marriage is quickly becoming a non-issue in a number of European countries but continues to be a hotly debated topic elsewhere in the world, and associated controversies over tax breaks, parental rights, reproductive rights, and transgender rights may come to play pivotal roles in queer crime stories. Readers will likely witness the articulation of specifically German and Austrian concerns as well, such as financial scandals involving politicians and the integration of immigrants from Turkey and southeastern Europe. At the same time, the challenges of transnationalism will doubtless have a more palpable presence in future queer mysteries, which are sure to thematize the economy of the European Union, racism and political extremism, Islam and multiculturalism, wars and unrest in the Middle East, and national and international terrorism.

Because this study has aimed above all to tease out the possibilities of interpretation and to initiate a scholarly conversation about a subgenre of crime fiction that has remained largely below the academic radar, but not to have the last word, I do not presume to impose a "conclusion." A shift in perspective made possible by pluralizing this heading nonetheless allows me to come to terms with what might otherwise be in this instance the inelegance of singularity: conclusions are multiple and necessarily open. While I have offered some possible solutions to the mysteries this book examines, their puzzles nonetheless continue to perplex, offering themselves to readers, critics, and scholars as mysteries to be solved and resolved anew.

Chapter Notes

Introduction

1. The term *genderqueer* references practices and embodiments that do not exclusively inhabit the territory conventionally described as male or female or that fall outside of gender norms altogether. It differs from *androgyny* in that the latter usually suggests a combination of masculine and feminine traits. Genderqueer can also signify resistance against the gender binary. See Joan Nestle, Clare Howell, and Riki Anne Wilchins, eds., *GenderQueer: Voices from Beyond the Sexual Binary* (Los Angeles: Alyson, 2002).

2. For definitions of *queer* that both emphasize its use as a noun to refer to gender and sexuality and gesture toward its function as a verb or adjective to imply a destabilizing approach, see Judith Butler, *Bodies That Matter: On the Discursive Limits of "Sex"* (New York: Routledge, 1993); David L. Eng, Judith Halberstam, and José Esteban Muñoz, "What's Queer about Queer Studies Now?" Introduction, *What's Queer about Queer Studies Now?*, ed. David L. Eng, Judith Halberstam, and José Esteban Muñoz, spec. issue of *Social Text* 84–85, 23.3–4 (2005): 1–17; Alice Kuzniar, Introduction, *The Queer German Cinema*, by Alice Kuzniar (Stanford: Stanford University Press, 2000), 1–20; Christoph Lorey and John L. Plews, "Defying Sights in German Literature and Culture: An Introduction to Queering the Canon," *Queering the Canon: Defying Sights in German Literature and Culture*, ed. Christoph Lorey and John L. Plews (Columbia: Camden House, 1998), xiii–xxiv; Holger A. Pausch, "Queer Theory: History, Status, Trends, and Problems," Lorey & Plews, eds. 1–19; Eve Kosofsky

Sedgwick, "Queer and Now," *Tendencies*, by Eve Kosofsky Sedgwick (Durham: Duke University Press, 1993), 1–20; and Michael Warner, Introduction, *Fear of a Queer Planet: Queer Politics and Social Theory*, ed. Michael Warner (Minneapolis: University of Minnesota Press, 1993), vii–xxxi.

3. Some scholars, such as Gill Plain, suggest that this tide change goes hand in hand with the advent of feminist approaches to crime fiction: "It is no longer possible to assume that any contemporary crime fiction will offer the secure, ratiocinative solutions that we associate with earlier manifestations of the genre, and (on an optimistic day) we might argue that feminist and lesbian crime fiction's refusal of androcentric bourgeois methodologies was instrumental in bringing about this change." Gill Plain, *Twentieth-Century Crime Fiction: Gender, Sexuality and the Body* (Chicago: Fitzroy, 2001), 204.

4. For discussions of queer methodologies as well as the fields of inquiry and interpretive possibilities they open up, see Judith Halberstam, "An Introduction to Female Masculinity: Masculinity Without Men," *Female Masculinity*, by Judith Halberstam (Durham: Duke University Press, 1998), 1–43; and Kath Browne and Catherine J. Nash, "Queer Methods and Methodologies: An Introduction," *Queer Methods and Methodologies: Intersecting Queer Theories and Social Science Research*, ed. Kath Browne and Catherine J. Nash (Burlington: Ashgate, 2010), 1–23.

5. Pieke Biermann and Ingrid Noll are the only two authors featured in this study whose crime fiction has been published in English translation. Though Biermann's popular Karin Lietze series begins with *Potsdamer*

Platz, only the second novel in series, the award-winning *Violetta*, has been translated into English, appearing under the same title (trans. Ines Rieder and Jill Hannum; New York: Serpent's Tail, 1996). Bestselling writer Noll has seen three of her novels translated into English, including the one I analyze in this study, *Die Häupter meiner Lieben*, which, as the italicized gloss in the main text indicates, came out under the name *Head Count* (trans. Ian Mitchell; London: Harper, 1997). Two other early novels by Noll, *Der Hahn ist tot* [*Hell Hath No Fury*] and *Die Apothekerin* [*The Pharmacist*], have also appeared in English translation with Harper.

6. English speakers interested in German feminist and queer crime literature can read, in addition to the translations of Biermann's and Noll's novels mentioned in the note above, published translations of novels by Doris Gercke (*How Many Miles to Babylon*) and Antje Rávic Strubel (*Snowed Under*). For those interested in other genres and media, Susanne Billig wrote the screenplay for the film *Verfolgt* [*Hounded*, directed by Angelina Maccarone], which is available with English subtitles; and a bilingual volume chronicling the history of Katrin Kremmler's interactive web cartoon, *Dykes on Dykes*, includes text in German and English.

7. Susan Stone recounts a bookseller's theory that German crime novels are "too local, too regional, just too German." Susan Stone, "Why German Crime Fiction Fails to Thrill US Readers," *PRI's The World*, PRI's The World, 28 Dec. 2012, accessed 15 May 2013, http://www.theworld.org/2012/12/why-german-thrillers-are-not-popular-in-us/.

8. Nicola Barfoot, *Frauenkrimi/polar féminin: Generic Expectations and the Reception of Recent French and German Crime Novels by Women* (Frankfurt am Main: Lang, 2007; MeLiS 5), 75.

9. Barfoot is not alone in pointing out that the concept *Frauenkrimi* is problematic; for instance, crime writers Biermann and Sabine Deitmer find the term ghettoizing and chauvinistic, while scholar Marianne Vogel argues that it not critically useful. See Pieke Biermann, "Warum ich *keine* Frauenkrimis schreibe," *Tagesanzeiger-Magazin* 8 Feb. 1992, *Krimikultur: Archiv*, accessed 12 Dec. 2012, http://krimikulturarchiv.files.wordpress.com/2009/07/warum-ich-keine-frauen krimis-schreibe-19912.pdf; Sabine Deitmer,

"Anna, Bella & Co.: Der Erfolg der deutschen Krimifrauen," *Frauen auf der Spur: Kriminalautorinnen aus Deutschland, Großbritannien und den USA*, ed. Carmen Birkle, Sabina Matter-Seibel, and Patricia Plummer (Tübingen: Stauffenburg, 2001; Frauen-/Gender-Forschung in Rheinland-Pfalz 3), 239–53; and Marianne Vogel, "Ein Unbehagen an der Kultur: Zur Kriminalliteratur deutschsprachiger Schriftstellerinnen in den 90er Jahren," *Zwischen Trivialität und Postmoderne: Literatur von Frauen in den 90er Jahren*, ed. Ilse Nagelschmidt, Alexandra Hanke, Lea Müller-Dannhausen, and Melani Schröter (Frankfurt am Main: Lang, 2002), 49–67.

10. Crime writer Thea Dorn contends that the popularity of the *Frauenkrimi* was so great in the 1980s and 1990s that even male authors considered publishing under female pseudonyms. Thea Dorn, *Die neue F-Klasse: Wie die Zukunft von Frauen gemacht wird* (Munich: Piper, 2006), 19. Dorn's comment may be a reference to Gronau, whose identity was the subject of controversy in the late 1990s and early 2000s, when readers and critics voiced suspicions that Gronau was actually a male writer using a female pseudonym in order to reach a female audience. For a discussion of the debate about Gronau's gender and identity, see Barfoot 191–94. For a discussion of the gendering of narrative voice in Gronau's work, see Evelyne Polt-Heinzl, "Frauenkrimis—Von der besonderen Dotation zu Detektion und Mord," *Ich kannte den Mörder wußte nur nicht wer er war: Zum Kriminalroman der Gegenwart*, ed. Friedbert Aspetsberger and Daniela Strigl (Innsbruck: StudienVerlag, 2004; Schriftenreihe Literatur des Instituts für Österreichkunde 15), 144–70; here, 158–59. For an analysis of the significance of gender and sexuality in Gronau's texts, see Faye Stewart, "Mother Sleuth and the Queer Kid: Decoding Sexual Identities in Maria Gronau's Detective Novels," *Questions of Identity in Detective Fiction*, ed. Linda Martz and Anita Higgie (Newcastle: Cambridge Scholars, 2007), 19–35.

11. Claudia Wessel, *Es wird Zeit* (Giessen: Wemü, 1984), 56. Translations in this book from the original German to English are mine throughout.

12. See "Marlowes Töchter," *Der Spiegel* 2 Jan. 1989: 148–50, *Der Spiegel*, accessed 18 July 2009, http://www.spiegel.de/spiegel/print/d-13493405.html. Barfoot also notes

that the late 1980s witnessed a change in the valence of gender on the crime fiction market (72).

13. Tielinen defines the *Frauenkrimi* as a specific type of feminist crime novel, suggesting that an understanding of the genre as feminist is commonly accepted. Kirsimarja Tielinen, "Ein Blick von außen: Ermittlungen im deutschsprachigen Frauenkriminalroman," *Verbrechen als Passion: Neue Untersuchungen zum Kriminalgenre*, ed. Bruno Franceschini and Carsten Würmann, spec. issue of *Juni-Magazin* 37–38 (2003): 41–68; here, 42. Similarly, Sabine Wilke's study indicates that the female gender of the writer, subject, and audience inevitably color the *Frauenkrimi*'s content, which, she implies, entails a feminist outlook. Sabine Wilke, "Wilde Weiber und dominante Damen: Der Frauenkrimi als Verhandlungsort von Weiblichkeitsmythen," Birkle, Matter-Seibel, and Plummer 255–71; see especially 255–57.

14. Anja Kemmerzell, "Was ist ein Frauenkrimi?" *Ariadne Forum* 4 (1996): 5–6; here, 6. Sally R. Munt advances a similar argument for Anglo-American women's crime writing: the fact that a text is written by a woman and narrated in a female voice, she demonstrates, does not necessarily mean that it adopts a feminist worldview. Sally R. Munt, *Murder by the Book? Feminism and the Crime Novel* (London: Routledge, 1994); see especially 1–29 and 191–207.

15. See Katrin Sieg, "Postcolonial Berlin? Pieke Biermann's Crime Novels as Globalization Critique," *Studies in Twentieth and Twenty-First Century Literature* 28.1 (2004): 152–82; and Sieg, "Women in the Fortress Europe: Feminist Crime Fiction as Antifascist Performative," *differences* 16.2 (2005): 138–66.

16. For this reason, Jean Bobby Noble and David V. Ruffolo instead map out a theoretical terrain called "post-queer." See Jean Bobby Noble, *Sons of the Movement: FtMs Risking Incoherence on a Post-Queer Cultural Landscape* (Toronto: Women's, 2006); and David V. Ruffolo, *Post-Queer Politics* (Farnham: Ashgate, 2009; Queer Interventions).

17. See Munt; Plain; Phyllis M. Betz, *Lesbian Detective Fiction: Woman as Author, Subject and Reader* (Jefferson, NC: McFarland, 2006); Lisa M. Dresner, "Lesbian Detectives Have Car Trouble," *The Female Investigator in Literature, Film, and Popular Culture*, by Lisa M. Dresner (Jefferson, NC: McFarland, 2007), 40–62; Brigitte Frizzoni, "Wer bin ich und wenn ja, wie viele? Verhandelte Identität(en)," *Verhandlungen mit Mordsfrauen: Geschlechterpositionierungen im "Frauenkrimi,"* by Brigitte Frizzoni (Zurich: Chronos, 2009), 125–44; and Paulina Palmer, "The Lesbian Feminist Thriller and Detective Novel," *What Lesbians Do in Books*, ed. Elaine Hobby and Chris White (London: Women's, 1991), 9–27.

18. For a discussion of the relationships among the three categories of feminist, lesbian, and queer crime, see Faye Stewart, "Dialogues with Tradition: Feminist-Queer Encounters in German Crime Stories at the Turn of the Twenty-First Century," *Contemporary Women's Writing and the Return of Feminism in Germany*, ed. Hester Baer, spec. issue of *Studies in Twentieth and Twenty-First Century Literature* 35.1 (2011): 114–35.

19. See Betz, *Lesbian*; Frizzoni; and Maureen T. Reddy, "Lesbian Detectives," *Sisters in Crime: Feminism and the Crime Novel*, by Maureen T. Reddy (New York: Continuum, 1988), 121–46.

20. Examples of texts that can be classified as lesbian rather than queer crime stories include Claudia Wessel's *Es wird Zeit* (1984), Yvonne Berger's *Schwarz überstrahlt Weiß* (1990), Kim Engels's *Zur falschen Zeit am falschen Ort* (1991), Andrea Keller's *Strömung* (1993), Angelika Aliti's *Kein Bock auf Ziegen* (1998), Alexandra von Grote's *Die Kälte des Herzens* (2000), Nanni Wachs's *Tanz der Leidenschaften* (2002), Lisa Pei's *Annas Umweg* (1996), and Andrea Karimé's *Zum Sterben nach Kairo* (2010).

21. Though my focus here is on German genre fiction and cultural history, much of the existing scholarship on crime fiction in general and on feminist and lesbian mysteries in particular analyzes Anglo-American texts and contexts. This should come as no surprise, given that many of the most famous fictional detectives in world literature—including Auguste Dupin, Sherlock Holmes, Miss Marple, and Sam Spade—come from Anglo-American traditions, and that American feminist and queer theory and politics have exerted a profound influence on the German women's and gay liberation movements.

22. In an earlier study, I defined the narrower category of the queer detective novel, linking it to queer theory. However, that ar-

ticle does not draw connections between queer mystery fiction and cultural critique, as I do here. See Faye Stewart, "Of Herrings Red and Lavender: Reading Crime and Identity in Queer Detective Fiction," *Lesbian Crime Fiction*, ed. Jacky Collins, spec. issue of *Clues* 27.2 (2009): 33–44.

23. Lisa Kuppler, ed., *Queer Crime: Lesbisch-schwule Krimigeschichten* (Berlin: Querverlag, 2002).

24. It should also be noted that a strict focus on gay and lesbian mysteries can lead to the exclusion of some queer crime stories. In her study *The Gay Detective Novel*, Judith Markowitz explains that her central criterion for selecting primary texts was the stable homosexual identities of their main characters. Markowitz emphasizes the limits of the categories of gay and lesbian to the exclusion of texts whose characters are more ambiguously sexualized: "The book contains only those series with main characters who are decidedly lesbian or gay. Series with characters whose sexual orientation is implied, coded, or (as yet) undetermined ... are not included." Markowitz's description suggests an understanding of sexuality as fixed and stable, which is not the case with my project and many of the texts it analyzes. Judith A. Markowitz, *The Gay Detective Novel: Lesbian and Gay Main Characters and Themes in Mystery Fiction* (Jefferson, NC: McFarland, 2004), 3.

25. "GLBT Fiction: Queer Mysteries and Thrillers," *Rainbow Sauce*, TurtleSauce Network, 2008, accessed 23 Apr. 2010, http://www.rainbowsauce.com/glbtfic/glbtmysthril.html.

26. GLBTI (often also LGBIT or LGBTQ) are commonly used abbreviations for a range of gender and sexual identities: gay, lesbian, bisexual, transgender, and intersexual (the Q stands for queer or questioning).

27. As an example of queer crime, Frizzoni cites Barbara Wilson's gender-bending feminist mystery *Gaudí Afternoon*. Frizzoni identifies Wilson's use of masquerade, mimicry, and parody as paradigmatic for the queer subgenre of crime fiction, and links these discourses to queer theory.

28. James W. Jones, "Gay Detectives and Victims in German Mystery Novels," *Monatshefte* 104.4 (2012): 570–92, *Project Muse*, accessed 22 May 2013, http://muse.jhu.edu/journals/monatshefte/summary/v104/104.4.jones.html.

Chapter 1

1. I am referring here to detective stories by authors such as Jakob Arjouni and Ralf König. Arjouni created the first German-Turkish detective in 1985 with *Happy Birthday, Türke!* [*Happy Birthday, Turk!*], and König's 1987 graphic novel *Kondom des Grauens* [*The Killer Condom*] helped popularize the figure of the gay male detective. Both of these works addressed contemporary political issues—racism and AIDS—and gained mainstream exposure when they were adapted into successful feature films.

2. Paragraph 218 galvanized both feminist and leftist movements of the early 1970s. Though the struggle to liberalize abortion laws had been a pivotal issue in leftist politics as early as the twenties and thirties, the campaign against Paragraph 218 gained renewed momentum in the feminist movement in the seventies, and many leftist and autonomous political groups aligned themselves with the cause. In 1971, West German journalist Alice Schwarzer started a project called "Frauen gegen den §218" [Women against Paragraph 218]. Taking inspiration from a similar campaign in France, Schwarzer was a motivating force behind the controversial June 6, 1971, issue of the popular German magazine *Stern* that sought to engage the public in a discussion of abortion. The magazine's cover page bore photographs of 28 prominent figures and the declaration, "Wir haben abgetrieben!" [We had abortions!]. See "Wir haben abgetrieben!" *Stern* 6 June 1971, *Deutsche Geschichte in Dokumenten und Bildern*, accessed 11 June 2013, http://germanhistorydocs.ghi-dc.org/sub_image.cfm?image_id=1592&language=german.

3. For a history of the German women's movement up to the late 1970s, see Hilke Schlaeger, "The West German Women's Movement," intro. Nancy Vedder-Shults, ed. Helen Fehervary, Renny Harrigan, and Nancy Vedder-Shults, Special Feminist Issue of *New German Critique* 13 (1978): 59–68, *JSTOR*, accessed 29 Aug. 2012, http://www.jstor.org/stable/3115187.

4. For a discussion of radical feminism and mainstreaming in the 1970s and 1980s, see Ute Gerhard, "Westdeutsche Frauenbewegung: Zwischen Autonomie und dem Recht auf Gleichheit," *Feministische Studien* 10.2 (1992): 35–55. For a review of the rela-

tionships between autonomism and feminism, see George Katsiaficas, *The Subversion of Politics: European Autonomous Social Movements and the Decolonization of Everyday Life* (Atlantic Highlands, NJ: Humanities, 1997; Revolutionary Studies).

5. Wilke, who notes that her list is not exhaustive, mentions the following writers in addition to Biermann: Susanne Billig, Sabine Deitmer, Doris Gercke, Christine Grän, Uta-Maria Heim, Edith Kneifl, Irene Rodrian, Viola Schatten, and Regula Venske (256).

6. See Rote Zora, "Interview mit der Roten Zora," Self-interview, *Emma* June 1984: 598–605, *Theorie als Praxis*, accessed 4 June 2012, http://theoriealspraxis.blog sport.de/images/Emma_Rote_Zora.pdf. In 1975, a bomb attack on the *Bundesverfassungsgericht* [Federal Constitutional Court] in Karlsruhe was perpetrated by a group that identified itself as the *Frauen aus den Revolutionären Zellen* [Women of the Revolutionary Cells]—referring to the left-wing terrorist organization with which they were affiliated—who later came to be known as Rote Zora. Members of the militant feminist group explain that its name bears the same initials as the *Revolutionären Zellen* in order to indicate their relationship and shared vision; both groups define themselves as illegal autonomous networks (Rote Zora 598). Their first action under the name of Rote Zora took place in 1977, when the group bombed the *Bundesärztekammer* [German Medical Association]. Cologne and the Ruhr Valley area were the geographical focus of a series of attacks executed by Rote Zora on government agencies, sex shops, law firms, and public transportation networks in the late 1970s and early 1980s. The final attack for which the group took responsibility was executed in 1995 against the shipbuilding company Lürssen Werft near Bremen.

7. Perta Bornhöft details the stations of Kawaters's exile and the conditions of her return to Germany. See Petra Bornhöft, "Als wenn es mich nicht gäbe," *Der Spiegel* 2 June 2001: 46–48, *Der Spiegel*, accessed 3 June 2012, http://www.spiegel.de/spiegel/print/d-19337146.html. Kawaters left Germany in December 1987 after a series of police raids targeting militant feminist groups, including a search of the Bochum office of the *taz* [*Tageszeitung*, Daily News] where she worked as an editorial assistant. She lived underground

in Spain and France for eight years before turning herself in to German officials. Among the charges Kawaters faced were membership in a terrorist organization and possession of a timing device for explosives. She was required to confess to her awareness of the intended use for the timing device, but was ultimately convicted only of membership in Rote Zora.

8. The name Rote Zora alludes to a 1941 classic children's book, *Die rote Zora und ihre Bande* [The Red Zora and Her Gang], by Kurt Held, whose redheaded title character is a young female version of Robin Hood. Held's book was adapted into a popular television series (Fritz Umgelter, 1979).

9. See Bornhöft; and Sören Grammel, "Rota Zora, a Video by Oliver Ressler," Review, *Videonale* 9 (2001): n. pag., *Installations, Videos and Projects in Public Space by Oliver Ressler*, accessed 14 June 2012, http://www.ressler.at/videonale-9/. Though these sources do not identify the novel by name, available information suggests that it was Kawaters's first book, *Zora Zobel findet die Leiche*, that was used against her in the terrorism trial. Bornhöft states that a Zora Zobel novel of the early eighties served in federal court as evidence of Kawaters's terrorist engagement (48), indicating that the 1984 book, and not its 1986 sequel, is the novel in question. According to Grammel, Oliver Ressler's video *Rote Zora* (2000) "documents how Corinna Kawaters' published fictive novel—Kawaters worked as a journalist and a writer—ironically became the main piece of evidence in the process against her."

10. When Deitmer identifies Kawaters as the creator of the *Frauenkrimi*, she makes specific reference to *Zora2*, in whose subtitle the term *Frauenkrimi* appears for the first time (245). Though Deitmer pays homage to Kawaters's *Zora2* as the first German crime novel with an all-female cast, she does not list it among the texts that formed an emerging feminist trend in the late 1980s: the early mystery fiction of Biermann, Christine Grän, and Doris Gercke, as well as her own (241–42).

11. For definitions of the *Frauenkrimi*, see, in addition to the aforementioned Wilke: Barfoot; Kemmerzell; Stewart, "Dialogues"; and Tielinen.

12. This is a common move in the reception of Kawaters's work, which tends to em-

phasize their narrator's militant leftist milieu over the texts' feminist content. See, for example, "Marlowes Töchter." The article mentions Kawaters's second book, highlights its setting in the "alternative milieu," and flattens its feminist content to the matter of lesbian complicity (150).

13. An entry on Kawaters in Karr's online *Lexikon der deutschen Krimi-Autoren* illustrates this viewpoint, describing the Zora Zobel series as an anarchist predecessor of the *Frauenkrimi* wave. H. P. Karr [Reinhard Jahn], "Kawaters, Corinna," *Lexikon der deutschen Krimi-Autoren: Internet-Edition*, accessed 30 May 2012, http://www.krimi lexikon.de/kawaters.htm.

14. Barfoot also mentions the significance of Kawaters's debut in popularizing the crime novel, but dismisses its content as insignificant to the genre question because neither is its main character a professional detective, nor does the series have longevity (70). Apparently unaware of the third installment in the series, Barfoot mistakenly claims that there were only two Zora Zobel novels and therefore identifies her as a short-lived heroine (70). While the span of Zora's career may not be comparable to that of Gercke's Bella Block, who has appeared in over a dozen novels, Zora has nonetheless investigated crime in three novels over the course of a decade and a half, which gives her some degree of literary longevity.

15. See Tielinen; Wilke; Gaby Pailer, "'Weibliche' Körper im 'männlichen' Raum: Zur Interdependenz von Gender und Genre in deutschsprachigen Kriminalromanen von Autorinnen," *Weimarer Beiträge* 46.4 (2000): 564–81; and Gabriela Wenke, "Sisters in Crime in deutschen Krimis," *Das Mordsbuch: Alles über Krimis*, ed. Nina Schindler (Hildesheim: Claassen, 1997), 283–93. None of these scholars mentions Kawaters in reviewing the history of German women's crime writing and the themes of the feminist *Frauenkrimi*. Vogel lists Kawaters among the female authors who began to publish around 1985, but relegates her to footnote, in a list that contains some twenty other names (50, note 5).

16. These characteristics of Kawaters's writing correspond to the interests that Deitmer asserts were shared among the early authors of feminist crime: they paid special attention to gender and social justice (242).

17. For a definition of the detective novel, see Richard Alewyn, "Anatomie des Detektivromans," *Der Kriminalroman: Poetik-Theorie-Geschichte*, ed. Jochen Vogt (Munich: Fink, 1998), 52–72.

18. As Barfoot alleges, Zora is not a professional investigator. However, the case can be made that the Zora Zobel texts belong to the detective genre despite the absence of a bona fide detective. *Frauenkrimi* investigators come in many forms, including amateurs and career hawkshaws. For instance, Deitmer lists Grän's Anna Marx books as early *Frauenkrimis*, even though Marx, by contrast with Biermann's Karin Lietze and Gercke's Bella Block, is not a police officer but a gossip journalist. Pailer also groups Grän's writing together with Biermann's and Gercke's in a category of novels with primary detective plots (567). Barfoot even points out that a "popular occupation for the serial heroine has been that of journalist" (71), perhaps because this profession also requires investigative work, and therefore qualifies Grän's novels for inclusion as detective stories. Examples of journalistic investigators include Christine Lehmann's Lisa Nerz, whom I discuss in chapter 3, and Susanne Billig's Helen Marrow, featured in chapter 4. Other fictional investigators who appear in my study include students and an accountant. As I demonstrate in chapter 2, the *Frauenkrimi* also includes another type of narrative that focuses on the criminal rather than the investigator. For a brief overview of scholarship on the messy relationships among crime fiction, detective novels, and thrillers, see Pailer 564–65.

19. Corinna Kawaters, *Zora Zobel findet die Leiche* (Frankfurt am Main: Zweitausendeins, 1984). Hereafter, parenthetical citations reference this text as *Zora1*.

20. For more on autonomism, protest cultures, and extremist violence on the left and right, see Katsiaficas; and Roger Karapin, *Protest Politics in Germany: Movements on the Left and Right since the 1960s* (University Park: Pennsylvania State University Press, 2007). Though similar militant protest movements, largely youth cultures influenced by the student revolts of the late 1960s, also developed in neighboring countries like the Netherlands and Switzerland, there was a distinctly West German inflection to this phenomenon, where the rise of the New Left and domestic terrorism manifested as forms of re-

sistance against the institutionalization of the Green Party and West German acceptance of American occupation forces as role models and guarantors of peace. Intellectually influenced by socialism and radical leftist philosophies, autonomism emerged as a decentralized movement embracing spontaneity, independence, and illegal, often violent, means. Certainly the best-known manifestation was the RAF [*Rote Armee Fraktion*, Red Army Faction], which was linked to other terrorist groups and factions in the autonomous movement born of the 1970s, such as the network RZ. Connections between autonomous factions and militant groups such as the RAF influenced the rise of militant autonomism in the 1980s. Violent clashes were typical of the movement, which organized demonstrations and protests around squat houses (protestors used barricades and Molotov cocktails to keep law enforcement from entering occupied buildings), visits by American politicians (Alexander Haig and Ronald Reagan in the early 1980s), nuclear power (such as the massive and ultimately bloody protests at Brokdorf), and large-scale construction projects (such as the airport runway in Frankfurt).

21. On feminist revisions of traditional gender dynamics in detective fiction, see Munt; Gabriele Dietze, *Hardboiled Woman: Geschlechterkrieg im amerikanischen Kriminalroman* (Hamburg: Europäische, 1997); Glenwood Irons, ed., *Feminism in Women's Detective Fiction* (Toronto: University of Toronto Press, 1995); Julie H. Kim, ed., *Murdering Miss Marple: Essays on Gender and Sexuality in the New Golden Age of Women's Crime Fiction* (Jefferson, NC: McFarland, 2012); Kathleen Gregory Klein, *The Woman Detective: Gender and Genre*, 2nd ed. (Urbana: University of Illinois Press, 1995); Kathleen Gregory Klein, ed., *Women Times Three: Writers, Detectives, Readers* (Bowling Green, OH: Bowling Green State University Popular Press, 1995); and Priscilla L. Walton and Manina Jones, *Detective Agency: Women Rewriting the Hard-Boiled Tradition* (Berkeley: University of California Press, 1999).

22. See, for instance, Betz, *Lesbian*; Dresner; Plain; Stewart, "Dialogues"; Palmer, "Lesbian Feminist"; and Paulina Palmer, "The Lesbian Thriller: Transgressive Investigations," *Criminal Proceedings: The Contemporary American Crime Novel*, ed. Peter Messent (London: Pluto, 1997), 87–110.

23. At times, the wording hints at attraction, as with Zora's unspoken remark that Rita looks "so appetitlich und frisch" [so appetizing and fresh, *Zora1* 130]. While the context here implies that a sick and exhausted Zora actually envies Rita's hygiene and well-being, the adjectives "appetizing" and "fresh" conjure up images of temptation and consumption that are not without sexual connotations.

24. Zora makes specific reference to the cult of motherhood in the context of rhetoric about the "Aussterben der bundesdeutschen Bevölkerung" [extinction of the German population, *Zora1* 76]. For a discussion of the debates among feminists and politicians about the German population, see Katsiaficas.

25. For a discussion of *Gleichschaltung* in National Socialist political culture, see Claudia Koonz, *The Nazi Conscience* (Cambridge: Belknap, 2003).

26. Munt notes that this is also common to Anglo-American socialist feminist crime fiction, where readers can witness the "characteristic socialist feminist swipe at the patriarchal Left" (70). For a discussion of the specifically German idiosyncrasies of the historical conflicts between feminists and the Left, see Edith Hoshino Altbach, "The New German Women's Movement," *Signs* 9.3 (Spring 1984): 454–69, *JSTOR*, accessed 20 Nov. 2012, http://www.jstor.org/stable/3173714.

27. Rote Zora addressed this point, alleging that militant leftist men are all too often "erschreckend weit davon entfernt, zu begreifen, was antisexistischer Kampf heißt und welche Bedeutung er für eine sozialrevolutionäre Perspektive hat" [frighteningly far away from understanding what antisexist struggle means and what significance it has for a social revolutionary perspective, 600].

28. For a more nuanced contextualization of this political shift, see Katsiaficas.

29. Many feminist groups saw feminism as part of a larger set of concerns dealing with oppression and inequality in general, racism, fascism, and imperialism. Rote Zora's perspective on the oppression of women as the basic foundation for all other forms of oppression (class struggle, racism, and imperialism, among others) is emblematic of this philosophy (601).

30. Despite the overt differences in genre,

narrative voice and structure, and date of publication, Kawaters's Zora Zobel series engages in a project similar to Stefan's *Häutungen*. See Verena Stefan, *Häutungen* (Munich, Frauenoffensive, 1975). For a discussion of Stefan's narrative and its political relationship to West Germany in the 1970s, see Monika Moyrer, "'Coming-to-herself': Diverging Representations of Female Subjectivity in Eastern and Western German Literary Texts in the 1970s," *Journal of Women's History* 15.3 (2003): 135–38, *Project Muse*, accessed 6 July 2012, http://muse.jhu.edu/journals/jowh/summary/v015/15.3moyrer.html.

31. This dynamic is further queered with Stefan's lover Ilona, whom Zora also perceives as attractive, but then she dies too. In line with my reading of the attractions to Werner and Stefan, such a structure indicates that any attraction or desire—whether for men or women—can lead to death. A literal link between death and desire comes in a reverse order with Hertha, the woman with whom Zora has a one-night stand in *Zora2*. Though Zora is later attracted to Hertha, her first impression is distinctly negative: she describes Hertha as "tödlich" [deadly]. Corinna Kawaters, *Zora Zobel zieht um* (Giessen: Focus, 1986), 14. Hereafter, parenthetical citations reference this text as *Zora2*.

32. Zora is not alone in desiring Stefan; her friend Resy discloses a past romantic interest in Stefan, though nothing came of their flirtation.

33. The adjective *hard* is an allusion to Hertha, whose name sounds similar to the German word *Härte* [hardness].

34. Anne Koedt attributes this lesbian feminist slogan to activist Ti-Grace Atkinson. Anne Koedt, *Lesbianism and Feminism* (Chicago: Chicago Women's Liberation Union, 1971), *Chicago Women's Liberation Union Herstory Website Archive*, accessed 10 June 2013, http://www.uic.edu/orgs/cwluher story/CWLUArchive/lesbianfeminism.html.

35. Like in *Zora1*, Rita is repeatedly identified by the first-person narrator as "meine Freundin" [my friend/girlfriend], a designation that suggests intimacy but also blurs the boundary between friendship and romance. However, in *Zora2*, there is more evidence that their relationship is not just platonic. When Rita appears halfway through the narrative for the first time after a trip, Zora perceives Rita as "unglaublich fremd" [unbeliev-

ably strange] and yet "so nah" [so close, *Zora2* 111], while Rita comments that Zora is "merkwürdig" [strange] and "verändert" [changed, *Zora2* 112]. Zora immediately tells her confidante everything that happened during her absence, with one notable exception: she keeps silent about her sexual encounter with Hertha. There is a queer tinge to this unexplained omission, as if there were a romantic commitment between the two friends that Zora feels she might be betraying with her silence. One of the final scenes in the novel offers further evidence of a queer attraction between Zora and Rita. Hertha comes on to Zora again but this time she meets with disinterest, and she correctly assumes that Zora's indifference has something to do with Rita's return, which the narrator confirms with silent unease. This interaction connects the three characters in a queer love triangle, not only with the physical presence of Zora, Rita, and Hertha in the same space, but also through the content of the dialogue, which highlights the triangulation of desire. A queer interpretation of the Zora-Rita alliance is further corroborated when Zora tells Hertha that she doesn't want Rita to find out about them—"Ich möchte nicht, daß Rita was von uns beiden mitkriegt" [I would not like for Rita to pick up on (what happened between) us two]—but then silently adds to herself that this is not the only thing she wishes to hide: "Und ich möchte auch nicht, daß Hertha was von mir und Rita erfährt, denke ich feindselig" [And I also wouldn't like for Hertha to find out about me and Rita, I think hostilely, *Zora2* 139]. This is one of the queerest moments in the novel: it unequivocally suggests that something is going on between Zora and Rita that parallels the dynamics of the Zora-Hertha affair, but it does not provide an unequivocal answer to the question of what kind of friendship or relationship the two women have.

36. A pregnancy counseling and family planning service named Pro Familia exists in Germany today, and Kawaters may have intentionally made reference to this real-life organization. Though today Pro Familia's website and advertising materials disavow affiliation with any religious sect or political party, there have been rumors in the past that the organization had connections to the Catholic Church in Germany.

37. Significantly, the representation of a

mother who suffers at the hand of her son is a reversal of the generational dynamic that many *Frauenkrimis* portray, according to Vogel, in which the abuse of children by their parents is a symbolic representation of individuals' fears of the state (65).

38. The police officers in *Zora1* are all male and prone to chauvinistic and condescending utterances.

39. Though the "Paragraphen" [paragraphs] mentioned here could be any part of the West German Basic Law, this might also be an implicit allusion to Paragraph 218.

40. For more on Hydra, see Sieg 178; and "Bald 'Bockscheine' für die Freier? Westdeutsche Prostituierte organisieren sich in Selbsthilfegruppen," *Der Spiegel* 19 Aug. 1985: 42–43, *Der Spiegel*, accessed 30 Nov. 2012, http://www.spiegel.de/spiegel/print/d-13515239.html. Throughout the 1980s and 1990s, Biermann and her collaborators in Hydra were associated with a number of events and campaigns, including political lobbying at the local and national levels, taking part in conferences on prostitution and the law, raising public awareness about AIDS, organizing whores' balls, publishing a newspaper, and the opening of a café and whores' support center in West Berlin.

41. See H. P. Karr [Reinhard Jahn], "Biermann, Pieke," *Lexikon der deutschen Krimi-Autoren: Internet-Edition*, accessed 11 June 2012, http://www.krimilexikon.de/biermann.htm.

42. Analyses of other texts by Biermann can be found in the contexts of wider discussions about the *Frauenkrimi*. See Barfoot (*Violetta*), Pailer (*Herzrasen*), Vogel (*Vier, fünf, sechs*), and Wilke (Biermann's edited short story collection *Wilde Weiber GmbH*).

43. See Stefanie Abt, *Soziale Enquête im aktuellen Kriminalroman: Am Beispiel von Henning Mankell, Ulrich Ritzel und Pieke Biermann*, Diss., University of Duisburg-Essen, 2004 (Wiesbaden: Deutscher Universitätsverlag, 2004; Literaturwissenschaft/Kulturwissenschaft); Christopher Jones, "Silence Is Golden? The Short Fiction of Pieke Biermann," *Sound Matters: Essays on the Acoustics of Modern German Culture*, ed. Nora M. Alter and Lutz Koepnick (New York: Berghahn, 2004), 142–51; and Klaus R. Scherpe, "Modern and Postmodern Transformations of the Metropolitan Narrative," trans. Mitch Cohen, *New German Critique*

55 (1992): 71–85, *JSTOR*, accessed 16 Aug. 2012, http://www.jstor.org/stable/488290. Abt's study focuses on social critique, narrative style, and realism in Biermann's fiction; feminism and the representation of gender are therefore not primary concerns, though the analysis does touch upon Biermann's representations of working women. Jones focuses on the acoustic worlds that Biermann's short fiction creates; his discussion almost completely overlooks the role of gender in Biermann's texts. Scherpe's brief discussion of Biermann exemplifies another trend, classifying her work as "Berlin literature" (84).

44. Pieke Biermann, *Potsdamer Ableben* (Berlin: Rotbuch, 1987), 38. Schwarzer became famous in Germany in 1975 with her bestselling book, *Der kleine Unterschied und seine großen Folgen* [The Little Difference and Its Big Consequences, 1975], about the oppression of women in sexual and romantic relationships. The book's success made Schwarzer one of the best-known names associated with women's emancipation. With the profits from *Der kleine Unterschied*, Schwarzer financed the establishment of the independent women's magazine *Emma*. One difference between Zaecke and Schwarzer is that the former has a son, while the latter has no known children; Zaecke's son may be a reference to the widespread rumor that Schwarzer did indeed have a son from her long-term relationship with a man, despite her public claims that she chose to devote her energies to activism rather than start a family. See Ruth Klüger, "Die schwere Entscheidung—Ein Kind oder 'Emma,'" *Die Welt*, Die Welt 15 Sept. 2011, accessed 19 Nov. 2012, http://www.welt.de/kultur/history/article13604494/Die-schwere-Entscheidung-ein-Kind-oder-Emma.html.

45. In 1978, antipornography advocate Schwarzer launched a massive campaign against *Stern* magazine and editor in chief Henri Nannen for publishing nude photos of women. In 1984, the television station WDR broadcast Schwarzer's interview of Rudolph Augstein, founder and editor in chief of *Spiegel*, which entailed a heated discussion of topics on which the two journalists held vastly differing opinions, including working women, discrimination and violence against women, and the feminist movement.

46. The irritation Zaecke's voice causes receives special emphasis in metaphors of

weaponry: her voice is described as "eine akustische Keule" [an acoustic mace, 18] and "eine akustische Splitterbombe" [an acoustic splitter bomb, 66]. Upon hearing Zaecke live, one radio listener wonders, "Was hat die denn an die Stimmbänder?" [What's with her vocal cords? 92], and asks her friend to turn down the volume.

47. Carrie Smith-Prei, "'Knaller-Sex für alle': Popfeminist Body Politics in Lady Bitch Ray, Charlotte Roche, and Sarah Kuttner," Baer 18–39; here, 19.

48. See Sieg; and Sara Lennox, "Divided Feminism: Women, Racism, and German National Identity," *German Studies Review* 18.3 (1995): 481–502, *JSTOR*, accessed 20 Nov. 2012, http://www.jstor.org/stable/1431776. Lennox critiques the racialization of Schwarzer's feminism, noting that Schwarzer's politics come from a white, Western European point of view that marginalizes women of color and non–German women.

49. Margaret McCarthy, "Feminism and Generational Conflicts in Alexa Hennig von Lange's *Relax*, Elke Naters's *Lügen*, and Charlotte Roche's *Feuchtgebiete*," Baer 56–73; here, 59. Universalist feminism is not uniquely German, nor is the critique thereof; Judith Butler also decries "the totalizing gestures of feminism." Judith Butler, *Gender Trouble: Feminism and the Subversion of Identity* (1990, New York: Routledge, 1999), 19.

50. See Meredith Haaf, Susanne Klingner, and Barbara Streidl, *Wir Alphamädchen: Warum Feminismus das Leben schöner macht* (2008, Munich: Blanvalet, 2009), 194–96.

51. Leslie A. Adelson, "The Price of Feminism: Of Women and Turks," *Gender and Germanness: Cultural Productions of Nation*, ed. Patricia Herminghouse and Magda Mueller (Providence: Berghahn, 1997; Modern German Studies 4), 305–19; here, 308.

52. Barfoot describes Zaecke's political perspective as "a grossly distorted vision of the world" (123). The description of Zaecke as "eine vernagelte Theologin des Feminismus" [a crucified theologian of feminism, 160] also resonates with an interpretation of her philosophies as antiquated and paralyzed.

53. I should note that what I call Zaecke's feminism—and liken to Schwarzer's feminism—generally refers to second-wave feminism, though scholarship on the topic has assigned various qualifiers to this political form, including radical, mainstream, universal(ist),

and utopian. I use these descriptors interchangeably. In line with much scholarship on German second-wave women's movements, Gerhard generally refers to this as radical feminism, though she also argues for a continuity with later "radical" forms (41). Lennox refers to "mainstream feminists" (484), a category with which she aligns Schwarzer, and cites Adelson's reference to "universal feminism" (quoted in Lennox 485). Sieg identifies Zaecke's particular stance in *Potsdamer Abeleben* as a "cultural-feminist ideology" (158) and argues that "Biermann's pre–1990 novels evince a deep skepticism of all utopian promises" (159).

54. Sieg takes Biermann's representation of feminism to task, arguing that despite the author's antagonistic positioning of Zaecke as representing universalist feminism in *Ableben*, her texts celebrate an implicitly white feminist perspective that is blind to the workings of race and ethnicity in gendered oppression; she further suggests that Biermann's vision could benefit from the insights of postcolonial theories (174–77).

55. See Lennox 484–85.

56. Claudia Breger, "Hegemony, Marginalization, and Feminine Masculinity: Antje Rávic Strubel's *Unter Schnee*," *Seminar* 44.1 (2008): 154–73, here, 159.

57. Lietze also imposes this linguistic turn on her lover by scolding him when he marks her femaleness by referring to her with words that carry the feminine suffix *-in*. Believing he may have unintentionally insulted Lietze, Jalta leaves a message on her answering machine apologizing for having called her a *Bullin* [(female) cop, 89].

58. In fact, the only financial transaction that takes place between Lietze and the prostitutes puts buying power in the whores' hands—Kim buys Lietze (and the other whores) breakfast after earning "die Mark des Monats" [the Mark of the month, 49]. Lietze, in contrast, has the social status and financial means to gain admission for the streetwalking trio into an exclusive restaurant (52).

59. With this opening sentence, the novel introduces a moment of copulation that does not end with the semantic turn of the verb *kommen* [to come] that typically suggests orgasm in a sexual setting, but, as one would perhaps expect, this *kommen* does bring about an end to the intercourse. Although she is "keineswegs fertig mit dem hübschen jungen

Mann" [in no way finished with the handsome young man, 9], Lietze terminates their sexual activity.

60. Kim's crush on Lietze also receives mention in *Ableben*'s sequel, *Violetta*. See Pieke Biermann, *Violetta* (Berlin: Rotbuch, 1990), 175.

61. Helga's retort to Kim's disappointed query about the male gender of Lietze's love object—"Weil die wirklich heißen Bräute auch nicht gebündelt anne Ecke stehen!" [Because the really hot broads don't stand all dolled up on the corner, 57]—leaves open the possibility that she is aware of same-sex desires on Lietze's part, but that she also knows Lietze would be unlikely to have relationships with people who await lovers "all dolled up on the corner," that is, prostitutes. The tension in this scene dissipates when Helga announces: "Ick geh ma für kleene Mädchen. Wer will mit?" [I'm going to the little girls'. Who wants to come? 57]. Helga's comical reference to "going to the little girls'" is, of course, a euphemism for going to the restroom and an invitation for homosocial bonding in a gender-specific space, but it could also be read as a suggestion of female sexual object choice.

62. Barfoot is making specific reference here to a passage in *Violetta*, though I believe that the suggestion of same-sex desire is stronger in *Ableben*.

63. *Potsdamer Ableben* is, however, the only novel in Biermann's series in which Kim's attraction to Lietze plays any significant role, though there are isolated references to Kim's crush in the later novels.

64. It is revealed later in Biermann's series that Helga raised Lietze, but this past does not come up in *Ableben*.

65. Zaecke and her teenage coconspirators deny the state the opportunity to function properly by serving justice when, instead of reporting what they know about Wielack's complicity in rape and murder, they act as vigilantes and take action against him. Lietze wishes that they had involved the law instead (149).

66. Lietze's team consists of four police officers: herself; Detlev Roboldt, a single gay man; Sonja Schade, who is revealed in the sequel *Violetta* to be in a committed lesbian relationship; and Lothar Fritz, a married straight man. Supporting the team is the Jewish assistant Mimi Jacob.

67. This contrasts with Munt's evaluation of the process typically embodied in the feminist crime novel's central figures: "The more successful of these novels fielded a critique of patriarchal society usually through a strong female hero who is *relatively* whole and centered. Fractured and fragmented *yet* authentic and autonomous, this fantasy figure provides a re-entry for the marginalized into society in order to regain power" (Munt 61, emphasis in original). Whereas Munt indicates that Anglo-American crime novels often emphasize the process of a strong woman coming to power, Biermann projects a vision of a woman who, having already attained a position of power, uses it to empower others.

68. Gerhard is not alone in noting this shift. Other scholars, such as Lennox, also provide critical assessments of West German feminisms in the 1980s and early 1990s: "The struggle over definitions within the German women's movement has forced growing numbers of German feminists to reassess their easy self-identification as victims of patriarchy and acknowledge their actual social location" (495–96).

Chapter 2

1. Birgit Rabisch, "Eier im Glas," *Mit Zorn, Charme & Methode oder: Die Aufklärung ist weiblich!* ed. Pieke Biermann (Frankfurt am Main: Fischer, 1992), 112–23; here, 115.

2. For an analysis of Rabisch's "Eier im Glas" as a feminist crime story, see Stewart, "Dialogues."

3. See Alfred Döblin, *Die beiden Freundinnen und ihr Giftmord* (1924, Reinbek: Rowohlt, 1978). For more detailed discussions of the Klein-Nebbe case and Döblin's portrayal thereof, see Veronika Fuechtner, *Berlin Psychoanalytic: Psychoanalysis and Culture in Weimar Republic Germany and Beyond* (Berkeley: University of California Press, 2011), 18–64; and Todd Herzog, *Crime Stories: Criminalistic Fantasy and the Culture of Crisis in Weimar Germany* (New York: Berghahn, 2009), 59–71.

4. John G. Cawelti, *Adventure, Mystery, and Romance: Formula Stories as Art and Popular Culture* (Chicago: University of Chicago Press, 1976), 52–53.

5. In particular, *Zwischen zwei Nächten* shares numerous themes and structures with

Bachmann's "Ein Schritt nach Gommorha" [A Step towards Gomorrah, 1961] and *Malina* (1971), and Jelinek's *Die Liebhaberinnen* [*Women as Lovers*, 1975] and *Die Klavierspielerin* [*The Piano Teacher*, 1983]. For discussions of Kneifl's work that compare it to Bachmann's and Jelinek's, see, for instance, Tielinen 63; Elena Agazzi, "Psychologie und Verbrechen in Edith Kneifls Kriminalromanen," *Mord als kreativer Prozess: Zum Kriminalroman der Gegenwart in Deutschland, Österreich und der Schweiz*, ed. Sandro M. Moraldo (Heidelberg: Universitätsverlag Winter, 2005; Beiträge zur Neueren Literaturgeschichte 222), 99–109; here, 107; and Klaus Ther, "Die Kritik zu *Zwischen zwei Nächten*," *Der Standard* 1991, *Das Syndikat: Autorengruppe deutschsprachige Kriminalliteratur*, accessed 25 Sept. 2006, http://www. das-syndikat.com/rom1992.htm. Bachmann thematizes the masculine gendering of the novel when her unnamed female narrator in *Malina* becomes a man at the story's end. See Ingeborg Bachmann, *Malina* (1971, Frankfurt am Main: Suhrkamp, 2004).

6. One German-language Austrian *Frauenkrimi* precedes this one, Austrian-born Christine Grän's *Weiße sterben selten in Samyana* [Whites Seldom Die in Samyana, 1986].

7. Czurda's novel is a postmodern adaptation of the Klein-Nebbe story. The Austrian queer feminist crime novel begins with Czurda's and Kneifl's 1991 texts. Later writers of the Austrian feminist, queer, and lesbian crime fiction include Angelika Aliti, Karin Rick, and Lisa Lercher, all of whom thematize desire, sexuality, and friendships and relationships among women.

8. Named after Swiss writer Friedrich Glauser (1896–1938), the Glauser Prize is one of the most prominent awards for German-language crime fiction (next to the German Crime Prize). Since 1987, it has been awarded annually by Das Syndikat [The Syndicate], a coalition of crime fiction authors.

9. A 1994 edition of the novel published with Heyne bore the term *Psychothriller* on its cover, and the almost identical word *Psy-Thriller* appears in Susan Ladika's review of Kneifl's novels. Susan Ladika, "Austrian Author's Psy-Thrillers," *Europe* March 2000: 43, *HighBeam Research*, accessed 25 Sept. 2006, http://www.highbeam.com/doc/1G1-61640821.html.

10. Edith Kneifl, *Zwischen zwei Nächten* (1991, Vienna: Milena, 2003), 7. The text implies that Ann-Marie's given name is Annemarie: "[Anna] durfte als einzige 'Annemarie' sagen. Seit ihre Freundin in den USA lebte, ließ sie das 'e' in der Mitte ihres Namens weg" [Anna alone was allowed to say "Annemarie." Since her friend had been living in the USA, she had dropped the "e" from the middle of her name, 9]. No explanation is given for Ann-Marie's distaste for the name or for her decision to change it.

11. Sigmund Freud, "Das Unheimliche" (1919), *Psychologische Schriften: Studienausgabe*, vol. 4, ed. Alexander Mitscherlich, Angela Richards, and James Strachey (Frankfurt am Main: Fischer, 1982), 241–74; here, 259.

12. Mark Anderson, "Death Arias in Vienna," Afterword, *Malina: A Novel*, by Ingeborg Bachmann, trans. Philip Boehm (New York: Holmes, 1990; Modern German Voices), 226–40; here, 239.

13. The connections among repression, female subjectivity, narrative authority, and violence in Kneifl's novel recall not only Bachmann's *Malina* but also Jelinek's *Die Klavierspielerin*, in which a woman copes with the trauma of long-term physical and psychological abuse. For a feminist reading of psychological themes in Bachmann's and Jelinek's work, see Nancy C. Erickson, "Writing and Remembering—Acts of Resistance in Ingeborg Bachmann's *Malina* and *Der Fall Franza*, and Elfriede Jelinek's *Lust* and *Die Klavierspielerin*: Case Studies in Hysteria," *Out from the Shadows: Essays on Contemporary Austrian Women Writers and Filmmakers*, ed. and intro. Margarete Lamb-Faffelberger (Riverside, CA: Ariadne, 1997; Studies in Austrian Literature, Culture, and Thought), 192–205. Barbara Neuwirth reads these feminist authors' psychological discourses within a larger social context: "The experiences they wrote about were no longer interpreted as case studies of pathological psychology, but instead as ways in which women were psychologically damaged by oppression, or even as typical experiences in the lives of Austrian women." Barbara Neuwirth, "Afterword: Literature by Austrian Women," *Escaping Expectations: Stories by Austrian Women Writers*, ed. Barbara Neuwirth, trans. Pamela S. Saur (Riverside, CA: Ariadne, 2001; Studies in Austrian Literature, Culture, and Thought: Translation Series), 151–63; here, 161.

14. Sabine Wilke suggests a similar reading of Alfred in her brief description of Kneifl's novel, which links Anna's unhappiness to geography, gender, and her professional and marital status: "Anna [versucht] aus ihrem Wiener Leben auszutreten ..., das durch die sexistische Kultur ihres Berufes und die Affären ihres Mannes bestimmt wird" [Anna tries to escape from her Vienna life, which is determined by the sexist culture of her profession and the affairs of her husband, 256].

15. Ann-Marie's rundown apartment and unsteady employment in New York and Frau Maricek's position as a housekeeper set them apart from the wealthy crowd at Anna's funeral. As with Ann-Marie, an unconventional hairstyle and alcoholism further differentiate Frau Maricek's nameless son from other guests. Ann-Marie's relocation to New York affirms that she does not belong in Vienna. Similarly, the difference of the Maricek surname from the Germanic-sounding names appearing in the novel (like Beckmann, Jonas, and Gerlich)—Maricek is likely of Slavic origin—marks it as foreign and carries with it the suggestion of marginality.

16. This headline recalls media representations of Anna's death, such as "Tod durch Selbstmord" and "Freiwillig aus dem Leben geschieden" [Death by suicide; Willingly departed from this life, 16], which are not only reductive, but—that is, if we ascribe to the theory that Alfred killed Anna—also mistaken.

17. This is one of the many passages in which Ann-Marie's perceptions and memory are depicted as unreliable: "Ihre Erinnerung ließ sie im Stich" [Her memory failed her, 165].

18. The limitations of Ann-Marie's point of view and her inability to see things clearly are thematized throughout the text. The novel's opening words, "Unscharf und verschwommen" [Out of focus and blurry, 5] doubly construct Ann-Marie's perspective as unreliable; due to her bad vision, she is able "ihre Umwelt nur äußerst eingeschränkt wahrzunehmen" [to perceive her environment only in an extremely limited way, 8]. The verb *verschwimmen* [to blur] from the opening sentence also appears at the novel's end, again in connection with Ann-Marie's vision, just before the dramatic conclusion (168). The discrepancy between Ann-Marie's perception of her own state of mind and the unembodied third-person narrator's description thereof also reinforces a reading of her as unreliable: while she asserts that, "selbst wenn ich betrunken bin, entgeht mir kaum was" [even when I'm drunk, I hardly miss a thing, 125], the external narrative depicts Ann-Marie at the end of the story as "nicht mehr in der Lage, zwischen Phantasie und Realität zu unterscheiden" [no longer in any condition to distinguish between fantasy and reality, 167].

19. Wilke twice emphasizes the friendship as the core of the novel: she initially introduces *Zwischen zwei Nächten* as "die Geschichte einer Frauenfreundschaft" [the story of a women's friendship, 256], and later describes the novel as narrating a friendship that is unable to develop fully (263).

20. See Bachmann; and Elfriede Jelinek, *Die Klavierspielerin* (1983, Reinbek: Rowohlt, 2001).

21. As B. Rudy Rich notes in a review of the film, Scott's *Thelma & Louise* is remarkable because it was one of the first explicitly heterosexual movies to introduce "the phenomenon of a lesbian audience claiming a mainstream film as an artifact of lesbian [culture]." B. Ruby Rich, "Two for the Road," *Advocate* 18 Feb. 2003: 48, *Academic Search Complete*, accessed 26 July 2012, http://ezproxy.gsu.edu:2048/login?url=http://search.ebscohost.com/login.aspx?direct=true&db=a9h&AN=9124085&site=ehost-live. See also *Thelma & Louise*, dir. Ridley Scott, writ. Callie Khouri, perf. Susan Sarandon and Geena Davis (MGM, 1991).

22. See Patricia Plummer, "'Die Blutspur fängt in frühester Jugend an': Interview mit Sabine Deitmer," Birkle, Matter-Seibel, and Plummer 87–99.

23. Though allusions to the psychological content of Noll's works are common in reception and scholarship, Verena Watzal further links gender with genre in creating the category of the *psychologische Frauenkrimi* [psychological women's crime novel]. See Verena Watzal, "Textimmanente Untersuchung des Romans 'Der Hahn ist tot' von Ingrid Noll und Versuch einer Zuordnung in das Subgenre 'psychologischer Frauenkrimi'" (Munich: GRIN, 2000), *Google Book Search*, accessed 20 July 2012, http://books.google.com/books?id=cSH8xD0OEOIC&printsec=frontcover&dq=Verena+Watzal&hl=en&

sa=X&ei=jRa2UZTfBsbw0QHW4oGYDA
&ved=0CFgQ6AEwBQ.

24. The few scholarly pieces available on Noll's work tend to focus on the interplay between the gendered construction of her female characters and their psychological profiles. Existing work emphasizes Noll's negotiation of gender and feminism; one example of this tendency can be found in Sigrid Schmid-Bortenschlager's essay, in which the author categorizes Noll's representations of female-embodied justice and power as psychological realism. Sigrid Schmid-Bortenschlager, "Violence and Woman's Status as Victim: Changing the Role Model or Being Caught in the Trap?" *Repensando la violencia y el patriarcado frente al nuevo milenio: Nuevas perspectivas en el mundo Hispanico y Germanico/Rethinking Violence and Patriarchy for the New Millennium: A German and Hispanic Perspective*, ed. Fernando de Diego and Agata Schwartz (Ottawa: University of Ottawa, 2002), 113–20. Other publications stress Noll's deconstruction of gendered stereotypes, as does Helga Arend's piece on teaching with Noll's crime novels. Helga Arend, "Nette alte Dame mit Leiche im Keller: Ingrid Nolls Kriminalromane als Unterrichtsthema," Birkle, Matter-Seibel, and Plummer 273–86. Cesare Giacobazzi's essay delves into philosophy, but does so by means of an analysis of the psychic characterization and evolution of Noll's female characters through the commission of violent crimes. He argues that her texts highlight "die Vergänglichkeit des Ethischen" [the ephemerality of the ethical, 48] and encourage their readers to interrogate the very conditions of possibility for ethical thinking, but he does not examine the legal or political implications of these issues. Cesare Giacobazzi, "'Mit Kind, Hund, warmen Decken und Leiche': Die Normalität des Mordes in Ingrid Nolls Kriminalromanen," Moraldo 41–49.

25. Ingrid Noll, *Die Häupter meiner Lieben* (1993, Zurich: Diogenes, 1994), 8.

26. Freud's concept of the doppelgänger comes into play here, though perhaps not as clearly with Cora and Carlo as with Carlo and his deceased uncle Karl. Carlo functions as a return of the repressed: in addition to having similar names, he and Karl bear a striking resemblance to one another. When Maja sees photographs and portraits of Karl, she mistakenly believes him to be Carlo's secret fa-

ther. She later learns that her own father, in a drunken daze, killed Karl, a mistake she is fated to repeat when she kills her own brother: "Mein Vater ist ein Mörder, ich bin eine Mörderin" [My father is a murderer, I am a murderess, 82].

27. Even before joining the Schwab family, Maja feels "als ob ich ständig in der Rolle einer ärmlichen Verwandten steckte" [as though I were repeatedly stuck in the role of a poor relative, 62]. The divided and reunited family as a metaphor for the split German nation during and after the Cold War is a theme that appears commonly in popular media and culture. In particular, East Germans are stereotyped as the poorer, needy, feminized counterparts to their richer, more fortunate, masculinized Western relatives, a discourse that became more pronounced during and after unification. Other examples of these nationally marked embodiments can be found, for instance, in the representation of the search for the sister lost in East Germany in Helga Schütz's *Vom Glanz der Elbe* (1995) and the comical portrayal of the West German uncle's visit in the *Ostalgie* film *Sonnenallee* (Leander Haussmann, 1999). See Ingrid Sharp, "Male Privilege and Female Virtue: Gendered Representations of the Two Germanies," *New German Studies* 18.1–2 (1994): 87–106; and N. Ann Rider, "The Journey Eastward: Helga Schütz' *Vom Glanz der Elbe* and the Mnemonic Politics of German Unification," *Textual Responses to German Unification: Processing Historical and Social Change in Literature and Film*, ed. Carol Anne Costabile-Heming, Rachel J. Halverson, and Kristie A. Foell (Berlin: de Gruyter, 2001), 17–34.

28. See Mary Fulbrook, *The People's State: East German Society from Hitler to Honecker* (New Haven: Yale University Press, 2005).

29. The GDR endorsed women entering the workforce and working in fields that had traditionally been occupied by men, for instance the medical and hard sciences, but as Fulbrook points out, some professions still remained largely the domain of female workers, such as healthcare, child care, social work and teaching (162–63). Nursing was one of these areas, and so Frau Westermann's work as a nurse's aide falls into this feminized domain. Caring for the elderly, however, is not as clearly feminized; even though it is, like nursing, a subcategory of health and social

services, this profession may have been more gender-neutral. It is quite possible that, in the GDR, more men worked in geriatric care than in nursing. Indeed, unlike the feminization of the field of nursing that is communicated in the title *Krankenschwester* [nurse; literally, sister of the sick], the term *Altenpflegerin* with its feminine *-in* ending implies the existence of a masculine version, *Altenpfleger*. In the home, however, women took on the bulk of the child care and elderly care responsibilities (Fulbrook 163).

30. The trope of the cultured, cosmopolitan West German, who edifies the less provincial, unworldly East German is common to post-unification literature and culture. Maja is painfully aware that access to culture and the comfortable lifestyle the Schwabs provide her come at a cost to them— "man bezahlte mir Eintrittskarten für kulturelle Veranstaltungen, man kaufte mir Kleider und Wäsche, Bücher und Kosmetika" [they paid for my tickets to cultural events, they bought me clothing and linens, books and cosmetics, 86]—but they make no issue of the money they spend on her. This representation might imply that the financially stable FRG had more than sufficient resources to share with its poorer counterpart—and perhaps it is even as an insinuation that the post-unification debates over slow economic growth and the decline of the welfare state were exaggerated or misdirected.

31. Patricia Anne Simpson, "Degrees of History in Contemporary German Narratives," *German Literature in a New Century: Trends, Traditions, Transitions, Transformations,* ed. Katharina Gerstenberger and Patricia Herminghouse (New York: Berghahn, 2008), 78–98; here, 80.

32. In her new family, Maja initially undergoes a reform: she stops stealing and becomes a model student in school. But she soon returns to her mendacious ways and remains dependent on theft and the benevolence of Cora and the Schwab parents for much of the time narrated in the novel.

33. Giacobazzi observes that Cora and Maja's reasons for killing are strategic and thus set them apart from other literary murderers (41). As Giacobazzi clarifies, murder is a means to an end: "Sie verwirklichen damit ihre Vorstellungen und ihre Träume" [Through it, they bring to life their visions and their dreams, 43]. By doing away with the

men that stand between them and their fantasies, the women clear their path to a financially independent, self-determined life.

34. This phrase, which became a rallying cry for feminists of color in the late 1970s and 1980s, was coined by Audre Lorde in a 1979 talk titled "The Master's Tools Will Never Dismantle the Master's House." Lorde argued in this speech that blindness to racism, classism, sexism, and homophobia was subverting the aims of the feminist movement, and that these patriarchal legacies needed to be addressed in order for women to achieve full emancipation. See Audre Lorde, "The Master's Tools Will Never Dismantle the Master's House," *Sister Outsider: Essays and Speeches,* by Audre Lorde (Trumansberg: Crossing, 1984; Crossing Press Feminist), 110–13.

35. As Fulbrook claims, "Around half the East German labour force in the 1980s was female; after unification, women were laid off disproportionately and affordable childcare facilities slashed, hitting East German women particularly hard" (142). For a discussion of the gender dynamics of cultural representations of German unification, see Sharp.

36. While all Germans in the former East and West were actually required to pay the *Soli,* the larger population and the higher average income in the former West meant that its citizens contributed greater sums of money to this fund-raising effort, which primarily sought to finance the rebuilding of the former East.

37. Further symbolic connections between Cora's wealth and (re)building include her husband Henning, who made his fortune in the construction business, and the Italian villa, which they come to own when Cora gets a tip about the death of its former owners "bevor Makler und Grundstückshaie Witterung aufnahmen" [before brokers and real estate sharks caught the scent, 133]. The reference to real estate speculation also evokes the eastward real estate rush after the fall of the Wall, when Western developers capitalized on the financial collapse of the GDR by investing in property at prices that were, by Western standards, extremely low.

38. For a discussion of the homosocial-homosexual continuum of desire, see Eve Kosofsky Sedgwick, *Between Men: English Literature and Male Homosocial Desire* (New York: Columbia University Press, 1985). There, Sedgwick theorizes "the potential un-

brokenness of a continuum between homosocial and homosexual" (1).

39. In the context of a discussion of the
feminist Bollywood film *Subhah*, Gopinath
argues for paying special critical attention to
narratives in which lesbianism is not overt but
rather implicit because of what they can reveal: "narratives that explicitly name female
same-sex desire as 'lesbian' may be less interesting than those moments within the narrative that represent female homoeroticism in
the absence of 'lesbians.'" Gayatri Gopinath,
*Impossible Desires: Queer Diasporas and South
Asian Public Cultures* (Durham: Duke University Press, 2005), 108.

40. In *Between Men*, Sedgwick analyzes
literary constructions of erotic triangles as
structures for organizing homosocial and homosexual desire between men via a female
proxy (21–27).

41. The Maastricht Treaty was signed
February 7, 1992, and went into effect on November 1, 1993. It announced the name of the
European Union and outlined plans for a single currency, or the EMU (European Monetary Union). In mid–1993, discussion regarding the possible expansion of the European
Union culminated in the establishment of a
set of conditions now commonly called the
Copenhagen criteria.

42. My interpretation of the text indicates
that Noll encourages her reader to examine
the connections between her work and its
wider political context. When Maja remi-
nisces about a geography teacher whom she
admired, she implies a desire for a certain
level of sociopolitical literacy: "Im Endkun-
deunterricht wurden historische, wirtschaft-
liche und politische Zusammenhänge betrach-
tet. Es ärgerte Herrn Becker, daß die meisten
Schüler nur den Sportteil und die Ki-
noanzeigen der Zeitung lasen, Politik und
Wirtschaft aber aussparten" [In geography
class, we examined historical, economic and
political relationships. It angered Mr. Becker
that most of the students only read the sports
section and the movie listings in the newspaper,
but passed over politics and the economy, 13].
This passage is evidence that Noll consciously
brings together such *Zusammenhänge* [rela-
tionships] and offers them up for her readers
to analyze.

43. From the 1980s until today, politicians
in the Federal Republic of Germany have repeatedly endorsed austerity policies as the key

to economic recovery in times of crisis. In
keeping with this quintessentially German
approach, Cora emphasizes the need for pru-
dence in financial matters. After she becomes
the executor of Henning's estate, Cora cuts
back on household spending, putting a halt
to the family's quotidian restaurant outings
and refraining from making major purchases.
When, for instance, Cora makes magnani-
mous gestures such as offering to buy shoes
for Don and clothing and a car for Emilia,
she justifies these purchases as timely and responsible investments. At the same time,
Cora suggests that her sober approach is more
of a performance than a financial necessity—
"nach außen müssen wir verhalten wirken"
[from the outside, we must appear restrained,
168]—and a means to another end, that of
getting away with murder. The notion that
Germany's austerity policies in economic
matters could be more of a performance than
a sincere ideology, as well as the implication
that it could be a means of masking other
weaknesses, might well strike a chord with
critics of Germany's role in the economy of
the European Union.

44. Cora considers Maja a family member
and regards her fortune as a resource they
share. When Maja moves in with Cora and
Henning in Florence, Henning treats her as a
temporary guest, but Cora reassures her:
"Sein Geld gehört mir und ist also auch dein
Geld" [His money is mine and is therefore
also your money, 155]. Immediately after
Henning's death, Cora announces to Maja
that their future is secure (168). Cora provides not only for Maja but for others too:
she purchases shoes and clothing for Don and
Emilia; she also finances outings to museums,
nice dinners, and trips to the beach. Maja describes her decision to seek employment outside of the home as a direct consequence of
the quarrels she and Cora have over Don and
Jonas. Rather than share the sexual resources
of these men with her friend and domestic
partner, Maja seeks to emancipate herself
from Cora's economic control—"Ich schwor
mir, in Zukunft nicht mehr in finanzieller
Abhängigkeit von Cora zu leben" [I swore to
myself to no longer live in financial dependency on Cora, 275]—but has not achieved
this goal by the novel's end.

45. The problem of consumers who "die
Nullen der Lire nicht rasch genug einschätzen
[können]" [cannot calculate the zeros of lire

fast enough, 7] reads as a sarcastic allusion to the massive speculation and fluctuations of the Italian lira and British pound on September 16, 1992, or Black Wednesday, which led to the renegotiation of the lira's membership in the ERM (European Exchange Rate Mechanism) and the revision of regulations regarding the stability of member state currencies. As a result of these events, the pound was excluded from the euro zone.

46. The child's name, which honors the Hungarian composer Béla Bartók, suggests yet another layer to this economic reading: that the former Soviet Bloc states could also become financial liabilities in international alliances.

47. In films of the economic miracle era, when the German middle-class dream entailed ownership of a vehicle and the financial flexibility to take family vacations, Italy repeatedly figured as a setting for class conflict and resolution and fantasies of entrepreneurism and independence. Several examples of these transnational themes can be found in the musical films *Der lachende Vagabund* (Thomas Engel, 1958), *Der Stern von Santa Clara* (Werner Jacobs, 1958), and *Conny und Peter machen Musik* (Werner Jacobs, 1960).

48. The German fascination with Italy evokes the Baroque and Classical traditions of the Grand Tour, a cultural education adventure in Southern Europe typically undertaken by noblemen and affluent intellectuals. Canonical authors like Goethe partook in this tradition, and his contemporaries Eichendorff, Platen, Schiller, and Heine either traveled to or were greatly influenced by the popular imagination of Italy, which appeared in their writings as the epitome of culture and civilization.

49. This is a reversal of the type of *Heimat* [homeland] fetishization that played a central role in Nazi ideology, which projected the fair-skinned Northern European as the embodiment of health and beauty, while the darker Southern European represented pathological corruption. By contrast, Maja's "kühles Vaterland" [chilly fatherland, 147] is far less attractive than Tuscany: "Mein Paradies war Florenz" [My paradise was Florence, 146].

50. This sets *Die Häupter meiner Lieben* apart from other feminist and queer crime novels in which Southern European men pose a threat to independent women and the es-

tablishment of female-dominated communities. For example, in texts like Claudia Wessel's self-published separatist novel *Es wird Zeit* [The Time Is Now, 1984] and Karin Rick's lesbian romance-adventure *Furien in Ferien* [Furies on Vacation, 2004], German-speaking women travel to Umbria and the Isle of Lesbos, where they encounter widespread misogyny, homophobia, abuse, and corruption, which are embodied in Italian and Greek men. These ethnocentric characterizations in Wessel's and Rick's stories set in motion the narrative conflicts to be resolved through the crime investigations.

51. A reading of Italy as a feminized paradise does cause friction with another gendered stereotype about Italy, namely that it is a land of machismo and that Italian men are oversexualized predators, especially of foreign women. These negative stereotypes, however, are absent from the novel's representation of Italian culture, which is aligned with female-embodied freedom and authority.

52. The three pillars of the European Union served as the legal structure of the EU from 1993 to 2009. The three pillars were European Communities, Common Foreign and Security Policy, and Police and Judicial Cooperation in Criminal Matters.

53. Katharina Gerstenberger, *Writing the New Berlin: The German Capital in Post-Wall Literature* (Rochester, NY: Camden House, 2008), 118.

Chapter 3

1. Ralf König, *Der bewegte Mann* (1987), *Der bewegte Mann/Pretty Baby: Der bewegte Mann 2* (Reinbek: Rowohlt, 1994), 48, ellipsis in original.

2. This line appears on the front cover of the *Maybe ... Maybe Not* [*Der bewegte Mann*] videocassette sold in the United States. *Maybe... Maybe Not* [*Der bewegte Mann*], dir. Sönke Wortmann, perf. Til Schweiger, Katja Riemann, and Joachim Król (Neue Constantin, 1994; United States: Orion, 1996).

3. For Ralf König's assessment of the sexual politics of both works and especially the differences between the original graphic novels and the film adaptation, see Ralf König, "Ralf König im Interview: 'Immer nur hei-tei-tei,'" Interview by Hans-Hermann Kotte, *Frankfurter Rundschau Online*, Frankfurter

Rundschau 25 June 2009, accessed 5 Apr. 2013, http://www.fr-online.de/panorama/ralf-koenig-im-interview—immer-nur-hei-tei-tei-,1472782,2935932.html. For discussions of the film's sexual politics, see Ute Lischke-McNab, "Gender, Sex, and Sexuality: The Use of Music as a Collateral Marketing Device in *Maybe... Maybe Not*," Lorey and Plews, eds. 403–19; and Les Wright, "The Genre Cycle of Gay Coming-Out Films, 1970–1994," Lorey and Plews, eds. 311–39.

4. For a timeline of gay and lesbian emancipation in Germany, see "Eine Chronik der Diskriminierung—und der Befreiung," *Die Zeit* 16 Aug. 2012: 2–3.

5. The ARD show *Lindenstraße* was a trailblazer in the prime-time portrayal of homosexuality: in its first year the series, which began in 1985, introduced the gay character Carsten Flöter (Georg Uecker). Though Uecker's character kissed a man in a 1987 episode, it was his second gay kiss on the show in 1990, with Robert Engel (Martin Armknecht), that set off a massive controversy, particularly in Bavaria, in the midst of which actors Uecker and his real-life lover Armknecht received death threats. By the late 1990s, the show regularly featured not only gay men but also lesbian characters. *Lindenstraße* was also one of the first German television shows to deal with other taboo themes such as AIDS.

6. For a contextualization and chronology of the parliamentary debate, which lasted from 1988 to 1990, see Luise F. Pusch, "Ein Streit um Worte? Eine Lesbe macht Skandal im Deutschen Bundestag," *Women in German Yearbook* 10 (1994): 239–66.

7. In 1992, Brandenburg became the first state in unified Germany to write a law protecting gays and lesbians from discrimination into its constitution, which went into effect in 1994. It was followed by similar debates and laws in Thuringia, Berlin, and Saxony-Anhalt. In the 2000s, Germany adopted a nationwide antidiscrimination law in order to conform with European Union regulations.

8. In 1991, Cornelia Scheel, daughter of former West German president Walter Scheel, came out publicly after attending a ball with her partner, comedian Hella von Sinnen. This event was widely reported and commented on in print media from *Die Bunte* to *Die Zeit*. The ensuing scandal culminated in Scheel's dismissal from her executive position with the nonprofit Deutsche Krebshilfe [German Cancer Aid]. Scheel and von Sinnen were intimately involved in pro-gay marriage activism and demonstrations throughout the 1990s. Film director Rosa von Praunheim's provocative public outing of closeted media personalities such as actor Hape Kerkeling and talk-show moderator Alfred Biolek on the RTL talk show *Explosiv—Der heiße Stuhl* in 1991 set off a heated debate about the politics of outing public figures against their will.

9. The 1994 Ikea television advertisement showed two men browsing for dining tables for their shared home. Though it aired not in Europe but in the United States, the commercial and the mixed reactions it received from the American public were the subject of discussions regarding gay representation in the German media. Ikea broadcast the first gay advertisement in Germany several years later in 1999.

10. Plain declares that "the presence of a validated desiring lesbian body within the framework of a popular genre cannot be other than radical" (207). However, a review of American hardboiled detective fiction of the early to mid-twentieth century demonstrates that the inclusion of gay characters does not necessarily serve to affirm homosexual desire or identity; indeed, the construction of gay characters as criminals can communicate extremely homophobic attitudes. One need only think of queer criminal Joel Cairo in Dashiell Hammett's *The Maltese Falcon* (1930) or gay blackmailer, pornographer, and murder victim Arthur Geiger in Raymond Chandler's *The Big Sleep* (1939). Gill Plain concedes that feminist and queer mysteries of the late twentieth and early twenty-first centuries convey a queer-inclusive vision not only by centering their narratives on homosexual investigators, but also by developing the implications of their sexual identities and desires throughout the texts: "In a genre predominantly controlled by the narrative voice of the detective-protagonist, who has the textual capacity to validate or invalidate the subjects of her investigation, the pleasures enjoyed by the detective herself will have repercussions far beyond the bedroom" (207).

11. See Plain; Palmer, "Lesbian Thriller"; Betz, *Lesbian*; Munt; and Anna Wilson, "Death and the Mainstream: Lesbian Detec-

tive Fiction and the Killing of the Coming-Out Story," *Feminist Studies* 22.2 (1996): 251–78, *JSTOR*, accessed 1 Feb. 2007, http://www.jstor.org/stable/3178413.

12. I use the term *identificatory* to refer to narratives that encourage reader identification or empathy with the main character and the fictional world she inhabits. For discussions of reader empathy in the context of narrative theory, see Jonathan Culler, *Literary Theory: A Very Short Introduction* (Oxford: Oxford University Press, 1997), 110–22; and Suzanne Keen, *Empathy and the Novel* (Oxford: Oxford University Press, 2007).

13. *Brigitte*, the most widely read German women's magazine, awarded Liertz second place in its Bettina von Arnim short story prize competition in 1997.

14. The balance between crime and romance, however, is different in each story. *Geheimnisse*'s "Erster Teil" [Part One], which begins with two corpses that turn up in rapid succession, adheres to the conventions of detective fiction more closely than the other two stories; romance becomes more central and increasingly displaces crime in each subsequent story.

15. Martina-Marie Liertz, *Die Geheimnisse der Frauen* (Munich: Goldmann, 1999), 259–61. Though they have no independent titles of their own, each narrative begins with the title and text of a foreign-language poem or song that introduces its themes; these could be seen as the titles of the individual stories as well. The first part begins with a poem by Antonio Machado, titled here "Spurrillen" [Tracks, 7]; and the second starts with the opening lines of the canzone "La donna è mobile" [Woman is Fickle, 133] from Giuseppe Verdi's opera *Rigoletto*.

16. This depiction of the cross-dresser resonates with Marjorie Garber's claim that economic success is among "the classic socioeconomic reasons for a woman's cross-dressing." Marjorie Garber, *Vested Interests: Cross-Dressing and Cultural Anxiety* (1992, New York: Routledge, 1997), 199. Though in Liertz's novel, Sascha's reasons are not strictly economical but rather professional, there is a correlation among these factors and the desire to gain "entry into a man's world of easy camaraderie and acceptance" (Garber 199), particularly when a woman would not have the same opportunities for career advancement, as is Sascha's case.

17. The masculine-gendered terms countertenor and contralto refer to the same vocal range as that of the feminine mezzo-soprano. Historically, the roles and ranges associated with the countertenor, contralto, and mezzo-soprano were sung by adolescent boys and castrati. Although male countertenors tend to be in high demand and play leading roles because they can sing many of the parts originally written for castrati, there is less demand for mezzo-sopranos: as Sascha notes, a countertenor is a far rarer phenomenon than a mezzo-soprano (411). Mezzo-sopranos, according to a common saying, usually play the supporting roles of "witches, bitches, and britches," the last of which refers to the so-called "breeches role" or "trouser role," in which a female singer performs a male part.

18. A number of scholars have examined both the role of reader identification (especially with the detective) in crime fiction and the function of empathy in lesbian literature; see, for instance, Betz, *Lesbian*. Kathryn Kent brings together theories of identification and sexuality in her discussion of identificatory erotics. Kathryn R. Kent, *Making Girls into Women: American Women's Writing and the Rise of Lesbian Identity* (Durham: Duke University Press, 2003).

19. Heteronormative and heterosexist perspectives engage an essentialist view of gender complementarity, the notion that maleness/masculinity and femaleness/femininity are complementary and complete each other through heterosexual coupling. See Warner, Introduction; and Erika Faith Feigenbaum, "Heterosexual Privilege: The Political and the Personal," *Hypatia* 22.1 (2007): 1–9, *JSTOR*, accessed 20 Sept. 2012, http://www.jstor.org/stable/4640040. Heteronormativity refers to the social processes that position heterosexuality as the normal sexual orientation: individuals are generally presumed to be heterosexual unless they demonstrate themselves to be otherwise. In *Geheimnisse*, Deborah calls upon the rhetoric of heterosexual normalcy when she suggests that coming out as gay allowed her to reassess the signficance of normalcy for her own life: "Mir nicht mehr beweisen mußte, daß ich doppelt so normal bin wie die anderen" [Didn't have to prove to myself anymore that I am twice as normal as others, 349]. The mention of normalcy points up the naturalization of heterosexuality as the norm, while

hegemonic culture still views homosexuality as a deviation from that norm. Heterosexism is the systemic bias toward heterosexual desires, acts, and relationships. Social institutions like marriage and the family, and the legal structures that protect them, are constructed according to this heterosexual expectation. Deborah notes that these qualities are alive and well in the theater world when she hears about a female director whose presence troubles operatic traditions. In response to a friend's anecdote about the gender confusion over who should initiate the ritual of bringing the director onto the stage during the applause, Deborah exclaims: "diese Sichtweise ist mir entschieden zu heterozentriert! Warum soll nicht die Primadonna die Dirigentin auf die Bühne holen? Seit wann bist du so ein Anhänger des Heterosexismus?" [this perspective is decidedly too heterocentric for me! Why shouldn't the prima donna escort the female director onto the stage? Since when are you such a fan of heterosexism? 364].

20. While discrimination, hate speech and oppressive violence are typically experienced as visible disruptions in the social order, privilege usually remains invisible to many. For discussions of visibility, whiteness, and male privilege, see Peggy McIntosh, "White Privilege and Male Privilege: A Personal Account of Coming To See Correspondences through Work in Women's Studies" (Wellesley: Wellesley College, Center for Research on Women, 1988; Working Paper 189), *Education Resources Information Center*, accessed 9 June 2013, http://www.eric.ed.gov:80/PDFS/ED335262.pdf; and Stephanie M. Wildman, *Privilege Revealed: How Invisible Preference Undermines America* (New York: New York University Press, 1996; Critical America).

21. By linking heterosexual privilege with the penetration of a guarded space, Liertz's text participates in a trope that Feigenbaum also identifies: "Privilege functions best when doling out access, admitting and rejecting claims at whim like a burly bouncer at the gates of justice" (7–8).

22. The relationship between masquerade, sexuality and seduction in Liertz's story is very different from what we find in classic examples of the popular texts that Chris Straayer calls temporary transvestite films. In such films, gender masquerade is a source of humor and the ultimate unmasking of the cross-dresser typically serves the purposes of advancing a heterosexual relationship. Chris Straayer, *Deviant Eyes, Deviant Bodies: Sexual Re-Orientations in Film and Video* (New York: Columbia University Press, 1996). Examples of the temporary transvestite film include *Queen Christina* (Rouben Mamoulian, 1933), *Viktor und Viktoria* (Reinhold Schünzel, 1933) and its English-language remake *Victor Victoria* (Blake Edwards, 1982), *Sylvia Scarlett* (George Cukor, 1935), *Some Like It Hot* (Billy Wilder, 1959), *Just One of the Guys* (Lisa Gottlieb, 1985), and *Mrs. Doubtfire* (Chris Columbus, 1993). There are also counterexamples to the type of scenario Straayer describes, such as the psychological thriller *The Crying Game* (Neil Jordan, 1992).

23. Phyllis M. Betz, "Re-Covered Bodies: The Detective Novel and Transgendered Characters," Collins 21–32; here, 30.

24. Yet another clue to Sascha's queerness might be found in the story of Orfeo, the queer dimensions of which are often omitted from operatic dramatizations of the myth that typically conclude with Orfeo's failure to bring his beloved Euridice back from the underworld—or, like Gluck's version, have a happy end in which the lovers are together again. In some mythical versions of his later life, however, Orfeo is so heartbroken at the loss of Euridice that he turns exclusively to young males for romantic companionship, and after his death, his body washes up on the isle of Lesbos, the mythical origin of lesbianism. Deborah is aware of these queer dimensions and contemplates them after seeing Sascha perform the role (279).

25. It is crucial to note that Sascha performs maleness in order to pass as male, rather than to parody masculinity. When asked if he would consider extending his repertoire beyond the trouser role to play "richtige Frauenrollen" [true women's roles], Sascha demurs, explaining that such performance "verkäme bestimmt zur unfreiwilligen Parodie" [would devolve into unintentional parody, 269]. This sets Sascha apart from characters such as Viktor in the Weimar film *Viktor und Viktoria*, who mobilizes the diegetically staged performance as a parody of femininity.

26. Judith Butler, "Performative Acts and Gender Constitution: An Essay in Phenomenology and Feminist Theory," *Theatre Journal* 40.4 (1988): 519–31; here, 520, *JSTOR*,

accessed 2 Feb. 2006, http://www.jstor.org/stable/3207893.

27. Though Butler draws parallels between the theatrical and the social staging of identity, she is careful not to conflate them. She points out that the stakes are very different: "Indeed, the sight of a transvestite onstage can compel pleasure and applause while the sight of the same transvestite on the seat next to us on the bus can compel fear, rage, even violence. The conventions which mediate proximity and identification in these two instances are clearly quite different" ("Performative" 527).

28. The name of the bar, La Belle [The Beauty], announces an emphasis on external appearances that is reinforced both at its entrance (by the bouncer who polices patrons for conformity with female gender) and within it (by the mirrors on the walls that encourage patrons to admire themselves and others). This fictional bar is likely a reference to the real-life women's bar Pour Elle [For Her] in the gay-friendly Schöneberg district of Berlin—which comes up explicitly in Gelien's *Eine Lesbe macht noch keinen Sommer*. In Liertz's book, the unknown and yet familiar-looking woman in the bar, whom Deborah calls the "blaue Lady," may be a reference to the performance of femininity and seduction in the film *Der blaue Engel* [*The Blue Angel*, Josef von Sternberg, 1930], based on the novel by Heinrich Mann, *Professor Unrat* [*Small Town Tyrant*, 1905].

29. By contrast with earlier scenes in which Sascha performs on stage and off, here it is not just Sascha/Alessandra who performs; Deborah is also a player in the erotic drama: "Beide standen wir auf der Bühne. Und waren beide Zuschauerinnen. Das Stück versprach spannend zu werden" [We were both standing on the stage. And both spectators. The play promised to be exciting, 413].

30. The novel takes male privilege to task along with heterosexual privilege. As Sascha argues, his cross-dressing success demonstrates that, given the same acting and singing talent and even the same roles, men have greater chances at achieving fame and fortune than women do in the novel's world of the opera. The text emphasizes sexism in other dimensions of operatic culture too. For instance, Deborah remarks that the backstage personnel form a boys' club, as there is no woman among them. Sascha's colleague Arno

also recounts an anecdote about a lone female director who has tired of being asked how she feels about working in a men's domain (364).

31. Mickey Spillane, *Vengeance Is Mine!* (1950), *The Mike Hammer Collection*, vol. 1, intro. Max Allan Collins (New York: New American, 2001), 345–513; here, 513.

32. Seduction is part and parcel of Hammer's daily detective routine, and Hammer views himself as a connoisseur of the female sex, "a guy what [*sic*] likes women, a guy who knows every one of their stunts" (512). However, he misreads Juno, even though clues of her queerness appear as early as their first date, when she takes Hammer to lunch in a restaurant that he remembers "used to be a fag joint" (410). One can read Juno's choice of venue either as an attempt to communicate to Hammer something about herself or as a way of testing his detective skills.

33. Many of the most popular crime stories in German-speaking countries were originally written in English and later translated into German; this is also true for feminist and lesbian texts. After the 1991 novels *Zur falschen Zeit am falschen Ort* [In the Wrong Place at the Wrong Time] by Kim Engels, and *Gestern, heute und kein Morgen* [Yesterday, Today and No Tomorrow] by Sonja Lassere, Gelien's *Lesbe* is the third German-language novel in the feminist Ariadne crime series. Aside from these debuts by Engels, Lasserre, and Gelien, all of the other Ariadne novels among the first forty were translations, the large majority of which had originally appeared in English (written by authors such as the British Anthony Gilbert; Canadian Marion Foster; Americans like Sarah Dreher and Katherine V. Forrest; Scottish Val McDermid; and Australian Rosie Scott). Since 2000, Ariadne has emphasized publishing a much larger percentage of texts originally written in German.

34. Frigga Haug, "Eine Lesbe macht noch keinen Sommer: Das Ungewöhnliche," Afterword, *Eine Lesbe macht noch keinen Sommer*, by Gabriele Gelien (Hamburg: Argument, 1993), 249–51; here, 249.

35. In order to avoid confusion in my analysis, I refer to the author with the surname Gelien and to the narrator-investigator in the novel by her first name, Gabriele.

36. This anecdote recalls the maxim taken from the title of the pop song, "Ohne Krimi geht die Mimi nie ins Bett" [Mimi Never

Goes to Bed without a Thriller, performed by Bill Ramsey, 1962], from the soundtrack of a comedy film by the same name (Franz Antel, 1962).

37. Gabriele Gelien, *Eine Lesbe macht noch keinen Sommer* (Hamburg: Argument, 1993), 77.

38. The colloquial term *Urlesbe* refers to a woman who knows from her first sexual self-awareness that she is gay and has seldom or never had sexual experiences with men. A *Junglesbe*, on the other hand, may spend her adolescence and even many of her adult years as a heterosexual, and only become aware of latent lesbian desires or come out much in later life. Gabriele explains this distinction in detail and lists the various criteria (with footnotes) for each classification (10–12).

39. Gabriele describes her desire for a man as a means of inserting herself into the images with which she is inundated on a daily basis: "all die Filme, Plakate, Gespräche und Pärchen in der U-Bahn, diese Welt, mit der ich nichts zu tun habe, die aber ständig um mich herum gelebt wird, die mir als das Wahre, Gesunde und Lebenswürdige gepriesen wird, muß ich irgendwie verarbeiten" [all the films, posters, conversations, and couples in the subway, this world, with which I have nothing to do but which is constantly lived around me, which is glorified as true, healthy, and worthy of life; all this I must somehow process, 17]. This same rhetoric comes up again when the narrator and her female lover imagine a world in which they can claim the right to live and to matter as lesbians: "Alles, stellten Hanne und ich fest, was wir wollen, ist lediglich, daß wir das leben dürfen—überall, in Kinos, Kneipen, S-Bahnen, der ganzen Öffentlichkeit—was diese anderen, die Mehrheit, auch leben" [All Hanne and I wanted, we determined, was simply to be permitted to live—everywhere, in theaters, bars, streetcars, the entire public sphere—that which these others, the majority, also live, 129]. Gabriele's desire to align external images with inner experiences resonates with the claim by Michael Warner, who is credited with having invented the term *heteronormativity*, that "Het culture thinks of itself as the elemental form of human association, as the very model of intergender relations, as the indivisible basis of all community, and as the means of reproduction without which society wouldn't exist" (Intro-

duction xxi). The notion of heterosexual normalcy also helps explain why Gabriele later dreams that her lover Hanne becomes a man (Gelien 184). Hanne is butch, but does not identify as a man, though she is sometimes mistaken for one.

40. See, for instance, Andrew Sullivan, *Virtually Normal: An Argument about Homosexuality* (New York: Knopf, 1995); and Michael Warner, *The Trouble with Normal: Sex, Politics, and the Ethics of Queer Life* (New York: Free, 1999).

41. Eve Kosofsky Sedgwick also suggests that queer positionalities affect all social interactions: coming out is not a one-time event; rather, it is something queer people must do again and again, depending on the context and whom they are speaking with. See Eve Kosofsky Sedgwick, *Epistemology of the Closet* (Berkeley: University of California Press, 1990).

42. Kunz goes to great pains to emphasize his alleged heterosexuality—and thus to hide his queer desires. He repeatedly makes reference to heterosexual desires and a past long-term relationship with a woman. For a critical discussion of gay shame, see Judith Halberstam, "Shame and White Gay Masculinity," Eng, Halberstam, and Muñoz, eds. 219–33.

43. This particular variant of the North-South conflict has a long history in German politics, dating back to the monarchical rivalry between the kingdoms of Prussia and Bavaria.

44. See Peter Schneider, *Der Mauerspringer* (Darmstadt: Luchterhand, 1982); and Schneider, "Tearing Down Berlin's Mental Wall," trans. The Times, *New York Times* 12 Aug. 2011: n. pag., *New York Times*, accessed 3 Nov. 2012, http://www.nytimes.com/2011/08/13/opinion/tearing-down-berlins-mental-wall.html?_r=0. The concept of the *Mauer im Kopf*, invented by writer Peter Schneider in the novel *Der Mauerspringer* [*The Wall Jumper*], is a common metaphor referring to the differences between the cultural experiences and collective consciousness of East and West Germans, resulting in stereotyped perceptions of *Ossis* and *Wessis*. In "Tearing Down," Schneider alleges that the wall in the mind still very much exists twenty years after unification, but it is slowly eroding, a process that will take a full generation to complete.

45. In contrast with its national sister

party, the CDU [*Christlich Demokratische Union Deutschlands*, Christian Democratic Union of Germany], which is represented in the other fifteen German states, the CSU is specific to Bavaria. In countrywide politics, the CSU usually works in a coalition with the CDU signified by the combined abbreviation CDU/CSU. The CSU, however, does have special representation as a state party at the national level in the *Bundestag* [Parliament].

46. Gabriele makes specific reference to conservative Bavarian politicians alleged to have described undesirable citizens in such pejorative terms—"sinngemäß, weil es mir zu mühselig ist, die Quellen von diesem Schrott aufzustöbern!" [I'm paraphrasing, because it's too much trouble to look up the sources of this garbage! 51]—such as Peter Gauweiler (CSU), Franz Schönhuber (Republican Party), and Hermann Fellner (CSU). There is also a historical dimension South-North/West-East diaspora in Germany. Because West Berlin did not formally belong to the Federal Republic, its male citizens were not required to complete the military service required of other citizens of the FRG. Many young men, especially leftists, from other parts of West Germany simply relocated to West Berlin in order to avoid mandatory conscription.

47. When Gabriele goes into a bar in Bavaria, she is disheartened to discover that she is its only female patron (and, aside from the server, its only female occupant), a gender dynamic that constructs the novel's Bavaria as one in which women have a marginalized presence in public spaces, particularly those traditionally viewed as male leisure spaces (221). Gabriele is also at pains to find evidence of gay culture in Munich. She cannot identify a hairdresser who can give her an "LKS" [*Lesbenkurzhaarschnitt*, a short hairstyle popular with lesbians in the late eighties and nineties] without requiring an explanation (109).

48. Angela Dwyer notes that this connection is neither new nor uncommon, asserting that "well regarded text books on sex crime continue to incorporate a chapter on homosexuality as a sex crime." Angela Dwyer, "Saving Schools from Abomination and Abnormal Sex: A Discourse Analysis of Online Public Commentary about 'Queering' School Spaces," *Queering Paradigms*, ed. Burkhard Scherer (Oxford: Lang, 2010), 197–215; here, 204.

49. In the original Prussian law, Paragraph 175 made homosexual acts and bestiality illegal. The law never mentioned or covered sex acts between women. During the Third Reich, the law was expanded to include not only homosexual acts but also the suspicion of homosexuality, and it was used to justify the persecution of thousands of alleged homosexuals between 1935 and 1945, as documented in the film *Paragraph 175* (Rob Epstein and Jeffrey Friedman, 2000). East Germany reduced the law to its prewar scope in 1950, as did West Germany in 1969. Both states further revised the law in the 1960s and 1970s so that it defined only homosexual acts with minors as illegal.

50. The description of lesbian love as "eine antisoziale Handlung" [an antisocial behavior, 102] is reminiscent of Nazi terminology. During the Third Reich, though lesbians were not viewed as posing the kind of political threat that male homosexuals represented, they were regarded as asocial because they were not fulfilling the ideologically correct duties of German women as wives and mothers.

51. The controversial debate over same-sex marriage lasted throughout the 1990s. Founded in 1990, the SVD was centrally concerned with the issue of gay marriage and acquired nationwide notoriety with the 1992 protests. (The organization, now called the LSVD [*Lesben- und Schwulenverband in Deutschland*, Lesbian and Gay Federation in Germany], has changed its name to include lesbians.) In 2001, a political compromise in the Federal Republic granted homosexual couples the right to legally registered partnerships. However, this type of liaison was still separate and distinct from marriage, a privilege reserved for heterosexual couples and allowing for other rights that remained unavailable to gays, such as adoption, insemination, and tax benefits.

52. Indeed, Dagmar Herzog claims that "Marriage is definitively in decline" even though monogamy and fidelity remain important values among post-unification German couples. Dagmar Herzog, "Post coitum triste est...? Sexual Politics and Cultures in Postunification Germany," *From the Bonn to the Berlin Republic: Germany at the Twentieth Anniversary of Unification*, ed. Jeffrey J. Anderson and Eric Langenbacher (New York: Berghahn, 2010), 131–59; here, 136.

53. Lisa Duggan, *The Twilight of Equality? Neoliberalism, Cultural Politics, and the Attack on Democracy* (Boston: Beacon, 2003), 50.

54. There are, however, also points in the novel where the discourse of the family is mobilized in order to normalize queerness. For instance, Gabriele enlists her large, conservative family to help convince her lover Hanne's homophobic mother to consent to their relationship. By demonstrating that she comes from a supportive and upstanding bourgeois environment, Gabriele assures Hanne's mother that homosexuals are not necessarily ill, abused, or neglected. But this scenario should not be viewed as a victory for queer politics; in fact, it is a repudiation of such politics in favor of an ideology of normalization.

55. It is noteworthy that Gabriele and her friends now live in the Franconian town of Atldorf (near Nuremberg). Franconians are wont to identify themselves as different from (other) Bavarians, even though a large part of the historical region of Franconia is in Bavaria. Living in Franconia simultaneously sets Gabriele, Hanne, and the other lesbian couple apart from the conservative Bavarian mainstream and situates them within the larger geographical space of the conservative state, where they could potentially challenge the political status quo.

56. Sara Ahmed, *Queer Phenomenology: Orientations, Objects, Others* (Durham: Duke University Press, 2006), 173.

57. However, the German word *quer* [diagonally], a term related to the English *queer*, comes up repeatedly. For instance, Gabriele explains to Hanne that her girlfriend Lisa has sex "querbeet" [all over, 135], meaning that she sleeps with other people.

58. This joke originally appeared in the May 1999 issue of *Emma* magazine and was reprinted in 2005 along with other jokes about men intended as feminist responses to the ever-popular blonde joke. "Die besten Männerwitze," *Emma* Jan.-Feb. 2005: n. pag., accessed 1 Oct. 2012, http://www.emma.de/?id=346.

59. After the success of *Harte Schule*, Ariadne reprinted Lehmann's original Nerz trilogy, with the first two novels appearing under new titles: *Der Masochist* was reissued as *Vergeltung am Degerloch* [Vengeance at Degerloch, 2006] and *Training mit dem Tod* came out as *Gaisburger Schlachthof* [Gaisburg

Slaughterhouse, 2006]. *Pferdekuss* retained its original name in the new Ariadne edition (2008). Perhaps the most successful novel in the series was the sixth book, *Allmachtsdackel* [Dumb Dogs, 2007]. The most recent installment is *Totensteige* [Death Climb, 2012].

60. For a discussion of gender and the hardboiled detective, see, for instance, Dietze; Klein; and Walton and Jones.

61. Thomas Wörtche, "Leichenberg 06/2007," *Kaliber .38: Krimis im Internet*, Thomas Wörtche, 2007, accessed 15 July 2012, http://www.kaliber38.de/woertche/leich0607.htm. This phrase, invented by literary critic Thomas Wörtche, has become a catchphrase to describe Lisa Nerz; author Lehmann embraces it too, using it on her personal blog to describe her fictional heroine. Lehmann's blog contains a link to her online shop, where one can buy Lisa Nerz paraphernalia, including a mug with a drawing of the butch heroine on one side and the words "Lisa Nerz: gendermäßig oszillierend" printed on the other. Christine Lehmann, "Christine Lehmann," Profile, *Christine Lehmann Blog*, accessed 20 July 2012, http://christine-lehmann.blogspot.com/.

62. Christine Lehmann, *Der Masochist* (Reinbek: Rowohlt, 1997), 5.

63. Christine Lehmann, *Training mit dem Tod* (Reinbek: Rowohlt, 1998), 24. All citations hereafter refer to this volume. In *Training*, Lisa recounts that she was once thrown out of a women's café because she was thought to be a man (24). She mobilizes her masculine appearance to her advantage in *Harte Schule* in order to investigate an underground gay pedophile scene up close: she infiltrates a men-only bar and flirts with a gay murder suspect who believes that she is a man. See Christine Lehmann, *Harte Schule* (Hamburg: Argument, 2005), 91–99.

64. Like the representations of transgendered figures in the detective novels that Betz analyzes, here, too, "open hostility [toward the transgendered individual] is missing" ("Re-Covered" 31). In Lehmann's *Training*, the portrayal of transgenderism as less socially accepted comes across largely through the contrast with drug trafficking and through Richard's narrative of his transition.

65. The deadly drug is named Llullallaco after the Andean village in which the fictional bacteria originates. The pill is invented by an international research team led by a Japanese

doctor, and the story of its development and distribution implicates American, French, Swiss and German doctors and research institutes (182–89).

66. The 2009 revision of the transsexual law took place in the wake of a 2008 legal case, the result of which was that the *Bundesverfassungsgericht* [Federal constitutional court] declared the *Transsexuellengesetz*, and in particular the part of the law governing marriage, incompatible with other dimensions of German law, and stipulated that it undergo revision.

67. In contrasting unhappily married heterosexuals characters with children with their happily single and childless queer counterparts, Lehmann may have been influenced by both the German gay marriage debates of the 1990s and by the International Bill of Gender Rights. The Bill, which was first drafted at the 1993 International Conference on Transgender Law and Employment Policy and adopted in 1996, served as an international petition for the extension of basic rights, including the rights to form marital contracts and to conceive, bear, or adopt children, for individuals with any gender or sexual identity, including transsexuals. For a discussion of the Bill and its implications, see Paisley Currah, Richard M. Juang, and Shannon Price Minter, eds., *Transgender Rights* (Minneapolis: University of Minnesota Pesss), 2006.

68. Lehmann's novel alludes to Nazi violence in its discussion of transgender legislation. Richard's narrative of his childhood and pre-operative past begins with the cultured environment of his parental home: "In den verglasten Bücherschränken reihte sich deutsches Kulturgut, ausgenommen Kästner, Ossietzky und Tucholsky und was sonst noch auf dem Scheiterhaufen gebrannt hatte" [In the glass-paned bookcases were rows of German cultural treasures, with the exceptions of Kästner, Ossietzky, and Tucholsky, and whatever else had burned on the pyre, 140]. This description recalls the National Socialist state's attempts to obliterate significant literary legacies that were not in line with party politics or that had been penned by Jewish writers. Richard's alienation from his parents after his surgery suggests that he too is an undesired cultural form. The stipulation for official gender reassignment, which Richard mentions on the following page, that transpeople be "dauernd fortpflanzungsunfähig"

[permanently sterile, 141], brings to mind the forced sterilization campaigns targeting Afro-Germans and people with mental and physical handicaps in the 1920s and 1930s.

69. Alice Schwarzer, "Transsexualität," *Emma* Mar.-Apr. 1994: 36–37; here, 36.

70. The novel's representation of this process again emphasizes the prevalent attitude in the medical establishment that, even if women do experience sexual desire, they are unworthy of discussion: "Niemand hatte [Richard] gesagt, daß die ersten Spritzen unsäglich geil machten" [No one had told Richard that the first (hormone) shots make you indescribably horny, 142].

71. Films such as Rainer Werner Fassbinder's *In einem Jahr mit 13 Monden* [*In a Year of 13 Moons*, 1978] and Oskar Roehler's *Agnes und seine Brüder* [*Agnes and His Brothers*, 2004] also depict transgendered people—in these cases, male to female—who leave Germany in order to gain access to reassignment surgery.

72. See Garber; Bernice L. Hausman, "Body, Technology, and Gender in Transsexual Autobiographies," *The Transgender Studies Reader*, ed. Susan Stryker and Stephen Whittle (New York: Routledge, 2006), 335–61; and Joanne Meyerowitz, "A 'Fierce and Demanding' Drive," Stryker and Whittle, 362–86.

73. The phallus takes on additional meaning in theories of sexuality as the primary symbol of gender differentiation: femaleness is defined as that which lacks a penis, while maleness means having the penis. See Sigmund Freud, *Three Essays on the Theory of Sexuality*, trans. James Strachey (New York: Basic, 1975); Luce Irigaray, *This Sex Which Is Not One*, trans. Catherine Porter (Ithaca: Cornell University, 1985); and Suzanne J. Kessler and Wendy McKenna, "Toward a Theory of Gender," Stryker and Whittle, 165–82.

74. Kate Bornstein points out that the converse transition of male-to-female transsexuality does not necessarily involve the sudden and complete loss of male privilege: "occasionally a male-to-female transsexual will carry more than a small degree of [male privilege] over into their newly-gendered life." Kate Bornstein, "Gender Terror, Gender Rage," Stryker and Whittle, 236–43; here, 239.

75. Donna J. Haraway, "A Cyborg Manifesto: Science, Technology, and Socialist-

Feminism in the Late Twentieth Century," *Simians, Cyborgs, and Women: The Reinvention of Nature*, by Donna J. Haraway (New York: Routledge, 1991), 149–83.

76. Susan Stryker, "My Words to Victor Frankenstein above the Village of Chamounix: Performing Transgender Rage," Stryker and Whittle, 244–56; here, 245.

77. Wolfgang Emmerich, ed., *Geschlechtertausch: Drei Geschichten über die Umwandlung der Verhältnisse* (1980, Darmstadt: Luchterhand, 1989). Wolf's story is not the only literary reference in Lehmann's text. By including characters named Schiller, Weber, and Weininger, Lehmann invokes both a humanistic philosophical tradition and antiquated theories of gender and sexuality (the latter in particular with Weininger, whose name references Jewish scholar Otto Weininger, author of the 1903 treatise *Geschlecht und Charakter* [Sex and Character]).

78. *Geschlechtertausch* comes up earlier in Lehmann's story too, though when it first appears the book functions as an unspoken indication of Lisa's emerging awareness that there is something queer about Richard. Lisa takes a copy of *Geschlechtertausch* when she visits a convalescing friend to whom she reads Wolf's feminist story (133). The appearance of the book is connected with Richard's appearance: as she leaves the hospital, Lisa runs into Richard, an encounter that indicates that there is indeed a link between him and Wolf's subject. The book comes up again later in conjunction with Richard's presence, but this time it is in the process of disappearing, a withdrawal that signals impending intimacy through its location (181).

79. See Christa Wolf, "Self-Experiment: Appendix to a Report," trans. Jeanette Clausen, intro. Helen Fehervary and Sara Lennox, Fehervary, Harrigan, and Vedder-Shults 109–31, *JSTOR*, accessed 17 Aug. 2008, http://www.jstor.org/stable/3115190. For a discussion of the political context of Wolf's short story, see Helen Fehervary and Sara Lennox, "Self-Experiment: Appendix to a Report," Introduction, Fehervary, Harrigan, and Vedder-Shults 109–12, *JSTOR*, accessed 17 Aug. 2008, http://www.jstor.org/stable/3115190.

80. Audre Lorde, perf., *Audre Lorde—The Berlin Years 1984–1992*, dir. Dagmar Schulz (Third World Newsreel, 2012).

81. See Pusch. Conservative politicians tended to prefer, in conjunction with the adjective *homosexuell*, the nominal form *Homosexuelle* [homosexuals] for male homosexuals and its somewhat antiquated feminine equivalent, *Lesbierinnen* [lesbians], for female homosexuals. Green politician Jutta Oesterle-Schwerin, who was backed by other members of her party, was an outspoken proponent of adopting the terms *schwul* and *lesbisch* (as well as the nouns *Schwule* and *Lesben*) for use in official records.

Chapter 4

1. Agatha Christie, *The Murder of Roger Ackroyd* (1926, New York: Garland, 1976; Fifty Classics of Crime Fiction, 1900–1950), 303, emphasis in original.

2. Susan Rowland maintains that the bond of trust that develops between the reader and the detective is a crucial element of this dynamic: "The detectives' evolving selves draw the reading consciousness into the imaginary world of the novel: that is, we make sense of the story partly through making sense of, learning to trust, the detective as a reassuring stable identity." Susan Rowland, *From Agatha Christie to Ruth Rendell: British Women Writers in Detective and Crime Fiction* (Basingstoke: Palgrave, 2001; Crime Files), 23. By contrast, Pierre Bayard claims that "*All mystery fiction in effect implies the narrator's bad faith.*" Pierre Bayard, *Who Killed Roger Ackroyd? The Mystery behind the Agatha Christie Mystery*, trans. Carol Cosman (New York: New, 2000), 54, emphasis in original. On the role of reader sympathy and distance in the effects of narrative and its interpretation, see Mark Currie, *Postmodern Narrative Theory* (New York: St. Martin's, 1998; Transitions).

3. This twist violates several conventions of detective fiction: the reader should have all of the clues necessary to solve the crime, no tricks or deceptions should be played on the reader, and the narrator-investigator should not be a criminal. These are the first, second, and fourth rules in S. S. Van Dine's canonical description of the genre. See S. S. Van Dine, "Twenty Rules for Writing Detective Stories," *American Magazine* Sept. 1928: n. pag., *Gaslight*, Mount Royal College, 2000, accessed 6 July 2011, http://gaslight.mtroyal.ca/vandine.htm.

4. There are indications of Sheppard's complicity early in the novel, but these are easily overlooked by an unsuspecting reader. On the first page, narrator Sheppard repeats the phrase "To tell the truth," as if it were necessary to emphasize the veracity of his claims here in opposition to other passages, in which he might not tell the truth, or tells only partial truths (1); and on the night of Ackroyd's murder, he admits that he "had to make up a slightly fictitious account of the evening in order to satisfy" his sister's curiosity (48). If the narrator must remind his reader that his account is "truth," and if he is willing to tell his sister tall tales, then why should readers expect to glean all the facts pertaining to the case from this narrative?

5. For an analysis of the ways in which closeting and outing interface with the genre of the lesbian detective novel, see Faye Stewart, "Out and Undercover: The Closeted Detective in Lisa Pei's *Die letzte Stunde*," *Sexual-Textual Border-Crossings: Lesbian Identity in German-Language Literature, Film, and Culture*, ed. Cordula Böcking-Politis and Carrie Smith-Prei, spec. issue of *Germanistik in Ireland* 5 (2010): 125–42. For a discussion of other closet metaphors that resonate with political significance, see Michael P. Brown, *Closet Space: Geographies of Metaphor from the Body to the Globe* (London: Routledge, 2000; Critical Geographies 12).

6. The first Helen Marrow novel, *Mit Haut und Handel*, was republished with Orlanda under the title *Angriff von Innen: Helen Marrows erster Fall* [Attack from Within: Hellen Marrow's First Case, 2002]. *Sieben Zeichen: Dein Tod* retained its original name in the Orlanda edition but acquired the subtitle *Helen Marrows zweiter Fall* [Helen Marrow's Second Case, 2003]. The third installment in the original Rowohlt series, *Im Schatten des schwarzen Vogels*, came out with Orlanda under the new name *angstherz: Helen Marrows dritter Fall* [Fearheart: Helen Marrow's Third Case, 2004].

7. While I read this novel as an allegory about Scientology's practices in Germany after the fall of the Wall, parallels can also be drawn with other global religions and historical eras. For instance, we can understand *Sieben Zeichen* as a critique of nineteenth-century colonialism and particularly the spread of Christianity in the colonies of Western European nations. Such an interpretation would be supported by the novel's symbolism, especially the number seven and the ritualistic use of water, which recalls the sacred symbols of Christianity. This reading would also fit well with the historical context of post-unification Germany, in which religion, in particular Catholicism, once deemed to be at odds with socialism and capitalism, offered new forms of faith for the citizens of former socialist countries whose belief systems had been called into question with the collapse of those states.

8. The jacket of the Orlanda edition of *Sieben Zeichen* quotes a review from the lesbian website www.lesarion.de. Susanne Billig, *Sieben Zeichen: Dein Tod: Helen Marrows zweiter Fall* (1994, Berlin: Orlanda, 2003), cited on back cover. While the inclusion of this review would seem to indicate an awareness of a lesbian readership for the author's work, the review cited does not explicitly link the novel with homosexuality.

9. Although authors' biographies do not determine their characters' sexual identities, it seems pertinent in this context to add that Billig herself lives in Berlin as an out lesbian, where she is active in lesbian culture. Billig's unnamed girlfriend receives mention in the short biography in *Queer Crime* (Kuppler 297). Queer desires find more explicit expression in other fiction by Billig: both *Ein gieriger Ort* and "Dora" feature romantic and erotic relationships among women. For a discussion of the queer dimensions of "Dora," see Stewart, "Dialogues."

10. The focus here is Helen's queer sexuality, but the contours of Helen's queerness also extend to her gender, which combines femininity and masculinity and might be categorized as feminine masculinity or female masculinity. In domestic dynamics, Helen plays roles traditionally aligned with masculinity: she is the more rational and orderly counterpart to her chaotic, flighty, and hysterical female roommates. At 1.80 meters in height, she towers over many men, and gender conventions of crime fiction receive a feminist rewriting in *Sieben Zeichen* and in *angstherz* when Helen must travel both inland and abroad to rescue male characters. Helen sports a "Kurzhaarschnitt" [short haircut, *Sieben* 44], like her male friend Ulf, which aligns her with masculinity and also recalls the *LKS* [*Lesbenkurzhaarschnitt*, lesbian short haircut] that appears in Gelien's *Lesbe*,

a stereotypical lesbian coif of the 1980s and 1990s. For a discussion of feminine masculinity, see Breger; and of female masculinity, see Halberstam, *Female Masculinity*.

11. The names Edna and Roy are highly symbolic. Edna, whose name signifies rebirth but also recalls the abbreviation for environmental DNA, is a deeply spiritual figure in tune with her surroundings, and develops into a protagonist by the novel's end. By contrast, Roy, whose name refers to monarchical authority, is revealed to be a power-mongering ruler who is in bed with the corrupt leadership of the S.A.L.

12. Although the presence of Scientology on German soil already dated back some twenty years when Billig's novel first came out, the international visibility of the Church increased markedly after the death of L. Ron Hubbard in 1986 and the ensuing advertising campaigns for Scientology in the 1990s. The rhetoric about Scientology in the German media tended to focus on its profit-earning interests and its connections to questionably legitimate businesses. See especially articles appearing in the popular magazine *Der Spiegel* in the early 1990s, such as: Jan Fleischhauer, "'Lieber tot als unfähig': *Spiegel*-Report über die Geschäfte der Scientology-Sekte," *Der Spiegel* 1 April 1991: 30–38, *Der Spiegel*, accessed 15 Dec. 2012, http://www.spiegel.de/spiegel/print/d-13487385.html; and "Ordentlicher Stromschlag," *Der Spiegel* 15 April 1991: 56–57, *Der Spiegel*, accessed 15 Dec. 2012, http://www.spiegel.de/spiegel/print/d-13489151.html.

13. For a discussion of the legal and political dimensions of the German debates about Scientology in the 1990s, see Stephen A. Kent, "The Globalization of Scientology: Influence, Control, and Opposition in Transnational Markets," *Religion* 29.2 (1999): 147–69.

14. In 1988, the United States Supreme Court upheld the IRS's 1967 retraction of the Church's tax-exempt status, but the IRS reversed its decision only five years later and granted tax exemptions to American Scientology organizations. The 1993 decision brought with it a discussion of the recognition of Scientology as a religion in other countries, and the United States Department of State criticized the discrimination against Scientologists in Germany. See United States, Dept. of State, *Germany Human Rights Prac-*

tices, 1993, 31 Jan. 1994, *State Department Electronic Archive*, accessed 7 Jan. 2013, http://dosfan.lib.uic.edu/ERC/democracy/1993_hrp_report/93hrp_report_eur/Germany.html. After a 1995 ruling in Germany that Scientology would not be recognized as a religion, the Church was kept under surveillance, and there were subsequent attempts to ban Scientology entirely. For a review of the legal situation Scientology has faced in Germany since the 1990s, see Andrew Purvis, "Germany's Battle against Scientology," *Time* 17 Dec. 2007: n. pag., *Time*, accessed 31 Dec. 2012, http://www.time.com/time/world/article/0,8599,1695514,00.html. For a more detailed history of Scientology in the United States, see Richard Behar, "The Thriving Cult of Greed and Power," *Time* 6 May 1991: n. pag., *Scientology: The Thriving Cult of Greed and Power*, Computer Science Dept., Carnegie Mellon University, accessed 12 Dec. 2012, http://www.cs.cmu.edu/~dst/Fishman/time-behar.html; and Hugh B. Urban, *The Church of Scientology: A History of a New Religion* (Princeton: Princeton University Press, 2011).

15. The novel can be read to theorize globalization as simply a modern form of colonialism, which brings to mind the discourse of colonizing the former East after 1989. For a contextualization of this discourse, see Paul Cooke, *Representing East Germany since Unification: From Colonization to Nostalgia* (Oxford: Berg, 2005). It should be noted that Billig's representation of globalization in *Sieben Zeichen* as a destructive force differs quite markedly from the feminist critique of globalization that Katrin Sieg identifies in Pieke Biermann's *Potsdamer Ableben* ("Postcolonial").

16. Helen is in some ways also an ideal target for brainwashing: not only is she emotionally vulnerable because she is also still mourning the death of her child, but she is single and recently relocated to a city where her only social contacts are with her roommates and her employer—and the latter are minimal because she works at home. It is not until the end of the novel that Helen discovers that the S.A.L. commune is meant to serve as the headquarters for a missionary campaign to cover the entirety of former East Germany (229).

17. Such an interpretation of the text resonates with Cooke's analysis of representations of the former East as forming a contin-

uum from neocolonialism in the East to post-socialist nostalgia for a lost culture.

18. According to Bornstein, the Fair Game policy was decreed by Scientology's founder L. Ron Hubbard in 1967, and though Hubbard retracted his directive a year later, the policy still remains unofficially in effect. Kate Bornstein, *A Queer and Pleasant Danger: A Memoir* (Boston: Beacon, 2012), xvi–xvii. For discussions of Scientology's attacks on critics, see also Behar, "Thriving"; Urban 1–25; and Janet Reitman, *Inside Scientology: The Story of America's Most Secretive Religion* (Boston: Houghton, 2011).

19. Billig's S.A.L. also evokes associations with other religious extremist movements of the early 1990s, such as the Branch Davidians in Waco, Texas, whose violent public confrontation with the FBI and ATF in 1993 ended in over eighty deaths.

20. For more on Vic's suicide and its aftermath in France, see Susan J. Palmer, "The Church of Scientology in France: Legal and Activist Counterattacks in the 'War on Sectes,'" *Scientology*, ed. James R. Lewis (Oxford: Oxford University Press, 2009), 295–322; here, 303–04. See also Behar's award-winning article, "Thriving," published a year after Lottick's suicide, which provides more detail about the circumstances of his death and issues a scathing critique of the Church.

21. For more on L. Ron Hubbard, the Sea Org, and the history of Scientology, see Bornstein; Reitman; Urban; and James R. Lewis, ed., *Scientology* (Oxford: Oxford University Press, 2009).

22. See Cooke; and Sonja Klocke, "Orientalisierung der DDR? Spuren von antifaschistischer Tradition und DDR-Literatur in Emine Sevgi Özdamars *Seltsame Sterne starren zur Erde* (2003)," *NachBilder der Wende*, ed. Inge Stephan and Alexandra Tacke (Cologne: Böhlau, 2008), 141–60.

23. See Ulrich Beck, *What Is Globalization?* trans. Patrick Camiller (Cambridge: Polity, 2000); and Jan Aart Scholte, *Globalization: A Critical Introduction*, 2nd ed. (Basingstoke: Palgrave, 2005).

24. This notion of globalization is quite different from the decentralized and multi-directional theory of globalization that Arjun Appadurai develops. See Arjun Appadurai, *Modernity at Large: Cultural Dimensions of Globalization* (Minneapolis: University of Minnesota Press, 1996; Public Worlds 1).

25. The novel neither equates Scientology/the S.A.L. with East German or Nazi institutions, nor does it suggest that there are similarities between the Gestapo and the Stasi, or the Hitler Youth and the Free German Youth. Rather, it employs symbolism and metaphors that recall the mechanisms of indoctrination and censorship in these two former iterations of German statehood, mobilizing these references as implicit critiques of the fictional dynamics it narrates.

26. See Purvis; and Richard Behar, "Pushing beyond the U.S.: Scientology Makes Its Presence Felt in Europe and Canada" *Time* 6 May 1991, intl. ed.: n. pag., *Scientology: The Thriving Cult of Greed and Power*, Computer Science Dept., Carnegie Mellon University, accessed 12 Dec. 2012, http://www.cs.cmu.edu/~dst/Fishman/time-behar.html. Scientologists reportedly responded to allegations of totalitarianism by mounting a campaign alleging that the discrimination they have experienced in Germany resembles Nazi discrimination against Jews (Purvis).

27. The children's commune in *Sieben Zeichen* is reminiscent of the special camps established by the Nazi regime in the early 1940s in rural parts of the German Reich, where children could be educated and maintain a regular routine safe from the dangers of the war. Another possible historical reference having to do with the Third Reich, but from the opposing side, is the *Kindertransport* [Refugee Children Movement] preceding World War II, an international mission to relocate Jewish children from areas of the German Reich to the United Kingdom. However, the connection to Nazi camps seems more fitting because in Billig's novel the displacement of the children to the Welsh coast both serves an ideological purpose and prevents them from falling victim to the violence plaguing the Brandenburg commune.

28. These parallels among spirituality, water, femininity, and sexuality evoke goddess worship, New Age feminism, and ecofeminism, while also recalling trends in Greek philosophy and pagan spirituality to align femininity with nature. See Shawn C. Jarvis, "Goddess," *The Feminist Encyclopedia of German Literature*, ed. Friederike Eigler and Susanne Kord (Westport, CT: Greenwood, 1997), 214–15; and Helga Stipa Madland, "Nature," Eigler and Kord 354–55.

29. The first recorded use of the phrase

"cherchez la femme" is attributed to Alexandre Dumas in *The Mohicans of Paris* (1854). It was then immortalized by O. Henry [William Sydney Porter] as the title of a 1909 story in which the central character, Dumas, repetitively utters the phrase. Henry's story also ends with these words.

30. The family metaphor also recalls the West German practice—particularly common among politicians during the Cold War—of showing solidarity with East Germans by referring to them as "Brüder und Schwestern" [brothers and sisters]. A recent novel by Birk Meinhardt, titled *Brüder und Schwestern* (2013), evokes this rhetorical turn to thematize life in the GDR.

31. In *angstherz*, Helen does reveal that she has developed a crush on a man, her client's husband, Martin Hamman-Haug. Nothing comes of this attraction, however, and the novel ends with Helen feeling only disgust for Martin when she learns about the skeletons in his closet.

32. Susanne Billig, *angstherz: Helen Marrows dritter Fall* (Berlin: Orlanda, 2004; Rpt. of *Im Schatten des Schwarzen Vogels*, 1995), 156.

33. See, for instance, Alyssa M. ElHage, "Homosexual Indoctrination: How Safety Is Used to Promote Homosexuality in Schools," *Findings* Dec. 2004: 1–4, *North Carolina Family Policy Council*, accessed 5 Jan. 2013, http://www.ncfpc.org/PolicyPapers/ Findings percent200412-HomosexualEd. pdf; and Ben Shapiro, *Brainwashed: How Universities Indoctrinate America's Youth* (Nashville: WND, 2004). For a gay-affirmative counterperspective, see Jason Cianciotto and Sean Cahill, "Education Policy: Issues Affecting Lesbian, Gay, Bisexual, and Transgender Youth" (New York: National Gay and Lesbian Task Force Policy Institute, 2003), *National Gay and Lesbian Task Force*, accessed 7 Jan. 2013, http://www. thetaskforce.org/downloads/reports/ reports/EducationPolicy.pdf; and, in the German context, Dirk Ch. Anglowski, *Homosexualität im Schulunterricht: Evaluation eines Lambda-Aufklärungsprojekts unter einstellungstheoretischer Perspektive*, 2nd ed. (Marburg: Tectum, 2000).

34. See "17th Jan: Puszta Cowboy and the Budapest Lesbian Film Collective," *Bildwechsel Glasgow* 2 Jan. 2007, *WordPress*, accessed 16 July 2011, http://bildwechselglasgow. wordpress.com/2007/01/02/puszta-cowboy-and-the-budapest-lesbian-film-collective/.

35. The Ariadne series consists exclusively of novels with female main characters, with equal numbers of texts featuring straight and lesbian characters. The heterosexual narratives are assigned even numbers, while the lesbian books have odd numbers, as if to signify their unevenness. Kremmler's novels are all odd-numbered: *Blaubarts Handy* is number 1131, *Die Sirenen von Coogee Beach* is number 1145, and *Pannonias Gral* is number 1153 in the series.

36. The Gay Games are an international, gender- and sexuality-inclusive sporting event and cultural festival. Like the Olympic Games that inspired them, the Gay Games are held every four years in a different city around the world. The plot of *Sirenen* unfolds in November and December 2002, during and after the Gay Games, which were held in Sydney from November 2 to 9, 2002.

37. Katrin Kremmler, *Die Sirenen von Coogee Beach* (Hamburg: Argument, 2003), 9.

38. This entire first opening passage is italicized in Kremmler's original text, but I have rendered the citations here in upright lettering for the sake of readability.

39. Stephen Knight, "Crimes Domestic and Crimes Colonial: The Role of Crime Fiction in Developing Postcolonial Consciousness," *Postcolonial Postmortems: Crime Fiction from a Transcultural Perspective*, ed. Christine Matzke and Susanne Mühleisen (Amsterdam: Rodopi, 2006; Internationale Forschungen zur Allgemeinen und Vergleichenden Literaturwissenschaft 102), 17–33; here, 17.

40. See also Xavier Pons, "'Redneck Wonderland': Robert G. Barrett's Crime Fiction," Matzke and Mühleisen, eds. 229–53.

41. SIEV is the official acronym for Suspected Illegal Entry Vessel, used by the Australian government to identify unauthorized maritime vessels in or near Australian territorial waters. The identification placeholder X is assigned to vessels that have not yet been catalogued under a tracking number. Though SIEV X is thus a common designation for unidentified boats, the phrase *SIEV X incident* has come to refer specifically to the events and controversy surrounding the 2001 sinking of a boat headed from Sumatra to Christmas Island.

42. The citation in Kremmler's novel

states that the boat initially held over 400 passengers, but does not mention that forty-five refugees were rescued after the boat sank. Many of the refugees were from the Middle East (primarily Iraq) and North Africa. For a detailed discussion of the incident and the controversy surrounding it, see Tony Kevin, *A Certain Maritime Incident: The Sinking of SIEV X* (Melbourne: Scribe, 2004).

43. In the Tampa affair of August 2001, Howard's government refused entry into Australian waters to a Norwegian freighter carrying over 400 rescued refugees fleeing Afghanistan; the event set off heated debates in Australia as well as a diplomatic argument with Norway. The Children Overboard affair of October 2001 involved a boat carrying over 200 refugees that sank between Indonesia and the Australian territory of Christmas Island; representatives of the Howard administration alleged that asylum seekers on the boat had thrown their own children overboard in an attempt to manipulate Australian authorities into rescuing them. The Howard administration responded to these events by emphasizing its stance on closing borders to illegal boat arrivals, which energized supporters and helped fuel its leader's successful bid for reelection on November 10, 2001. For a discussion of these events in the context of discourses about asylum and immigration during this era, see Michael Leach, "'Disturbing Practices': Dehumanizing Asylum Seekers in the Refugee 'Crisis' in Australia, 2001–2002," *Refuge* 21.3 (2003): 25–33, *Refuge*, accessed 31 Dec. 2012, http://pi.library.yorku.ca/ojs/index.php/refuge/article/viewFile/21301/19972.

44. See, for instance, Kevin; Steve Biddulph, "Tragic Legacy of SIEVX's Fatal Sinking," *The Age*, The Age 19 Oct. 2009, accessed 31 Dec. 2012, http://www.theage.com.au/opinion/politics/tragic-legacy-of-sievxs-fatal-sinking-20091019-h38e.html; and Linda Tenenbaum, "The Tragedy of SIEV X: Did the Australian Government Deliberately Allow 353 Refugees to Drown?" *World Socialist Web Site* 13–16 Aug. 2002, World Socialist Web Site, 2013, accessed 28 Aug. 2012, http://www.wsws.org/en/articles/2002/08/siel-a13.html.

45. The Amnesty International text Kremmler cites does not name a specific law, but ends with an allusion to legislation enacted in the months following the SIEV X in-

cident which stipulated that all asylum seekers be in the possession of legal documents (8). In late 2001, other measures were also taken to secure Australian borders. The Border Protection Bill, passed in the days following the Tampa affair, ostensibly aimed to regulate the procedure for turning away foreign ships seeking permission to enter Australian territorial waters. The Bill gave government and military officials the authority to refuse entry and docking rights to unauthorized vessels and their passengers. Following the Tampa affair, the government also formed a border protection initiative called Operation Relex, which was operated by the Australian Defense Force and focused specifically on oceanic activity to the north.

46. Gab explains that an ethnocentric definition of culture also makes its way into the racial politics of memory, where *history* and *heritage* are aligned exclusively with whiteness and non-indigenous culture: "In Studien zur Denkmalwürdigkeit bestimmter Stadtbezirke, ... wird 'Geschichte' methodisch abgegrenzt von 'Natur' und 'aboriginal.' Laut dieser Definition ist aboriginale Geschichte nicht denkmalwürdig, nicht historisch, nicht Teil der offiziellen Geschichte. *Heritage*, kulturelles Erbe, ist weißes kulturelles Erbe, für die *aboriginalen* Orte und Artefakte eines Bezirks ist eine andere Behörde zuständig" [In studies on the monument-worthiness of particular city districts, 'history' is methodologically separated from 'nature' and 'aboriginal.' According to this definition, aboriginal history is not monument-worthy, not historical, not a part of official history. *Heritage*, cultural heritage, is white cultural heritage; another agency is responsible for a district's *aboriginal* sites and artifacts, 102, emphasis in original]. For a historical contextualization of these discourses, see James Jupp, *From White Australia to Woomera: The Story of Australian Immigration* (New York: Cambridge University Press, 2002).

47. Simon Green, "Towards an Open Society? Citizenship and Immigration," *Developments in German Politics 3*, ed. Stephen Padgett, William E. Paterson, and Gordon Smith (Durham: Duke University Press, 2003), 227–47; here, 231.

48. The Woomera Immigration Reception and Processing Centre served as an overflow detention center for unauthorized arrivals from 1999 to 2003, during which

multiple controversies surrounded its operations due to riots, hunger strikes, and allegations of human rights abuses. In *Sirenen*, Hawa breaks out of Woomera during the Easter protests, a reference to the historical 2002 demonstrations when approximately forty refugees escaped. The text explicitly likens Woomera to a concentration camp: "Die leben da wie im KZ. Wie damals bei den Nazis" [They live there like in a concentration camp. Like back then with the Nazis, 168].

49. Symbolically, both types of camps served to separate one ethnic population from another. However, it should be noted that Kremmler's comparison seeks not to equate Australian and Nazi institutions, but rather to underline the problematic facets of Australian immigration policies. Crucial distinctions exist between immigration detainment centers such as Woomera—both as it is depicted in Kremmler's novel and in real life—and Nazi concentration camps. Above all, Woomera and other such centers never served as labor camps or extermination camps. Detainment in Australia's immigration centers was compulsory only for those immigrants who arrived illegally, and lasted only until the refugees' claims could be processed, though this often took a year or longer. The detained refugees were eventually repatriated or deported to other countries, but there is no evidence that genocide figured among the Australian government's goals.

50. Iran and Southern Asia is the region designated by the German *Mittlerer Osten*. The lack of direct English equivalent for the German term makes it difficult to translate; the English term *Middle East* and the German *Mittlerer Osten* have the same literal meaning but refer to different geographic regions. German speakers typically distinguish the *Mittleren Osten* from the *Nahen Osten* [literally, Near East, but corresponding geographically to the Middle East] and the *Fernen Osten* [Far East] in that it references the area between the "near" and "far" East. The *Mittlere Osten* stretches from Iran, Afghanistan, and Pakistan in the west to the Southern Asian lands of India, Nepal, Bangladesh, and Myanmar in the east.

51. With the unification of Germany and the Yugoslav Wars, a wave of refugees in the early 1990s brought about a revision of the *Ausländergesetz* [foreigner law] and a new

Asylkompromiss [asylum compromise] governing immigration and asylum. The new laws, which prioritized immigrants and refugees into different groups, effectively reduced the number of qualified applicants, while also withholding many civil rights and protections. In the early 2000s, updating these laws became a priority under the chancellorship of Social Democrat Gerhard Schröder, whose coalition sought sweeping reforms. In 2000, a controversial new *Staatsangehörigkeitsgesetz* [citizenship law] went into effect, allowing for dual citizenship and recognizing the rights of second-generation migrants to citizenship. A new federal *Zuwanderungsgesetz* [immigration law], consisting of a more liberal *Aufenthaltsgesetz* [residency law] and *Asylverfahrengesetz* [asylum law], went into effect in 2005. See Green; Harald Bauder, *Immigration Dialectic: Imagining Community, Economy, and Nation* (Toronto: University of Toronto Press, 2011); and Joyce Marie Mushaben, "From Ausländer to Inlander: The Changing Faces of Citizenship in Post-Wall Germany," Anderson and Langenbacher 160–82. Another facet of these developments was the "Kinder statt Inder" [children instead of Indians] campaign initiated in 2000 by Christian Democratic politician Jürgen Rüttgers and the ensuing controversy over Chancellor Schröder's plan to grant work permits to foreigners with desirable computer skills. See "'Kinder statt Inder': Rüttgers verteidigt verbalen Ausrutscher," *Der Spiegel Online* 9 Mar. 2000, accessed 20 May 2013, http://www.spiegel.de/politik/deutschland/kinder-statt-inder-ruettgers-verteidigt-verbalen-ausrutscher-a-68369.html; and Dietmar Henning, "Treading in Haider's Footsteps: Germany's CDU Veers to the Right as State Elections Approach," *World Socialist Web Site* 29 Mar. 2000, World Socialist Web Site, 2013, accessed 20 May 2013, http://www.wsws.org/en/articles/2000/03/cdu-m29.html.

52. Christine Matzke and Susanne Mühleisen, "Postcolonial Postmortems: Issues and Perspectives," Introduction, Matzke and Mühleisen, eds. 1–16; here, 5.

53. Several of these dimensions of global citizenship resonate with contemporary theories about globalization and citizenship, in particular Jan Aart Scholte's recommendations for future globalizations and John Schwarzmantel's theory of the new republic.

See Scholte 382–423; and John Schwarzman-tel, *Citizenship and Identity: Towards a New Republic* (London: Routledge, 2003; Routledge Innovations in Political Theory 11).

54. Stephen Castles and Alastair Davidson, *Citizenship and Migration: Globalization and the Politics of Belonging* (New York: Routledge, 2000), 2.

55. The representation of bureaucratic corruption and inefficacy in investigating crimes recalls not only clichés about Australia's convict heritage, but also stereotypical representations of frontier life in the American Wild West. See Pons; and Richard Slotkin, *Gunfighter Nation: The Myth of the Frontier in Twentieth-Century America* (1992, Norman: University of Oklahoma Press, 1998).

56. See Van Dine, rule number seven. Kremmler's novel, like many feminist, lesbian, and queer detective novels, also breaks Van Dine's third rule, which stipulates that there be no romance in the detective story.

Conclusions

1. Carolyn G. Heilbrun, "Nancy Drew: A Moment in Feminist History," *Rediscovering Nancy Drew*, ed. Carolyn Stewart Dyer and Nancy Tillman Romalov (Iowa City: University of Iowa Press, 1995), 11–21; here, 11.

2. My understanding of the history of the series is based on Dyer and Romalov; Michael G. Cornelius and Melanie E. Gregg,

eds., *Nancy Drew and Her Sister Sleuths: Essays on the Fiction of Girl Detectives* (Jefferson, NC: McFarland, 2008); and Melanie Rehak, *Girl Sleuth: Nancy Drew and the Women Who Created Her* (Orlando: Harcourt, 2005).

3. A number of studies have linked laughter and feminism, among other countercultural movements. See, for instance, Regina Barreca, Introduction, *The Penguin Book of Women's Humor*, ed. Regina Barreca (New York: Penguin, 1996), 1–10; Gail Finney, ed., *Look Who's Laughing: Gender and Comedy* (Langhorne, PA: Gordon, 1994; Studies in Humor and Gender 1); and Gloria Kaufman, "Introduction: Humor and Power," *In Stitches: A Patchwork of Feminist Humor and Satire*, ed. Gloria Kaufman (Bloomington: Indiana University Press, 1991), viii–xii.

4. The most popular and prolific venue for the publication of queer crime fiction is undoubtedly Argument's Ariadne series, established in 1988, which specializes in feminist and lesbian crime literature. Other publishers and series where multiple feminist, lesbian, and queer crime novels have appeared include Rowohlt, Rotbuch, Milena, Elles, Frauenoffensive, and Fischer's longstanding series, Die Frau in der Gesellschaft [The Woman in Society]. The ongoing popularity of the genre is also evident in the number of recent volumes that have come out in a new thriller series with the lesbian-friendly publisher Konkursbuch, and in the Quer Criminal [Oblique Criminal] series established in 2009 by the gay and lesbian publisher Querverlag.

Works Cited

Primary Literature and Related Works Published in English

Biermann, Pieke. *Violetta*. Trans. Ines Rieder and Jill Hannum. New York: Serpent's Tail, 1996. Trans. of *Violetta*. Berlin: Rotbuch, 1990.

Billig, Susanne, writ. *Hounded [Verfolgt]*. Dir. Angelina Maccarone. Perf. Kostja Ullmann and Maren Kroymann. MMM, 2007. (United States: Picture This! 2007.)

Gercke, Doris. *How Many Miles to Babylon*. Trans. Anna Hamilton. Seattle: Women in Translation, 1991. Trans. of *Weinschröter, du mußt hängen*. Hamburg: Galgenberg, 1988.

Kremmler, Katrin. *Dykes on Dykes: The First Interactive Dyke-Cartoon*. Tübingen: Konkursbuch, 1998.

Noll, Ingrid. *Head Count*. Trans. Ian Mitchell. London: Harper, 1997. Trans. of *Die Häupter meiner Lieben*. Zurich: Diogenes, 1993.

_____. *Hell Hath No Fury*. Trans. Ian Mitchell. London: Harper, 1996. Trans. of *Der Hahn ist tot*. Zurich: Diogenes, 1991.

_____. *The Pharmacist*. Trans. Ian Mitchell. London: Harper, 1998. Trans. of *Die Apothekerin*. Zurich: Diogenes, 1994.

Strubel, Antje Rávic. *Snowed Under: An Episodic Novel*. Trans. Zaia Alexander. Los Angeles: Red Hen, 2008. Trans. of *Unter Schnee: Episodenroman*. Munich: Deutscher Taschenbuch, 2001.

Works Cited

Abt, Stefanie. *Soziale Enquête im aktuellen Kriminalroman: Am Beispiel von Henning Mankell, Ulrich Ritzel und Pieke Biermann*. Diss. University of Duisburg-Essen, 2004. Wiesbaden: Deutscher Universitätsverlag, 2004. Literaturwissenschaft/Kulturwissenschaft.

Adleson, Leslie A. "The Price of Feminism: Of Women and Turks." *Gender and Germanness: Cultural Productions of Nation*. Ed. Patricia Herminghouse and Magda Mueller. Providence: Berghahn, 1997. Modern German Studies 4. 305–19.

Agazzi, Elena. "Psychologie und Verbrechen in Edith Kneifls Kriminalromanen." *Moraldo* 99–109.

Ahmed, Sara. *Queer Phenomenology: Orientations, Objects, Others*. Durham: Duke University Press, 2006.

Alewyn, Richard. "Anatomie des Detektivromans." *Der Kriminalroman: Poetik-Theorie-Geschichte*. Ed. Jochen Vogt. Munich: Fink, 1998. 52–72.

Altbach, Edith Hoshino. "The New German Women's Movement." *Signs* 9.3 (1984): 454–69. *JSTOR*. Accessed 20 Nov. 2012. http://www.jstor.org/stable/3173714.

Anderson, Jeffrey J., and Eric Langenbacher, eds. *From the Bonn to the Berlin Republic: Germany at the Twentieth Anniversary of Unification*. New York: Berghahn, 2010.

Anderson, Mark. "Death Arias in Vienna." Afterword. *Malina: A Novel*. By Ingeborg Bachmann. Trans. Philip Boehm. New York: Holmes, 1990. Modern German Voices. 226–40.

Anglowski, Dirk Ch. *Homosexualität im Schulunterricht: Evaluation eines Lambda-Aufklärungsprojekts unter einstellungstheoretischer Perspektive*, 2d ed. Marburg: Tectum, 2000.

Appadurai, Arjun. *Modernity at Large: Cul-

tural Dimensions of Globalization. Minneapolis: University of Minnesota Press, 1996. Public Worlds 1.

Arend, Helga. "Nette alte Dame mit Leiche im Keller: Ingrid Nolls Kriminalromane als Unterrichtsthema." Birkle, Matter-Seibel, and Plummer 273–86.

Bachmann, Ingeborg. *Malina*. 1971. Frankfurt am Main: Suhrkamp, 2004.

Baer, Hester, ed. *Contemporary Women's Writing and the Return of Feminism in Germany*. Spec. issue of *Studies in Twentieth and Twenty-First Century Literature* 35.1 (2011): 1–176.

"Bald 'Bockscheine' für die Freier? Westdeutsche Prostituierte organisieren sich in Selbsthilfegruppen." *Der Spiegel* 19 Aug. 1985: 42–43. *Der Spiegel*. Accessed 30 Nov. 2012. http://www.spiegel.de/spiegel/print/d-13515239.html.

Barfoot, Nicola. *Frauenkrimi/polar féminin: Generic Expectations and the Reception of Recent French and German Crime Novels by Women*. Frankfurt am Main: Lang, 2007. MeLiS 5.

Barreca, Regina. Introduction. *The Penguin Book of Women's Humor*. Ed. Regina Barreca. New York: Penguin, 1996. 1–10.

Bauder, Harald. *Immigration Dialectic: Imagining Community, Economy, and Nation*. Toronto: University of Toronto Press, 2011.

Bayard, Pierre. *Who Killed Roger Ackroyd? The Mystery Behind the Agatha Christie Mystery*. Trans. Carol Cosman. New York: New, 2000.

Beck, Ulrich. *What Is Globalization?* Trans. Patrick Camiller. Cambridge: Polity, 2000.

Behar, Richard. "Pushing beyond the U.S.: Scientology Makes Its Presence Felt in Europe and Canada." *Time* 6 May 1991, intl. ed.: n. pag. *Scientology: The Thriving Cult of Greed and Power*. Computer Science Dept., Carnegie Mellon University. Accessed 12 Dec. 2012. http://www.cs.cmu.edu/~dst/Fishman/time-behar.html.

_____. "The Thriving Cult of Greed and Power." *Time* 6 May 1991: n. pag. *Scientology: The Thriving Cult of Greed and Power*. Computer Science Dept., Carnegie Mellon University. Accessed 12 Dec. 2012. http://www.cs.cmu.edu/~dst/Fishman/time-behar.html.

"Die besten Männerwitze." *Emma* Jan.-Feb. 2005: n. pag. *Emma*. Accessed 1 Oct. 2012. http://www.emma.de/?id=346.

Betz, Phyllis M. *Lesbian Detective Fiction: Woman as Author, Subject and Reader*. Jefferson, NC: McFarland, 2006.

_____. "Re-Covered Bodies: The Detective Novel and Transgendered Characters." Collins 21–32.

Biddulph, Steve. "Tragic Legacy of SIEVX's Fatal Sinking." *The Age*. The Age 19 Oct. 2009. Accessed 31 Dec. 2012. http://www.theage.com.au/opinion/politics/tragic-legacy-of-sievxs-fatal-sinking-20091019-h38e.html.

Biermann, Pieke. *Potsdamer Ableben*. Berlin: Rotbuch, 1987.

_____. *Violetta*. Berlin: Rotbuch, 1990.

_____. "Warum ich keine Frauenkrimis schreibe." *Tagesanzeiger-Magazin* 8 Feb. 1992. *Krimikultur: Archiv*. Accessed 12 Dec. 2012. http://krimikulturarchiv.files.wordpress.com/2009/07/warum-ich-keine-frauenkrimis-schreibe-19912.pdf.

Billig, Susanne. *angstherz: Helen Marrows dritter Fall*. Berlin: Orlanda, 2004. Rpt. of *Im Schatten des schwarzen Vogels*. 1995.

_____. *Sieben Zeichen: Dein Tod: Helen Marrows zweiter Fall*. 1994. Berlin: Orlanda, 2003.

Birkle, Carmen, Sabina Matter-Seibel, and Patricia Plummer, eds. *Frauen auf der Spur: Kriminalautorinnen aus Deutschland, Großbritannien und den USA*. Tübingen: Stauffenburg, 2001. Frauen-/Gender-Forschung in Rheinland-Pfalz 3.

Bornhöft, Petra. "Als wenn es mich nicht gäbe." *Der Spiegel* 2 June 2001: 46–48. *Der Spiegel*. Accessed 3 June 2012. http://www.spiegel.de/spiegel/print/d-19337146.html.

Bornstein, Kate. "Gender Terror, Gender Rage." Stryker and Whittle 236–43.

_____. *A Queer and Pleasant Danger: A Memoir*. Boston: Beacon, 2012.

Breger, Claudia. "Hegemony, Marginalization, and Feminine Masculinity: Antje Rávic Strubel's *Unter Schnee*." *Seminar* 44.1 (2008): 154–73.

Brown, Michael P. *Closet Space: Geographies of Metaphor from the Body to the Globe*. London: Routledge, 2000. Critical Geographies 12.

Browne, Kath, and Catherine J. Nash. "Queer Methods and Methodologies: An Introduction." *Queer Methods and Methodologies: Intersecting Queer Theories and Social Science Research*. Ed. Kath Browne and Catherine J. Nash. Burlington: Ashgate, 2010. 1–23.

Butler, Judith. *Bodies That Matter: On the Discursive Limits of "Sex."* New York: Routledge, 1993.

_____. *Gender Trouble: Feminism and the Subversion of Identity.* 1990. New York: Routledge, 1999.

_____. "Performative Acts and Gender Constitution: An Essay in Phenomenology and Feminist Theory." *Theatre Journal* 40.4 (1988): 519–31. *JSTOR.* Accessed 2 Feb. 2006. http://www.jstor.org/stable/3207893.

Castles, Stephen, and Alastair Davidson. *Citizenship and Migration: Globalization and the Politics of Belonging.* New York: Routledge, 2000.

Cawelti, John G. *Adventure, Mystery, and Romance: Formula Stories as Art and Popular Culture.* Chicago: University of Chicago Press, 1976.

Christie, Agatha. *The Murder of Roger Ackroyd.* 1926. New York: Garland, 1976. Fifty Classics of Crime Fiction, 1900–1950.

"Eine Chronik der Diskriminierung—und der Befreiung." *Die Zeit* 16 Aug. 2012: 2–3.

Cianciotto, Jason, and Sean Cahill. "Education Policy: Issues Affecting Lesbian, Gay, Bisexual, and Transgender Youth." New York: National Gay and Lesbian Task Force Policy Institute, 2003. *National Gay and Lesbian Task Force.* Accessed 7 Jan. 2013. http://www.thetaskforce.org/downloads/reports/reports/EducationPolicy.pdf.

Collins, Jacky, ed. *Lesbian Crime Fiction.* Spec. issue of *Clues* 27.2 (2009): 1–119.

Cooke, Paul. *Representing East Germany since Unification: From Colonization to Nostalgia.* Oxford: Berg, 2005.

Cornelius, Michael G., and Melanie E. Gregg, eds. *Nancy Drew and Her Sister Sleuths: Essays on the Fiction of Girl Detectives.* Jefferson, NC: McFarland, 2008.

Culler, Jonathan. *Literary Theory: A Very Short Introduction.* Oxford: Oxford University Press, 1997.

Currah, Paisley, Richard M. Juang, and Shannon Price Minter, eds. *Transgender Rights.* Minneapolis: University of Minnesota Press, 2006.

Currie, Mark. *Postmodern Narrative Theory.* New York: St. Martin's, 1998. Transitions.

Deitmer, Sabine. "Anna, Bella & Co.: Der Erfolg der deutschen Krimifrauen." Birkle, Matter-Seibel, and Plummer 239–53.

Dietze, Gabriele. *Hardboiled Woman:*
Geschlechterkrieg im amerikanischen Kriminalroman. Hamburg: Europäische, 1997.

Dresner, Lisa M. "Lesbian Detectives Have Car Trouble." *The Female Investigator in Literature, Film, and Popular Culture.* By Lisa M. Dresner. Jefferson, NC: McFarland, 2007. 40–62.

Döblin, Alfred. *Die beiden Freundinnen und ihr Giftmord.* 1924. Reinbek: Rowohlt, 1978.

Dorn, Thea. *Die neue F-Klasse: Wie die Zukunft von Frauen gemacht wird.* Munich: Piper, 2006.

Duggan, Lisa. *The Twilight of Equality? Neoliberalism, Cultural Politics, and the Attack on Democracy.* Boston: Beacon, 2003.

Dwyer, Angela. "Saving Schools from Abomination and Abnormal Sex: A Discourse Analysis of Online Public Commentary about 'Queering' School Spaces." *Queering Paradigms.* Ed. Burkhard Scherer. Oxford: Lang, 2010. 197–215.

Dyer, Carolyn Stewart, and Nancy Tillman Romalov, eds. *Rediscovering Nancy Drew.* Iowa City: University of Iowa Press, 1995.

Eigler, Friederike, and Susanne Kord, eds. *The Feminist Encyclopedia of German Literature.* Westport, CT: Greenwood, 1997.

ElHage, Alysse M. "Homosexual Indoctrination: How Safety Is Used to Promote Homosexuality in Schools." *Findings* Dec. 2004: 1–4. *North Carolina Family Policy Council.* Accessed 5 Jan. 2013. http://www.ncfpc.org/PolicyPapers/Findings percent200412-HomosexualEd.pdf.

Emmerich, Wolfgang, ed. *Geschlechtertausch: Drei Geschichten über die Umwandlung der Verhältnisse.* 1980. Darmstadt: Luchterhand, 1989.

Eng, David L., Judith Halberstam, and José Esteban Muñoz. "What's Queer About Queer Studies Now?" Introduction. Eng, Halberstam, and Muñoz, eds. 1–17.

_____, eds. *What's Queer About Queer Studies Now?* Spec. issue of *Social Text* 84–85, 23.3–4 (2005): 1–308.

Erickson, Nancy C. "Writing and Remembering—Acts of Resistance in Ingeborg Bachmann's *Malina* and *Der Fall Franza,* and Elfriede Jelinek's *Lust* and *Die Klavierspielerin*: Case Studies in Hysteria." *Out from the Shadows: Essays on Contemporary Austrian Women Writers and Filmmakers.* Ed. and intro. Margarete Lamb-Faffelberger. Riverside, CA: Ariadne, 1997. Studies in Austrian Literature, Culture, and Thought. 192–205.

Fehervary, Helen, Renny Harrigan, and Nancy Vedder-Shults, eds. Special Feminist Issue of *New German Critique* 13 (1978): 1–196. *JSTOR*. Accessed 17 Aug. 2008. http://www.jstor.org/stable/3115182.

Fehervary, Helen, and Sara Lennox. "Self-Experiment: Appendix to a Report." Introduction. Fehervary, Harrigan, and Vedder-Shults 109–12. *JSTOR*. Accessed 17 Aug. 2008. http://www.jstor.org/stable/3115190.

Feigenbaum, Erika Faith. "Heterosexual Privilege: The Political and the Personal." *Hypatia* 22.1 (2007): 1–9. *JSTOR*. Accessed 20 Sept. 2012. http://www.jstor.org/stable/4640040.

Finney, Gail, ed. *Look Who's Laughing: Gender and Comedy*. Langhorne, PA: Gordon, 1994. Studies in Humor and Gender 1.

Fleischhauer, Jan. "'Lieber tot als unfähig': *Spiegel*-Report über die Geschäfte der Scientology-Sekte." *Der Spiegel* 1 Apr. 1991: 30–38. *Der Spiegel*. Accessed 15 Dec. 2012. http://www.spiegel.de/spiegel/print/d-13487385.html.

Freud, Sigmund. *Three Essays on the Theory of Sexuality*. Trans. James Strachey. New York: Basic, 1975.

_____. "Das Unheimliche." 1919. *Psychologische Schriften: Studienausgabe*. Vol. 4. Ed. Alexander Mitscherlich, Angela Richards, and James Strachey. Frankfurt am Main: Fischer, 1982. 241–74.

Frizzoni, Brigitte. "Wer bin ich und wenn ja, wie viele? Verhandelte Identität(en)." *Verhandlungen mit Mordsfrauen: Geschlechterpositionierungen im "Frauenkrimi."* By Brigitte Frizzoni. Zurich: Chronos, 2009. 125–44.

Fuechtner, Veronika. *Berlin Psychoanalytic: Psychoanalysis and Culture in Weimar Republic Germany and Beyond*. Berkeley: University of California Press, 2011.

Fulbrook, Mary. *The People's State: East German Society from Hitler to Honecker*. New Haven: Yale University Press, 2005.

Garber, Marjorie. 1992. *Vested Interests: Cross-Dressing and Cultural Anxiety*. New York: Routledge, 1997.

Gelien, Gabriele. *Eine Lesbe macht noch keinen Sommer*. Hamburg: Argument, 1993.

Gerhard, Ute. "Westdeutsche Frauenbewegung: Zwischen Autonomie und dem Recht auf Gleichheit." *Feministische Studien* 10.2 (1992): 35–55.

Gerstenberger, Katharina. *Writing the New Berlin: The German Capital in Post-Wall Literature*. Rochester, NY: Camden House, 2008.

Giacobazzi, Cesare. "'Mit Kind, Hund, warmen Decken und Leiche': Die Normalität des Mordes in Ingrid Nolls Kriminalromanen." Moraldo 41–49.

"GLBT Fiction: Queer Mysteries and Thrillers." *Rainbow Sauce*. TurtleSauce Network, 2008. Accessed 23 Apr. 2010. http://www.rainbowsauce.com/glbtfic/glbtmysthril.html.

Gopinath, Gayatri. *Impossible Desires: Queer Diasporas and South Asian Public Cultures*. Durham: Duke University Press, 2005.

Grammel, Sören. "Rota Zora, a Video by Oliver Ressler." Review. *Videonale* 9 (2001): n. pag. *Installations, Videos and Projects in Public Space by Oliver Ressler*. Accessed 14 June 2012. http://www.ressler.at/videonale-9/.

Green, Simon. "Towards an Open Society? Citizenship and Immigration." *Developments in German Politics* 3. Ed. Stephen Padgett, William E. Paterson, and Gordon Smith. Durham: Duke University Press, 2003. 227–47.

Haaf, Meredith, Susanne Klingner, and Barbara Streidl. *Wir Alphamädchen: Warum Feminismus das Leben schöner macht*. 2008. Munich: Blanvalet, 2009.

Halberstam, Judith. "An Introduction to Female Masculinity: Masculinity without Men." *Female Masculinity*. By Judith Halberstam. Durham: Duke University Press, 1998. 1–43.

_____. "Shame and White Gay Masculinity." Eng, Halberstam, and Muñoz, eds. 219–33.

Haraway, Donna J. "A Cyborg Manifesto: Science, Technology, and Socialist-Feminism in the Late Twentieth Century." *Simians, Cyborgs, and Women: The Reinvention of Nature*. By Donna J. Haraway, New York: Routledge, 1991. 149–83.

Haug, Frigga. "Eine Lesbe macht noch keinen Sommer: Das Ungewöhnliche." Afterword. Gelien 249–51.

Hausman, Bernice L. "Body, Technology, and Gender in Transsexual Autobiographies." Stryker and Whittle 335–61.

Heilbrun, Carolyn G. "Nancy Drew: A Moment in Feminist History." Dyer and Romalov 11–21.

Henning, Dietmar. "Treading in Haider's Footsteps: Germany's CDU Veers to the Right as State Elections Approach." *World*

Socialist Web Site 29 Mar. 2000. World Socialist Web Site, 2013. Accessed 20 May 2013. http://www.wsws.org/en/articles/2000/03/cdu-m29.html.

Herzog, Dagmar. "Post coitum triste est...? Sexual Politics and Cultures in Postunification Germany." Anderson and Langenbacher 131–59.

Herzog, Todd. *Crime Stories: Criminalistic Fantasy and the Culture of Crisis in Weimar Germany.* New York: Berghahn, 2009.

Irigaray, Luce. *This Sex Which Is Not One.* Trans. Catherine Porter. Ithaca: Cornell University Press, 1985.

Irons, Glenwood, ed. *Feminism in Women's Detective Fiction.* Toronto: University of Toronto Press, 1995.

Jarvis, Shawn C. "Goddess." Eigler and Kord 214–15.

Jelinek, Elfriede. *Die Klavierspielerin.* 1983. Reinbek: Rowohlt, 2001.

Jones, Christopher. "Silence Is Golden? The Short Fiction of Pieke Biermann." *Sound Matters: Essays on the Acoustics of Modern German Culture.* Ed. Nora M. Alter and Lutz Koepnick. New York: Berghahn, 2004. 142–51.

Jones, James W. "Gay Detectives and Victims in German Mystery Novels." *Monatshefte* 104.4 (2012): 570–92. *Project Muse.* Accessed 22 May 2013. http://muse.jhu.edu/journals/monatshefte/summary/v104/104.4.jones.html.

Jupp, James. *From White Australia to Woomera: The Story of Australian Immigration.* New York: Cambridge University Press, 2002.

Karapin, Roger. *Protest Politics in Germany: Movements on the Left and Right Since the 1960s.* University Park: Pennsylvania State University Press, 2007.

Karr, H. P. [Reinhard Jahn]. "Biermann, Pieke." *Lexikon der deutschen Krimi-Autoren: Internet-Edition.* Accessed 11 June 2010. http://www.krimilexikon.de/biermann.htm.

_____. "Kawaters, Corinna." *Lexikon der deutschen Krimi-Autoren: Internet-Edition.* Accessed 30 May 2012. http://www.krimilexikon.de/kawaters.htm.

Katsiaficas, George. *The Subversion of Politics: European Autonomous Social Movements and the Decolonization of Everyday Life.* Atlantic Highlands, NJ: Humanities, 1997. Revolutionary Studies.

Kaufman, Gloria. "Introduction: Humor and Power." *In Stitches: A Patchwork of Feminist Humor and Satire.* Ed. Gloria Kaufman. Bloomington: Indiana University Press, 1991. viii–xii.

Kawaters, Corinna. *Zora Zobel findet die Leiche.* Frankfurt am Main: Zweitausendeins, 1984.

_____. *Zora Zobel zieht um.* Giessen: Focus, 1986.

Keen, Suzanne. *Empathy and the Novel.* Oxford: Oxford University Press, 2007.

Kemmerzell, Anja. "Was ist ein Frauenkrimi?" *Ariadne Forum* 4 (1996): 5–6.

Kent, Kathryn R. *Making Girls into Women: American Women's Writing and the Rise of Lesbian Identity.* Durham: Duke University Press, 2003.

Kent, Stephen A. "The Globalization of Scientology: Influence, Control and Opposition in Transnational Markets." *Religion* 29.2 (1999): 147–69.

Kessler, Suzanne J., and Wendy McKenna. "Toward a Theory of Gender." Stryker and Whittle 165–82.

Kevin, Tony. *A Certain Maritime Incident: The Sinking of SIEV X.* Melbourne: Scribe, 2004.

Kim, Julie H., ed. *Murdering Miss Marple: Essays on Gender and Sexuality in the New Golden Age of Women's Crime Fiction.* Jefferson, NC: McFarland, 2012.

"'Kinder statt Inder': Rüttgers verteidigt verbalen Ausrutscher." *Der Spiegel Online* 9 Mar. 2000. Accessed 20 May 2013. http://www.spiegel.de/politik/deutschland/kinder-statt-inder-ruettgers-verteidigt-verbalen-ausrutscher-a-68369.html.

Klein, Kathleen Gregory. *The Woman Detective: Gender and Genre.* 2d ed. Urbana: University of Illinois Press, 1995.

_____, ed. *Women Times Three: Writers, Detectives, Readers.* Bowling Green, OH: Bowling Green State University Popular Press, 1995.

Klocke, Sonja. "Orientalisierung der DDR? Spuren von antifaschistischer Tradition und DDR-Literatur in Emine Sevgi Özdamars *Seltsame Sterne starren zur Erde* (2003)." *NachBilder der Wende.* Ed. Inge Stephan and Alexandra Tacke. Cologne: Böhlau, 2008. 141–60.

Klüger, Ruth. "Die schwere Entscheidung— Ein Kind oder 'Emma.'" *Die Welt.* Die Welt 15 Sept. 2011. Accessed 19 Nov. 2012. http://

www.welt.de/kultur/history/article 13604494/Die-schwere-Entscheidung-ein-Kind-oder-Emma.html.

Kneifl, Edith. *Zwischen zwei Nächten.* 1991. Vienna: Milena, 2003.

Knight, Stephen. "Crimes Domestic and Crimes Colonial: The Role of Crime Fiction in Developing Postcolonial Consciousness." Matzke and Mühleisen, eds. 17–33.

Koedt, Anne. *Lesbianism and Feminism.* Chicago: Chicago Women's Liberation Union, 1971. *Chicago Women's Liberation Union Herstory Website Archive.* Accessed 10 June 2013. http://www.uic.edu/orgs/cwlu herstory/CWLUArchive/lesbianfeminism. html.

König, Ralf. *Der bewegte Mann.* 1987. *Der bewegte Mann/Pretty Baby: Der bewegte Mann 2.* Reinbek: Rowohlt, 1994.

_____. "Ralf König im Interview: 'Immer nur hei-tei-tei.'" Interview by Hans-Hermann Kotte. *Frankfurter Rundschau Online.* Frankfurter Rundschau 25 June 2009. Accessed 5 Apr. 2013. http://www.fr-online. de/panorama/ralf-koenig-im-interview—immer-nur-hei-tei-tei-,1472782,2935932. html.

Koonz, Claudia. *The Nazi Conscience.* Cambridge: Belknap, 2003.

Kremmler, Katrin. *Die Sirenen von Coogee Beach.* Hamburg: Argument, 2003.

Kuppler, Lisa, ed. *Queer Crime: Lesbisch-schwule Krimigeschichten.* Berlin: Querverlag, 2002.

Kuzniar, Alice. Introduction. *The Queer German Cinema.* By Alice Kuzniar. Stanford: Stanford University Press, 2000. 1–20.

Ladika, Susan. "Austrian Author's Psy-Thrillers." *Europe* Mar. 2000: 43. *HighBeam Research.* Accessed 25 Sept. 2006. http:// www.highbeam.com/doc/1G1–61640821. html.

Leach, Michael. "'Disturbing Practices': Dehumanizing Asylum Seekers in the Refugee 'Crisis' in Australia, 2001–2002." *Refuge* 21.3 (2003): 25–33. *Refuge.* Accessed 31 Dec. 2012. http://pi.library.yorku.ca/ojs/ index.php/refuge/article/viewFile/21301/ 19972.

Lehmann, Christine. "Christine Lehmann." Profile. *Christine Lehmann Blog.* Accessed 20 July 2012. http://christine-lehmann. blogspot.com/.

_____. *Harte Schule.* Hamburg: Argument, 2005.

_____. *Der Masochist.* Reinbek: Rowohlt, 1997.

_____. *Training mit dem Tod.* Reinbek: Rowohlt, 1998.

Lennox, Sara. "Divided Feminism: Women, Racism, and German National Identity." *German Studies Review* 18.3 (1995): 481–502. *JSTOR.* Accessed 20 Nov. 2012. http:// www.jstor.org/stable/1431776.

Lewis, James R., ed. *Scientology.* Oxford: Oxford University Press, 2009.

Liertz, Martina-Marie. *Die Geheimnisse der Frauen.* Munich: Goldmann, 1999.

Lischke-McNab, Ute. "Gender, Sex, and Sexuality: The Use of Music as a Collateral Marketing Device in *Maybe ... Maybe Not.*" Lorey and Plews, eds. 403–19.

Lorde, Audre. "The Master's Tools Will Never Dismantle the Master's House." *Sister Outsider: Essays and Speeches.* By Audre Lorde. Trumansberg: Crossing, 1984. Crossing Press Feminist. 110–13.

_____, perf. *Audre Lorde—The Berlin Years 1984–1992.* Dir. Dagmar Schulz. Third World Newsreel, 2012.

Lorey, Christoph, and John L. Plews. "Defying Sights in German Literature and Culture: An Introduction to Queering the Canon." Lorey and Plews, eds. xiii–xxiv.

_____, eds. *Queering the Canon: Defying Sights in German Literature and Culture.* Columbia: Camden House, 1998.

Madland, Helga Stipa. "Nature." Eigler and Kord 354–55.

Markowitz, Judith A. *The Gay Detective Novel: Lesbian and Gay Main Characters and Themes in Mystery Fiction.* Jefferson, NC: McFarland, 2004.

"Marlowes Töchter." *Der Spiegel* 2 Jan. 1989: 148–50. *Der Spiegel.* Accessed 18 July 2009. http://www.spiegel.de/spiegel/print/d-13493405.html.

Matzke, Christine, and Susanne Mühleisen. "Postcolonial Postmortems: Issues and Perspectives." Introduction. Matzke and Mühleisen, eds. 1–16.

_____, eds. *Postcolonial Postmortems: Crime Fiction from a Transcultural Perspective.* Amsterdam: Rodopi, 2006. Internationale Forschungen zur Allgemeinen und Vergleichenden Literaturwissenschaft 102.

Maybe... Maybe Not [*Der bewegte Mann*]. Dir. Sönke Wortmann. Perf. Til Schweiger, Katja Riemann, and Joachim Król. Neue

Constantin, 1994. (United States: Orion, 1996.) Videocassette.

McCarthy, Margaret. "Feminism and Generational Conflicts in Alexa Hennig von Lange's *Relax*, Elke Naters's *Lügen*, and Charlotte Roche's *Feuchtgebiete*." Baer 56–73.

McIntosh, Peggy. "White Privilege and Male Privilege: A Personal Account of Coming to See Correspondences through Work in Women's Studies." Wellesley: Wellesley College, Center for Research on Women, 1988. Working Paper 189. *Education Resources Information Center*. Accessed 9 June 2013. http://www.eric.ed.gov:80/PDFS/ED 335262.pdf.

Meyerowitz, Joanne. "A 'Fierce and Demanding' Drive." Stryker and Whittle 362–86.

Moraldo, Sandro M., ed. *Mord als kreativer Prozess: Zum Kriminalroman der Gegenwart in Deutschland, Österreich und der Schweiz.* Heidelberg: Universitätsverlag Winter, 2005. Beiträge zur Neueren Literaturgeschichte 222.

Moyrer, Monika. "'Coming-to-herself': Diverging Representations of Female Subjectivity in Eastern and Western German Literary Texts in the 1970s." *Journal of Women's History* 15.3 (2003): 135–38. *Project Muse.* Accessed 6 July 2012. http://muse.jhu.edu/journals/jowh/summary/v015/15.3moyrer.html.

Munt, Sally R. *Murder by the Book? Feminism and the Crime Novel.* London: Routledge, 1994.

Mushaben, Joyce Marie. "From Ausländer to Inlander: The Changing Faces of Citizenship in Post-Wall Germany." Anderson and Langenbacher 160–82.

Nestle, Joan, Clare Howell, and Riki Anne Wilchins, eds. *Gender Queer: Voices from Beyond the Sexual Binary.* Los Angeles: Alyson, 2002.

Neuwirth, Barbara. "Afterword: Literature by Austrian Women." *Escaping Expectations: Stories by Austrian Women Writers.* Trans. Pamela S. Saur. Ed. Barbara Neuwirth. Riverside, CA: Ariadne, 2001. Studies in Austrian Literature, Culture, and Thought: Translation Series. 151–63.

Noble, Jean Bobby. *Sons of the Movement: FtMs Risking Incoherence on a Post-Queer Cultural Landscape.* Toronto: Women's, 2006.

Noll, Ingrid. *Die Häupter meiner Lieben.* 1993. Zurich: Diogenes, 1994.

"Ordentlicher Stromschlag." *Der Spiegel* 15 Apr. 1991: 56–57. *Der Spiegel.* Accessed 15 Dec. 2012. http://www.spiegel.de/spiegel/print/d-13489151.html.

Pailer, Gaby. "'Weibliche' Körper im 'männlichen' Raum: Zur Interdependenz von Gender und Genre in deutschsprachigen Kriminalromanen von Autorinnen." *Weimarer Beiträge* 46.4 (2000): 564–81.

Palmer, Paulina. "The Lesbian Feminist Thriller and Detective Novel." *What Lesbians Do in Books.* Ed. Elaine Hobby and Chris White. London: Women's, 1991. 9–27.

———. "The Lesbian Thriller: Transgressive Investigations." *Criminal Proceedings: The Contemporary American Crime Novel.* Ed. Peter Messent. London: Pluto, 1997. 87–110.

Palmer, Susan J. "The Church of Scientology in France: Legal and Activist Counterattacks in the 'War on *Sectes*.'" Lewis 295–322.

Pausch, Holger A. "Queer Theory: History, Status, Trends, and Problems." Lorey and Plews, eds. 1–19.

Plain, Gill. *Twentieth-Century Crime Fiction: Gender, Sexuality and the Body.* Chicago: Fitzroy, 2001.

Plummer, Patricia. "'Die Blutspur fängt in frühester Jugend an': Interview mit Sabine Deitmer." Birkle, Matter-Seibel, and Plummer 87–99.

Polt-Heinzl, Evelyne. "Frauenkrimis—Von der besonderen Dotation zu Detektion und Mord." *Ich kannte den Mörder wußte nur nicht wer er war: Zum Kriminalroman der Gegenwart.* Ed. Friedbert Aspetsberger and Daniela Strigl. Innsbruck: StudienVerlag, 2004. Schriftenreihe Literatur des Instituts für Österreichkunde 15. 144–70.

Pons, Xavier. "'Redneck Wonderland': Robert G. Barrett's Crime Fiction." Matzke and Mühleisen, eds. 229–53.

Purvis, Andrew. "Germany's Battle against Scientology." *Time* 17 Dec. 2007: n. pag. *Time.* Accessed 31 Dec. 2012. http://www.time.com/time/world/article/0,8599,1695514,00.html.

Pusch, Luise F. "Ein Streit um Worte? Eine Lesbe macht Skandal im Deutschen Bundestag." *Women in German Yearbook* 10 (1994): 239–66.

Rabisch, Birgit. "Eier im Glas." *Mit Zorn, Charme & Methode oder: Die Aufklärung ist weiblich!* Ed. Pieke Biermann. Frankfurt am Main: Fischer, 1992. 112–23.

Reddy, Maureen T. "Lesbian Detectives." *Sisters in Crime: Feminism and the Crime Novel.* By Maureen T. Reddy. New York: Continuum, 1988. 121–46.

Rehak, Melanie. *Girl Sleuth: Nancy Drew and the Women Who Created Her.* Orlando: Harcourt, 2005.

Reitman, Janet. *Inside Scientology: The Story of America's Most Secretive Religion.* Boston: Houghton, 2011.

Rich, B. Ruby. "Two for the Road." *Advocate* 18 Feb. 2003: 48. *Academic Search Complete.* Accessed 26 July 2012. http://ezproxy.gsu.edu:2048/login?url=http://search.ebscohost.com/login.aspx?direct=true&db=a9h&AN=9124085&site=ehost-live.

Rider, N. Ann. "The Journey Eastward: Helga Schütz' *Von Glanz der Elbe* and the Mnemonic Politics of German Unification." *Textual Responses to German Unification: Processing Historical and Social Change in Literature and Film.* Ed. Carol Anne Costabile-Heming, Rachel J. Halverson, and Kristie A. Foell. Berlin: de Gruyter, 2001. 17–34.

Rote Zora. "Interview mit der Roten Zora." Self-interview. *Emma* June 1984: 598–605. *Theorie als Praxis.* Accessed 4 June 2012. http://theoriealspraxis.blogsport.de/images/Emma_Rote_Zora.pdf.

Rowland, Susan. *From Agatha Christie to Ruth Rendell: British Women Writers in Detective and Crime Fiction.* Basingstoke: Palgrave, 2001. Crime Files.

Ruffolo, David V. *Post-Queer Politics.* Farnham: Ashgate, 2009. Queer Interventions.

Scherpe, Klaus R. "Modern and Postmodern Transformations of the Metropolitan Narrative." Trans. Mitch Cohen. *New German Critique* 55 (1992): 71–85. *JSTOR.* Accessed 16 Aug. 2012. http://www.jstor.org/stable/488290.

Schlaeger, Hilke. "The West German Women's Movement." Intro. Nancy Vedder-Shults. Fehervary, Harrigan, and Vedder-Shults 59–68. *JSTOR.* Accessed 29 Aug. 2012. http://www.jstor.org/stable/3115187.

Schmid-Bortenschlager, Sigrid. "Violence and Woman's Status as Victim: Changing the Role Model or Being Caught in the Trap?" *Repensando la violencia y el patriarcado frente al nuevo milenio: Nuevas perspectivas en el mundo Hispanico y Germanico/Rethinking Violence and Patriarchy for the New Millennium: A German and Hispanic Perspective.* Ed. Fernando de Diego and Agata Schwartz. Ottawa: University of Ottawa, 2002. 113–20.

Schneider, Peter. *Der Mauerspringer.* Darmstadt: Luchterhand, 1982.

_____. "Tearing Down Berlin's Mental Wall." Trans. The Times. *New York Times* 12 Aug. 2011: n. pag. *New York Times.* Accessed 3 Nov. 2012. http://www.nytimes.com/2011/08/13/opinion/tearing-down-berlins-mental-wall.html?_r=0.

Scholte, Jan Aart. *Globalization: A Critical Introduction,* 2d ed. Basingstoke: Palgrave, 2005.

Schwarzer, Alice. "Transsexualität." *Emma* Mar.-Apr. 1994: 36–37.

Schwarzmantel, John. *Citizenship and Identity: Towards a New Republic.* London: Routledge, 2003. Routledge Innovations in Political Theory 11.

Sedgwick, Eve Kosofsky. *Between Men: English Literature and Male Homosocial Desire.* New York: Columbia University Press, 1985.

_____. *Epistemology of the Closet.* Berkeley: University of California Press, 1990.

_____. "Queer and Now." *Tendencies.* By Eve Kosofsky Sedgwick. Durham: Duke University Press, 1993. 1–20.

"17th Jan: Puszta Cowboy and the Budapest Lesbian Film Collective." *Bildwechsel Glasgow* 2 Jan. 2007. *WordPress.* Accessed 16 July 2011. http://bildwechselglasgow.wordpress.com/2007/01/02/puszta-cowboy-and-the-budapest-lesbian-film-collective/.

Shapiro, Ben. *Brainwashed: How Universities Indoctrinate America's Youth.* Nashville: WND, 2004.

Sharp, Ingrid. "Male Privilege and Female Virtue: Gendered Representations of the Two Germanies." *New German Studies* 18.1–2 (1994): 87–106.

Sieg, Katrin. "Postcolonial Berlin? Pieke Biermann's Crime Novels as Globalization Critique." *Studies in Twentieth and Twenty-First Century Literature* 28.1 (2004): 152–82.

_____. "Women in the Fortress Europe: Feminist Crime Fiction as Antifascist Performative." *differences* 16.2 (2005): 138–66.

Simpson, Patricia Anne. "Degrees of History in Contemporary German Narratives." *German Literature in a New Century: Trends, Traditions, Transitions, Transformations.* Ed. Katharina Gerstenberger and Patricia Herminghouse. New York: Berghahn, 2008. 78–98.

Slotkin, Richard. *Gunfighter Nation: The Myth of the Frontier in Twentieth-Century America*. 1992. Norman: University of Oklahoma Press, 1998.

Smith-Prei, Carrie. "'Knaller-Sex für alle': Popfeminist Body Politics in Lady Bitch Ray, Charlotte Roche, and Sarah Kuttner." Baer 18–39.

Spillane, Mickey. *Vengeance Is Mine!* 1950. *The Mike Hammer Collection*. Vol. 1. Intro. Max Allan Collins. New York: New American, 2001. 345–513.

Stefan, Verena. *Häutungen*. Munich: Frauenoffensive, 1975.

Stewart, Faye. "Dialogues with Tradition: Feminist-Queer Encounters in German Crime Stories at the Turn of the Twenty-First Century." Baer 114–35.

_____. "Mother Sleuth and the Queer Kid: Decoding Sexual Identities in Maria Gronau's Detective Novels." *Questions of Identity in Detective Fiction*. Ed. Linda Martz and Anita Higgie. Newcastle: Cambridge Scholars, 2007. 19–35.

_____. "Of Herrings Red and Lavender: Reading Crime and Identity in Queer Detective Fiction." Collins 33–44.

_____. "Out and Undercover: The Closeted Detective in Lisa Pei's *Die letzte Stunde*." *Sexual-Textual Border-Crossings: Lesbian Identity in German-Language Literature, Film, and Culture*. Ed. Cordula Böcking-Politis and Carrie Smith-Prei. Spec. issue of *Germanistik in Ireland* 5 (2010): 125–42.

Stone, Susan. "Why German Crime Fiction Fails to Thrill US Readers." *PRI's The World*. PRI's The World, 28 Dec. 2012. Accessed 15 May 2013. http://www.theworld.org/2012/12/why-german-thrillers-are-not-popular-in-us/.

Straayer, Chris. *Deviant Eyes, Deviant Bodies: Sexual Re-Orientations in Film and Video*. New York: Columbia University Press, 1996.

Stryker, Susan. "My Words to Victor Frankenstein above the Village of Chamounix: Performing Transgender Rage." Stryker and Whittle 244–56.

Stryker, Susan, and Stephen Whittle, eds. *The Transgender Studies Reader*. New York: Routledge, 2006.

Sullivan, Andrew. *Virtually Normal: An Argument about Homosexuality*. New York: Knopf, 1995.

Tenenbaum, Linda. "The Tragedy of SIEV X: Did the Australian Government Deliberately Allow 353 Refugees to Drown?" Parts 1–4. *World Socialist Web Site* 13–16 Aug. 2002. World Socialist Web Site, 2013. Accessed 28 Aug. 2012. http://www.wsws.org/en/articles/2002/08/siel-a13.html.

Thelma & Louise. Dir. Ridley Scott. Writ. Callie Khouri. Perf. Susan Sarandon and Geena Davis. MGM, 1991.

Ther, Klaus. "Die Kritik zu *Zwischen zwei Nächten*." *Der Standard* 1991. *Das Syndikat: Autorengruppe deutschsprachige Kriminalliteratur*. Accessed 25 Sept. 2006. http://www.das-syndikat.com/rom1992.htm.

Tielinen, Kirsimarja. "Ein Blick von außen: Ermittlungen im deutschsprachigen Frauenkriminalroman." *Verbrechen als Passion: Neue Untersuchungen zum Kriminalgenre*. Ed. Bruno Franceschini and Carsten Würmann. Spec. issue of *Juni-Magazin* 37–38 (2003): 41–68.

United States. Dept. of State. *Germany Human Rights Practices, 1993*. 31 Jan. 1994. *State Department Electronic Archive*. Accessed 7 Jan. 2013. http://dosfan.lib.uic.edu/ERC/democracy/1993_hrp_report/93hrp_report_eur/Germany.html.

Urban, Hugh B. *The Church of Scientology: A History of a New Religion*. Princeton: Princeton University Press, 2011.

Van Dine, S. S. "Twenty Rules for Writing Detective Stories." *American Magazine* Sept. 1928: n. pag. *Gaslight*. Mount Royal College, 2000. Accessed 6 July 2011. http://gaslight.mtroyal.ca/vandine.htm.

Vogel, Marianne. "Ein Unbehagen an der Kultur: Zur Kriminalliteratur deutschsprachiger Schriftstellerinnen in den 90er Jahren." *Zwischen Trivialität und Postmoderne: Literatur von Frauen in den 90er Jahren*. Ed. Ilse Nagelschmidt, Alexandra Hanke, Lea Müller-Dannhausen, and Melani Schröter. Frankfurt am Main: Lang, 2002. 49–67.

Walton, Priscilla L., and Manina Jones. *Detective Agency: Women Rewriting the Hard-Boiled Tradition*. Berkeley: University of California Press, 1999.

Warner, Michael. Introduction. *Fear of a Queer Planet: Queer Politics and Social Theory*. Ed. Michael Warner. Minneapolis: University of Minnesota Press, 1993. vii–xxxi.

_____. *The Trouble with Normal: Sex, Poli-*

tics, and the Ethics of Queer Life. New York: Free, 1999.

Watzal, Verena. "Textimmanente Untersuchung des Romans 'Der Hahn ist tot' von Ingrid Noll und Versuch einer Zuordnung in das Subgenre 'psychologischer Frauenkrimi.'" Munich: GRIN, 2000. *Google Book Search.* Accessed 20 July 2012. http://books.google.com/books?id=cSH8xD0OEOIC&printsec=frontcover&dq=Verena+Watzal&hl=en&sa=X&ei=jRa2UZTfBsbw0QHW4oGYDA&ved=0CFgQ6AEwBQ.

Wenke, Gabriela. "Sisters in Crime in deutschen Krimis." *Das Mordsbuch: Alles über Krimis.* Ed. Nina Schindler. Hildesheim: Claassen, 1997. 283–93.

Wessel, Claudia. *Es wird Zeit.* Giessen: Wemü, 1984.

Wildman, Stephanie M. *Privilege Revealed: How Invisible Preference Undermines America.* New York: New York University Press, 1996. Critical America.

Wilke, Sabine. "Wilde Weiber und dominante Damen: Der Frauenkrimi als Verhandlungsort von Weiblichkeitsmythen." Birkle, Matter-Seibel, and Plummer 255–71.

Wilson, Anna. "Death and the Mainstream: Lesbian Detective Fiction and the Killing of the Coming-Out Story." *Feminist Studies* 22.2 (1996): 251–78. *JSTOR.* Accessed 1 Feb. 2007. http://www.jstor.org/stable/3178413.

"Wir haben abgetrieben!" *Stern* 6 July 1971. *Deutsche Geschichte in Dokumenten und Bildern.* Accessed 11 June 2013. http://germanhistorydocs.ghi-dc.org/sub_image.cfm?image_id=1592&language=german.

Wolf, Christa. "Self-Experiment: Appendix to a Report." Trans. Jeanette Clausen. Intro. Helen Fehervary and Sara Lennox. Fehervary, Harrigan, and Vedder-Shults 109–31. *JSTOR.* Accessed 17 Aug. 2008. http://www.jstor.org/stable/3115190.

Wörtche, Thomas. "Leichenberg 06/2007." *Kaliber .38: Krimis im Internet.* Thomas Wörtche, 2007. Accessed 15 July 2012. http://www.kaliber38.de/woertche/leich0607.htm.

Wright, Les. "The Genre Cycle of Gay Coming-Out Films, 1970–1994." Lorey and Plews, eds. 311–39.

Index

abortion 22, 28, 30, 36, 38, 46, 66, 182*n*2; *see also* Paragraph 218

abuse 3, 12, 23, 40, 46, 57–58, 60, 64–65, 72, 75–76, 78, 94, 110–11, 117, 145, 163, 168, 190*n*13, 195*n*50, 202*n*54; child 110–11, 117, 122, 163, 176, 187n37; emotional/psychological 72, 78, 190*n*13; sexual 23, 57, 110–11, 117, 122, 162–63, 171; substance 62; *see also* violence

activism 8, 17, 21–23, 25–28, 30–32, 34, 37, 40–45, 53–54, 111–13, 115–16, 118–19, 127, 135, 139, 156, 163, 165, 167, 174–75, 186*n*34, 187*n*44, 196*n*8; *see also* autonomism; feminism; Rote Zora; Schwarzer, Alice

Adelson, Leslie 46, 188*n*53

Agazzi, Elena 60, 65, 70–72

Ahmed, Sara 120

amateur investigator 8, 26–27, 36, 40, 42, 54, 98, 100, 102, 110, 112-13, 115, 121-22, 124, 139, 156, 184*n*18

Anderson, Mark 65

Anglo-American crime fiction 7–8, 13, 22, 112, 123, 181*n*14, 181*n*21, 185*n*26, 189*n*67, 196*n*10; *see also* hardboiled detective fiction; United States

angstherz 142, 153–54, 205*n*6, 205*n*10, 208*n*31; *see also* Billig, Susanne

Appadurai, Arjun 126, 207*n*24

Ariadne (crime series) 110–11, 120, 123, 156, 199*n*33, 202*n*59, 208*n*35, 211*n*4

asylum 4, 18–19, 157–58, 160–67, 172, 175, 209*n*43; laws 157, 164, 209*n*45, 210*n*51; politics 4, 18–19, 138, 157, 160–61, 163, 166; seekers 158, 160–62, 165–67, 209*n*43; 209*n*45; *see also* refugee

Australia 19, 138, 156–67, 169, 208*n*41, 209*n*43–46, 210*n*49, 211*n*55

Austria 2, 7, 12, 17–18, 59, 66, 68, 72, 94, 175–76, 190*n*13; crime fiction 8, 12, 17–18, 60, 190*n*6–7; history 8, 60, 66–67, 72–73; literature 60, 72–73

autonomism 8, 10, 15, 17, 22–23, 25–27, 30–

34, 37, 40–41, 44, 46, 53–55, 174, 182*n*2, 182–83*n*4, 183*n*6, 184–85*n*20; *see also* activism; Rote Zora; terrorism

Bachmann, Ingeborg 60, 73; *Malina* 65, 72, 190*n*5, 190*n*13

Barfoot, Nicola 9, 26, 43, 51, 75, 180*n*9–10, 180–81*n*12, 184*n*14, 184*n*18, 188*n*52, 189*n*62

Bavaria 113, 116–17, 119, 121, 196*n*5, 200*n*43, 201*n*45–47, 202*n*55

Beck, Ulrich 148

Berlin 42–43, 46, 99, 111–12, 116–17, 120–21, 140, 143–44, 151, 175, 187*n*43, 199*n*28, 205*n*9; dialect 50; East 47, 121; post-unification 78, 144–45, 196*n*7; West 22, 27, 43, 47, 100, 116, 187*n*40, 201*n*46

Berr, Annette 16, 176

Betz, Phyllis M. 12–13, 98–99, 103, 125, 202*n*64

Biermann, Pieke 7, 9, 11, 15, 19, 23–24, 39, 42–43, 54–55, 174, 179*n*5, 180*n*6, 180*n*9, 183*n*5, 183*n*10, 184*n*18, 187*n*40, 187*n*42–43, 188*n*53–54, 206*n*15; *Herzrasen* 42; *Potsdamer Ableben* 7–8, 12, 15, 17, 23–24, 42–55, 76, 149, 174; *Violetta* 42, 180*n*5, 189*n*60, 189*n*62, 189*n*66

Billig, Susanne 1, 15, 139–40, 142, 145–46, 174, 180*n*6, 183*n*5, 184*n*18, 205*n*9; *angstherz* 142, 153–54, 205*n*6, 205*n*10, 208*n*31; "Dora" 14, 140, 205*n*9; *Ein gieriger Ort* 140, 205*n*9; *Im Schatten des schwarzen Vogels* 140, 142, 205*n*6; *Mit Haut und Handel* 139, 205*n*6; *Sieben Zeichen* 12, 15, 18–19, 138–56, 171–72, 175, 205*n*6–10; *Die Tage der Vergeltung* 140

bisexuality 2, 5, 14, 97–98, 107, 122–23, 131, 135, 142

Bochum 22, 27, 183*n*7

body/embodiment: dead 28, 36, 71, 80–81, 86, 132, 170, 198*n*24; gendered/transgendered 14–16, 18, 28, 36, 39–40, 54, 59, 80, 91, 97, 105, 108, 123, 126–27, 129–31, 133, 170, 192*n*24, 195*n*50–51, 196*n*10; physicality of